GERMANY

GERMANY

EDITED BY MICHAEL RAY, ASSISTANT EDITOR, GEOGRAPHY

Britannica
Educational Publishing

IN ASSOCIATION WITH

ROSEN
EDUCATIONAL SERVICES

Published in 2014 by Britannica Educational Publishing
(a trademark of Encyclopædia Britannica, Inc.)
in association with Rosen Educational Services, LLC
29 East 21st Street, New York, NY 10010.

Distributed exclusively by Rosen Educational Services.
For a listing of additional Britannica Educational Publishing titles, call toll free (800) 237-9932.

First Edition

Britannica Educational Publishing
J.E. Luebering: Director, Core Reference Group
Adam Augustyn: Assistant Manager, Core Reference Group
Marilyn L. Barton: Senior Coordinator, Production Control
Steven Bosco: Director, Editorial Technologies
Lisa S. Braucher: Senior Producer and Data Editor
Yvette Charbonneau: Senior Copy Editor
Kathy Nakamura: Manager, Media Acquisition
Michael Ray, Assistant Editor, Geography

Rosen Educational Services
Nicholas Croce: Editor
Nelson Sá: Art Director
Cindy Reiman: Photography Manager
Brian Garvey: Designer, Cover Design
Introduction by Nicki Peter Petrikowski

Library of Congress Cataloging-in-Publication Data

Germany/edited by Michael Ray.
     pages cm.—(The Britannica guide to countries of the European Union)
"In association with Britannica Educational Publishing, Rosen Educational Services."
Includes bibliographical references and index.
ISBN 978-1-61530-965-8 (library binding)
1. Germany—Juvenile literature. 2. European Union—Germany—Juvenile literature. I. Ray,
Michael (Michael J.), 1973–
DD17.G474 2014
943—dc23

                                                                      2012043293

Manufactured in the United States of America

On the cover: The European Central Bank in Frankfurt, Germany. © *iStockphoto.com/
Patrick Poendl (euro symbol),* © *iStockphoto.com/Wittelsbach bernd (tower)*

On page xii: Map of Germany. *Pavalena/Shutterstock.com*

Cover, p. iii (map contour, stars), back cover, multiple interior pages (stars) © iStockphoto.
com/pop_jop; cover, multiple interior pages (background graphic) Mina De La O/Digital
Vision/Getty Images

CONTENTS

CHAPTER 4: GOVERNMENT AND SOCIETY

CHAPTER 5: CULTURAL LIFE

55

79

82

99

110

118

151

165

172

CHAPTER 9: GERMANY FROM 1871 TO THE MODERN ERA

278

314

DENMARK

North Sea

Sylt

Hamburg

Bremen

NETHERLANDS

Hanover

BERLI

Elbe

Dusseldorf

Cologne

Leipzig

Dresden

BELGIUM

Rhine

GERMANY

Koblenz

Frankfurt

Wiesbaden

Mainz

CZECI

Heidelberg

Danube

Baden-Baden

Stuttgart

FRANCE

Freudenstadt

Freiberg

Munich

SWITZERLAND

It was a surprise for many Germans when the World Service Poll conducted by the British Broadcasting Corporation in 2009 came to the conclusion that Germany was the most favourably viewed nation in the world, a title the country has been able to retain in subsequent years. It was a surprise because the history of the first half of the 20th century cast a long shadow. The World Wars and the Shoah were the first things many people would connect with Germany, which was understandable considering the extraordinary severity of these historic events. For Germans abroad it was not an uncommon experience to be met with resentment or outright hostility, even for those who had been born after 1945. Germany has accepted its special responsibility not only for its own history, but also for not allowing anything similar to happen again, a responsibility that is conveyed thoroughly in German schools. While it is not possible for Germany to simply put history behind it, the results of the BBC poll show that the outside perception no longer reduces the country to its darkest hour, but that people all over the globe believe that Germany can and will play a positive role in our world today.

In this book readers will find information about Germany, its geography, its society and culture, and especially its rich history, which spans over two millennia from the first contact of Germanic tribes with Ancient Rome to Germany's position today as one of the biggest economies in the world and—together with France—the driving force behind the European Union.

Of course it took a long time for Germany to reach its current form. The Germanic tribes encountered by the Romans did not form a single, unified entity, although there existed alliances between smaller tribes. During the Migration Period starting in the 4th century CE, Huns invading from the East pushed Germanic tribes into the Roman Empire, which led to its decline in the West. Several Germanic tribes founded kingdoms on former Roman territory, but most of these successor states were short-lived. The Franks, a confederation of tribes that had settled in Romanized Gaul and western Germany, were able to expand their kingdom under the Merovingian and Carolingian dynasties until it reached its heyday under the rule of Charlemagne, who was crowned emperor in the year 800. After his heir, Louis the Pious, had died in 840, the empire was divided into three realms. While the middle kingdom soon fell apart and was partially absorbed by its neighbours, the western and the eastern kingdoms survived and eventually became France and Germany, respectively. Charlemagne's grandson Louis II, the first ruler of the eastern Frankish kingdom, was given the byname "the German" by 19th-century historians; this is misleading because there did not exist a sense of German national identity yet. That only developed over time and one cannot point to a single date upon which the eastern kingdom stopped being Frankish and started being German.

One important factor, though, was the end of the Carolingian dynasty with the death of Louis IV in 911. Instead of joining the western kingdom, which was still ruled by a Carolingian, or breaking the realm apart into smaller pieces, several of the Germanic peoples—not only Franks, but also Saxons, Bavarians, and Swabians —elected Conrad, duke of the Franks, to be their new king. His successor, Henry I, the duke of Saxony, was the first non-Frank to hold the title of Rex Francorum. His son, Otto I, was the first ruler of the eastern Frankish kingdom to be crowned emperor in 962. From then until the end of the Empire in 1806, his successors claimed this prerogative for themselves, making them the worldly leaders of Christianity in the West. This often applied only in theory and not in practice, not least because this claim, along with territorial claims in Italy and the struggle over influence on the church in the Empire, was a constant cause of conflict with the papacy, which had the power to bestow or withhold the imperial coronation.

The discrepancy between ambitions and reality became increasingly more apparent after the end of the Hohenstaufen dynasty in the mid-13th century. Due to the monarchy being elective rather than hereditary, more and more power shifted from the king to the territorial princes, who did not necessarily have an interest in supporting a strong king and usually let themselves be paid for their compliance.

The Reformation started in 1517, adding another dividing line, as some took up the new denomination while others did not. It also brought on a unification in the form of language. The influence of Martin Luther's works and especially his translation of the Bible on the development of the German language and its standardization can hardly be overestimated. The wide distribution of Luther's Bible was possible thanks to Johannes Gutenberg's invention of movable type printing some sixty years earlier. For the time being, though, the dividing factor won out, as the violent conflicts that erupted in the wake of the Reformation made clear.

The Peace of Augsburg (1555) regularised the coexistence of Catholicism and Lutheranism in Germany, but it failed to address lingering problems. Therefore it was only a matter of time until the tensions would break out again. When that happened during the Thirty Years' War, not only did German rulers fight each other (for religious as well as political reasons), but several European powers intervened to further their own goals. Large parts of the Empire were devastated, not only by the fighting, but by the epidemics that followed the armies through the land. The regions hit hardest would not recover until the 19th century. The Peace of Westphalia, signed in 1648, mainly benefitted France and Sweden, while the Empire and especially its monarchy were weakened. Switzerland became independent and the princes whose lands remained part of the Empire began to assert their sovereignty.

The Empire comprised 300 principalities, two of which took the leading role over the next few centuries: Austria and Prussia. The Habsburg house from Austria was the ruling dynasty in the Empire from 1438 to 1806, but they also accumulated territories that were not part of the Empire, in Italy, in the Netherlands, and in eastern Europe.

The Hohenzollern house of Brandenburg was able to secure for itself several territories in western Germany as well as Prussia to the east; in 1701 the elector of Brandenburg obtained from the emperor the right to style himself King of Prussia. The two powers clashed in the War of the Austrian Succession (1740–1748) and the Seven Years' War (1756–1763), which further cemented Prussia's position as the dominating power in northern Germany. With the partitions of Poland, Prussia continued to grow.

In this age of absolutism and particularism, even the rulers of the small principalities tried to copy the style of the bigger royal courts. They spared no expense to erect magnificent buildings, but they also supported universities and the arts. A prime example is the court of Saxe-Weimar and the nearby university of Jena, where in the late 18th and early 19th centuries were gathered some of the greatest writers and philosophers of their time (Wieland, Goethe, Herder, Schiller, Fichte, Hegel, Schelling, etc.).

The downside of this particularism became apparent when the Empire proved to be no match for French armies during the French Revolutionary and Napoleonic wars, and the Empire was dissolved in 1806. Only after Napoleon's defeat in Russia in 1812 were the German states able to shake off French control as part of the Wars of Liberation. At the Congress of Vienna in 1815, the map of Europe was redrawn by rulers intent on restoration and confining any revolutionary ideas. Only a few of the states comprising the newly founded German Confederation established representative assemblies, Prussia and Austria not among them. But the times were changing. The incipient industrialization saw the rise of a rich middle class interested in establishing political influence, while the poor, drawn in great number to the cities to find work, were increasingly dissatisfied by their situation, which was exacerbated by overpopulation and crop failures in the 1840s. The result was the revolution of 1848, inspired by the overthrowing of King Louis-Philippe in France, and the election of a national assembly. This assembly wanted to unify Germany with Prussia as a leader—Austria was to be excluded because of its interests in eastern Europe and Italy—but the Prussian king turned down the crown offered to him as he objected to becoming emperor by the grace of the people. It took another twenty years and a series of wars against Denmark in 1864, against Austria in 1866, and against France in 1870–71 before Germany was unified under Prussian rule.

The population and the industrial power of the German Empire grew rapidly, but the attempt to establish global influence had only limited success because the other European powers had left little room for German colonies to be founded overseas. Chancellor Otto von Bismarck, the architect of the formation of the Empire, had tried to prevent further wars through shrewd diplomacy, but his policies were abandoned in favour of an increasingly aggressive stance in the early 20th century. When the heir to the throne of their ally Austria was assassinated in June of 1914 by a nationalist Serb, the political leaders of Germany did not try to defuse the crisis, but embraced the chance to go to war, and the German people followed suit. But the hope for a quick, decisive victory soon gave way to the reality of a drawn-out war of unprecedented proportions. In November 1918, revolution broke out in Germany, the emperor abdicated, a republic was declared, and an armistice signed.

The circumstances of its formation were a huge burden for the fledgling democracy of the Weimar Republic (the constitutional assembly took place in Weimar to make it the spiritual heir to the cultural high point of the Weimar court in the late 18th century). The political right blamed those who had stepped up to form a democratic government for the loss of the war, while the Communists pushed for a political system akin to the one in Russia. Hence the Republic was under constant attack from both sides.

A few short years of political stability came to an end in 1929 with the beginning of the worldwide depression that caused massive unemployment. Political extremists gained popularity, particularly Hitler's NSDAP. The Republic effectively came to an end when President Paul von Hindenburg invoked his emergency powers in 1930 to appoint a new chancellor. After three different chancellors failed to establish stability in as many years, Hindenburg appointed Hitler, who in 1932 had lost the election for president to the 84-year-old Hindenburg, to be chancellor on January 30, 1933. His political rivals had hoped to be able to check Hitler's radical tendencies, but instead the Nazi party was able to quickly eliminate the political opposition and establish a totalitarian dictatorship propagating its racist ideology. Steps for the preparation of war were taken early on and the Third Reich's intention to expand was made abundantly clear in 1938 with the annexation of Austria and the Sudetenland. The invasion of Poland on September 1, 1939, started World War II, which saw astounding German successes early on, but as the war went on a German victory became less and less likely. When the surrender was signed on May 7, 1945, Germany lay in ruins.

The Allied powers occupying Germany divided the country into four zones, while the provinces in the east were stripped from Germany and given to Poland and the Soviet Union. From these zones emerged two German states in 1949: the Federal Republic of Germany in the west and the German Democratic Republic, formerly the zone occupied by the Soviet Union, in the east.

The conflict between the world's two superpowers, the United States and the Soviet Union, played out in the divided

Germany, with West Germany joining NATO and East Germany becoming a charter member of the Warsaw Pact. The erection of the Berlin Wall starting in 1961 was a manifestation of the Iron Curtain that Germans found themselves guarding from both sides. When Germany was finally reunified in 1990, it was cause for celebration, but also for concern. Some of its neighbours were wary of a unified Germany, but the leading role Germany took in the EU showed that it was no threat to a peaceful Europe, but rather a driving force behind it. The Nobel Peace Prize awarded to the EU in 2012 not only honours the pacific path Germany and its neighbours have taken over the last decades, but also encourages Europe to stay on that path in the future. Another concern was—and still is —the expense associated with the reunification. Two decades have passed, yet the economic gap between east and west has not yet been fully closed. High unemployment has been a problem for Germany, although the reforms of the welfare system and the economy undertaken in the early years of the new millennium have left Germany in better shape than most of Europe during the global financial crisis of recent years.

Over the course of its history Germany has been disunified and unified again. It has been destroyed and risen from the ashes time and again, thanks to the hard and precise work of the German people that is valued highly all over the world. Germany has evolved to be a peaceful and prosperous nation that this book invites you to get to know.

CHAPTER 1

LAND

One of Europe's largest countries, Germany encompasses a wide variety of landscapes: the tall, sheer mountains of the south; the sandy, rolling plains of the north; the forested hills of the urbanized west; and the plains of the agricultural east. At the spiritual heart of the country are the magnificent east-central city of Berlin, which rose phoenix-like from the ashes of World War II and now, after decades of partition, is the capital of a reunified Germany, and the Rhine River, which flows northward from Switzerland and is celebrated in visual art, literature, folklore, and song. Along its banks and those of its principal tributaries—among them the Neckar, Main, Moselle, and Ruhr—stand hundreds of medieval castles, churches, picturesque villages, market towns, and centres of learning and culture, including Heidelberg, the site of one of Europe's oldest universities (founded in 1386), and Mainz, historically one of Europe's most important publishing centres. All are centrepieces of Germany's thriving tourist economy, which brings millions of visitors to the country each year, drawn by its natural beauty, history, culture, and cuisine (including its renowned wines and beers).

Germany is bounded at its extreme north on the Jutland peninsula by Denmark. East and west of the peninsula, the Baltic Sea (Ostsee) and North Sea coasts, respectively, complete the northern border. To the west, Germany borders the Netherlands, Belgium, and Luxembourg; to the southwest it borders France. Germany shares its entire southern boundary with Switzerland and Austria. In the southeast the border

Germany.

with the Czech Republic corresponds to an earlier boundary of 1918, renewed by treaty in 1945. The easternmost frontier adjoins Poland along the northward course of the Neisse River and subsequently the Oder to the Baltic Sea, with a westward deviation in the north to exclude the former German port city of Stettin (now Szczecin, Poland) and the Oder mouth. This border reflects the loss of Germany's eastern territories to Poland, agreed to at the Yalta Conference (February 1945), mandated at the Potsdam Conference (July–August 1945) held among the victorious World War II Allies, and reaffirmed by subsequent governments.

Barge on the Rhine River, with vineyards in the background, at the town of Kaub, Germany. E. Streichan—Shostal Associates/ Superstock

RELIEF

The major lineaments of Germany's physical geography are not unique. The country spans the great east-west morphological zones that are characteristic of the western part of central Europe. In the south Germany impinges on the outermost ranges of the Alps. From there it extends across the Alpine Foreland (Alpenvorland), the plain on the northern edge of the Alps. Forming the core of the country is the large zone of the Central German Uplands, which is part of a wider European arc of territory stretching from the Massif Central of France in the west into the Czech Republic, Slovakia, and Poland in the east. In Germany it manifests itself as a landscape with a complex mixture of forested block mountains, intermediate plateaus with scarped edges, and lowland basins. In the northern part of the country the North German Plain, or Lowland, forms part of the greater North European Plain, which broadens from the Low Countries eastward across Germany and Poland into Belarus, the Baltic states, and Russia and extends northward through Schleswig-Holstein into the Jutland peninsula of Denmark. The North German Plain is fringed by marshes, mudflats, and the

Eastern summit of the Zugspitze, Germany.
Hans Huber

islands of the North and Baltic seas. In general, Germany has a south-to-north drop in altitude, from a maximum elevation of 9,718 feet (2,962 metres) in the Zugspitze of the Bavarian Alps to a few small areas slightly below sea level in the north near the coast.

It is a common assumption that surface configuration reflects the underlying rock type; a hard resistant rock such as granite will stand out, whereas a softer rock such as clay will be weathered away. However, this assumption is not always borne out. The Zugspitze, for example, is Germany's highest summit not because it is composed of particularly resistant rocks but because it was raised by the mighty earth movements that began some 37 to 24 million years ago and created the Alps, Europe's highest and youngest fold mountains. Another powerful force determining surface configuration is erosion, mainly

by rivers. In the Permian Period (some 290 million years ago) an earlier mountain chain—the Hercynian, or Variscan, mountains—had crossed Europe in the area of the Central German Uplands. Yet the forces of erosion were sufficient to reduce these mountains to almost level surfaces, on which a series of secondary sedimentary rocks of Permian to Jurassic age (about 300 to 145 million years old) were deposited. The entire formation was subsequently fractured and warped under the impact of the Alpine orogeny. This process was accompanied by some volcanic activity, which left behind not only peaks but also a substantial number of hot and mineral springs. Dramatic erosion occurred as the Alpine chains were rising, filling the furrow that now constitutes the Alpine Foreland. The pattern of valleys eroded by streams and rivers has largely given rise to the details of the present landscape. Valley glaciers emerging from the Alps and ice sheets from Scandinavia had some erosive effect, but they mainly contributed sheets of glacial deposits. Slopes outside the area of the actual ice sheets—those under tundra conditions and unprotected by vegetation—were rendered less steep by the periglacial slumping of surface deposits under the influence of gravitation. Winds blowing over unprotected surfaces fringing the ice sheets picked up fine material known as loess; once deposited, it became Germany's most fertile soil-parent material. Coarser weathered material was carried into alluvial cones and gravel-covered river terraces, as in the Rhine Rift Valley (Rhine Graben).

The detailed morphology of Germany is significant in providing local modifications to climate, hydrology, and soils, with consequent effects on vegetation and agricultural utilization.

THE CENTRAL GERMAN UPLANDS

Geographically, the Central German Uplands form a region of great complexity. Under the impact of the Alpine orogeny, the planed-off remnants of the former Hercynian mountains were shattered and portions thrust upward to form block mountains, with sedimentary rocks preserved between them in lowlands and plateaus. The Central German Uplands may be divided into three main parts: a predominantly lowland country in the south, an arc of massifs and plateaus running from the Rhenish Uplands to Bohemia, and a fairly narrow northern fringe, composed of folded secondary rocks.

SOUTHERN GERMANY

In southern Germany Hercynian massifs are of restricted extent. The Black Forest (Schwarzwald) was once continuous with the Vosges massif in what is now France, but they were broken apart through the sinking of a central strip to form the Rhine Rift Valley, which extends 185 miles (300 km) in length. The Black Forest reaches its greatest elevation at Mount Feld (Feldberg; 4,898 feet [1,493 metres]) in the south and declines northward beneath secondary sediments before rising to the smaller Oden Forest. For the most part, however, southern Germany consists of scarplands, mainly of Triassic age (about 250 to 200 million years old). The work of erosion on eastward-dipping strata has left the sandstones standing out as west- or northwest-facing scarps, overlooking valleys or low plateaus of clays or Muschelkalk (Triassic limestone formed from shells). The sequence of Triassic rocks ends south and east against the great Jurassic scarp of the Swabian Alp (Schwäbische Alb), rising to more than 3,300 feet (1,000 metres), and its continuation, the lower Franconian Alp (Fränkische Alb). Large parts of the plateaus and lowlands in the eastern region are covered with loess and are farmed, but the massive Bunter Sandstone fringing the Black Forest and the Keuper scarp are mainly wooded. West of the Rhine there are again wide stretches of forested Bunter Sandstone, with more open country in the Saar region and along the foot of the Hunsrück upland.

THE BARRIER ARC

The open land of southern Germany ends against a great barrier arc of Hercynian massifs and forested sandstone plateaus. In the west the Rhenish Uplands (Rheinisches Schiefergebirge) consist mainly of resistant slates and shales. The complex block is tilted generally northwestward, with a steep fault-line scarp

BLACK FOREST

 Located in southwestern Germany's Baden-Württemberg *Land* (state), the Black Forest (German: Schwarzwald) is the source of the Danube and Neckar rivers. The mountainous region occupies an area of 2,320 square miles (6,009 square km) and extends toward the northeast for about 100 miles (160 km) from Säckingen on the Upper Rhine River (at the Swiss border) to Durlach (east of Karlsruhe). Its width varies from 10 to 25 miles. Structurally and topographically, it forms the counterpart of the Vosges, which lies west of the Rhine valley. The Black Forest drops abruptly to the Rhine plain but slopes more gently toward the Neckar and Nagold valleys to the east.

Black Forest, Germany. © 2009 EB, Inc.

 It is mainly a granite highland with rounded summits, although its northern part comprises forested sandstone, and it is bordered to the south by a narrow band of lower and more fertile limestone. Divided into two parts by the deep Kinzig valley, its highest summits—Feldberg (4,897 feet [1,493 metres]), Herzogenhorn, and Blössling—are to the south. Its northern half has an average height of 2,000 feet.

 The raw climate of the higher districts supports only hardy grains, but the valleys are mild with good pastureland. Oak and beech woods clothe the lower slopes, while the extensive fir

forests, which gave the range its name, climb to 4,000 feet. Traditional economic activities—such as lumbering, woodworking, and the manufacture of watches, clocks, and musical instruments—continue. Newer manufactures include electronic equipment and precision machinery. Tourism and winter sports are also prominent, and there are many mineral springs and spas, such as Baden-Baden and Wildbad. Principal cities are Freiburg im Breisgau, Offenburg, Rastatt, and Lahr.

The Black Forest region, Baden-Württemberg, Germany © Huber/Press and Information Office of the Federal Government of Germany

in the south. The intensely folded rocks are planed off by erosion surfaces that give the massif a rather monotonous appearance, broken only by quartzite ridges, especially in the south, where the Hunsrück rises to 2,684 feet (818 metres) and the Taunus to 2,884 feet (879 metres).

The valleys are quite different. They range from narrow forested slots—a great hindrance to passage—to the spectacular gorge of the Rhine, the most important natural routeway through the barrier arc. The most dramatic section of the gorge runs from Bingen to the vicinity of Koblenz; hilltop castles look down over vineyards to picturesque valley towns. In this section is the Lorelei rock, from which a legendary siren is said to have lured fishermen to their death on the rocks.

Until highways were constructed over the plateau tops, access to the uplands was difficult. The landscape gained some variety from past volcanic activity responsible for the eroded volcanic necks of the Siebengebirge (Seven Hills) near Bonn, the flooded craters and cinder cones of the Eifel Upland, and the sombre basalt flows of the Westerwald. Westward the Rhenish Uplands continue into Belgium as the Ardennes. In the Carboniferous Period (about 360 to 300 million years ago), when the Hercynian uplands were still young folded mountains, great deltaic swamps developed to the north and south; these were the basis of the great Ruhr coalfield and the smaller Aachen and Saar fields.

The eastern end of the barrier arc is buttressed by the great and complex

Bohemian Massif, which Germany shares only marginally. On the southwestern fringe of the massif, German territory includes the remote and thinly populated Bohemian Forest and the Bavarian Forest. Along part of the Czech border are the Ore Mountains (Erzgebirge), where the centuries-old mining tradition still continued during the period of the German Democratic Republic before ending in the 1990s. The Bohemian Massif is prolonged northwestward by the long spur of the Thuringian Forest (Thüringer Wald), which separates the scarplands of northern Bavaria from the Thuringian Lowland. The barrier arc is completed by the great eroded cone of the Vogelberg, rising to 2,536 feet (773 metres), the volcanic Rhön mountains, and the forested Bunter Sandstone plateaus of northern Hessen. The Rhine Rift Valley continues northward through Hessen, with a series of discontinuous basins filled with sediments from the Paleogene and Neogene periods (i.e., about 65 to 2.6 million years ago) that allow a slightly difficult traverse to the North German Plain.

THE NORTHERN FRINGE OF THE CENTRAL GERMAN UPLANDS

North of the upland barrier there are a number of regions, generally of folded limestones, sandstones, and clays, that mark the transition to the expanse of the North German Plain. Balanced on either side of the plateau of Hessen are two basins of subdued scarpland relief, the Westphalian Basin to the northwest and the Thuringian Basin to the southeast, both partially invaded by glacial outwash from the North German Plain. Hessen and the Westphalian Basin are succeeded northward by the hills of Lower Saxony. The breakthrough of the Weser River into the North German Plain at the Porta Westfalica, south of Minden, is overlooked by the giant monument of Emperor William I (built in 1896). North of the Thuringian Basin is one of the smaller Hercynian massifs, the Harz, which reaches an elevation of 3,747 feet (1,142 metres) in the Brocken.

THE NORTH GERMAN PLAIN

Less than 90 miles (145 km) wide in the west, the North German Plain, or Lowland, broadens eastward across the whole of northern Germany. Although relief is subdued everywhere, the landscape is varied and beautiful. Unconsolidated Paleogene and Neogene deposits, gravels, sands, and clays, with overlying glacial drift, have buried the previous landscape of secondary rocks. These make only two brief appearances, in the chalk cliffs of the island of Rügen in the Baltic Sea and in the cliffs of Triassic Bunter Sandstone of the island of Helgoland, located some 40 miles (65 km) northwest of Cuxhaven in the North Sea. In the Paleogene and Neogene periods large swamps developed, and the underlying deposits of lignite (brown coal) are mined in Saxony, in Lower Lusatia (Niederlausitz), and west of the city of Cologne.

The North German Plain is divided into contrasting eastern and western portions, the division marked approximately by the Elbe valley. The northern and eastern regions were molded by southward-moving ice sheets in the last (Weichsel, or Vistula) glaciation. The advancing ice sheets pushed up material that remains today as terminal moraines, stretching across the country in a generally southeast-to-northwest direction and rising to some 500 feet (150 metres) above the general level. Within the terminal moraines the decay of the ice sheets typically left behind sheets of till (ground moraine). They are studded with ponds, often resulting from the decay of buried "dead ice," and littered with boulders of all sizes brought by the ice from Scandinavia. In a region otherwise lacking in stone, these boulders were used as building material and are to be found forming the walls of the oldest churches. Outside the moraines, meltwater laid down sheets of outwash sands, which, offering poorer soils, are frequently forested. In the moraine country there are large, long, and branching lake systems, usually believed to have been formed by water moving under the ice sheets.

The unique character of the region east of the Elbe is further enhanced by the fact that the ice sheets of the last glaciation coming from the north blocked the river's natural flow to the Baltic, forcing it to escape laterally around the margin of the ice toward the North Sea; the river cut a deep trench as it did so. The landscape in the western portion of the plain tends to be monotonous. Much of it was formerly heath; the few patches that have escaped afforestation, agricultural improvements, or damage caused by military training have a wistful beauty, especially when the heather is in bloom. At 554 feet (169 metres), Wilseder Hill (Wilseder Berg), a fragment of a former moraine, is the highest elevation in the Lüneburg Heath (Lüneburger Heide), a plateau extending on a morainic belt between Hamburg and Hannover. Toward the maritime northwest, large areas of peat bogs have been reclaimed for agriculture. The southern edge of the plain extending to the Thuringian Basin is marked by a belt of mainly loess, which supports highly productive agricultural activity.

THE COASTS

The western and eastern coastlines vary considerably in their forms. The coast of the North Sea continues the type familiar in the northern Netherlands; an offshore bar, crowned with sand dunes, has been shattered and left as the chain of the East Frisian Islands off the coast of Lower Saxony and the North Frisian Islands off the Schleswig-Holstein portion of the Jutland peninsula. These islands form a favourite vacation area in summer. The sea has encroached upon the land behind the islands, forming tidal flats (known as

Wattenmeer), which become exposed at low tide. The coast is broken by the estuaries of the Elbe, Weser, and Ems rivers and by drowned inlets such as the Jade and Dollart bays. Much of this area is now protected within three adjoining national parks (Schleswig-Holstein, Hamburg, and Lower Saxony Wadden Sea national parks).

Along the Baltic coast, the boulder-clay plains shelve rather tamely beneath the sea. However, the typically varied relief of minor moraines, depressions, and other glacial features gives diversity to the coastline. In Schleswig-Holstein long inlets (fjords), carved by water moving beneath the ice sheets, extend to the sea. Farther east the coast gains in complexity; there are peninsulas and sea inlets known as Bodden, and sandy beach bars dominate the landscape. Several islands line the shore, including Usedom, Hiddensee, Poel, and Rügen, Germany's largest island.

THE ALPS AND THE ALPINE FORELAND

Very small portions of the outer limestone (or calcareous) Alps extend from Austria into Germany. From west to east these are the Allgäuer Alps, the Wetterstein Alps—with Germany's highest mountain, the Zugspitze—and the Berchtesgadener Alps. Like the North German Plain, the Alpine Foreland is fundamentally a depression filled with Paleogene and Neogene gravels, sands, and clays, which are derived from the Alpine orogeny.

In contrast to the North German Plain, however, the Paleogene and Neogene deposits are more visible on the surface. Along the foot of the limestone Alps but particularly in the Allgäuer Alps in the west, the older Paleogene and Neogene deposits (flysch, molasse) were caught up in the later stages of the Alpine folding, forming a pre-Alpine belt of hills and low mountains consisting mainly of sandstone. The Paleogene and Neogene sands and clays also emerge at a much lower elevation in the northeast, forming a subdued landscape.

Glaciers emerging from the main Alpine valleys formed lobes stretching some 20 to 35 miles (30 to 55 km) into the plain. Crescentic moraines mark the points where the lobes came to rest; within the moraines are irregular deposits of till and many lakes. Outside the moraines, floodwaters deposited sheets of outwash gravel, which extend as river terraces along the courses of tributaries flowing north to the Danube. The Alps and the Bavarian lakes are among Germany's most favoured tourist areas.

DRAINAGE

Most German rivers follow the general north-northwestward inclination of the land, eventually entering the North Sea. The major exception to the rule is the Danube, which rises in the Black Forest and flows eastward, marking approximately the boundary between the Central German Uplands and the Alpine Foreland.

The Danube draws upon a series of right-bank Alpine tributaries, which, through reliance on spring and summer snow-melt, make its regime notably uneven. Further exceptions are the Altmühl and the Naab, which follow a southerly direction until becoming north-bank tributaries of the Danube, and the Havel, which flows south, west, and north before emptying into the Elbe River. River flow relates mainly to climate, albeit not in a simple way; for example, in all but Alpine Germany, maximum river flow occurs in winter when evaporation is low, though in the lowlands the peak rainfall is in summer.

The most majestic of the rivers flowing through Germany is the Rhine. It has its source in east-central Switzerland and flows west through Lake Constance (Bodensee), skirting the Black Forest to turn northward across the Central German Uplands. Below Bonn the Rhine emerges into a broad plain, and west of Emmerich it enters the Netherlands to issue into the North Sea. The Rhine belongs to two types of river regimes. Rising in the Alps, it profits first from the extremely torrential Alpine regime, which causes streams to be swollen by snowmelt in late spring and summer. Then, by means of its tributaries—the Neckar, Main, and Moselle (German Mosel)—the Rhine receives the drainage of the Central German Uplands and the eastern part of France, which contributes to a maximum flow during the winter. As a result, the river has a remarkably

Isar River at its source in the Karwendelgebirge (mountains), Bavaria, Germany. Charles Bear/ Shostal Associates

powerful and even flow, a physical endowment that caused it to become the busiest waterway in Europe. Only in occasional dry autumns are barges unable to load to full capacity to pass the Rhine gorge.

The Weser and Elbe rise in the Central German Uplands, crossing the North German Plain to enter the North Sea. The northward-flowing Oder (with its tributary, the Neisse) passes through the northeastern part of the country and a small section of Poland before emptying into the Baltic Sea. The navigation of these rivers is often adversely affected in the summer by low water and in the winter by ice, which increases eastward.

River courses in the northern lowlands have a notably trellised pattern—rivers follow the ice-margin stream trenches (Urstromtäler) carved outside the fringes of the retreating ice sheets before breaking

Meander in the Rhine River valley at Boppard, Germany, just south of the confluence with the Moselle River. The J. Allan Cash Photolibrary

through the next moraine ridge to the north. This pattern greatly facilitated the cutting of canals linking the Rhine River with Berlin and the Elbe and Oder rivers.

Germany has relatively few lakes. The greatest concentration comprises the shallow lakes of the postglacial lowland of the northeast. The largest natural lake in the region is Lake Müritz (44 square miles [114 square km]) in the Weichsel glacial drift of Mecklenburg–West Pomerania. In addition to Dümmer and Steinhude in Lower Saxony, a few small lakes of glacial origin dot Schleswig-Holstein. The remainder of Germany's lakes are concentrated at the extreme southeastern corner of Upper Bavaria, many of these in outstandingly beautiful surroundings. Germany shares Lake Constance, its largest lake (having the proportions of an inland sea), with Switzerland and Austria.

SOILS

Most of Germany has temperate brown and deep brown soils. Their formation is dependent on relief, hydrologic conditions, vegetation, and human intervention.

Germany's finest soils are developed on the loess of the northern flank of the Central German Uplands, the Magdeburg Plain, the Thuringian Basin and adjoining areas, the Rhine valley, and the Alpine Foreland. They range from black to extremely fertile brown soil types, and most of them are arable land under cultivation. The till (ground moraine) of the

LAKE CONSTANCE

Lake Constance (German: Bodensee), which borders Switzerland, Germany, and Austria, occupies an old glacier basin at an elevation of 1,299 feet (396 metres). It has an area of 209 square miles (541 square km) and is about 40 miles (65 km) long and up to 8 miles (13 km) wide, with an average depth of 295 feet (90 metres) and a maximum depth of 827 feet (252 metres). It has about 125 miles (200 km) of shoreline. In the west, near Konstanz (Constance), it is divided by the Bodan mountain ridge into two parts: the Unter Lake (south) and the Überlinger Lake (north). The lake's main body southeast of Konstanz is called the Ober Lake. The lake forms part of the course of the Rhine River, which enters it in the southeast near Bregenz and leaves it at the west via the Unter Lake. The island of Mainau is north of Konstanz in the Überlinger Lake, and the island of Reichenau is west of the city in the Unter Lake. Konstanz itself is a "political island," for it is the only part of Germany on the lake's southwestern shore; it is entirely surrounded by Swiss territory, except on the northeast where it fronts on the lake.

Boat on Lake Constance, near Lindau, Germany © Huber/Press and Information Office of the Federal Government of Germany

The name Bodensee probably derives from the Carolingian imperial palatinate of Bodman at the northwest end of the Überlinger Lake. By the Middle Ages, the lake was a major traffic centre as the meeting place of roads from all directions. There are remains of Neolithic lake dwellings in the area.

The lake stores and reflects heat, contributing to the unusually sunny and mild climate along its shores. The fertile slopes along its shores support fruit-growing and wine production, and there is fishing for lake trout and salmon. Spectacular Alpine scenery combines with the mild climate to make the lake a popular resort area. The major lakeside cities are Konstanz, Lindau, and Friedrichshafen, Germany; Bregenz, Austria; and Kreuzlingen, Switzerland.

North German Plain and Alpine Foreland has heavy but fertile soil. Other productive soils include those based on fluvial deposits in river valleys (e.g., those in the Rhine floodplain from Mainz to Basel, Switzerland). Brown soil covers much of the Central German Uplands and is used for agriculture and grazing. With increasing elevation, soils are suitable only for grazing or forestation. In the northern plains the soil types are sand, loam, and brown podzols, which are heavily leached of mineral matter and humus by deforestation and grazing. Along the North Sea littoral in the northwest there are some extensive areas of sand, marsh, and mudflats that are covered with rich soil suitable for grazing and growing crops.

Because of the preponderance of mountainous and forested areas, the remainder of German soil types range from sand to loam, from loam to clay, and from clay to rocky outcrops. Timber production thrives where the land is all but unarable, and viticulture in the southern hill regions flourishes in an otherwise inhospitable type of soil.

CLIMATE

Germany is favoured with a generally temperate climate, especially in view of its northerly latitudes and the distance of the larger portions of its territory from the warming influence of the North Atlantic Current. Extremely high temperatures in the summer and deep, prolonged frost in the winter are rare. These conditions, together with a more-than-abundant and well-distributed amount of rainfall, afford ideal conditions for raising crops. As throughout western Europe in general, however, Germany's climate is subject to quick variations when the moderate westerly winds from the Atlantic Ocean collide with the cold air masses moving in from northeastern Europe. Whereas in the open coastlands near the North

and Baltic seas the maritime component prevails, continental elements gain in importance moving toward the east and southeast.

Seasonal weather is subject to great variations from year to year. Winters may be unusually cold or prolonged, particularly in the higher elevations in the south, or mild, with the temperatures hovering only two or three degrees above or below the freezing point. Spring may arrive early and extend through a hot, rainless summer to a warm, dry autumn with the threat of drought. In other years, spring—invariably interrupted by a frosty lapse in May, popularly known as *die drei Eisheiligen* ("the three ice saints")—may arrive so late as to be imperceptible and be followed by a cool, rainy summer. One less-agreeable feature of the German climate is the almost permanent overcast in the cool seasons, only infrequently accompanied by precipitation; it sets in toward the latter part of autumn and lifts as late as March or April. Thus, for months on end, little sunshine may appear.

Despite the country's generally temperate climate, there are specific regional patterns associated with temperature, frequency of sunshine, humidity, and precipitation. Germany's northwestern and lowland portions are affected chiefly by the uniformly moist air, moderate in temperature, that is carried inland from the North Sea by the prevailing westerly winds. Although this influence affords moderately warm summers and mild winters, it is accompanied by the disadvantages of high humidities, extended stretches of rainfall, and, in the cooler seasons, fog. Precipitation diminishes eastward, as the plains open toward the Eurasian interior and the average temperatures for the warmest and coldest months become more extreme. The hilly areas of the central and southwestern regions and, to an even greater degree, the upland and plateau areas of the southeast are subject to the more pronounced ranges of hot and cold from the countervailing continental climate. The mountains have a wetter and cooler climate, with westward-facing slopes receiving the highest rainfall from maritime air masses. The Brocken in the Harz mountains receives annual precipitation of some 60 inches (1,500 mm) at an altitude in excess of 3,700 feet (1,100 metres). The sheltered lee slopes and basins have, by contrast, rainfall that is extremely low—Alsleben receives about 17 inches (432 mm) annually—and hot summers—July mean temperatures above 64 °F (18 °C)—that necessitate crop irrigation. Southeastern Germany may intermittently be the coldest area of the country in the winter, but the valleys of the Rhine, Main, Neckar, and Moselle rivers may also be the hottest in the summer. Winters in the North German Plain tend to be consistently colder, if only by a few degrees, than in the south, largely because of winds from Scandinavia. There is also a general decrease of winter temperature from west to east, with Berlin having an average temperature in January of 31.5 °F (-0.3 °C).

One anomaly of the climate of Upper Bavaria is the occasional appearance of warm, dry air passing over the northern Alps to the Bavarian Plateau. These mild winds, known as foehns (Föhn), can create an optical phenomenon that makes the Alps visible from points where they normally would be out of sight, and they also are responsible for the abrupt melting of the snow.

Annual mean precipitation varies according to region. It is lowest in the North German Plain, where it fluctuates from 20 to 30 inches (500 to 750 mm); in the Central German Uplands it ranges from nearly 30 to about 60 inches (750 to 1,500 mm) and in the Alpine regions up to and exceeding 80 inches (2,000 mm).

PLANT AND ANIMAL LIFE

Since Germany is a somewhat arbitrary south-north slice across central Europe, it does not have vegetation and animal life greatly different from that of neighbouring countries. Before being settled, Germany was almost totally forested, except for a few areas of marsh. There is now little truly natural vegetation; both the cultivated areas and the country's extensive forests, which account for about one-fifth of the total land area, are man-made.

PLANTS

After the Ice Age the loess areas were covered by oak and hornbeam forests, which are now largely gone. The sandy areas of the North German Plain were originally covered by a predominantly mixed oak-birch woodland. They were cleared and replaced by heather (*Calluna vulgaris*) for sheep grazing, with associated soil erosion. In the 19th century artificial fertilizer was introduced to improve some of this land for agriculture, and large stretches were forested, mainly with Scotch pine (*Pinus sylvestris*). The Central German Uplands are traditionally the domain of the beech (*Fagus sylvatica*), a tree with a leaf canopy so dense that few plants can survive beneath it. Although beech trees survive well on the poor soils covering the limestones and the Bunter Sandstone, many have been replaced by pine in the lowlands and spruce in the uplands. Other conifers, such as the Douglas and Sitka spruces, Weymouth pine, and Japanese larch, also have been introduced. In the highest elevations of the Alps, mixed forests and pasture provide grazing for cattle. German forests have suffered greatly from acid rain pollution, generally blamed on emissions (of sulfur dioxide and nitrogen oxide) from power plants, industrial operations, and motor-vehicle emissions. Damage has also been severe in southeastern Germany near the Ore Mountains, which border on the Czech Republic and its lignite-burning industries.

ANIMALS

The vast tracts of forest and mountainous terrain, with only scattered habitation, contribute to a surprising variety of wildlife. Game animals abound in most regions—several varieties of deer, quail, and pheasant and, in the Alpine regions, the chamois and ibex—and their numbers are protected by stringent game laws. The wild boar population, which soared after World War II because of restrictions on hunting, has now been reduced so that it no longer represents a danger to people or crops. The hare, a favoured game animal, is ubiquitous. Although the bear and wolf are now extinct in the wild, the wildcat has had a resurgence since World War II, especially in the Eifel and Hunsrück regions and in the Harz mountains. The lynx reappeared in the areas near the Czech border, and the elk and wolf are occasional intruders from the east. The polecat, marten, weasel, beaver, and badger are found in the central and southern uplands, and the otter and wildcat are among the rarer animals of the Elbe basin. Common reptiles include salamanders, slow worms, and various lizards and snakes, of which only the adder is poisonous.

Germany has several internationally recognized bird reserves. The tidal flats of Lower Saxony (Niedersächsisches Wattenmeer) and Schleswig-Holstein along the North Sea coast, the lakes of the Mecklenburg plains, and glacially formed lakes of the North German Plain are vital areas for the European migration of ducks, geese, and waders. The nature protection park at Lüneburg Heath is a haven for various species of plants, birds, insects, and reptiles. The rare white-tailed eagle can be found in the lakes of the North German Plain, whereas the golden eagle can be seen in the Alps. White storks have decreased in number, but they can still be seen, perched on enormous piles of sticks on chimneys or church towers in areas where unpolluted and undrained marsh is still found. One newly designated reserve area is now within a national park in the lower Oder River valley, which is flooded annually. The park was established as part of an effort to preserve Germany's unique eco-system and its hundreds of species of native birds and plants.

CHAPTER 2

PEOPLE

The German-speaking peoples—which include the inhabitants of Germany as well as those of Austria, Liechtenstein, and the major parts of Switzerland and Luxembourg; small portions of France, Belgium, the Netherlands, and Italy; and the remnants of German communities in eastern Europe—are extremely heterogeneous in their ethnic origins, dialectal divisions, and political and cultural heritage, in which the split between Protestantism and Roman Catholicism has played a significant role since the Protestant Reformation and Catholic Counter-Reformation in the 16th century.

Throughout its history Germany has been characterized by a lack of clearly defined geographic boundaries. Both the area occupied by the German peoples and the boundaries of the German state (at such times as it existed) have fluctuated constantly. The German people appear to have originated on the coastal region of the Baltic Sea and in the Baltic islands in the Bronze and early Iron ages. From about 500 BCE they began to move southward, crushing and absorbing the existing Celtic kingdoms; from 58 BCE they clashed with Rome along the line of the Rhine and Danube rivers. With the fall of the Roman Empire, German peoples, predominantly under Frankish tribal leadership, closely settled a large area west of the Rhine River in what is still German territory; they also penetrated deeply into Belgium and areas that later became France. The Merovingian and Carolingian empires made no distinction between what are now France and western Germany, and thus it is understandable that Charlemagne

German delegates in Versailles, France, in 1919 listening to a speech by French Prime Minister Georges Benjamin Clemenceau. © Everett Collection/SuperStock

(Karl der Grosse) is recognized as an important figure in the history of both countries.

The weakness of Charlemagne's successors was revealed in their inability to handle the waves of invaders that poured into the empire at the end of the 9th century. In despair, people turned to local leaders able to offer protection. In the German heartland the old tribal divisions still retained their validity, and the tribes looked for defense to an army of their own people, led by a duke. Indeed, the names of these dukedoms are still used for some of the German states (*Länder*), notably Bavaria, Thuringia, and (Lower) Saxony. In the 10th and 11th centuries they were brought under the power of a single monarch, but this precocious centralization did not survive. The dukedoms were progressively subdivided until Germany became notorious for its Kleinstaaterei— its swarm of frequently tiny states, each with its court borne on the backs of the peasantry. The states, and particularly their boundaries, were of considerable social and economic significance, introducing contrasts that are still somewhat perceptible.

The rise of France extinguished most of Germanic control west of the Rhine, a process facilitated by German divisions; German dialects remain in use in France only in Alsace and parts of Lorraine. However, driven by population pressure during the Middle Ages, Germans cleared large areas of forest for the expansion of cultivation and extended their settlements far to the east. From about 800 in the south and about two centuries later in the centre and north, the Germans moved east in an advance that divided into three prongs: down the Danube through Austria, north of the Central German Uplands through Silesia, and along the Baltic shore. Between the prongs were the partially isolated Slavic areas of Bohemia and Poland; this development held the potential for conflict that lasted into the 20th century. Islands of German people were at various times established beyond the continuously settled area as far as the Volga. Many of their descendants later moved farther east into Asia under harsh decrees and policies instituted by Soviet leader Joseph Stalin. Over the centuries these groups tenaciously retained their German language and culture.

The German Empire created in 1871 did not include all German-speaking peoples. In particular, the Germans of the Austro-Hungarian Empire were excluded from the new Reich, and Switzerland, with its majority of German speakers, retained its independence. After World War I large numbers of Germans who had lived under German or Austrian rule found themselves under French rule—Alsace and Lorraine, German since 1871, were returned to France—or in the states created by the Treaty of Versailles in 1919, notably Poland and Czechoslovakia. The presence of German ethnic minorities in these countries was later used by Adolf Hitler as a pretext for military occupation. After World War II the German populations were largely expelled from Czechoslovakia and Poland, making the distribution of German-speaking people more nearly coincidental with the boundaries of the German state, although Austria and German-speaking Switzerland still remained outside.

ETHNIC GROUPS

The Germans, in their various changes of territory, inevitably intermingled with other peoples. In the south and west they overran Celtic peoples, and there must at least have been sufficient communication for them to adopt the names of physical features such as rivers and hills; the names Rhine, Danube, and Neckar, for example, are thought to be of Celtic origin. Similarly, in occupying the Slavic lands to the east, Germans seem to have taken over and reorganized the Slavs along with their established framework of rural and urban settlements, many of which, along with numerous physical features, still bear names of Slavic origin. The same is true of family names. In addition, large numbers of immigrants added to the mixture: French Huguenots at the end of the 16th century, Polish mine workers in the Ruhr at the end of the 19th, White Russians in Berlin after the communist revolution of 1917, and stateless "displaced persons" left behind by World War II.

Prior to the 1950s there were few ethnic minorities in Germany, except Jews, whose population was decimated during the Holocaust. A population of Slavic-speaking Sorbs (Wends), variously estimated at between 30,000 and an improbable 100,000, have survived in the Lusatia (Lausitz) area, between Dresden and Cottbus, and a small number of Danish speakers can still be found in Schleswig-Holstein, even after the Versailles boundary changes there. Of the so-called "guest workers" (Gastarbeiter) and their families who immigrated to Germany beginning in the mid-1950s, the largest group is of Turkish ancestry. Distinct both culturally and religiously, they are scattered throughout German cities. Even more culturally distinct groups have been added by asylum seekers from countries such as Sri Lanka and Vietnam, and the opening of the eastern frontiers brought many more immigrants, including several thousand Jews seeking religious and ethnic tolerance and economic opportunity. By the beginning of the 21st century nearly one-tenth of the population—some eight million people—were non-Germans.

LANGUAGES

The dialectal divisions of Germany, once of conspicuous significance for the ethnic and cultural distinctions they implied, persist despite leveling and standardizing influences such as mass education and communication and despite internal migration and the trend among the younger, better-educated, and more-mobile ranks of society to speak a standard, "accentless" German. The repository of dialectal differences now lies more with the rural populace and the longtime native inhabitants of the cities.

Standard German itself is something of a hybrid language in origin, drawn from elements of the dialects spoken in the central and southern districts but with the phonetic characteristics of the north predominating. Indeed, the pronunciation of standard German is an arbitrary compromise that gained universal currency only in the late 19th century. Even today the most "accent-conscious" of the well-educated speak with the coloration of their native district's dialect, especially so if they are from the southern regions.

The three major dialectal divisions of Germany coincide almost identically with the major topographic regions: the North German Plain (Low German), the Central German Uplands (Central German), and the southern Jura, Danube basin, and Alpine districts (Upper German). Of the

GERMAN LANGUAGE

German is the official language of both Germany and Austria and one of the three official languages of Switzerland. German belongs to the West Germanic group of the Indo-European language family, along with English, Frisian, and Dutch (Netherlandic, Flemish).

The recorded history of Germanic languages begins with their speakers' first contact with the Romans, in the 1st century BCE. At that time and for several centuries thereafter, there was only a single "Germanic" language, with little more than minor dialect differences. Only after about the 6th century CE can one speak of a "German" (i.e., High German) language.

German is an inflected language with four cases for nouns, pronouns, and adjectives (nominative, accusative, genitive, dative), three genders (masculine, feminine, neuter), and strong and weak verbs. Altogether German is the native language of more than 90 million speakers and thus probably ranks sixth in number of native speakers among the languages of the world (after Chinese, English, Hindi-Urdu, Spanish, and Russian). German is widely studied as a foreign language and is one of the main cultural languages of the Western world.

As a written language German is quite uniform; it differs in Germany, Austria, and Switzerland no more than written English does in the United States and the British Commonwealth. As a spoken language, however, German exists in many dialects, most of which belong to either the High German or Low German dialectal groups. The main difference between High and Low German is in the sound system, especially in the consonants. High German, the language of the southern highlands of Germany, is the official written language.

HIGH GERMAN (HOCHDEUTSCH)

Old High German, a group of dialects for which there was no standard literary language, was spoken until about 1100 in the highlands of southern Germany. During Middle High German times (after 1100), a standard language based on the Upper German dialects (Alemannic and Bavarian) in the southernmost part of the German speech area began to arise. Middle High German was the language of an extensive literature that includes the early 13th-century epic *Nibelungenlied*.

Modern standard High German is descended from the Middle High German dialects and is spoken in the central and southern highlands of Germany, Austria, and Switzerland. It is used as the language of administration, higher education, literature, and the mass media in the Low German speech area as well. Standard High German is based on, but not identical to, the Middle German dialect used by Martin Luther in his 16th-century translation of the Bible. Within the modern High German speech area, Middle and Upper German dialect groups are differentiated, the latter group including Austro-Bavarian, Alemannic (Swiss German), and High Franconian.

LOW GERMAN (PLATTDEUTSCH, OR NIEDERDEUTSCH)

Low German, with no single modern literary standard, is the spoken language of the lowlands of northern Germany. It developed from Old Saxon and the Middle Low German speech of the citizens of the Hanseatic League. The language supplied the Scandinavian languages with many loanwords, but, with the decline of the league, Low German declined as well.

Although the numerous Low German dialects are still spoken in the homes of northern Germany and a small amount of literature is written in them, no standard Low German literary or administrative language exists.

OTHER MAJOR DIALECTS

Alemannic dialects, which developed in the southwestern part of the Germanic speech area, differ considerably in sound system and grammar from standard High German. These dialects are spoken in Switzerland, western Austria, Swabia, and Liechtenstein and in the Alsace region of France. Yiddish, the language of the Ashkenazic Jews (Jews whose ancestors lived in Germany in the European Middle Ages), also developed from High German.

Upper German dialects, the Alemannic branch in the southwest is subdivided into Swabian, Low Alemannic, and High Alemannic. Swabian, the most widespread and still-ascending form, is spoken to the west and south of Stuttgart and as far east as Augsburg. Low Alemannic is spoken in Baden-Württemberg and Alsace, and High Alemannic is the dialect of German-speaking Switzerland. The Bavarian dialect, with its many local variations, is spoken in the areas south of the Danube River and east of the Lech River and throughout all of Austria, except in the state of Vorarlberg, which is Swabian in origin.

The Central German, or Franconian, dialect and the Thuringian dialect helped to form the basis of modern standard German. The present-day influence of Thuringian is of greatest significance in Thuringia, Saxony, and Saxony-Anhalt states. East Franconian is spoken in northern Bavaria, South Franconian in northern Baden-Württemberg. The Rhenish Franconian dialect extends northwest from approximately Metz, in French Lorraine, through the states of Rhineland-Palatinate and Hessen. Moselle Franconian extends from Luxembourg through the Moselle valley districts and across the Rhine into the Westerwald. Ripuarian Franconian begins roughly near Aachen, at the Dutch-Belgian border, and spreads across the Rhine between Düsseldorf and Bonn into the Sauerland.

The dialect known as Low German, or Plattdeutsch, historically was spoken in all regions occupied by the Saxons and spread across the whole of the North German Plain. Although it has been largely displaced by standard German, it is still widely spoken, especially among elderly and rural inhabitants in the areas near the North and Baltic seas, and is used in some radio broadcasts, newspapers, and educational programs. Tiny pockets of Frisian, the German dialect most closely related to English, persist. Foreign immigration, more widespread education, the influence of the United States, and globalization also have helped create a polyglot of languages in major German cities.

RELIGION

The Reformation initiated by Martin Luther in 1517 divided German Christians between Roman Catholicism and Protestantism. The Peace of Augsburg (1555) introduced the principle that (with some exceptions) the inhabitants of each of Germany's numerous territories should follow the religion of the ruler; thus, the south and west became mainly Roman Catholic, the north and east Protestant. Religious affiliation had great effect not only on subjective factors such as culture and personal attitudes but also on social and economic developments. For example, the willingness of Berlin to receive Calvinist religious refugees (Huguenots) from Louis XIV's France meant that by the end of the 17th century one-fifth of the city's inhabitants were of French extraction. The Huguenots introduced numerous new branches of manufacture to the city and strongly influenced administration, the army, the advancement of science, education, and fashion. The Berlin dialect still employs many terms of French derivation.

Population movements during and after World War II brought many Protestants into western Germany, evening the numbers of adherents of the two religions. In the former West Germany most people, whether or not they attended church, agreed to pay the church tax levied with their income tax; the revenue from this tax has been used to support community centres, hospitals, senior citizens' centres and group homes, and the construction of church buildings in the former East Germany. The centrality of religion in Germany has meant that religious leaders, especially the Roman Catholic hierarchy, sometimes exercise considerable influence on political decisions on social issues such as abortion.

In East Germany Protestants outnumbered Roman Catholics about seven to one. Although the constitution nominally guaranteed religious freedom, religious affiliation was discouraged. Church membership, especially for individuals who were not members of the ruling Socialist Unity Party (SED), was a barrier to career advancement. Similarly, youth who on religious grounds did not join the Free German Youth (Freie Deutsche Jugend) lost access to recreational facilities and organized holidays and found it difficult, if not impossible, to secure admission to universities. Not surprisingly, formal church affiliation was relatively low, amounting to only about half the population, compared with nearly seven-eighths in West Germany. However, Protestant (Lutheran) churches did act as rallying

MARTIN LUTHER

The German priest Martin Luther (born November 10, 1483, Eisleben, Saxony [Germany]—died February 18, 1546, Eisleben) sparked the Reformation. Through his words and actions, Luther precipitated a movement that reformulated certain basic tenets of Christian belief and resulted in the division of Western Christendom between Roman Catholicism and the new Protestant traditions, mainly Lutheranism, Calvinism, the Anglican Communion, the Anabaptists, and the Antitrinitarians. He is one of the most influential figures in the history of Christianity.

Luther studied philosophy and law before entering an Augustinian monastery in 1505. He was ordained two years later and continued his theological studies at the University of Wittenberg, where he became a professor of biblical studies. On a trip to Rome in 1510 he was shocked by the corruption of the clergy and was later troubled by doubts centring on fear of divine retributive justice. His spiritual crisis was resolved when he hit on the idea of justification by faith, the doctrine that salvation is granted as a gift through God's grace. He urged reform of the Roman Catholic Church, protesting the sale of indulgences and other abuses, and in 1517

Martin Luther. Imagno/Hulton Fine Art Collection/Getty Images

he distributed to the archbishop of Mainz and several friends his Ninety-five Theses (according to legend, Luther nailed the theses to the door of the castle church in Wittenberg); the theses questioned Roman Catholic teaching and called for reform. In 1521 he was excommunicated by Pope Leo X and declared an outlaw at the Diet of Worms. Under the protection of the elector of Saxony, Luther took refuge in Wartburg. There he translated the Bible into German; his superbly vigorous translation has long been regarded as the greatest landmark in the history of the German language. He later returned to Wittenberg, and in 1525 he married the former nun Katherine of Bora, with whom he raised five children. Though his preaching was the principal spark that set off the

Peasants' War (1524–25), his vehement denunciation of the peasants contributed to their defeat. His break with Rome led to the founding of the Lutheran Church; the Lutheran confession of faith, or Augsburg Confession, was produced with Luther's sanction by Philipp Melanchthon in 1530. Luther's writings included hymns, a liturgy, and many theological works.

points for supporters of unofficial protest groups, leading ultimately to the demonstrations that toppled the communist government in 1989.

Lutherans and Roman Catholics in Germany now are about equal in number. Small percentages of Germans belong to what are known as the free churches, such as Evangelical Methodists, Calvinists, Old Catholics, Jehovah's Witnesses, and (by far the largest) Eastern Orthodox. The number of people professing no religion (Konfessionslose) has sharply increased and now represents about one-fifth of all Germans. Because of large-scale Turkish immigration, Muslims now account for some 5 percent of the total population. Only a few thousand German Jews survived the Holocaust. During the 1990s, however, Germany's Jewish population quadrupled, the result of significant immigration from eastern Europe (especially Russia). There are now some 100,000 Jews in the country, and Berlin, with Germany's largest concentration of Jews, has experienced a modest rebirth of its once thriving Jewish community.

SETTLEMENT PATTERNS

Since medieval times Germany has been politically fragmented, with numerous states competing with one another to develop lucrative market centres and to create capitals, large and small. As a result, the country inherited a profusion of towns and cities. Most of these remained frozen within their circuits of walls until the 19th century, with only the larger princely capitals (e.g., Berlin and Munich) developing distinctive government quarters in the early modern period.

RURAL SETTLEMENT

The most striking feature of the rural settlement pattern in western Germany is probably the concentration of farmyards into extremely large villages, known as Haufendörfer. These villages are surrounded by unenclosed fields divided into often hundreds of striplike units. The Haufendorf is particularly characteristic of Hessen and southwestern Germany, areas that have a tradition of partible inheritance. During periods of population pressure, land holdings—as well as farmhouses and farmyards—were repeatedly divided on inheritance, becoming progressively smaller and more fragmented. As a result, villages became increasingly huddled and chaotic. In areas with a tradition of undivided inheritance (e.g., Bavaria and Lower Saxony), the holdings—the individual field parcels and the farmhouses—remained larger.

During the period of high medieval prosperity in the 11th to 13th centuries, population pressure brought about the advance of peasant settlements into the forests, where isolated farms and hamlets were the usual settlement form, and the colonization of the predominantly Slavic lands beyond the line of the Elbe and Saale rivers. Because this was an organized colonization under the control of the lords and their agents, the haphazard structure of the western Haufendorf could be streamlined into a few well-planned forms. Thus farmhouses in the eastern regions were customarily arranged along either a single village street (Strassendorf) or an elongated green, on which stood the church (Angerdorf); long unfenced strips of land were allotted at right angles to the road or green.

The evolution of rural settlement has not been uniform. Instead, there have been phases of advance and retreat. In particular, the decline of medieval prosperity, accompanied by the Black Death that decimated much of Europe's population in the 14th century, led to a stage of retreat, in which many hundreds of villages—the so-called "lost villages"—were abandoned in western Germany. In eastern Germany lords often appropriated deserted farms and added them to their own land, thus initiating that characteristic feature of the area beyond the Elbe, the large Junker estate farm (Gut).

The organization of agriculture and settlement in eastern and western Germany diverged considerably after World War II. In western Germany federal and state governments provided large subsidies to improve the existing structure. Land consolidation created larger holdings, and in some places farmers were moved to new farmsteads dispersed outside the villages. An increased average size of holding was associated with a massive movement of people out of agriculture. But instead of leaving for the cities, as occurred in the 19th century, people mostly remained in their existing homes and commuted to work. Part-time "Sunday" farming remained, but on a reduced scale. Land was actually left uncultivated by the new urban workers (social fallow). Some of this land was cultivated by the few remaining full-time farmers, but marginal areas were abandoned, being either afforested or reverting to rough grass and scrub.

In East Germany the Junker estates were confiscated and either divided among peasants or turned into state farms. This development was only the first stage in a process of collectivization; from 1958 to 1960, private holdings were regrouped under heavy political pressure into vast "cooperative" farms. New buildings marked the introduction of mechanized cultivation or large-scale animal husbandry, and multistory apartments and community centres reflected a politically inspired attempt to create a new concept of rural life. After unification

Munich, Germany, with (left) *the twin towers of the Church of Our Lady and* (right) *the New Town Hall.* Camerique/H. Armstrong Roberts

rural settlement patterns and agriculture were once again transformed in eastern Germany, with a decline of about three-fourths in agricultural employment. Few private farms were reestablished, however, and very large areas were fallowed.

URBAN SETTLEMENT

Germany's great urban explosion came late in the 19th century. Because industrialization was linked largely to the development of the railways, urban expansion was not confined to areas near the coalfields, such as the Ruhr region, but was distributed among many cities. Typically, the new urban workers were herded into dismal five-story apartment blocks built on a monotonous grid of straight-line streets. Today, especially in eastern Berlin and cities such as Dresden,

Halle, and Leipzig, these blocks present an urgent problem of urban renewal.

World War II was followed by a period of rapid urban growth as evacuees returned to the bombed cities. After 1949, however, contrasting government policies led to divergent urban development in eastern and western Germany. In West Germany many people abandoned the old city cores in favour of suburbs and urbanized villages within commuting range. Thus, in many agglomerations, notably in the Ruhr region, population loss was associated with peripheral gain. By contrast, the East German government pursued a policy of population concentration, whereby people were moved into concentrated peripheral settlements of 50,000 to 100,000, consisting of uniform prefabricated high-rise housing blocks built at the immediate outskirts of larger towns and cities. Economic growth and change in postwar Germany led to the loss of a considerable heritage of historic buildings, compounding the losses suffered during the war. However, during the last decades of the 20th century, virtually all western German towns and cities began to restore historic buildings from a variety of eras and architectural styles. The same process occurred much more slowly in the east prior to unification, but preservation efforts increased beginning in the 1990s.

DEMOGRAPHIC TRENDS

Excepting Russia, Germany is Europe's most populous country. Its population density is high in comparison with those of most other European countries, although less than those of Belgium and the Netherlands. Germany has one of the world's lowest birth rates, and its life expectancy—some 75 years for males and 80 for females—is among the world's highest. Over the last decades of the 20th century and the first decade of 21st century, Germany has witnessed years of both positive and negative population growth. From the mid-1970s to the mid-1980s the country's population dropped; however, Germany experienced significant population growth—largely because of immigration—over the following decade. Thereafter the country's population growth was slight. To stem long-term population decline, governments at all levels have attempted to develop policies aimed at encouraging an increase in the birth rate, in particular by subsidizing child care and providing benefits and other tax incentives to families.

MIGRATION

After World War II Germany received more than 12 million refugees and expellees from former German territory east of the Oder and from areas with substantial German ethnic populations in central and eastern Europe. These numbers were swollen by the ranks of "displaced persons"—non-Germans unwilling to return to their former homelands. After Germany was partitioned in 1949, the demographic histories of the two parts of the country diverged, with West Germany becoming the prime target of continuing migration flows. Although immigrants, principally ethnic Germans, continued to drift in from the east, their numbers were overshadowed by a mass desertion of some two million people from East Germany. Because these immigrants from East Germany were mostly young and highly skilled, their arrival was a major gain to the booming West German economy but a grievous loss to the much smaller East Germany. In 1961 the East German government blocked further desertion of its people by building strong defenses along the inner-German border and around West Berlin (including the Berlin Wall). East Germany enjoyed relative demographic tranquillity for most of the following three decades. After the disintegration of communist regimes throughout central and eastern Europe, however, the population of West Germany began to surge again because of flows first from newly liberalized Hungary and Czechoslovakia and then from East Germany after the inner-German boundary was opened and the Berlin Wall fell on November 9, 1989. In 1989–90 alone nearly 700,000 East Germans poured into West Germany; thereafter the stream continued, though from 1994 to 1997 net immigration occurred at a sharply reduced rate before increasing again because of ongoing economic problems in eastern Germany.

The arrival of these new migrants caused some resentment among western Germans because of the pressures placed on an already overburdened housing market and on social services. Because the new arrivals were mainly young and skilled, they fueled a postunification boom in western Germany and continued to drain the economy and society in the east, which still faces economic and social problems. Several hundred thousand eastern Germans also commuted to jobs in western Germany.

To spur economic growth, West Germany began as early as the mid-1950s to encourage workers to migrate from other countries. At first these migrants were to be "guest workers," coming to work for a limited period of time only, but increasingly they sent for their families; thus, even when economic recession occurred in 1973 and the further immigration of workers was discouraged, the number of foreign residents continued to grow, reaching more than seven million people—nearly one-tenth of the total—by the beginning of the 21st century. Because of higher birth rates among the foreign-born population, non-Germans have accounted for a majority of natural population growth since the 1950s. The Turks represent the largest group of foreign residents, followed by Yugoslavs (Serbs and Montenegrins), Italians, Greeks, Poles, Croats, Austrians, and Bosnians. Immigrants typically were employed in the heaviest, dirtiest, and least-remunerative jobs, and in times of economic difficulty they generally were the first to lose their jobs and the last to be reemployed. Their children—of whom more than four-fifths have been born in

Germany—are among the last to be considered for an apprenticeship or training place. Immigrants also inhabit the least-desirable housing. Turks, in particular, have formed distinctive quarters in the poorest "inner city" areas. Although the East German state prided itself on its nonreliance on guest workers, some Poles, Vietnamese, Angolans, Cubans, and Mozambicans were imported, ostensibly for "education and training."

With the opening of the eastern frontiers and a more liberal attitude of the Soviet Union toward emigration, the influx of ethnic Germans became a veritable flood. Nearly 400,000 came in 1989, followed by more than 200,000 annually between 1991 and 1995; subsequently the number of immigrants fell but remained substantial. These new immigrants were less easily assimilated into western German culture than those from eastern Germany; many had difficulties with the German language and lacked marketable skills. With some apprehension, united Germany realized that a further million ethnic Germans could arrive from eastern Europe in the future, and there was a further fear that the freedom to travel and political or economic problems might produce a flow of untold millions of non-German residents of the former Soviet Union. Partially in response to these concerns, Germany's relations with Russia focused on attempting to improve the lot of ethnic Germans living in Russia, thereby diminishing the likelihood of mass emigration to Germany.

West Germany's constitution guaranteed the right of asylum to those forced to flee their native countries because of political oppression. This privilege was regarded as compensation for the asylum granted to 800,000 German victims of political and ethnic persecution during World War II. Criticism of this constitutional provision mounted in the 1980s with the arrival of asylum seekers from non-European countries such as Sri Lanka, Iran, Lebanon, Ghana, and India, together with stateless Palestinians; it was difficult to distinguish those hoping to better themselves economically or to avoid compulsory military service from genuine victims of oppression. The issue of asylum became even more pressing when the eastern borders were opened, admitting a flood of foreigners—most prominently Poles, Romanian Roma (Gypsies), and Bosniaks (Bosnian Muslims). Between 1990 and 1993, one million people sought asylum in Germany, and, as antagonism toward immigrants increased, there was a surge of violent attacks against foreigners. Although the government and citizen groups condemned such xenophobic sentiment and behaviour, foreigners continued to be subjected to discrimination and sporadic violence. Beginning in 1991, legislation brought Germany in line with the more restrictive policies practiced by other members of the European Community (since 1993 the European Union) regarding immigration from outside the Community.

But while cooperation with neighbouring states reduced the flow of illegal immigrants and somewhat abated the problem, Germany nevertheless became embroiled in a domestic debate over the rights of noncitizen residents, including the right to naturalization, which had become somewhat easier for long-term residents in the late 1990s.

POPULATION STRUCTURE

As in most industrialized countries, the proportion of the population under age 15 is quite low, accounting for about one-sixth of the total; in contrast, the proportion of those over age 60 has increased dramatically, representing more than one-sixth of the population. That women predominate in the older population is largely a reflection of their higher life expectancy and of the significant losses of men during World War II, but the discrepancy has become less pronounced with time. In eastern Germany the disproportion of elderly citizens increased significantly after the desertion of the young before the erection of the Berlin Wall and after its destruction in 1989.

POPULATION DISTRIBUTION

Because Germany has for centuries had a profusion of states (each with towns and cities), its population is more widely dispersed than that of countries, such as France, in which centralization occurred early. It is possible, however,

As birth rates continued to decline, Germany's aging population presented the country with a demographic challenge. Sean Gallup/Getty Images

to discern two major population axes. The main axis runs from the Rhine-Ruhr region southward through the Rhine-Main (Frankfurt) and Rhine-Neckar (Heidelberg-Mannheim-Ludwigshafen) agglomerations, the great cities of southern Germany, and to Basel (Switzerland) and the Alpine passes. This is the main axis not only for Germany but also the European Union (EU). The second axis runs from the Rhine-Ruhr region eastward north of the Central German Uplands through Hannover, Braunschweig, and Magdeburg to the great urban concentration of Saxony. Some major cities stand in isolation outside the two axes, notably Augsburg and Nürnberg to the south and Bremen, Hamburg, and the capital city of Berlin, the last three forming islands in the thinly populated North German Plain. Before unification, population redistribution from the agglomeration cores in western Germany was accompanied by a marked drift of population from the north to the booming cities and attractive environment of southern Germany. In eastern Germany, early gains by migration were experienced in areas of planned industrial development (Eisenhüttenstadt, Rostock, Schwedt, Hoyerswerda). After initial postwar recovery, the cities of the south lost population, reflecting industrial decline, rationalization of production, and unattractive environments. East Berlin and its satellite towns were the principal targets of migration until western Germany became accessible in 1989.

CHAPTER 3

ECONOMY

The German constitution, the Basic Law (Grundgesetz), guarantees the right to own property, freedom of movement, free choice of occupation, freedom of association, and equality before the law. However, the constitution modified the operation of the unfettered free market by means of its "social market economy" (Soziale Marktwirtschaft). With a "safety net" of benefits—including health protection, unemployment and disability compensation, maternity and child-care provisions, job retraining, pensions, and many others—paid for by contributions from individuals, employers, and public funds, Germany has an economic order supported by most workers and businesses.

In the social market economy the government attempts to foster fair play between management and labour and to regulate the relationship between the capitalist participants in the market, particularly with regard to competition and monopolies. Works councils have been established, and workers have representation on the boards of businesses. The social market economy was created by policy makers with a vivid memory of market distortions and social tensions caused by the giant industrial trusts before 1939. Legislation against monopolies appeared in 1958 and has been criticized as ineffective. For example, it has proved impossible to restrict the indirect coordination, through which individuals, banks, and other financial institutions build up "diagonal" share holdings linking a range of firms that are nominally independent. Moreover, where a whole branch of industry has experienced difficulties (e.g., the Ruhr coal industry), even the federal government has encouraged concentration. The emergence of very large monopolistic firms has been unavoidable because, in an increasingly international economy, large firms that enjoy economies of scale are better positioned to survive. With globalization, governments are less able to regulate businesses at the national level or even at the transnational level of the EU.

The social market economy is regulated not exclusively by the federal government but by a plurality of agencies. For example, there are numerous insurance institutions that deliver social benefits. The most important institution in post-World War II Germany is the Frankfurt-based Deutsche Bundesbank (German Federal Bank). With memories of the runaway inflation of 1922–23, the West German government decided that it should never again have a license to print money and that the central bank should be independent of political control. Consequently, Germany's adoption of the euro, the EU's single currency, in 1999 raised some concerns in the country that the European Central Bank would be subject to political influence and manipulation. The Chambers of Trade, at every level of the administrative hierarchy, are also influential, and the state governments play a significant economic role (e.g., the government of North Rhine–Westphalia is intimately concerned with the survival of the Ruhr coal industry). Federal and state governments also participate in the ownership of some enterprises, notably public utilities. The Basic Law, however, prevents the arbitrary intervention of the central government.

As Germany has numerous economic actors, a high degree of coordination has been required to achieve adequate growth, balanced foreign trade, stable prices, and low unemployment. A variety of consultative bodies unite federal and state governments, the Deutsche Bundesbank, representatives of business and of the municipalities, and trade unions. The Board of Experts for the Assessment of Overall Economic Trends, established in 1963 and known as the "five wise men," produces an evaluation of overall economic developments each year to assist in national economic decision making. Moreover, the federal government submits an annual economic report to the legislature that contains a response to the annual evaluation of the Board of Experts and an outline of the economic and financial policies it is pursuing.

Although the free market operates in Germany, the federal government plays an important role in the economy. It is accepted as self-evident that it should underwrite the capital and operating costs of the economic and social infrastructure, such as the autobahn network, waterways, the postal system and telecommunications, and the rail system. The federal government, the states, and the cities also contribute to the regional and local rapid transit systems. Government collaborates with industry in bearing the costs of research and development, as, for example, in the nuclear power industry. Federal intervention is particularly strong in the defense industry. The coal industry is perhaps the most notable example of subsidization, and agriculture has traditionally been massively protected by the state, though the sector is now governed by EU institutions. Regional planning is another significant field of government intervention; the federal government fosters economic developments in rural and industrial "problem" regions. States and cities also intervene with schemes to foster regional or local development.

Germany has a varied tax system, with taxes imposed at the national, state, and local levels. Because of the generous system of social services, tax rates on corporations, individuals, and goods and services are all relatively high in comparison with other countries. Germany employs a system of tax equalization, through which tax revenues are distributed from wealthier regions to less-prosperous ones. After unification these transfers were resented among many western Germans.

MODERN ECONOMIC HISTORY: FROM PARTITION TO REUNIFICATION

Following the German military leaders' unconditional surrender in May 1945, the country lay prostrate. The German state had ceased to exist, and sovereign authority passed to the victorious Allied powers. The physical devastation from Allied bombing campaigns and from ground battles was enormous: an estimated one-fourth of the country's housing was destroyed or damaged beyond use, and in many cities the toll exceeded 50 percent. Germany's economic infrastructure had largely collapsed as factories and transportation systems ceased to function. Rampant inflation was undermining the value of the currency, and an acute shortage of food reduced the diet of many city dwellers to the level of malnutrition. These difficulties were compounded by the presence of millions of homeless German refugees from the former eastern provinces. The end of the war came to be remembered as "zero hour," a low point from which virtually everything had to be rebuilt anew from the ground up.

THE WEST GERMAN SYSTEM

After the devastation of World War II, West Germany rebounded with a so-called "economic miracle" that began in 1948. The subsequent combination of growth and stability made West Germany's economic system one of the most respected in the world, though it began to suffer strains beginning in the 1990s, exacerbated by the costs of unification. Germany's remarkable economic performance was largely a result of effective economic management, but temporary factors were especially important in spurring economic growth in the immediate post-World War II era. In particular, a large force of unemployed workers—returned servicemen

Brown-coal (lignite) pit in Eschweiler in the Rhenish field between Cologne and Aachen, Germany.
Gunter Brinkmann/Bavaria

and displaced persons—were available and eager to rebuild their own lives and willing to work hard at a rate of remuneration that left a considerable investment surplus in their employers' hands. In addition, the country reaped benefits from the joint economic planning for the American, British, and French zones of occupation that culminated in the vital and essential currency reform that introduced the deutsche mark in June 1948 and the U.S.-financed Marshall Plan (1948–52), which helped to rebuild war-torn Europe.

From 1951 to 1961 West Germany's gross national product (GNP) rose by 8 percent per year—double the rate for Britain and the United States and nearly double that of France—and exports trebled. Despite some occasional economic downturns (e.g., during the oil crisis of 1973–74), West Germany's economy followed an upward trend. Indeed, when East and West Germany reunited in 1990, West Germany's economy was enjoying a cycle of business expansion that had lasted since the early 1980s and continued into 1992. By that time Germany had one of the largest economies in the world and was a leader in world trade. All this was achieved while maintaining low inflation.

THE EAST GERMAN SYSTEM

East Germany also had experienced an economic miracle of sorts. Unlike the other Soviet-style states of eastern Europe, East Germany had been part of an advanced capitalist economy before the war, which gave it a considerable advantage in reconstruction. Even though it had emerged from World War II and the postwar Soviet demolitions economically ravaged, its surviving industrial infrastructure, inherited skills, and high level of scientific and technical education enabled it to develop the economy and to advance the standard of living to a level markedly higher than those of most other socialist countries, though living standards were still well below those of western Europe. East Germany became the principal supplier of advanced industrial equipment to the communist countries, though it became apparent after unification that it produced poor-quality goods and caused environmental devastation.

East Germany had a command economy, in which virtually all decisions were made by the governing communist party, the Socialist Unity Party (SED). The system of planning was inflexible and eventually caused ruinous economic conditions. Power, influence, and personal connections (Beziehungen, or "vitamin B") drove economic decisions, and all groups, including trade unions, were expected to collaborate to achieve the SED's economic objectives.

East Germany's industrial sector lacked quality controls and technological innovation. The cynicism, apathy, and inertia that were common among workers and enterprise managers contributed to low rates of East German technological change. Despite excellent training, workers were not rewarded with increased earnings for ingenuity; the result was a general malaise.

Supply and distribution were controlled by state-owned companies, and the centralized provision of services through nationalized concerns and local administrations was a generally recognized weakness. This was partially addressed by a "gray market" for goods and services in short supply (e.g., automobiles and automobile and house repairs), particularly when payment was made in hard currency; for example, repairmen offered much faster service for an extra fee or favours, and sales clerks also kept certain goods "under the counter." By the 1970s and '80s, particularly as contacts with the West increased, this gray market grew in significance.

ECONOMIC UNIFICATION AND BEYOND

The implementation of Mikhail Gorbachev's glasnost (political liberalization) and perestroika (economic restructuring) policies in the Soviet Union fueled sentiment in Germany that reunification could become a reality, and the basic steps toward German economic unity were accomplished with astonishing speed. The unexpected opening of the frontier between East and West Germany and the breaching of the Berlin Wall on November 9, 1989, were a heavy blow to the East German economy, as the relatively small numbers of migrants, who in previous years had left the country by way of Hungary or Czechoslovakia, rose dramatically. Exacerbating the problem was the fact that most of those who left were the younger, more active members of the population and those with marketable skills. The economic unification, achieved by July 1, 1990, swept away all customs barriers and introduced the deutsche mark as the sole currency in Germany.

Following Germany's official reunification on October 3, 1990, the western German economy continued to grow rapidly until 1992, after which it began to experience an economic slowdown before growth resumed in the mid-1990s. During the decade following 1992, the German economy grew at an average annual rate of 1.4 percent—among the lowest rates in western Europe. Many economists attributed the slowdown to rigid labour policies, high taxes, marginal incentives for investment, and generous incentives for workers to retire, miss work, or be unemployed. The slowdown was also related to unification, which wholly revealed the economic deficiencies of East Germany—the extent of its technological backwardness, its low productivity, and the faltering state of its manufacturing plants. Disillusionment in eastern Germany rose sharply as manufacturing output and employment declined rapidly. The federal government's insistence that eastern German firms compete immediately in the free market led to economic devastation in the east. By spring 1991, mass demonstrations against unemployment occurred regularly in Leipzig, and there was concern that economic despair would cultivate the rise of political extremism. Indeed, the Berlin office of the Treuhandanstalt (a government-owned but independent trust agency for the privatization of eastern German industry with wide powers of disposal) was firebombed, and in April 1991 its head was murdered by the West German Red Army Faction.

The Deutsche Bundesbank believed that the government had introduced the deutsche mark into eastern Germany too precipitately, with practically no preparation or possibility of adjustment, and at too favourable a rate. The effect of currency conversion and subsequent wage pressure deprived industry in the east of one of its few advantages, low labour costs. The favourable exchange rate and relatively high wages and salaries did, on the other hand, help achieve a sociopolitical goal—encouraging eastern Germans to remain in the east rather than migrating to the west, where people feared being overwhelmed by migrants. There were commercial bankruptcies in eastern Germany, and the eastern economy was further decimated by the tendency of easterners to buy the better-presented and technically superior consumer goods from western Germany or abroad rather than the generally drab products of eastern German industry; by the end of the decade, however, high-quality goods produced in eastern Germany bolstered the economy, and there was a wave of regional consciousness that favoured the patronage of local products.

Economic unification caused particularly severe hardships for eastern German workers; unemployment rose sharply and industrial output fell by two-thirds in the years after unification. Decline was greatest in the food-processing sector, metallurgy, building materials, machinery and vehicles, electronics and related equipment, and textiles. Eastern German agriculture also was devastated, with employment dropping by some three-fourths. Although the eastern economy later rebounded, at the beginning of the 21st century more than one-sixth of its labour force was unemployed—more than double the rate for western Germany. Unemployment also rose disproportionately for women. As a result of job losses, migration from east to west continued throughout the 1990s and into the early 21st century.

The slowness of economic recovery in eastern Germany was the result of a variety of factors. The haste of change, especially regarding the currency conversion and the breakup of the great industrial combines, and the fact that East Germany had no effective government for a period of three months following the economic union in July 1990 hampered economic reconstruction efforts. Even after political unification, progress was disappointing. Firms removed from ministerial control and transformed into limited companies found themselves unable to compete in the free market, burdened not only with outdated plants but with debt because the East German government had appropriated their profits while requiring them to borrow their capital. The federal government had assumed that the reconstruction of eastern German industry would essentially come about by the takeover of plants by Western, predominantly western German, firms. In reality, however, the Treuhandanstalt set up to dispose of some 10,000 formerly nationalized firms made extremely slow progress, partly as a result of an excessively legalistic approach and partly because of the shortage of experienced administrators afflicting the reconstituted public service in the east. Western German firms were under no great financial pressure to move in, and, with the help of the additional labour available from eastern German migrants, they expanded production at their existing plants without having to become involved in the difficulties of actually setting up a branch in the east. Protesters warned that eastern Germany was turning into an internal colony; however, this overly pessimistic outlook was exaggerated, and about 1992 some economic revival began to occur.

Land ownership was a significant barrier to establishing plants in eastern Germany. Following the principles of the German constitution, after unification, former owners were assured that they could repossess their property or at least be compensated for their losses. However, this did not apply to property expropriated by the Soviet military administration (1945–47), including many large estates that not everybody would be happy to see returned to their original aristocratic owners. Where a plant had originally been owned by a family or firm in western Germany but had received additional investment from the East German government and had perhaps expanded over land originally in a number of hands, western German firms were deterred from moving in, there being a lack of clear title to ownership.

The production-focused East German communist system had ignored environmental considerations. Firms seeking to take over electrical generation based on brown coal, any part of the chemical industry, or any other plant where dangerous chemicals had been used in processing faced enormous costs in attempting to meet federal government standards. Firms were also discouraged from taking over plants because the inevitable reductions in surplus labour would involve the payment of unemployment compensation. As a result, the few western German firms setting up in the east preferred to establish a completely new plant on a green-field site, allowing them to avoid these excessive costs.

The federal government initially believed that the costs of unification could be borne by borrowing and without increases in taxation. Despite these assurances by Chancellor Helmut Kohl at the 1990 all-German elections, by 1991 additional taxation was required. If people in the east were disillusioned by the economic results of union, those in the west grew increasingly resentful of the cost of paying for it.

During the 1990s Germany made a number of dramatic changes in its energy sector—e.g., higher taxes, lower subsidies for coal mining, and privatization of huge eastern German energy firms. In 2002 the government passed legislation that stipulated the end of the nuclear power industry by 2022, though in 2010 it extended the deadline into the 2030s. In 2007 it also tentatively planned to phase out coal mining within about a decade. Massive reconstruction projects in the east (Aufbau Ost), funded largely by higher taxes in the west, helped to improve infrastructure in the eastern regions. Telecommunications systems were upgraded, and there were generous subsidies to encourage capital investment.

Quite apart from the costs and problems associated with unification, Germany and its economy faced a number of interrelated problems at the beginning of the 21st century. High unemployment—which regularly exceeded four million people—became the chief political issue.

Extremely high wages—among the world's highest—generous social services, and high taxation also dampened the economy. Unification caused the public debt to grow dramatically, and at the beginning of the 21st century some one-fifth of the annual federal budget went toward interest payments on the accrued national debt.

Although unification was more than a decade old, at the beginning of the 21st century its effects still weighed heavily on the German economy and its political institutions. However, in large measure unification gave way to other issues, such as globalization, the introduction of the euro as the single currency of the EU in 2002, and the enlargement of the EU to central and eastern Europe. Germany's domestic economic problems and opportunities are complexly bound up with global and regional processes over which it has only varying levels of influence and control—a somewhat unsettling situation for a society that became very prosperous by following accustomed patterns and having firm control of the major levers of its own economy.

AGRICULTURE

As in other sectors of the economy, the division of Germany was reflected in a dramatic divergence of agricultural development. West Germany remained essentially a country of small family farms; in the 1980s only about 5 percent of holdings had more than 124 acres (50 hectares), though they accounted for nearly one-fourth of the total agricultural area. By the beginning of the 21st century, however, large farms represented about half of the total agricultural area in western Germany and some two-thirds in eastern Germany. The change in western Germany is reflective of a rationalization of agriculture, with many small landholders leaving farming and the remaining farms often increasing in size. The larger farms in the west are mainly concentrated in Schleswig-Holstein and eastern Lower Saxony, with smaller groupings in Westphalia, the lowland west of Cologne, and southern Bavaria. Small farms predominated in the central and southern parts of West Germany. The process of steady enlargement decreased the total number of holdings by more than three-fourths from 1950 to the end of the 20th century. The number of people employed in agriculture also declined substantially, from about one-fifth of the total workforce in 1950 to less than 3 percent by the end of the 20th century. Wage labourers virtually disappeared from all but the largest farms, and smaller farms were cultivated on a part-time basis.

By contrast, in the east, following conquest by the Soviet army at the end of World War II, many large estates were split up or retained as state farms. From 1952 to 1960 virtually all the small farms in East Germany were united, under strong political pressure, to form agricultural cooperatives. Agricultural production was increasingly concentrated into extremely

Hops growing near Mainburg, in the Hallertau district, Niederbayern, Germany. Ulrich Hofmann/© Silvestris

large specialized units; by the mid-1980s state-run or cooperative crop-producing enterprises averaged more than 11,000 acres (4,450 hectares). Despite a marked decrease in agricultural employees, modern machinery and technological innovation led to increased production. After unification agricultural employment in eastern Germany plunged by about three-fourths.

In areas of high natural fertility, wheat, barley, corn (maize), and sugar beets are the principal crops. The poorer soils of the North German Plain and of the Central German Uplands are traditionally used for growing rye, oats, potatoes, and fodder beets. Technological changes have altered much of the traditional spatial pattern of German agriculture. Sugar beets, formerly confined to deep fertile soils such as the loess lands on the northern fringe of the Central German Uplands, are now much more widespread. With the availability of chemical fertilizers, light soils have become more highly valued because of their suitability for machine cultivation; for example, fodder corn is now widely grown on the North German Plain, replacing potatoes. The two most widespread forms of agricultural land use are cereal cultivation (including corn for its grains) and permanent pasture; both are important sources of animal feed. Dairying formerly was concentrated in the area of mild climate in the northern coastal lowlands and in the Alpine foothills, but it is now widespread in all areas where small farms predominate. East Germany concentrated milk production into vast specialist holdings in arable areas where food was available and urban markets accessible. In both the western and eastern sectors, chickens, eggs, pigs, and veal calves are concentrated into large battery units, divorced from immediate contact with the soil. Besides concern for the plight of the animals under this system of concentrated production, Germans are distressed by the groundwater pollution associated with it.

In the areas surrounding western German cities, crops such as fruits, vegetables, and flowers are grown. The warm lowlands of the southwest favour tobacco and seed corn. They also support vegetables, as do the Elbe marshes south of Hamburg and the marshy Spreewald south of Berlin. Fruit grows abundantly in southern Germany; other important areas of specialization include the "Altes Land" on the Elbe south of Hamburg, the Havel lake country near Potsdam, and the Halle area. Vineyards are located in the west, especially in or near the valleys of the Rhine, Moselle, Saar, Main, and Neckar rivers, although the slopes of the Elbe valley near Dresden also produce wine grapes.

At the time of reunification, western Germany produced some four-fifths of its food requirements, and increased productivity and guaranteed prices resulted in vast surpluses (especially of butter, meat, wheat, and wine). At the beginning of the 21st century, Germany's production of major agricultural products (e.g., grains, sugar, oils, milk, and meat) exceeded domestic consumption, resulting in both exports and continued surpluses.

FORESTRY

Some three-tenths of Germany's total land area is covered with forest. In the Central German Uplands and the Alps, forests are particularly plentiful, but they are notably absent from the best agricultural land, such as the loess areas of the North German Plain. The western part of the North German Plain also has little forest cover, but there are substantial wooded stretches farther east. Conifers predominate in the forest area; spruce now accounts for much of the plantings because of its rapid growth and suitability for building purposes and for the production of paper and chipboard. Domestic production covers about half of the demand for wood from temperate forests, but producers face severe competition from Austria, Scandinavia, and eastern Europe. The federal government, states, and municipalities own about half the forest in western Germany, with the remainder in private hands; eastern German forests are primarily publicly owned.

FISHING

Fishing in western Germany began to decline markedly from the 1970s because of overutilization of traditional fishing grounds and the extension of the exclusive economic zone to 200 miles (320 km) offshore. The greatly reduced deep-sea fleet now uses freezer vessels and accompanying catchers; Bremerhaven, Cuxhaven, and Hamburg are the home ports and processing centres. During the 1990s, high-seas catches by German fishermen declined by about half. The North Sea herring fishery has almost disappeared, and now the German appetite for pickled herring is satisfied mainly by imports. There are well over 100 fishing ports on the North Sea and Baltic coasts. Fishing for shrimp and mussels is important on the mud flats fringing the North Sea. Prior to unification East Germany had a substantial deep-sea fishing fleet, but most of it has since been scrapped; its shore base for fish processing was at Sassnitz on the island of Rügen.

RESOURCES AND POWER

Germany, which has relatively few domestic natural resources, imports most of its raw materials. It is a major producer of bituminous coal and brown coal (lignite), the principal fields of the latter being west of Cologne, east of Halle, south and southwest of Leipzig, and in Lower Lusatia in Brandenburg. Other minerals found in abundance are salt and potash, mined

Fishermen's huts (Fischerhäuser) on the west coast of Lake Müritz near Röbel, Mecklenburg-West Pomerania. Wilhelm Irsch/© Silvestris

at the periphery of the Harz mountains. The mining of most metallic minerals ceased for economic reasons in western Germany before unification; in the 1990s the centuries-old mining and processing of copper ores in the Mansfeld area of eastern Germany and the mining and processing of uranium ores for the benefit of the Soviet Union in the Ore Mountains also stopped. There are small reserves of oil and natural gas in northern Germany.

As in all industrialized countries, water supply is a constant problem. The filtration of water on riverbanks (e.g., those of the Rhine) is one source. It is supplemented by reservoirs in the uplands. For example, the Harz mountains provide water to much of the North German Plain as far as Bremen, and the Ore Mountains supply the central German industrial region.

Oil is Germany's principal source of energy. As domestic production is quite limited, most crude oil is imported. Many petroleum products also are imported, transported from Rotterdam by product lines, barges, and rail. Until the mid-1950s the refining of oil took place at the coast, notably at Hamburg and Rotterdam; however, refineries have been developed at inland locations close to markets, mostly on rivers such as the Rhine and Danube, which are served by pipelines from Wilhelmshaven, Rotterdam (Netherlands), Lavéra (near Marseille, France), Genoa (Italy), and Trieste (Italy). Eastern Germany receives oil delivered by pipeline from Russia to a refinery at Schwedt on the Oder, which supplies the central German industrial region; there is also a pipeline from Rostock that provides industry with oil. German supplies of natural gas are significant, but most gas is imported. Principal sources are the Friesian and North Sea fields of the Netherlands and the Norwegian North Sea. Gas is imported from Russia via a pipeline from the Czech Republic, with a branch serving eastern Germany and Berlin.

Bituminous coal, Germany's second most important source of energy, is available from the Ruhr field and from the smaller Saar, Aachen, and Ibbenbüren fields, though extraction is costly and often subsidized. In the last half of the 20th century, however, output shrank by some two-thirds. Coal now has two major uses: the generation of electricity and the production of metallurgical coke. A striking feature of the German economy is the significance of brown coal (lignite). This low-grade, waterlogged fuel can be worked economically in vast open pits, which are mined with massive machines. About seven-eighths of all the coal is fed straight to electric-power generating stations that are situated on the field itself. A relatively small quantity of the coal is pressed into briquettes for domestic heating. Electricity generation is also the principal use of the main fields in eastern Germany; however, during partition lignite was a major basis of the chemical industry as well as a source of gas and briquettes for urban consumption. After unification many eastern German pits closed, particularly those producing the most sulfurous coal. The shortfall in energy output led the federal government to subsidize additional imports of gas from Russia.

The largest producers of electric energy are the thermal plants that are located primarily in the Ruhr and the Rhenish brown-coal fields and in the brown-coal fields of the east, especially in Lower Lusatia. During partition all western German plants were required to significantly reduce the emissions of the dust, sulfur dioxide, and nitrogen oxide formerly emitted into the atmosphere. Plants in the east were not similarly regulated and thus contributed to general atmospheric pollution; after unification a number of them were closed and others were upgraded.

Nuclear power plants rival thermal plants in significance; in western Germany they are typically located on the coast or on rivers far from the coalfields. Plants in eastern Germany, built on the Soviet (Chernobyl) model, were closed for safety reasons. At the turn of the 21st century the German government committed to phasing out all of the country's nuclear power plants. In 2010, however, claiming that nuclear plants would be necessary until renewable energy technologies became sufficiently productive, the government extended the life span of the country's existing plants. This plan was quickly abandoned in the wake of the 2011 Fukushima nuclear accident in Japan, and Germany's remaining plants were scheduled to be shut down by 2022.

The canalization of such rivers as the Main, Neckar, and Moselle, together with hydroelectric power plants in the Alps, produce relatively minor amounts of electric power; pumped storage schemes in mountain areas are important in meeting peak electricity demands. Before unification, East and West Germany had distinct transmission grids without interconnection. The West German network was linked to that of neighbouring countries, allowing it to import surplus power from the French nuclear system and, during the Alpine snow melt, especially from Austria. West Berlin formerly was forced to generate its own power, adding to urban pollution. The eastern and western German grids were connected in the 1990s, and West Berlin was connected to the network in 1994.

MANUFACTURING

Industrial employment in western Germany declined steadily from a postwar peak. However, deindustrialization was not as precipitous in Germany as it was in some other European countries. Western German industry benefited from the willingness of banks to take a long-term view on investment and of the federal government to underwrite research and development. German industrial products are viewed with great prestige on world markets and are in strong demand overseas. By contrast, unification revealed that most of eastern German industry was incapable of competing in a free market.

Germany is one of the world's leading manufacturers of steel, with production concentrated in the Ruhr region; however, since the peak output of the early 1970s, a number of plants have closed. (The steel industry in eastern Germany was largely abandoned after unification, though some production was reestablished at a renovated plant at Eisenhuettenstadt.) Germany's principal industries include machine building,

VOLKSWAGEN AG

German automobile manufacturer Volkswagen AG was founded by the German government in 1937 to mass-produce a low-priced "people's car." The company was originally operated by the German Labour Front (Deutsche Arbeitsfront), a Nazi organization; and Ferdinand Porsche was brought in to design the car. Production was interrupted by World War II, and by the end of the war both the Volkswagen factory and the city of Wolfsburg were in ruins. Allied attempts to revive the West German auto industry after the war centred on the Volkswagen, and in little more than a decade the company was producing half of West Germany's motor vehicles.

Exports to most parts of the world were strong, but because of the car's small size, unusual rounded appearance, and historical connections with Nazi Germany, sales in the United States were originally slow. This changed in 1959, when an American advertising agency, Doyle Dane Bernbach, began a landmark advertising campaign, dubbing the car the Beetle because of its shape and pointing to its size as an advantage to the consumer. This campaign was very successful, and for some years following, the Beetle was the leading automobile import sold in the United States.

The Volkswagen hardly changed from its original design, however, and by 1974, with increasing competition from other compact foreign cars, Volkswagen came near bankruptcy. This spurred the company to develop newer, sportier car models, among them the Rabbit and its successor, the Golf.

Although the company had been founded by the German government, in 1960 the state essentially denationalized it by selling 60 percent of its stock to the public. Volkswagen acquired the Audi auto company in 1965. Volkswagen and its affiliates operate plants throughout most of the world. In addition to cars, the company produces vans and minibuses, automotive parts, and industrial engines. It owns several other auto companies, including Audi in Germany and SEAT (Sociedad Espanola de Automoviles de Turismo) in Spain, and it also makes and markets cars with Fiat of Italy and Škoda of the Czech Republic. Its headquarters are in Wolfsburg.

automobiles, electrical engineering and electronics, chemicals, and food processing. Automobile manufacturing is concentrated in Baden-Württemberg, Lower Saxony, Hessen, North Rhine–Westphalia, Bavaria, the Saarland, and Thuringia. Leading automobile manufacturers in Germany include Audi, BMW, Daimler AG (formerly Daimler-Benz and DaimlerChrysler), Ford, Opel, and Volkswagen. Following unification, production of the environmentally unfriendly Trabant and Wartburg cars in eastern Germany ceased. Volkswagen, Opel, and Daimler-Benz were quick to establish assembly or parts production in the east. Shipbuilding, once a major industry, has declined significantly.

Since the late 19th century Germany has been a world leader in the manufacture of electrical equipment. As the home of internationally known firms such as Siemens, AEG, Telefunken, and Osram, Berlin was the industry's principal centre until World War II, after which production was largely transferred to Nürnberg-Erlangen, Munich, Stuttgart, and other cities in southern Germany. The output of these centres made Germany one of the world's leading exporters of electrical and electronic equipment.

In East Germany electrical and electronic production was concentrated in East Berlin, with Dresden forming a second important centre. The country was a major supplier of equipment (e.g., computer-controlled robots) to the communist world. Although eastern German plants were outdated in comparison with those in the west, both Dresden and Erfurt achieved some success in developing microelectronics production following unification.

With the discovery of synthetic dyestuffs in the late 19th century, Germany became a world leader in the chemical industry. Most of the western German chemical industry is concentrated along the Rhine or its tributaries, notably in Ludwigshafen, Hoechst (near Frankfurt), and Leverkusen (together with a row of other plants along the Rhine in North Rhine–Westphalia). Chemical plants also operate in the Ruhr region. The majority of East German chemical plants were on the two brown-coal fields of Lower Lusatia and Halle-Leipzig; after unification some plants were closed because of environmental reasons, and others were upgraded.

Germany is also particularly strong in the field of optical and precision industries. The once-mighty textile industry has suffered from overseas competition but is still significant. Principal centres are in North Rhine–Westphalia (Mönchen-Gladbach, Wuppertal) and southern Germany. After unification many textile plants were closed in eastern Germany, where employment in the sector plunged by some nine-tenths.

FINANCE

Germany's financial sector is robust, and it represents more than one-fourth of the country's gross domestic product. Frankfurt am Main is widely regarded as the financial capital of continental Europe, and the Frankfurt Stock Exchange is one of the world's largest securities markets.

THE CENTRAL BANKING SYSTEM

Germany's central bank, the Deutsche Bundesbank, is headquartered in Frankfurt am Main, which is the country's main financial centre and also the base of the European Central Bank, the EU's chief financial institution. Before the circulation of the euro, the common currency of the EU, in 2002, the Bundesbank issued the deutsche mark (the country's former currency) and oversaw its circulation. As the EU's most powerful national central bank, the Bundesbank played a pivotal role in the planning of and preparation for the euro. One of its primary roles now is to implement the monetary policies of the European System of Central Banks to help maintain the euro's stability.

Upon the establishment of the Bundesbank, its preeminent characteristic was its independence from government control, instituted to prevent a recurrence of the severe inflation experienced in 1922–23, when the government resorted to the printing press for finance. The federal bank maintained a policy of careful control of credit and concern for the international exchange rate of the deutsche mark, which had made West Germany the leading financial power in post-World War II Europe. The Bundesbank demonstrated its genuine independence in 1991 when it insisted that additional government expenditure for the eastern sector be covered by unwelcome tax increases rather than by borrowing. Individual Land (state) central banks are the Bundesbank's representatives at state level.

THE PRIVATE BANKING SECTOR

There are hundreds of commercial banks, of which the most important are the Deutsche Bank, the KfW Bankengruppe, and the Commerzbank, though mergers have tended to shrink the number of major banks. Apart from conducting normal banking business, German banks provide financing for private businesses. As a result, the stock exchanges in Frankfurt, Düsseldorf, and other cities are less influential in providing finance for industry than parallel institutions in other countries.

PUBLIC AND COOPERATIVE INSTITUTIONS

Germany has several types of public financial institutions, including credit and personal checking institutions and cooperative banks. Under public law, credit institutions operate as savings banks, and the state banks act as central banks and clearinghouses for the savings banks and focus on regional financing. The state-owned Kreditanstalt für Wiederaufbau ("Development Loan Corporation") channels public aid to developing countries.

The cooperative banks are headed by the DZ Bank (Deutsche Zentral-Genossenschaftsbank, or "German Central Cooperative Bank"), which serves as a central bank for some 1,500 industrial and agricultural credit cooperatives. There are also public and private mortgage banks, installment credit institutions, and the now-privatized postal check and postal savings systems, which were once operated by the federal postal service.

In East Germany the state bank was subordinate to the Ministry of Finance and designed to be a tool of central planning. It was part of a unified system that embraced not only central and local government but also banks, insurance companies, and industries, all of which were directed in their use of funds.

DEUTSCHE BANK AG

One of the world's largest banks, Deutsche Bank AG was founded in 1870 in Berlin and it has been headquartered in Frankfurt am Main since 1957. It has a number of foreign offices and has acquired controlling interests in several foreign banks in Europe, North and South America, and Australia.

The first bank was licensed by King William I of Prussia on March 10, 1870, and it began operation in Berlin on April 9. Branches were opened in Bremen in 1871, in Hamburg, Shanghai, and Yokohama, Japan, in 1872, and in London in 1873. By the end of the century, it had absorbed a number of other German banks and multiplied its capital about 10-fold under its managing director, Georg von Siemens. More mergers were capped in 1929 by the amalgamation of Deutsche Bank with its older rival, DiscontoGesellschaft. After experiencing difficulties at the onset of the Great Depression, the company prospered hugely under the Nazi regime.

With the collapse of the Third Reich, Deutsche Bank's offices in Berlin and eastern Germany were closed by the Russian occupation forces or were expropriated; branches in western Germany were "decartelized," coalescing in 1947–48 as 10 independent banks. As the Cold War progressed and as the economic growth and cooperation of what by then was West Germany became a priority, the North Atlantic Treaty Organization reduced its opposition to West German economic consolidation. By 1952 the 10 banks had been reduced to 3; and in 1957 the 3 successor institutions were reunited to form a single Deutsche Bank AG. The bank made several significant acquisitions in the 1990s, including U.S.-based Bankers Trust. Its primary interests are in Europe, and it has additional operations in Asia, North America, and South America. By the early 21st century, it served more than 12 million customers in more than 70 countries.

With economic union on July 1, 1990, East Germany came under the central banking system of the Deutsche Bundesbank, which effected the conversion of the eastern system to the West German mark. Progressively, the western German commercial banks, insurance companies, and all the other financial institutions moved in. The ruined East German economy, the unemployment assistance fund, and the bankrupt state and local administrations all required massive financial transfusions from the federal government and the West German states. In stages, consumer subsidies have been removed, while wages, social insurance payments, and taxes have been progressively raised toward western levels.

TRADE

One of the world's leading exporters, Germany has consistently maintained a surplus with its trading partners. More than half of its trade is with members of the

EU. Germany's principal export markets are France, the United States, the United Kingdom, Italy, and the Netherlands. Trade with eastern and central Europe has increased, and Germany has replaced the former Soviet Union and Russia as the primary trading partner for most countries in the region. Major exports include transport equipment (including automobiles), electrical machinery, and chemicals, as well as some food products and wine. Imports fall into remarkably similar categories, but in addition they include raw materials and semifinished products for industry. Germany's major sources of imports include France, the Netherlands, Italy, the United States, the United Kingdom, and Belgium.

Before unification East Germany specialized as a supplier of advanced industrial equipment, electronics, ships, and rail rolling stock to the communist bloc countries. Following economic unification, the countries of the former communist bloc were virtually unable to pay for equipment in hard currency, with disastrous consequences for eastern German industry. However, unlike the other former communist countries, eastern Germany, as part of united Germany, automatically received the benefits of full EC membership, though its factories also immediately faced overwhelming competition from western producers.

SERVICES

As is the case in many other countries with an advanced economy, Germany's service sector (i.e., trade, transport, banking, finance, and administration) is a leading employer. This is abundantly clear in urban centres throughout western Germany, with their concentration of retailing, banking, and insurance. The transformation of eastern Germany along these lines is in progress, and the sector's importance has grown considerably there. For example, while the economies of most eastern and western German states were still dominated by manufacturing in the early 1990s, by the end of the decade a majority of states, and the country as a whole, had economies with a higher level of output by private firms providing services (even excepting trade and transport, which are categorized separately). In short, the German economy, for years one of the world's most manufacturing-oriented economies, has become dominated by services. This is particularly well illustrated by Berlin, where manufacturing's importance has declined sharply; indeed, the city has become an increasingly significant centre for both public and private international and national service-sector institutions.

Although foreign tourism to Germany is substantial, receipts from German tourists abroad exceed the receipts from foreign visitors to the country. In comparison with many of its neighbours, Germany does not rely heavily on tourism for income. The Alps and the Rhine and Moselle valleys are leading destinations, though urban areas (e.g., Frankfurt, Munich, and Berlin) also attract many visitors, and local festivals in places such as Bayreuth also entice tourists. Tourism to eastern Germany, particularly to the beaches along the Baltic Sea, has increased significantly since unification.

LABOUR AND TAXATION

Germany's highly urban and industrialized character is reflected in its employment patterns. Services, including trade and finance, account for the largest share of employment. At the turn of the 21st century, about one-fifth of workers were employed in manufacturing, and just over 2 percent were employed in agriculture-related industries.

Prior to World War II most German labour unions were organized along partisan lines. After the war, however, trade unions were reconstituted to represent an entire industrial branch rather than simply a single trade or skill, thus avoiding interunion jostling within plants, and an independent German Trade Union Federation (Deutscher Gerwerkschaftsbund; DGB), which represents nearly all the country's unionized industrial employees, was established. The federation is an agglomeration of mostly blue-collar unions (though there are some white-collar unions), the largest of which are the United Service Industries Union (Vereinte Dienstleistungsgewerkschaft), the Metalworkers' Union (IG Metall), the Public Services and Transport Workers' Union (Gewerkschaft Nahrung-Genuss-Gastätten), the Mining, Chemical, and Energy Union (Industriewerkschaft Bergbau, Chemie, Energie), and the Federation of Civil Servants (DBB–Beamtenbund und Tarifunion).

Although Germany's social economy allows collective bargaining, unions are generally viewed as partners rather than opponents of business. The common interests of management and labour are expressed in works councils. Labour also has a right of codetermination (Mitbestimmungsrecht) through representation on managerial boards. About one-third of all German workers belong to a trade union. German's average labour costs are among the highest in the world.

Taxes are the major source of revenue for all levels of government. Five types of taxes—value-added, wage, assessed income, energy, and corporate—account for nearly four-fifths of all revenues. The federal government and the states each receive more than two-fifths of the principal taxes, leaving the remainder for local councils. A host of lesser taxes are specific to either the federal level (such as the tax on tobacco and alcohol and customs duties), the states (tax on beer and motor vehicle licenses), or the local authorities (tax on real estate, trade, and public entertainment). The states also benefit from property taxes. Because the taxing potential of the states is unevenly distributed, the economically weaker or smaller states share in the tax revenue of the richer or more populous states through a process of "horizontal financial equalization," which became an especially controversial matter after unification, when the poorer eastern German states

GERMAN TRADE UNION FEDERATION

Germany's dominant union organization, the German Trade Union Federation (Deutscher Gewerkschaftsbund; DGB), was founded in Munich in 1949 and soon became the largest labour organization in West Germany, with 16 constituent unions. With the reunification of Germany in 1990, workers of the former East Germany were incorporated into the DGB.

The DGB is primarily a blue-collar organization, but it also includes a large number of white-collar workers and civil servants. It has avoided ties with political parties, although on policy issues it has tended to support the Social Democrats. By the year 2000 the federation had a total membership of about 8 million workers (including about 3.8 million workers from the former East Germany), which constituted about one-third of the total German workforce.

became entitled to subsidies from western Germany. The federal corporate tax rate is about 25 percent, and, when local taxes are included, the overall tax burden reaches about 40 percent. Germany imposes a value-added tax of 16 percent to most goods and services. To spur economic growth, the German government reduced personal and business taxes in the late 1990s.

The federal government is obligated to transmit certain revenues to the EU. Germany's disproportionately large payments to the EU have become a significant domestic and EU-wide political issue. As one of the world's richest countries, Germany feels obliged to supplement its regular contributions to the United Nations with complex international aid programs of its own.

TRANSPORTATION AND TELECOMMUNICATIONS

Germany has a dense network of communication facilities. Its geographic location in the heart of Europe also makes Germany responsible for facilitating the transit traffic serving neighbouring countries.

WATERWAYS

The Rhine has the great advantage of having a remarkably even flow, with a spring-summer high water from the Alpine snowmelt supplemented by autumn-winter rains in the Central German Uplands. It is navigable from its mouth to above Basel, Switzerland, with the support in its upper course of the French Grand Canal d'Alsace. Typically, river transport is accomplished by using push units propelling several barges. Since World War II the Rhine tributaries have been opened up for travel and transport. Navigation on the Moselle has been improved to the Saar region and Lorraine, on the Neckar to Stuttgart, and on the Main to provide a major European link to the Danube. Canals through the Ruhr region allow access to the northern

German ports of Emden, Bremen, and Hamburg; waterway connections eastward to Berlin were once inadequate, especially at the crossing of the Elbe, but are being improved.

SEAPORTS

Hamburg, which handles some one-third of the overall tonnage by weight, is Germany's principal port, accommodating the largest share of containers, as well as various ores and a wide range of general cargo. But because the largest tankers can no longer reach the Hamburg refining centre, Wilhelmshaven has become the prime destination for Germany's oil imports, as well as a major port in general. The Weser ports (Bremen and Bremerhaven) also handle a significant amount of total tonnage and containers; Bremen has an important general cargo trade. Although Hamburg, the Weser ports, and Emden are able to transship heavy goods to the interior by waterway, they play a less important role in this area than Rotterdam (in the Netherlands) and other ports located at the mouth of the great Rhine waterway and closer to the Rhine-Ruhr area than the northern German ports are. Because the Elbe River leads to the port of Hamburg in what was West Germany and the Oder River to Szczecin (Stettin) in Poland, East Germany developed a new deep-sea port at Rostock, which was served by motorway and rail but had no waterway link. Some commodities needing fast service continued to arrive at special East

The Kiel Canal, which runs from the mouth of the Elbe River to the Baltic Sea, at Kiel, Germany. A.G.E. FotoStock

German quays at Hamburg. Hamburg has regained much of its former Elbe trade since unification, but Rostock remains busy. Ferries for passengers, road vehicles, or railcars link Germany with Scandinavian destinations.

RAILWAYS

During the country's partition, the rail system was divided as well. In West Germany the Deutsche Bundesbahn (German Federal Railroad) reconstructed the old system, converting it to electric and diesel traction. The configuration of the country placed the emphasis on north-south routes. The burdened Rhine valley lines and the difficult routes through Hessen were augmented by a superbly engineered (and extremely expensive) high-speed track that permitted speeds up to 155 miles (250 km) per hour.

East Germany retained the old name of Deutsche Reichsbahn ("German Imperial Railroad") for its system. Postwar reconstruction was slow, with efforts centring on rail links with the country's eastern European neighbours and the port of Rostock. The once-important east-west routes across the inner-German boundary were either removed or neglected. The Berlin outer-ring railroad was completed, enabling mainline and local traffic to avoid West Berlin. Unification revealed the dilapidated state of the system. Within Berlin, the trains, buses, and trams of the public transport were totally divided. Yet, when the border reopened, both the S-Bahn (Stadtbahn), an elevated railway system, and the U-Bahn (Untergrundbahn), the subway, were immediately able to resume service from east to west. (Two U-Bahn lines had continued to cross through areas of East Berlin but were not permitted to make stops at intermediate stations.)

A lengthy and costly process of fully restoring a unified system, both within Berlin and nationally, began in late 1989 and resulted in significant progress for eastern Germany's railway network. Deutsche Bundesbahn and Deutsche Reichsbahn were officially merged under the name Deutsche Bahn in 1994. The railway operated under state ownership into the 21st century, although plans were made to privatize at least a portion of it. High-speed passenger rail service now links major German urban centres with one another and with other European destinations.

HIGHWAYS

Germany's first high-speed roadway was actually a closed-circuit experimental racetrack that covered some 12 miles (19 km) near Berlin. Unveiled in 1921, this proto-autobahn inspired several other countries to follow with their own versions of high-speed expressways. In the 1930s Hitler exploited the autobahn for economic, military, and propaganda purposes, but during World War II this German innovation—regarded as a model for modern expressways—was battered. The West German government greatly extended the system from 700 miles (1,125 km) in 1950 to more than 5,000 miles (8,000 km) by the time of unification. With powerful German automobiles able to cruise at their top speeds without speed limits, the autobahn gained an aura of automobile-centred romanticism throughout the world in the second half of the 20th century. However, road construction has encountered serious opposition from the country's environmentalist movement, and in inhabited areas the roads sometimes have been narrowed rather than widened to reduce traffic speed. Because the growth of the system

AUTOBAHN

The high-speed, limited-access German highway known as the autobahn (German: "automobile road") is famous the world over for its speeding motorists. Planned in Germany in the early 1930s, these roads were extended to a national highway network (Reichsautobahnen) of 1,310 miles (2,108 km) by 1942 and in the process established the template for modern national expressway systems. West Germany embarked on an ambitious reconstruction of the system after World War II, and after German reunification in 1989 the West German system (Bundesautobahnen) absorbed the East German system. The current length of the entire network is more than 7,400 miles (12,000 km), making it the third largest system in the world, after those of the United States and China.

has been slower than the growth of traffic, congestion is a serious problem, especially on motorways in industrial areas. Attempts to divert shipment of goods to the railways have not prevented a steady rise in the transport of goods by road. Western German motorways have direct transfrontier connections with the similar systems of Denmark, the Netherlands, Belgium, France, and Austria.

With a lower growth rate of motor traffic (and an official policy of giving preference to the railroads), postwar construction of motorways was less advanced in East Germany. There were some improvements in central Germany, and new links to the ports of Rostock and Hamburg were constructed. The Berliner Ring, a circle of expressways around the city, was completed in 1979. With reunification, many transboundary roads were reopened and road surfaces improved. However, the construction of new roads has been hindered by conflicts between those seeking greater accessibility for automobiles and those seeking to protect the landscape and reduce air pollution.

AIR TRANSPORT

Germany's major long-distance airline is Lufthansa, though there also are a number of other carriers that service European and North American destinations. Frankfurt's airport, one of the world's busiest, is the country's largest; airports in Düsseldorf, Munich, and Berlin (Tegel) are also of major importance. During the period of partition, passenger traffic from West Germany to West Berlin was restricted to the airlines of France, the United Kingdom, and the United States. After unification Berlin was opened to German carriers (and indeed to carriers of other countries). East Germany discouraged internal air traffic and the growth of regional airports, using the rail and Berlin subway systems to serve its major international airport, Berlin-Schönefeld, south of the city. During the late 1990s, expansion of Schönefeld began. The expanded Schönefeld would, upon its completion, be renamed Berlin Brandenburg Airport. With the closing of Templehof Airport in 2008 and the planned closing of Tegel, Berlin Brandenburg would become Berlin's only commercial airport.

TELECOMMUNICATIONS

After World War II West Germany developed an advanced telecommunications system. By contrast, the East German telephone system was completely insufficient; people requesting a telephone often were faced with a wait of up to 12 years. The deficiencies of the telecommunications system were a major impediment to the restructuring of the administration and the economy following unification, but by the late 1990s rapid reconstruction of the system using current technology made eastern Germany a world leader in advanced telecommunications infrastructure.

The leading German telecommunications company is Deutsche Telekom AG. During the late 1990s the entire sector was liberalized, increasing the number of telecommunications firms and competition for Deutsche Telekom from companies such as Vodafone and Telefónica Germany. The adoption of telecommunications services by German consumers has been widespread, particularly for cellular services. By the second decade of the 21st century, cellular subscriptions outnumbered people in Germany by a ratio of more than 1.25 to 1. By 2009 almost 80 percent of the population used the Internet regularly.

CHAPTER 4

GOVERNMENT AND SOCIETY

The structure and authority of Germany's government are derived from the country's constitution, the Grundgesetz (Basic Law), which went into force on May 23, 1949, after formal consent to the establishment of the Federal Republic (then known as West Germany) had been given by the military governments of the Western occupying powers (France, the United Kingdom, and the United States) and upon the assent of the parliaments of the Länder (states) to form the Bund (federation). West Germany then comprised 11 states and West Berlin, which was given the special status of a state without voting rights. As a provisional solution until an anticipated reunification with the eastern sector, the capital was located in the small university town of Bonn. On October 7, 1949, the Soviet zone of occupation was transformed into a separate, nominally sovereign country (if under Soviet hegemony), known formally as the German Democratic Republic (and popularly as East Germany). The five federal states within the Soviet zone were abolished and reorganized into 15 administrative districts (Bezirke), of which the Soviet sector of Berlin became the capital.

Full sovereignty was achieved only gradually in West Germany; many powers and prerogatives, including those of direct intervention, were retained by the Western powers and devolved to the West German government only as it was able to become economically and politically stable. West Germany finally achieved full sovereignty on May 5, 1955.

East Germany regarded its separation from the rest of Germany as complete, but West Germany considered its

The German Bundestag, Berlin. © Bundesbildstelle/ Press and Information Office of the Federal Government of Germany

eastern neighbour as an illegally constituted state until the 1970s, when the doctrine of "two German states in one German nation" was developed. Gradual rapprochements between the two governments helped regularize the anomalous situation, especially concerning travel, transportation, and the status of West Berlin as an exclave of the Federal Republic. The dissolution of the communist bloc in the late 1980s opened the way to German unification.

As a condition for unification and its integration into the Federal Republic, East Germany was required to reconstitute the five historical states of Brandenburg, Mecklenburg–West Pomerania, Saxony, Saxony-Anhalt, and Thuringia. As states of the united Germany, they adopted administrative, judicial, educational, and social structures parallel and analogous to those in the states of former West Germany. East and West Berlin were reunited and now form a single state.

With the country's unification on October 3, 1990, all vestiges of the Federal Republic's qualified status as a sovereign state were voided. For example, Berlin was no longer technically occupied territory, with ultimate authority vested in the military governors.

Germany's constitution established a parliamentary system of government that incorporated many features of the British system; however, since the Basic Law created a federal system, unlike the United Kingdom's unitary one, many political structures were drawn from the models of the United States and other federal governments. In reaction to the centralization of power during the Nazi era, the Basic Law granted the states considerable autonomy. In addition to federalism, the Basic Law has two other features similar to the Constitution of the United States: (1) its formal declaration of the principles of human rights and of bases for the government of the people and (2) the strongly independent position of the courts, especially in the right of the Federal Constitutional Court to void a law by declaring it unconstitutional.

The formal chief of state is the president. Intended to be an elder statesman of stature, the president is chosen for a five-year term by a specially convened assembly. In addition to formally signing all federal legislation and treaties, the president nominates the federal chancellor and the chancellor's cabinet appointments, whom the president may dismiss upon the chancellor's recommendation. However, the president cannot dismiss either the federal chancellor or the Bundestag (Federal Diet), the lower chamber of the federal parliament. Among other important presidential functions are those of appointing federal judges and certain other officials and the right of pardon and reprieve.

The government is headed by the chancellor, who is elected by a majority vote of the Bundestag upon nomination by the president. Vested with considerable independent powers, the chancellor is responsible for initiating government policy. The cabinet and its ministries also enjoy extensive autonomy and powers of initiative. The chancellor can be deposed only by an absolute majority of the Bundestag and only after a majority has been assured for the election of a successor. This "constructive vote of no confidence"—in contrast to the vote of no confidence employed in most other parliamentary systems, which only require a majority opposed to the sitting prime minister for ouster—reduces the likelihood that the chancellor will be unseated. Indeed, the constructive vote of no confidence has been used only once to remove a chancellor from office (in 1982 Helmut Schmidt was defeated on such a motion and replaced with Helmut Kohl). The cabinet may not be dismissed by a vote of no confidence by the Bundestag. The president may not unseat a government or, in a crisis, call upon a political leader at his discretion to form a new government. The latter constitutional provision is based on the experience of the sequence of events whereby Adolf Hitler became chancellor in 1933.

Most cabinet officials are members of the Bundestag and are drawn from the majority party or proportionally from the parties forming a coalition, but the chancellor may appoint persons without party affiliation but with a certain area of technical competence. These nondelegate members speak or answer questions during parliamentary debates.

The Bundestag, which consists of about 600 members (the precise number of members varies depending on election results), is the cornerstone of the German system of government. It exercises much wider powers than the 69-member upper chamber, known as the Bundesrat (Federal Council). Bundesrat delegations represent the interests of the state governments and are bound to vote unanimously as instructed by their provincial governments. All legislation originates in the Bundestag; the consent of the Bundesrat is necessary only on certain matters directly affecting the interests of the states, especially in the area of finance and administration and for legislation in which questions of the Basic Law are involved. It may restrain the Bundestag by rejecting certain routine legislation passed by the lower chamber; unless a bill falls within certain categories that enable the Bundesrat to exercise an absolute veto over legislation, its vote against a bill may be overridden by a simple majority in the Bundestag, or by a two-thirds majority in the Bundestag should there be a two-thirds majority

REICHSTAG

The Reichstag is the meeting place of the Bundestag ("Federal Assembly"), the lower house of Germany's national legislature. One of Berlin's most famous landmarks, it is situated at the northern end of the Ebertstrasse and near the south bank of the Spree River. Tiergarten Park is directly west of the building, and the Brandenburg Gate is to the south.

The Neo-Renaissance building was designed by Paul Wallot and was completed in 1894. It was the home of the Reichstag ("Imperial Diet") from 1894 to 1933, during the periods of the German Empire (1871–1918) and the Weimar Republic (1919–33). A fire at the Reichstag on February 27, 1933, one month after Adolf Hitler assumed the chancellorship, triggered events that led to Hitler's assumption of dictatorial powers in Germany. The disused building sustained additional damage from Allied bombing during World War II, and neglect in postwar years led to further deterioration. By the 1970s it had undergone partial restoration and became a museum of German history. More extensive restoration and renovation took place under the direction of British architect Sir Norman Foster after the reunification of West and East Germany in 1990. The building's huge glass dome, once its most recognizable feature, was rebuilt. An interior ramp spirals to the top of the dome, affording excellent views of the surrounding city. After the restoration was completed, the Reichstag became one of Berlin's most prominent tourist attractions, drawing hundreds of thousands of visitors each year.

The Reichstag, with renovations by Sir Norman Foster, in Berlin. © Bundesbildstelle/Press and Information Office of the Federal Government of Germany

The building became the focus of the art world in June 1995 when it was wrapped in more than one million square feet (more than 90,000 square meters) of silver fabric by the environmental sculptors Christo and Jeanne-Claude. More than five million people viewed the installation, which was regarded as one of Christo and Jeanne-Claude's most ambitious projects.

The Reichstag (Berlin) wrapped in silver fabric by Christo, June 1995. © Bilderberg/Press and Information Office of the Federal Government of Germany

On October 4, 1990, the Bundestag of the newly reunified German state met for the first time in the Reichstag and the following year voted to transfer the seat of government from Bonn to Berlin, with the Reichstag becoming the Bundestag's permanent home. Though the use of the Reichstag was met with some criticism, the Bundestag opened its inaugural session there on September 7, 1999.

In the 21st century the Reichstag became a symbol of Germany's commitment to renewable energy. The Reichstag's iconic dome was designed to bathe the Bundestag chamber in natural light, and a massive solar array on its roof further increased the building's energy independence. Biofuel generators provided for a significant amount of the Reichstag's power needs, and in 2008 the Bundestag approved a plan to power the building with 100 percent renewable resources.

opposed in the Bundesrat. To amend the Basic Law, approval by a two-thirds vote in each chamber is required.

The powers of the Bundestag are kept in careful balance with those of the Landtage, the state parliaments. Certain powers are specifically reserved to the republic—for example, foreign affairs, defense, post and telecommunications, customs, international trade, and matters affecting citizenship. The Bundestag and the states may pass concurrent legislation in such matters when it is necessary and desirable, or the Bundestag may set out certain guidelines for legislation; drawing from these, each individual Landtag may enact legislation in keeping with its own needs and circumstances. In principle, the Bundestag initiates or approves legislation in matters in which uniformity is essential, but the Landtage otherwise are free to act in areas in which they are not expressly restrained by the Basic Law.

REGIONAL AND LOCAL GOVERNMENT

Certain functions (e.g., education and law enforcement) are expressly the responsibility of the states, yet there is an attempt to maintain a degree of uniformity among the 16 states through joint consultative bodies. The state governments are generally parallel in structure to that of the Bund but need not be. In 13 states the head of government has a cabinet and ministers; each of these states also has its own parliamentary body. In the city-states of Hamburg, Bremen, and Berlin, the mayor serves simultaneously as the head of the city government and the state government. In the city-states the municipal senates serve also as provincial parliaments, and the municipal offices assume the nature of provincial ministries.

The administrative subdivisions of the states (exclusive of the city-states and the Saarland) are the Regierungsbezirke (administrative districts). Below these are the divisions known as Kreise (counties). Larger communities enjoy the status of what in the United Kingdom was formerly the county borough. The counties themselves are further subdivided into the Gemeinden (roughly "communities" or "parishes"), which through long German tradition have achieved considerable autonomy and responsibility in the administration of schools, hospitals, housing and construction, social welfare, public services and utilities, and cultural amenities. Voters may pass laws on certain issues via referenda at the municipal and state levels.

JUSTICE

The German court system differs from that of some other federations, such as the United States, in that all the trial and appellate courts are state courts while the courts of last resort are federal. All courts may hear cases based on law enacted on the federal level, though there are some areas of law over which the states have exclusive control. The federal courts assure the uniform application of national law by the state courts. In addition to the courts of general jurisdiction for civil and criminal cases, the highest of which is the Federal Court of Justice, there are four court systems with specialized jurisdiction in administrative, labour, social security, and tax matters. The jurisdiction of the three-level system of administrative courts extends, for example, to all civil law litigation of a nonconstitutional nature unless other specialized courts have jurisdiction.

Although all courts have the power and obligation to review the constitutionality of government action and legislation within their jurisdiction, only the Federal Constitutional Court (Bundesverfassungsgericht) in Karlsruhe may declare legislation unconstitutional. Judges on the Federal Constitutional Court are chosen for nonrenewable 12-year terms. The Bundestag and Bundesrat each select half of the court's 16 judges; in each case, a nominee must win two-thirds support to secure appointment. The court sits in two eight-member Senates, which handle ordinary cases. Important cases are decided by the entire body.

Judges play a more prominent and active role in all stages of legal proceedings than do their common-law counterparts, and proceedings in German courts tend to be less controlled by prosecutors and defense attorneys. There is less emphasis on formal rules of evidence, which in the common-law countries is largely a by-product of the jury system, and more stress on letting the facts speak for what they may be worth in the individual case. There is no plea bargaining in criminal cases. In Germany, as in most European countries, litigation costs are relatively low compared with those in the United States, but the losing party in any case usually must pay the court costs and attorney fees of both parties.

Although codes and statutes are viewed as the primary source of law in

The Federal Constitutional Court. Michael Latz/AFP/Getty Images

Germany, precedent is of great importance in the interpretation of legal rules. German administrative law, for example, is case law in the same sense that there exists no codification of the principles relied upon in the process of reviewing administrative action. These principles are mostly the law as determined by previous judicial rulings. Germans see their system of judicial review of administrative actions as implementation of the rule of law. In this context an emphasis is placed on the availability of judicial remedies.

Unification brought about the integration and adaptation of the administration of justice of East and West Germany; however, this was complicated by the large number of judges who were incapacitated by the union. Many judges were dismissed either because they owed their appointment as judges primarily to their loyalty to the communist government or because of their records. To fill the many vacancies created in the courts of the new states, judges and judicial administrators were recruited from former West Germany. Indeed, a large number were "put on loan" from the western states and many others urged out of retirement to help during the transition.

POLITICAL PROCESS

The Basic Law established a mixed electoral system, consisting of elements of both plurality and proportionality. Half of the Bundestag's members are elected to represent single-seat constituencies, and half are elected through proportional representation. The system is designed to simultaneously provide a link between citizens and elected representatives and a legislature that reflects a consensus of opinions in the country.

THE ELECTORATE

National elections to the Bundestag are held once every four years. All German citizens at least age 18 are eligible to vote (this was reduced from age 21 in 1970), and 16-year-olds are eligible to vote in municipal elections in some Länder. In 2011 Bremen became the first Land to extend suffrage to 16-year-olds for state elections. Voters cast two ballots. Constituency representatives are elected by the distribution of votes on the first ballot; the candidate winning the most

votes secures election to the Bundestag. Voters cast ballots for political parties at the regional level with their second vote (Zweitstimme), which determines overall party representation. A party must win at least 5 percent of the national vote (or win at least three constituencies) to secure representation, and the number of seats it is allocated is based on its proportion of second votes. Bundesrat members are appointed by the state governments, and the body exercises its authority to protect the rights and prerogatives of the state governments. Each state is allocated between three and six members of the Bundesrat, depending on population.

The quadrennial general and provincial elections as well as local elections are attended with the greatest interest and involvement by the electorate. The public is kept informed on political issues through intense media coverage, and political affairs are frequently debated among German citizens. Although voting is not compulsory, the participation rate is high, with about three-fourths of eligible voters casting ballots. Since elections in the states are staggered throughout the life of each Bundestag, they act as a bellwether of public opinion for the incumbent federal government. German citizens, along with German residents who are citizens of other EU countries, also elect representatives to the European Parliament, although voter participation in these contests tends to be lower than in general or state elections.

POLITICAL PARTIES

The sheer proliferation of Germany's political parties contributed to the downfall of the Weimar Republic in 1933, but they have shown an increasing tendency toward consolidation since the early days of the Federal Republic. Smaller parties generally either have allied themselves with the larger ones, have shrunk into insignificance, or simply have vanished. Reunified Germany has, in effect, only two numerically major parties, the Christian Democratic Union (Christlich-Demokratische Union; CDU) and the Social Democratic Party of Germany (Sozialdemokratische Partei Deutschlands; SPD), neither of which can easily attain a parliamentary majority. In addition, there are four smaller but still important parties: the Christian Social Union (Christlich-Soziale Union; CSU), the Bavarian sister party of the CDU; the Free Democratic Party (FDP), which has served as a junior coalition partner in most German governments since World War II; Alliance '90/The Greens (Bündnis '90/Die Grünen), a party formed in 1993 by the merger of the ecologist Green Party and the eastern German Alliance '90; and the Left Party, formerly the Party of Democratic Socialism (Partei des Demokratischen Sozialismus; PDS), the successor of the Socialist Unity Party of Germany (SED), which later allied itself with left groups in western Germany. Fringe political parties, such as The Republicans (Die Republikaner), the German People's Union (Deutsche Volksunion; DVU), and the Pirate Party of Germany (Piratenpartei Deutschland) have scored some success at the local and state levels but have not won representation at the national level. The 5 percent threshold for elections has proved a highly effective instrument in excluding radical parties of whatever stripe and in preventing the formation of splinter parties. However, the proportional element of the electoral system has necessitated the formation of coalition governments. Since 1966 all federal governments have been composed of at least two parties. Dissent within the major parties is contained in the wings and factions of each respective party.

THE CHRISTIAN DEMOCRATIC PARTIES

The CDU is a centre-right party that endorses conservative social values and the social market economy. In government for much of Germany's post-World War II history, it headed governments from 1949 to 1966 and from 1982 to 1998 (in alliance with the FDP and CSU); it returned to power in 2005 in a coalition with the CSU and the SPD. Beginning in 2009, the CDU headed a new coalition with the CSU and the FDP. The CDU is a successor of the old Catholic Centre Party and kindred bourgeois parties, either Protestant or nonsectarian. In a country in which one's religion often determined one's politics, the party's strongest constituencies are still in the Roman

Catholic districts, although the sectarian Christian aspect is of only incidental emphasis, chiefly among older voters. The party strongly endorses Germany's leading role in the EU, its membership in the North Atlantic Treaty Organization (NATO), a free market economy, and vigorous material assistance to the countries of the former communist bloc, especially the onetime Soviet republics. It is established in all states except Bavaria, where the more conservative CSU functions as its counterpart in effectively a permanent coalition.

A branch of the CDU (known as CDU-Ost) existed in East Germany throughout that country's history. However, it was only tolerated to preserve the facade of a multiparty system. With the overthrow of the ruling communist regime in East Germany's first free elections, on March 18, 1990, it was this rump party that took power by a large mandate, with Lothar de Maizière as minister president presiding over the six-month transitional period to unification.

THE SOCIAL DEMOCRATS

The SPD, in government from 1966 to 1982 (1966–69 with the CDU and 1969–82 with the FDP) and from 1998 to 2009 (1998–2005 with the Greens and 2005–09 with the CDU-CSU), is the heir to the Marxist parties of the 19th century. In East Germany, which historically was the stronghold of the socialist movement in Germany, the SPD was subsumed by the formation of the SED in 1946. Ostensibly a combination of the old Communist Party of Germany (Kommunistische Partei Deutschlands; KPD) and the Socialist Party, the SED was in fact simply the ruling communist party. In West Germany the SPD's early postwar leadership, drawing strength from its record of opposition to Nazism, adhered to a rigorously orthodox Marxism, opposed vehemently the communist movement from which it had split in the early 20th century, and rejected West Germany's rearmament and the country's integration into the Western military defense system. In 1959, however, the SPD, in the so-called Bad Godesberg Resolution, discarded its doctrinaire approach; nationalization of industry was dropped in favour of gradualist reform, and appeals to class warfare were abandoned. The party broadened its base to attract increasingly greater segments of the middle class. The SPD was cautious about unification, fearing that it would unleash enormous financial and emotional costs. Unlike the CDU, the SPD did not initially gain a windfall of votes in eastern Germany.

THE FREE DEMOCRATS

Because neither the CDU-CSU nor the SPD have generally been able to win enough votes to capture a majority of seats in the Bundestag, the balance of power has often rested with the FDP. The successor of the older German liberal parties, the FDP has generally adopted free trade, pro-business, and anticlerical positions. The party now serves as a liberal, bourgeois alternative to the CDU and SPD and often exercises a power far beyond the 6 to 10 percent support it regularly receives in national elections. For example, FDP leader Hans-Dietrich Genscher, Germany's foreign minister from 1974 to 1992, was often viewed as the architect of German unification. In 2009 it won its best-ever electoral results—14.6 percent of the national vote—and formed a governing coalition with the ruling CDU-CSU.

THE GREENS

The ecologist Green Party was formed in West Germany in 1980 and merged with the eastern German Alliance '90 in 1993. It has been the only completely new party to win national representation in the post-World War II era. Formed by mainly younger groups of environmentalists, opponents of nuclear power, and pacifists, the Greens successfully broke the 5 percent barrier in the 1983 election. On the heels of the accident at the nuclear power plant in Chernobyl, Ukraine, in 1986, the Greens captured in excess of 8 percent of the overall vote and sent 22 delegates to the Bundestag. However, internal disputes between the "realists" (Realos), who took a pragmatic approach to environmental policies, and the "fundamentalists" (Fundis), who eschewed compromise in favour of ideological purity, and dissension over

individual issues weakened the cohesion of the party's constituent factions. In 1990 the Green Party failed to surpass the 5 percent threshold. Its union with Alliance '90 enabled it to reenter the Bundestag beginning in 1994, and from 1998 to 2005 it served as a junior partner in an SPD-led coalition. In office, the party continued to face internal dissension between the realists and fundamentalists, though the former have been dominant since the early 1990s. The party increased its representation in the Bundestag to 68 seats in the 2009 election. A catastrophic accident at Japan's Fukushima nuclear plant in 2011 sparked a massive surge in support for Greens at the state level. In March 2011 an impressive showing in Baden-Württemberg, traditionally a CDU stronghold, won the Greens their first state government at the head of a coalition with the SPD.

THE LEFT PARTY

The Left Party formed as an alliance between the PDS and the disillusioned members of the SPD and of the Green Party who had established the Electoral Alternative for Labour and Social Justice (Wahlalternative Arbeit und soziale Gerechtigkeit) in western Germany. The PDS was the successor party to East Germany's former ruling party, the SED, which controlled the entire government apparatus until the system's demise in 1989–90. After unification the SED lost most of its supporters and members.

The PDS won 11 percent of the vote in eastern Germany in the first all-German election in 1990, giving it 17 seats in the Bundestag. During the 1990s the party gained strength in eastern Germany, where unemployment remained stubbornly high and economic conditions lagged. Although it did not surpass the 5 percent threshold in 1994, the PDS won enough constituency seats to gain Bundestag representation, and in 1998 it captured 5.1 percent of the vote, including some 20 percent in the former East German territories. The PDS largely remained a regional party, but it scored successes in eastern German states and even formed a coalition government with the SPD in Berlin in 2002. In 2002 it again failed to cross the 5 percent threshold, but in 2005 the PDS and its left allies in western Germany—together known as the Left Party—captured nearly 9 percent of the national vote and won more than 50 seats in the Bundestag. Support for the Left Party continued to grow, and in 2009 it won nearly 12 percent of the national vote and increased its number of seats in the Bundestag to 76.

FRINGE PARTIES

In the late 20th century the rightist Republican Party and the DVU were the most visible of Germany's fringe parties. With their tiny memberships, neither of these parties has been able to surmount the 5 percent barrier in national elections. The National Democratic Party of Germany (Nationaldemokratische Partei Deutschlands; NPD), the oldest of the country's right-wing parties, was formed in 1964 and gained little support in national elections, though it was able to enter several state parliaments in the late 1960s. In the 1980s and '90s the Republicans and the DVU won seats in several state legislatures, with the Republicans' support particularly concentrated in Bavaria, Baden-Württemberg, and Berlin. The DVU, originally formed in 1971, achieved its electoral breakthrough in the 1990s, when it won representation in Schleswig-Holstein and fared particularly well in eastern Germany, where it won 13 percent in Saxony-Anhalt's state election in 1998. Although the rightist parties have distinct policies and have been unable to coalesce around a united platform, they share an antipathy toward Germany's liberal immigration policies and have generally been regarded as neofascist in orientation. The NPD and DVU attempted to merge in 2010, but a legal challenge by a group of state DVU organizations successfully blocked the move.

The Pirate Party of Germany, an outgrowth of the larger Pirate Party movement that began in Sweden in 2006, promoted a broadly populist platform that focused on copyright reform and Internet freedom. The Pirate Party used open-source software to facilitate group decision making, a process the party called "liquid democracy." In essence, the party's entire platform was subject to electronic referendum by its members. Riding a wave of antiestablishment sentiment, the Pirates scored a string of electoral successes at the state level in 2011–12, winning representation in regional legislatures in Berlin, Saarland, Schleswig-Holstein, and North Rhine–Westphalia.

SECURITY

Germany has been a member of the North Atlantic Treaty Organization (NATO) since May 1955. Until unification West Germany was the only NATO country with territory bordering two members of the Warsaw Pact, the Soviet bloc's anti-Western defense alliance, and NATO strategy was founded on West Germany's vulnerability to an armed invasion. The dissolution of the Soviet Union and the Warsaw Pact and the admission of Poland and the Czech Republic to NATO have eased Germany away from this "front-line" status.

The German contribution to the Western defense system takes the form of its combined arm of defense known as the Federal Armed Forces (Bundeswehr). The German military forces are divided into an army, navy, and air force. From its inception the Federal Armed Forces was envisioned as a citizens' defense force, decisively under civilian control through the Bundestag, and its officers and soldiers trained to be mindful of the role of the military in a democracy. Conscription for males was universal until July 2011, when the country adopted an all-volunteer force. Germany maintains a separate Coast Guard and Federal Police (Bundespolizei) force.

After unification the former East German People's Army (Volksarmee) was integrated into the Federal Armed Forces. The special troops who had guarded the Berlin Wall and the boundary with West Germany, together with the factory militia, were disarmed and dissolved. In the 21st century there was much discussion about the future of the German military, particularly regarding the role of the Eurocorps, a pan-European ready-reaction force, and expansion of the role of German forces in international activities (e.g., the NATO-led war in Afghanistan). As the focus of the armed services shifted from border defense to operations abroad, a massive plan for the reorganization and downsizing of German forces was undertaken. Beginning in 2006, the German military began its transformation into a smaller, all-volunteer force, and cuts were made to reduce spending across all three branches of service. Additionally, the Bundeswehr was restructured into three broad joint-operations command categories: response forces, designed for high-intensity combat operations; stabilization forces, intended for lower-intensity peacekeeping missions; and support forces—the largest of the three groups—tasked with command, control, logistics, and training.

Germany's national police force, the Federal Police, handles emergencies outside the jurisdiction of state police forces, such as border control and air and rail security. Law enforcement remains a province primarily reserved to the states, and each state maintains its own police force, which is charged with all phases of enforcement, except where its function is assumed by a municipal force. In the event of a national emergency, the federal government may commandeer the services of various state police units, along with the standby police reserve that is trained and equipped by each state for action during civil emergencies.

The federal government investigates certain actions, particularly those related to the internal security of the state and crimes that transcend state boundaries. National agencies include the Berlin-based Federal Intelligence Service (Bundesnachrichtendienst; BND), which combats external threats; the Federal Office for the Protection of the Constitution (Bundesamt für Verfassungsschutz; BfV), headquartered in Cologne, which compiles information regarding threats posed to security by domestic groups; the Customs Criminological Office (Zollkriminalamt; ZKA), also based in Cologne, which investigates customs violations; and the Federal Criminal Investigation Office (Bundeskriminalamt), headquartered in Wiesbaden, which provides forensic and research assistance to federal and state agencies investigating crime, as well as coordinating efforts among various state, national, and international police forces. The BfV is particularly noteworthy for tracking the activities of extremist groups and publishing statistics annually, while the BKA has taken on a more prominent counterterrorism role in the wake of the September 11, 2001, attacks in the United States.

The People's Police of East Germany was dissolved upon unification, and its members were integrated into the police forces of the new states. The loathed Ministry for State Security (Ministerium für Staatssicherheit, popularly known as Stasi) was also dissolved, and its files were removed into Western custody.

HEALTH AND WELFARE

Germany's system of social benefits is among the world's most elaborate and all-embracing. A pioneer in establishing social welfare benefits, imperial Germany in the 1880s became the first country to provide health and accident insurance, workers' and employees' benefits and pensions, and miners' insurance. (Under German labour law, a categorical distinction is made between hourly wage earners and salaried employees.) Ostensibly, the programs were introduced both to meet the needs of workers and to stem the influence of socialism. The German welfare system has served as a model for similar programs in other countries.

INSURANCE AND SERVICES

By the end of the 20th century some nine-tenths of the population was covered by statutory (public) health insurance, and the country ranked among the world's highest in terms of the proportion of health care costs covered by the government—about 90 percent of all incurred costs. Reforms in the early 21st century made health insurance compulsory for all people living in Germany. Although the vast majority of Germans remain covered by the government-sponsored health system, employees above a certain salary level or self-employed persons may decline public insurance and purchase full private insurance that is as comprehensive as the government-sponsored plans. Once an individual opts for private insurance, however, it is difficult to return to the public program. Those participating in a government health scheme also may purchase supplemental private insurance. Contributions to government health insurance, which amount to more than one-tenth of wages or salaries, are shared by employees and employers.

Medical care in Germany is excellent, and even rural areas are well served. Hospitals are usually operated by municipalities or religious organizations or as proprietary institutions owned by one or more physicians. The conquering of tuberculosis, once endemic in Germany but now rarely encountered, was a triumph of the health system. The extensive health care system that operated in East Germany—where universal free health care, medication, child care, nursing, and pensions were funded by an obligatory state insurance system—was reorganized from the exclusive management of the system by the trade unions to alignment with the various employment, health, and retirement insurance systems of western Germany.

Introduced by Otto von Bismarck in the 1880s, Germany's old-age pension program provided retirement benefits that were funded by a combination of worker, employer, and government contributions. The program became unsustainable as it was structured, however, when longer life expectancies and lower birth rates reduced the worker-to-pensioner ratio in the late 20th century. A series of reforms were undertaken in the early 21st century to reduce the government's share of the pension load while preserving existing benefits through additional worker contributions. Tax incentives were provided for workers who chose to invest in private or occupation-based pension plans, and the retirement age was increased to 67.

ADDITIONAL BENEFITS

Germany also provides several special systems of coverage for groups such as war widows, orphans, and farmers. Unemployment insurance is funded through deductions from wages and salaries. Allowances are made for families with one or more children. Additional public allowances are granted to persons suffering disabilities from wartime injury, whether as military personnel or as civilians. Some small indemnification has been made to property owners whose holdings lay in former German territories now outside the country.

WAR REPARATIONS

Under agreements concluded with 12 European countries, Germany has paid compensation to the nationals of those countries who were victims of Nazi oppression or to their families and successors. In particular, the government has assumed the immense financial responsibility of making restitution to the Jewish victims of Adolf Hitler's Germany. Claims for property confiscated during the Third Reich have been honoured, and Jewish refugees and expellees from that era, the vast majority of whom reside abroad, have been paid indemnifications and pensions. Massive reparations have been paid to Israel in the name of the Jewish people at large. East Germany ignored all such claims until 1990, when the transition government of Lothar de Mazière undertook similar restitution. In 2000 the German government, more than 3,000 German companies, the Evangelical Church in Germany, and a number of other institutions and governments established a multibillion-dollar fund to compensate those forced to perform labour during Nazi internment. These roughly one million rapidly aging people, living primarily in central and eastern Europe, were among the last large groups of victims of the Nazi era who had received no previous payments or support from Germany. The fund was intended both to provide some restitution to the forced labourers and to shield German companies from potential individual lawsuits.

STANDARDS OF LIVING

Western Germany's standard of living is among the highest in the world. The distribution of wealth compares favourably with that of other advanced countries. Powerful incentives to save are offered by the state not only in the form of housing subsidies and tax concessions but also through bonus saving schemes. For those whose income does not exceed a certain level, savings of up to a fixed amount kept in a bank or savings institution for seven years are granted a generous bonus by the government. The accumulation of capital assets is encouraged under a plan whereby workers below a certain earning level who agree to pay into a longer-term savings agreement, such as a home-savings contract, are given a "worker savings grant" by the state.

Earning power for both workers and employers assures an adequate income to meet the cost of living. There is no exaggerated difference between the compensation for blue-collar workers and white-collar employees, although upper levels of management earn generous incomes and benefits. Because a major portion of tax revenue is derived from excise levies and the value-added tax—as in most EU countries—low- and medium-income workers collectively bear a greater relative tax burden.

The absorption of the eastern German population and economy had no more than a marginal effect on living standards in the regions of the western sector despite a rise in unemployment, a housing shortage, and tax increases. Even the exorbitant costs of unification, which brought about a tax increase, seemed to cause few changes in western Germany. The deutsche mark held its strength and grew even stronger. By contrast, the introduction of the mark in East Germany in July 1990—far from being the "magic bullet" hoped for—tended to have a depressing effect. The eastern population with its much lower earning power suddenly had to pay Western prices for food and other commodities. The wholesale shutdown of former state factories and enterprises caused vast unemployment in industrial cities in Thuringia, Saxony-Anhalt, and Saxony and resulted in much hardship and discontent that persisted long after unification.

During its 40 years, the East German government produced a society in which employment was guaranteed and in which most of the requirements of life were often provided free or at low cost. The demands of work were different than in West Germany and were relatively lax; competitiveness, initiative, and individuality were not qualities highly prized or rewarded. The working population was even more ill-suited than workers in Poland, Czechoslovakia, or Hungary for the plunge into a free market economy—largely because eastern German workers needed to learn new technologies, were under new management, had to accommodate the rules and culture of West German labour unions, and were forced to compete with their western German counterparts. But, unlike other former Soviet bloc countries, East Germany had a prosperous neighbour that bailed it out. As a result, in the two decades that followed reunification, the standard of living in the east rose dramatically. Household incomes almost doubled over this period, although unemployment remained significantly higher in the east than in the west, and a wave of migration resulted in a brain drain, as tens of thousands of people left the east for destinations in the west and abroad.

HOUSING

German housing stock is generally of good quality, though there is a considerable discrepancy between eastern and western Germany. In the territory of the former West Germany, the stock is modern, some three-fourths of its dwellings having been built since the end of World War II. In contrast, eastern German housing stock is significantly older, about half of it having been built prior to the end of the war. Home ownership rates also vary considerably; almost half of dwellings are owner-occupied in western Germany compared with less than one-third in eastern Germany.

In principle, under the communist government of East Germany, every citizen and family had the right to adequate accommodations. Rents everywhere, together with charges for heating and electricity, were held at extremely low levels. The need for new housing after the war was solved by erecting massive apartment blocks of cheap material, places that are now generally out of favour with people who have the means to choose their style of housing.

After unification, the government devoted significant resources to modernizing eastern Germany's stock and alleviating the housing shortages caused by the extensive immigration of the 1990s. Significant tax incentives were offered to spark investment in the real estate sector of the former East Germany, and a speculative boom followed, eventually resulting in a housing supply that far outstripped demand. When the tax incentives expired in 1998, the real estate bubble burst, and housing prices across Germany slumped. This had the unintended consequence of insulating Germany from the exuberance that fueled 21st-century housing bubbles across the industrialized world. As a result, German banks and investors were far less exposed to the shocks of the economic crisis than their American, British, Spanish, and Irish counterparts.

The private sector provides most of the capital for new housing. However, the federal government's building savings policy offers loans to those who save for a prescribed period to build or purchase a home. Much of the housing built with government subsidies is allocated to "social housing"—dwellings provided at "cost rent" far below the market rental value to families with many children, people with disabilities, the elderly, and persons with low incomes. Stringent definitions of tenants' rights, including injunctions against arbitrary or unfair evictions and protection against precipitous rent increases, balance the rights of tenants and landlords.

The rebuilding of the cities in the 1950s and '60s, coupled with increased automobile ownership, invariably led to the desertion of older city centres by many residents. Easier access and parking near town centres, improved public transportation, large-scale refurbishing of historic buildings, and the creation of pedestrian zones offering special entertainments, festivals, and attractions were among the attempts to reverse this trend and lure the public back downtown in the evening. Nonetheless, suburbanization has continued, particularly in eastern Germany since unification.

The physical appearance of villages and towns throughout western Germany was improved on a grand scale beginning in the 1970s through extensive renovation programs undertaken by the states; grants, subsidies, and matching funds were made available to restore the exteriors of historic monuments and older buildings to pristine condition. The process also occurred in eastern Germany after unification.

EDUCATION

Full-time schooling is free and compulsory for children aged 6 to 15 or 16; the exact age is determined at the state level. Although the control of education rests with the states, there is a national commission that strives for uniformity of curriculum, requirements, and standards. Some books and study materials are free, and financial assistance and other forms of support are available in cases of hardship.

PRESCHOOL, ELEMENTARY, AND SECONDARY

Preschooling, to which the notably German contribution in modern times is enshrined in the universal word *kindergarten*, can begin at 3 years of age. Some four-fifths of children attend kindergarten. All children attend the Grundschule ("basic school") from age 6 until about age 10. Somewhat less than half continue elementary schooling in a junior secondary school called the Hauptschule ("head school") until about age 15 or 16. Afterward students are assigned to a Berufsschule ("vocational school") that they attend part-time in conjunction with an apprenticeship or other on-the-job training. This program makes it possible for virtually every young person in the vocational track to learn a useful skill or trade, constantly adapted to the actual demands of the employment market.

Children who receive a commercial or clerical education, somewhat less than one-third of the school-age population, attend an intermediate school called the Realschule (roughly meaning "practical school") and earn an intermediate-level

certificate that entitles them to enter a Fachschule ("technical" or "special-training school"), the completion of which is a prerequisite for careers in the middle levels of business, administration, and the civil service.

Approximately one-third of all children are chosen to study at a Gymnasium (senior secondary school, equivalent to a grammar school in the United Kingdom), in which a rigorous program lasting for nine years (levels 5 to 13) prepares them—with emphasis variously on the classics, modern languages, mathematics, and natural science—for the Abitur or Reifezeugnis ("certificate of maturity"), the prerequisite for matriculation at a German university. The traditional structure of the German Gymnasium has mainly shifted from being built around a single branch of studies to offering a "reformed upper phase" with a choice of courses.

Many so-called Gesamtschulen (equivalent to British comprehensive schools), which were established beginning in the 1960s, are now operated in each state, though conservative areas were generally resistant to them. These Gesamtschulen are intended as an alternative to the previously rigid division into three levels, often criticized for forcing the choice of a child's future at too early an age, a choice that, once entered upon, was almost impossible to change. These schools offer a large range of choices and permit pupils more freedom in seeking the level best suited for them.

HIGHER EDUCATION

German universities, famed in history and noted for their enormous contributions to learning, especially in the 19th and early 20th centuries, have been severely strained by the swelling numbers of students and changing social conditions that have taxed the traditional structures of the universities beyond their capacities or accustomed functions. Today, it has become all but impossible for students to take as long as they wish to complete their studies or to move from university to university. Lecture rooms, seminars, and libraries are greatly overburdened. In response, a small number of specialized private universities were founded, and there has been considerable debate about the financing of education, particularly whether tuition charges should be introduced.

To meet the rapidly rising demand for higher education, the number of universities also has increased. Entirely new academic universities have been added to the ranks of the ancient institutions, and the status of institutes and colleges of technology, education, and art have been upgraded to university rank. At the same time, new specialized or technical institutions such as the Fachhochschule, a higher technical college specializing in a single discipline, such as engineering, architecture, design, art, agriculture, or business administration, have been created. Little difference in prestige is attached to whether a student has studied at Heidelberg, founded in 1386, or at the University of Hagen, Westphalia, established in 1976, a distance-learning university that supplemented online lessons with meetings at regional study centres. Among Germany's leading universities are the Humboldt University of Berlin (founded 1809–10), the Free University of Berlin (founded 1948), the University of Cologne (founded 1388), the Johann Wolfgang Goethe University of Frankfurt (founded 1914), the University of Göttingen (founded 1737), the University of Leipzig (founded 1409), and the University of Tübingen (founded 1477). At the beginning of the 21st century Germany had more than 300 universities or institutions of equivalent rank (about half of which were Fachhochschule).

The rough equivalent of a bachelor's degree is a Diplom, though some consider the degree a closer equivalent to the American master's degree. A fairly large number of students also earn degrees in education (by way of the Lehramtspruefung) and in technical schools. A small number of institutions have begun offering an American-style bachelor's degree.

There is an extensive range of possibilities for extended education or extramural studies. Each year about 1,000 Volkshochschulen (adult education centres) enroll some 10 million adults for complete courses or individual subjects, whether in preparation for or furtherance of a career or out of personal interest. The government has also promoted the retraining and further vocational education of workers.

University Library, part of the University of Heidelberg in Germany. © Heidelberger Kongress und Tourismus GmbH

PROBLEMS OF TRANSITION

Integration of the former East German educational system brought a host of problems. As the focus of education was to inculcate the values of the communist state, even textbooks and some school materials were unsuitable for the educational aims of united Germany. English replaced Russian as the primary foreign language taught, forcing unemployment for untold numbers of Russian teachers and creating a shortage of qualified English teachers. The reorientation of primary and secondary schoolteachers to the standards and aims of the republic became an important concern and a focus of retraining.

At the university level the issue of competence became acute. Since many of the faculty of East Germany's universities had been appointed based on their soundness in Marxism-Leninism or loyalty to the SED, upon unification their qualifications became obsolete. The federal authority for qualifying universities to confer degrees and diplomas was unable to give recognition to some institutions of university rank, while the ministers of education of the new states were subjected to great pressures to reconfirm existing appointments. Reappointment committees staffed largely by western Germans reassessed the qualifications of eastern faculty. These committees failed to rehire many easterners, and institutions in eastern Germany were flooded with westerners. Whereas the former East German research institutions had generally been separate from universities, the western system combining research and teaching was implemented nationally following unification.

CHAPTER 5

CULTURAL LIFE

The birthplace of the modern printing press and of influential schools of philosophy and artistic styles, Germany has long played an important role in Western culture. The arts have been central to Germany's idea of itself; indeed, the historian Hagen Schulze has observed that

> the German nation was born in the minds of the intelligentsia, as a cultural entity without direct ties to politics. It was therefore only logical that its great heroes were not princes and military leaders as in France and England but rather a collection of poets and philosophers…. Germany's extraordinary cultural flowering made it the new Greece, said both Friedrich von Schiller and Wilhelm von Humboldt—powerless but intellectually supreme.

That ideal fell only when the German nation began to experiment with power and expand militarily, but it remains fondly held by contemporary German intellectuals as a model worthy of emulation in a new Europe.

CULTURAL MILIEU

During the period of partition, West Germany, as heir to Germany's older regions, was custodian of the greater portion of the country's rich cultural legacy. The majority of Germany's architectural monuments—of Roman Germany

Costumes with wooden masks worn during the pre-Lenten celebrations in Rottweil, Germany. Otto Stadler/© Silvestris

and of the medieval Romanesque and southern German Baroque styles—fell within its borders, as did many of the great libraries, archives, and facilities for the performing arts. Yet some of the greatest monuments of German cultural and historical achievement were located in East Germany, including the Wartburg of Martin Luther, the Weimar of Johann Wolfgang von Goethe, and the Leipzig of Johann Sebastian Bach; a large share of prewar Germany's art treasures also rested in East Germany, especially in East Berlin and Dresden. After the division of Germany, many of the cultural assets originally from the eastern sector were removed to the West or to Russia, which generally refused to return them after unification. For example, it is estimated that some 200,000 works of art were taken from Germany after World War II, and German sources estimate that more than 4.6 million books were taken; Russian holdings include a Gutenberg bible and thousands of works from the Berlin Museum's East Asian collection. Nonetheless, some materials, such as a stained-glass window from the Marienkirche in Frankfurt, have been returned. Many of East Germany's artists, writers, and institutions, including entire publishing houses, relocated to West Germany or set up successor organizations there.

Despite the political division, the German cultural and artistic tradition remained identifiably the same. In the German-speaking world, a writer or painter or composer or playwright or sculptor was German whether holding a passport from the Federal Republic or from the Democratic Republic. Moreover, in art and literature the adjective *deutsch* ("German") has no strict political boundaries. For example, the Austrian composer Gustav Mahler, the Czech novelist Franz Kafka, the Romanian poet Paul Celan, and the Swiss playwright Friedrich Dürrenmatt all are considered

"German" because their work falls within the German cultural tradition.

During the four decades of separation it was inevitable that some divergence would occur in the cultural life of the two Germanys. Both followed traditional paths of the common German culture, but West Germany, obviously more susceptible to influences from western Europe and North America, became more cosmopolitan. Conversely, East Germany, while remaining surprisingly conservative in its adherence to some aspects of tradition, was powerfully molded by the dictates of a socialist ideology of predominantly Soviet inspiration. The state, as virtually the sole market for artistic products, inevitably had the last word.

Admirably enough, the cultural commissars of East Germany steadfastly protected certain cultural monuments contained within East German borders—even though their provenance was regal, aristocratic, liberal, bourgeois, or religious and the content hardly reconcilable with the aspirations of the "State of Workers and Peasants." The Goethe House and Goethe National Museum on the Frauenplanstrasse in Weimar were carefully restored after the war and meticulously maintained; the Thomanerchor at the St. Thomas Church in Leipzig, the boys' choir made famous by Bach, continued to perform the cantatas and motets of the master in exactly the style of two and a half centuries previously; Dresden, though devastated by wartime bombing, made it an early priority to restore its opera house; and the

The Wartburg, on a hill above Eisenach, Germany © Caio Garrubba/Madeline Grimoldi

music ensembles of East Germany, especially the Dresden Philharmonic and the Dresdner Staatskapelle, together with the Gewandhaus and Rundfunk orchestras of Leipzig, remained part of the mainstream of European music, touring in the West and freely exchanging performers, conductors, and producers. It has been remarked that during their separation the two Germanys diverged not at all in music and only slightly in literature and the theatre but sharply in architecture and the plastic arts.

DAILY LIFE AND SOCIAL CUSTOMS

The incursions of modern patterns of life and global forms of entertainment,

Goethe's garden house, Weimar, Germany; detail of a photomechanical print, c. 1890–1900. Library of Congress, Washington, D.C. (neg. no. LC-DIG-ppmsca-01163)

from fast food to Hollywood films, have weakened the traditional arts, entertainments, and customs of regional and rural Germany, although this has occurred somewhat less so in southern Germany, where the older arts and usages have persisted concurrently with a gradual adaptation to a modern urban pattern of life; the old and the new coexist in an incongruous compatibility. In late summer in the Alpine regions, colourful and festive parades still celebrate the successful return of cattle from mountain pastures to lowland farms. The wood-carvers, violin makers, and gunsmiths of Upper Bavaria continue, under great economic pressure, to follow their trades, not because doing so is quaint but because they still believe in the work itself. Similarly, some women in the Black Forest still wear an elaborate costume known as a Tracht on festival days because they have always done so rather than to amaze tourists. However, even in more traditional communities, where the tourist industry is often highly developed, many folk usages have all but disappeared: older women now seldom wear black dresses and scarves, and the village men no longer appear in top hat and cutaway for a funeral procession.

Popular festivals continue to abound in the west, southwest, and south, the regions that have clung most to the practices of a traditional, preindustrial age. For example, the donning of elaborate wooden masks during the pre-Lenten celebrations in the southwest remains unchanged despite being televised; hundreds of smaller towns and larger villages in the south still commemorate an anniversary from the Thirty Years' War with a parade in 17th-century costume or, in Roman Catholic areas, march in full procession on Corpus Christi Day. What is remarkable is not merely that these traditions survive but that the homelier and less celebrated of them remain truly genuine in the observance.

Traditional German cuisine, though varying considerably from region to region, makes generous use of meat—pork is especially popular, both cured and fresh. Beef, poultry, game such as rabbit and venison, and both freshwater and ocean fish are also widely consumed. German dairies produce a variety of excellent cheeses, and fresh soft cheeses find their way into many dishes. Starches are supplied by bread (wheat and rye) and by potatoes, noodles, and dumplings. The necessity of preserving foods for the northern winter has led to a highly developed array of cured, smoked, and pickled meats, fish, and vegetables

such as sauerkraut (fermented cabbage). German hams and sausages (Wurst) are world-famous and widely imitated, produced in an impressive variety. Mustard, caraway, dill, juniper berries, and marjoram are favoured spices and herbs. Tortes, kuchen, cookies, and other pastries produced in the Konditorei (pastry shop) or home kitchen are served as a conclusion to a meal or an accompaniment to coffee. Holidays bring an array of seasonal sweets such as stollen, gingerbread, and anise cookies. Few meals of the traditional sort, whether presented in the home or in a Gasthaus (inn) or restaurant, are unaccompanied by locally produced wine, beer, brandy, or schnapps. By the early 21st century German cuisine had become more cosmopolitan with the influence of immigrant cultures, and a meal out was as likely to involve Italian, Chinese, Vietnamese, or Turkish foods as traditional German dishes such as sauerbraten, schnitzel, or spaetzle.

As in many other Western countries, family life has undergone many changes. In contrast to past generations, when families had numerous children, an estimated 30 percent of married German couples never become parents, and most of the remainder have only one or two children. Thus, German birth rates are low and below replacement levels. More people are living together before or instead of marrying, the number of marriages is declining, and the number of divorces has increased. More than one-third of all births now occur outside of marriage. Changing marriage patterns have also influenced gender roles. Traditionally, German families had highly differentiated gender roles within marriage—men worked outside the home and women undertook most homemaking activities and child care. During the last decades of the 20th century, however, this pattern shifted, with more than 70 percent of working-age women employed outside the home—though they still are underrepresented within the elite professions.

THE ARTS

For several centuries Germany has enjoyed a tradition of governmental support of the arts. Before the founding of the German Empire in 1871, the many small kingdoms, principalities, duchies, bishoprics, and free cities that preceded it—as well as Austria and German-speaking Switzerland—supported the arts; they established theatres, museums, and libraries, and their leaders acted as patrons for poets, writers, painters, and performers. The institutions thus founded and the convention of generous public support have continued uninterrupted to the present.

GOVERNMENT AND AUDIENCE SUPPORT

The quantitative dimensions of Germany's cultural life astound non-Germans. Several hundred theatres are subsidized by the federal government, the states, and the cities, and there also are many privately financed theatres. Unlike the United States, Britain, and France, in which theatre is more often than not centred in one city, no single German city predominates. Also, productions in Vienna, Austria, and in Zürich, Switzerland, are significant to Germany's artistic life, and artists and resources move easily and freely among the theatrical and operatic companies within the German-speaking regions. Only in Vienna, the capital in which the arts arouse far more intense passions than do politics, does theatre have a broader audience base than in Germany. Audiences in Germany are not limited to a small intellectual or social elite but are drawn from all ranks of society. Season tickets, group arrangements, bloc tickets bought by business firms, and theatre clubs constitute the major patronage of such production companies as the People's Independent Theatre (Theater der Freien Volksbühne), dating from 1890 in Berlin. Going to the theatre or opera in Germany is nearly as affordable and as unremarkable as attending the cinema is elsewhere. The same is also true of concert music. Every major city has at least one symphony orchestra offering many concerts and recitals each week, and many smaller cities and towns also have concerts.

In few countries are the arts so lavishly cultivated as in Germany in terms of the proliferation of cultural amenities, the funds allotted to them, and the attendance upon them. Although this abundance and generous support have not called forth a new era of brilliance to rival that of the Weimar Republic—when Germany (especially Berlin) experienced a resurgence in the arts and a proliferation of creative talents unparalleled since German Classicism and Romanticism—there are a number of noteworthy individual talents and movements dotting the contemporary landscape.

LITERATURE AND THEATRE

Arguably, German literature holds less than its deserved status in world literature in part because the lyrical qualities of its poetry and the nuances of its prose defy translation. Even the most sublime figures in German literary history—Goethe (the author of *Faust*), whose genius not only created poetry, novels, and drama but extended to scientific study as well, and his friend Friedrich von Schiller, poet, dramatist, and literary theorist—are doomed to remain known to the world outside the German-speaking regions largely by reputation. The same is true for a host of remarkable writers through all periods of German literary history, including Friedrich Hölderlin, whose lyric poetry, heavily influenced by the Greek and Latin classics, invigorated early modern German writing; Hermann Broch, whose *Der Tod des Vergil* (1945; *The Death of Virgil*) is a profound meditation on the collapse of the spirit in the scientific age; Ernst Jünger, whose futuristic novel *Auf den Marmorklippen* (1939; *On the Marble Cliffs*) is an allegorical

critique of Nazism; and even Karl May, perhaps the most popular of all German writers, who in the late 19th century wrote a succession of best-selling westerns after serving a prison sentence for fraud.

Four German poets and writers from the early 20th century won permanent niches in world literature: Franz Kafka, whose fantastical works explored the dark side of modernism; Thomas Mann, who explored the psychology of the modern condition in his novels; Rainer Maria Rilke, who developed a new style of lyric poetry influenced by the work of the French Symbolists; and Bertolt Brecht, known for his brilliant Marxist dramas. Four other German novelists became Nobel laureates while winning a popular following abroad in translation—Hermann Hesse, who celebrated Eastern mysticism, Heinrich Böll and Günter Grass, who explored the effects of World War II on German lives and psyches; and Herta Müller, who reflected on the oppressive atmopshere of her native Romania during the dictatorship of Nicolae Ceauşescu. Among other writers who gained widespread recognition in the late 20th and early 21st centuries were Siegfried Lenz, Peter Weiss, Uwe Johnson, Hans Magnus Enzensberger, Patrick Süskind, Peter Handke, Gabriele Wohmann, and W.G. Sebald. During partition many writers fled East Germany, some after serving prison terms; the poet and songwriter Wolf Biermann was exiled in 1976 while on tour in West Germany. Among those of

JOHANN WOLFGANG VON GOETHE

German poet, novelist, playwright, statesman, and scientist Johann Wolfgang von Goethe (born August 28, 1749, Frankfurt am Main—died March 22, 1832, Weimar, Saxe-Weimar) is considered the greatest German literary figure of the modern era. In 1773 Goethe provided the Sturm und Drang movement with its first major drama, *Götz von Berlichingen*, and in 1774 with its first novel, *The Sorrows of Young Werther*, an extraordinarily popular work in its time, in which he created the prototype of the Romantic hero. In 1775 he arrived at Weimar, where he accepted an appointment to the ducal court; he would remain there for the rest of his life, and his presence helped to establish Weimar as a literary and intellectual centre. His poetry includes lyrics in praise of natural beauty and ballads that echo folk themes. His contact with ancient Classical culture during an Italian sojourn (1786–88) deeply influenced his later work. From 1794 Friedrich Schiller became his most important and influential friend. *Wilhelm Meister's Apprenticeship* (1795–96) is often called the first bildungsroman (a class of novel that deals with its protagonist's moral and psychological maturation process); it was followed many years later by *The Wanderings of Wilhelm Meister* (1821; 2nd ed. 1829). Many of Goethe's works were inspired by a series of passionate loves for women. His chief masterpiece, the drama *Faust* (*Part One*, 1808; *Part Two*, 1832), represents Faust tragically, as a singularly modern figure who is condemned to remain unsatisfied by life. Goethe also wrote extensively on botany, colour theory, and other scientific topics. In his late years he was celebrated as a sage and visited by world luminaries. The greatest figure of German Romanticism, he is regarded as a giant of world literature.

international significance who remained in East Germany were Stefan Heym, Anna Seghers, and Christa Wolf.

The German theatre has long been faced with the dilemma of either being bold and innovative or relying on the rich repertoire of German classics from the 18th and 19th centuries, a limited number of established 20th-century dramas from artists such as Brecht, Carl Zuckmayer, or Max Frisch, and contemporary plays in translation from Britain, France, and the United States. While the system of public subsidies and ticket subscriptions favours a steady diet of Goethe, Schiller, Gotthold Ephraim Lessing, William Shakespeare, George Bernard Shaw, Jean Anouilh, Anton Chekhov, and Brecht, it also allows for risks and for the plays of late 20th-century dramatists such as Martin Walser and Patrick Süskind to be performed. Small experimental theatres enjoy a lively, if hazardous, existence in the major cities and often closely resemble Germany's still vibrant political cabaret.

In East Germany all theatres were state-owned. The German Theatre (Deutsches Theater) in Berlin reopened in September 1945 and was the first

German theatre to perform following the Nazi collapse. The old German National Theatre (Deutsches Nationaltheater) in Weimar was the first to be rebuilt after 1945. Understandably, Berlin dominated theatrical developments, especially because of the work of Brecht at the Theater am Schiffbauerdamm. Given a haven in East Germany—a theatre and a company, along with the political and artistic latitude he required—Brecht was able to produce and perform his own works exclusively. Nevertheless, the Berliner Ensemble, as his group was named, possibly commanded more critical and popular attention in the West, where his plays are still widely performed, than on its home ground.

MUSIC AND DANCE

In the 12th and 13th centuries, German poets and musicians known as minnesingers, influenced by the troubadours and trouvères of France, composed and performed songs of courtly love for the Hohenstaufen dukes of Franconia and Swabia. Their most prominent representative, Walther von der Vogelweide, is recognized for his didactic moral and religious poetry as well as for his poems of love. Later, fraternities of mostly middle-class singers developed into singing schools (Singschulen), organized as craft guilds, in free cities such as Mainz, where the first such school is said to have been founded in the early 13th century by the minnesinger Frauenlob. The schools of the Meistersingers, as they came to be known, spread to other German cities, notably Nürnberg. The outstanding 16th-century Meistersinger Hans Sachs is celebrated in the opera *Die Meistersinger von Nürnberg* by Richard Wagner.

In the mid-16th century the leader of the Protestant Reformation, Martin Luther, composed chorales, many of them based on older Latin hymns and secular tunes, for performance in religious services. The chorale, a musical form characteristic of the Protestant church in Germany, was developed in sophisticated ways in the early 17th century by the composer and musicologist Michael Praetorius. Heinrich Schütz, widely considered the greatest German composer of the 17th century, produced sacred vocal music that melded the newer styles of his Italian teachers (notably Giovanni Gabrieli) with traditional German forms; his *Dafne* was the first German opera.

The late Baroque period of musical history (the first half of the 17th century) was dominated by Johann Sebastian Bach, a brilliant and prolific composer for the organ and harpsichord, who produced masterpieces of instrumental and sacred vocal music, including the six *Brandenburg Concertos* and the *Mass in B Minor*, and by the German-born English composer George Frideric Handel, who is best remembered for his operas and oratorios, especially the *Messiah*, and for the instrumental pieces *Water Music* and *Music for the Royal Fireworks*. Another major figure, Georg Philipp Telemann was considered Germany's leading composer during his lifetime and is arguably the most prolific and versatile composer in history.

Germanic music until the early 20th century is understood to include the contributions of Austrian composers. Indeed, Ludwig van Beethoven, whose work bridged the 18th and 19th centuries, is generally regarded as the pivotal transitional figure between the Classical period—best represented by the works of Austrians Franz Joseph Haydn and Wolfgang Amadeus Mozart—and the Romantic period. Mozart, considered by many the greatest of all musical geniuses, was the master of all genres, especially the symphony, chamber music for strings, and opera. Beethoven developed the major forms of Classical instrumental music—especially the symphony, the sonata, and the quartet—in radically new directions. The passion and heroic individualism of his music, and Beethoven's own uncompromising commitment to the purity and integrity of his art, inspired many composers and writers of the Romantic Movement. Also influential was Beethoven's contemporary the Austrian Franz Schubert, remembered principally for his chamber music.

Felix Mendelssohn (*Overture to a Midsummer Night's Dream*), the first of the major German Romantic composers,

LUDWIG VAN BEETHOVEN

A child of a musical family, Ludwig van Beethoven (born December 17, 1770, Bonn, archbishopric of Cologne—died March 26, 1827, Vienna, Austria) was a precociously gifted pianist and violist. After nine years as a court musician in Bonn, he moved to Vienna to study with Joseph Haydn and remained there for the rest of his life. He was soon well known as both a virtuoso and a composer, and he became the first important composer to earn a successful living while forsaking employment in the church or court. He uniquely straddled the Classical and Romantic eras. Rooted in the traditions of Haydn and Mozart, his art also encompassed the new spirit of humanism expressed in the works of German Romantic writers as well as in the ideals of the French Revolution, with its passionate concern for the freedom and dignity of the individual. His astonishing *Third* (*Eroica*) *Symphony* (1804) was the thunderclap that announced the Romantic century, and it embodies the titanic but rigorously controlled energy that was the hallmark of his style. He began to lose his hearing from *c.* 1795; by *c.* 1819 he was totally deaf. For his last 15 years he was unrivaled as the world's most famous composer. In musical form he was a considerable innovator, widening the scope of the sonata, symphony, concerto, and string quartet. His greatest achievement was to raise instrumental music, hitherto considered inferior to vocal, to the highest plane of art. His works include the celebrated 9 symphonies; 16 string quartets; 32 piano sonatas; the opera *Fidelio* (1805, rev. 1814); 2 masses, including the *Missa Solemnis* (1823); 5 piano concertos; a violin concerto (1806); 6 piano trios; 10 violin sonatas; 5 cello sonatas; and several concert overtures.

was also a conductor and led a 19th-century revival of interest in Bach, whose music had been neglected for nearly 100 years. Other significant 19th-century German composers included Robert Schumann and his wife Clara Schumann, Carl Maria von Weber, Johannes Brahms, who, with the Russian Pyotr Ilyich Tchaikovsky, was one of the most important symphonic composers of the second half of the 19th century, and Richard Wagner, who created a revolutionary new form of musical drama grounded in complicated psychological, religious, and philosophical symbolism.

In the late 19th and the early 20th century Richard Strauss composed operas and operettas but is best remembered for his tone poems, especially *Don Juan* and *Also sprach Zarathustra*. His contemporary the Austrian Gustav Mahler anticipated the compositional techniques of the 20th century and is generally regarded as the last great composer in the Austro-German tradition. In the early 20th century the Austrian Arnold Schoenberg invented the atonal method of composition known as serialism, or the 12-tone technique, to which German composer Paul Hindemith responded by developing a system of composition that expanded traditional tonality. Also shaped by Schoenberg, the Austrian composer Alban Berg produced exceptional works—notably his operas *Wozzeck* and *Lulu*—in atonal style. Carl Orff, in addition to composing, created an innovative system of musical education for children.

In the late 1920s Kurt Weill collaborated with Brecht to satirize the corruption of modern capitalism in *Die Dreigroschenoper* (*The Threepenny Opera*; including the standard "Mack the Knife") and *Aufstieg und Fall der Stadt Mahagonny* ("Rise and Fall of the City of Mahagonny"). In these and other works, Weill employed a "cabaret" style incorporating popular tunes, jazz, and ragtime. The rise of the Nazis in 1933 forced many German composers and musicians to flee to the United States. In the decades after World War II, Karlheinz Stockhausen, the most eminent of contemporary German composers, produced avant-garde electronic music that radically extended the expressive possibilities of serialism. Other significant German composers of the second half of the 20th century included Bernd Alois Zimmerman, best known for his opera *Die Soldaten* ("The Soldiers"), and Hans Werner Henze.

The Berlin Philharmonic, led for more than three decades by Herbert von Karajan, is among the world's leading orchestras, as are the Gewandhaus Orchestra of Leipzig, formerly conducted by Kurt Masur; the Bamberg Symphonic Orchestra; the Bavarian Radio Symphony Orchestra; and the Stuttgart Chamber Orchestra. Many German musicians, including the conductor and pianist Christian Thielemann and the violinist Anne-Sophie Mutter, and concert vocalists, including Elisabeth Schwarzkopf and Peter Schreir, enjoy international reputations. Moreover, the opera houses of Hamburg (the oldest), Berlin, Cologne,

Frankfurt, and Munich are among the world's most renowned. The system of state-supported opera has allowed many young North American and British singers lacking opportunities at home to train in Germany, and some remain in the permanent companies there.

Germany has also been proving ground for foreign rock musicians, from the Beatles apprenticeship in clubs along Hamburg's Reeperbahn in the early 1960s to fellow Englishman David Bowie's landmark recordings in Berlin and the collaborations of Italian producer Giorgio Moroder and American disco diva Donna Summer in Munich's Musicland Studios in the 1970s. German performers have also left their mark on rock, not least the influential groups Can, Faust, and Tangerine Dream, whose innovative music emerged in the early 1970s and was dubbed "Krautrock" by Anglo-American critics. A wave of other German groups followed, making important contributions to a variety of genres. Kraftwerk helped lay the foundation for modern electronic music and influenced the development of hip-hop. The Scorpions, powered by the virtuosic playing of lead guitarist Uli Jon Roth, became Germany's most-enduring heavy metal act. Germany was also a centre for industrial music, with acts like Einstürzende Neubauten and KMFDM achieving global popularity. Curiously, East Germany's best-known rock performer was leftist American expatriate Dean Reed (the "Red Elvis"), who was especially popular in the Soviet Union in the 1970s and '80s.

Dance also has been an important part of German cultural life. In the 18th century the waltz, a ballroom dance for couples, developed from regional social dances of southern Germany and Austria, such as the Dreher, Ländler, and Deutscher. The waltz quickly gained popularity in other European countries, perhaps because it appeared to represent some of the abstract values of the Romantic era, the ideals of freedom, character, passion, and expressiveness. Vienna became the city of the waltz. The early 19th century was the age of the Viennese waltz kings, most notably the composers of the Strauss family.

Ballet in Germany was generally relegated to various court opera productions. During the French choreographer Jean-Georges Noverre's appointment at Stuttgart (1760–67), Germany briefly became a significant centre for ballet. However, German theatrical dance lacked a unified movement until the 20th century.

Modern dance was embraced in Germany, where it was known as Ausdruckstanz ("expressionistic dance"). Early modern dance pioneers such as Mary Wigman, Kurt Jooss, and Hanya Holm had a broad influence on dance practice, particularly in the United States. The Stuttgart Ballet at the Württemberg State Theatre rose to world prominence in the 1960s under its South African-born director John Cranko, and its success continued under Marcia Haydée and Reid Anderson after Cranko's death in 1973. In Wuppertal in the 1970s the choreographer Pina Bausch pioneered the innovative form known as Tanztheater ("dance theatre"), which was widely influential into the 1980s. The Hamburg Ballet is also a lively centre of world ballet.

THE VISUAL ARTS

Germany has a strong, rich tradition in the visual arts. In the medieval era, the reign of Charlemagne introduced German artists to the three-dimensionality of Roman art. Paintings and sculptures, often in the Gothic style popularized in France and Germany, were generally made to decorate churches, and illuminated manuscripts and stained glass were also created. In the 15th century, the design of altarpieces, which combined the arts of painting, sculpture, and architecture, became a popular pursuit, and the rise of book printing led to the design of many fine woodcut illustrations. In the late 15th and the 16th centuries, a generation of German artists emerged that included Albrecht Dürer, Lucas Cranach, Matthias Grünewald, and Hans Holbein the Younger, all of whom worked in a style influenced by the Italian Renaissance; their work represented a golden age in German art. During this era, the Protestant Reformation of the 1520s brought about the destruction of some art that was deemed idolatrous and led to more secular subject matter, as seen in the numerous self-portraits by Dürer.

Subsequent generations of artists explored French and Italian variations on the Baroque and Rococo, but German art did not develop a definite national character again until the mid-18th century, when a staid Neoclassicism, advocated by theorist Johann Winckelmann and a series of new art academies, took hold. At the turn of the 19th century, Romanticism blossomed, perhaps best exemplified in the work of Caspar David Friedrich and Philipp Otto Runge, who in the first quarter of the century explored nature with a passionate, almost religious fervour. By the late 19th century, artists began to form groups that seceded from the conservative teachings and exhibition opportunities of the academies. Nevertheless, the staid Neoclassical style mostly dominated until the late 19th century, when secessionist groups formed in Munich (1892), Berlin (1898), and, under the leadership of Gustav Klimt, Vienna (1897).

German painters of the 20th century, especially groups such as Die Brücke ("The Bridge") and Der Blaue Reiter ("The Blue Rider"), developed a new Expressionist current in European art. Beginning in 1916, Kurt Schwitters, George Grosz, Hannah Höch, John Heartfield, and others explored the more theoretical concerns of Dada, while in the 1920s artists such as Otto Dix and photographer August Sander worked in the realistic, socially critical style known as Neue Sachlichkeit ("New Objectivity").

These and other developments came to a halt in 1933 with the rise of the National Socialists. Hitler and the Nazi regime condemned most modern art, holding the infamous Entartete Kunst ("Degenerate Art") show in 1937 in an attempt to make a mockery of artists such as Wassily Kandinsky, Emil Nolde, and Ernst Ludwig Kirchner. Conservative, "heroic" German landscape art was instead promoted as an ideal art form.

After World War II, German art struggled to regain a sense of direction, challenged by the emigration of many important German artists to France or the United States. In East Germany a form of Socialist Realism dominated artistic practice, a trend that would continue until reunification. In West Germany, however, many artists experimented with avant-garde movements such as Abstract Expressionism, Pop art, minimalism, and Op art. Beginning in the 1960s, Joseph Beuys created sculpture, performance art, and installation art that challenged the very definition of "high art." Incorporating materials such as fat and felt, Beuys's work represented an individual take on Pop art's goal of bringing art into the realm of the everyday experience; his example influenced a new generation of artists. Perhaps the most notable German figure of the 1970s was Gerhard Richter, who became known for his paintings based on photographs. Blurring the lines between the media of photography and painting, his beautifully executed works anticipated the challenge to traditional forms that would characterize postmodern art. German art was again at the centre of the international art world when Neo-Expressionism became the dominant international trend of the 1980s. Building upon German art's long-standing interest in Expressionism, artists such as Georg Baselitz (who had been making important work since the 1960s), Anselm Kiefer, and Sigmar Polke combined a raw, expressive application of paint with challenging subject matter.

At the turn of the 21st century, photography became the international medium of choice. German artists who won international art prizes and had their work featured in the world's most prominent museums included Wolfgang Tillmans, who gained attention for his portraits of youth culture; Bernd and Hilla Becher, who adopted a formalist approach and won a coveted lifetime achievement prize at the Infinity Awards in 2003; Thomas Struth, who became especially well known for his series of photographs set within major museum galleries; and Andreas Gursky, who became known for his large-scale photographs of public spaces.

ARCHITECTURE

Throughout its history, German architecture combined influences from elsewhere in Europe with its own national character. During the medieval period, the Romanesque style dominated. In the 13th century, as the Gothic style took hold, some of Germany's most notable structures were built, including the cathedrals at Cologne (begun 1248) and Strasbourg (planned 1277). Variations on the Gothic and Renaissance styles predominated through the 15th and 16th centuries, but, after the Protestant Reformation, commissions for elaborate religious structures decreased for a time. A revival of the Gothic began in the 17th century, when an increasing amount of ornamentation became the chief characteristic of churches and palaces; this decorative bent in German design reached a crescendo in the first half of the 18th century with the influence of the French and Italian Rococo style. Such lightness evaporated by the 19th century, when a forbidding sort of Neoclassicism came to represent the Prussian military spirit of the time. The Romantically tinged Neoclassicism of Karl Friedrich Schinkel, who became state architect of Prussia in 1815, embodied this era. Although radical architecture was generally suppressed during this period, some architects, inspired in part by the Jugendstil movement and figures such as Henry van de Velde and Peter Behrens, questioned by the turn of the century the validity of architecture that appeared so disengaged from modernity; such questioning opened the door for the radical experiments that characterized German architecture in the 20th century.

Contemporary German architecture—indeed world architecture—is very much the creature of the Bauhaus school that originated in Weimar in the 1920s

The Römer, the old town hall, Frankfurt am Main, Germany. The J. Allan Cash Photolibrary, London

and is associated with the names of Walter Gropius and Ludwig Mies van der Rohe. In the postwar years the dogmas of the Bauhaus school—the insistence on strict harmony of style with function and on the intrinsic beauty of materials, as well as a puritan disdain of decorativeness—were dutifully applied in building after building in city after city. Yet in West Germany, as elsewhere in the 1960s and '70s, the stark Bauhaus style began to yield to the more free-ranging postmodernism, which took as its precept "not just function but fiction as well." The unremitting rectangularity of the

BAUHAUS

The Bauhaus school of design, architecture, and applied arts existed in Germany from 1919 to 1933. It was based in Weimar until 1925, Dessau through 1932, and Berlin in its final months. The Bauhaus was founded by the architect Walter Gropius, who combined two schools, the Weimar Academy of Arts and the Weimar School of Arts and Crafts, into what he called the Bauhaus, or "house of building," a name derived by inverting the German word *Hausbau,* "building of a house." Gropius's "house of building" included the teaching of various crafts, which he saw as allied to architecture, the matrix of the arts. By training students equally in art and in technically expert craftsmanship, the Bauhaus sought to end the schism between the two.

Beginning in the mid-19th century, reformers led by the English designer William Morris had sought to bridge the same division by emphasizing high-quality handicrafts in combination with design appropriate to its purpose. By the last decade of that century, these efforts had led to the Arts and Crafts Movement. While extending the Arts and Crafts attentiveness to good design for every aspect of daily living, the forward-looking Bauhaus rejected the Arts and Crafts emphasis on individually executed luxury objects. Realizing that machine production had to be the precondition of design if that effort was to have any impact in the 20th century, Gropius directed the school's design efforts toward mass manufacture.

Before being admitted to the workshops, students at the Bauhaus were required to take a six-month preliminary course taught variously by Johannes Itten, Josef Albers, and László Moholy-Nagy. The workshops—carpentry, metal, pottery, stained glass, wall painting, weaving, graphics, typography, and stagecraft—were generally taught by two people: an artist (called the Form Master), who emphasized theory, and a craftsman, who emphasized techniques and technical processes. After three years of workshop instruction, the student received a journeyman's diploma.

The Bauhaus included among its faculty several outstanding artists of the 20th century. In addition to the above-mentioned, some of its teachers were Paul Klee (stained glass and painting), Wassily Kandinsky (wall painting), Lyonel Feininger (graphic arts), Oskar Schlemmer (stagecraft and sculpture), Marcel Breuer (interiors), Herbert Bayer (typography and advertising), Gerhard Marcks (pottery), and Georg Muche (weaving). A severe but elegant geometric style carried out with great economy of means has been considered characteristic of the Bauhaus, though in fact the works produced were richly diverse.

Although Bauhaus members had been involved in architectural work from 1919 (notably, the construction in Dessau of administrative, educational, and residential quarters designed by Gropius), the department of architecture, central to Gropius's program in founding this unique school, was not established until 1927; Hannes Meyer, a Swiss architect, was appointed chairman. Upon Gropius's resignation the following year, Meyer became director of the Bauhaus until 1930. He was asked to resign because of his left-wing political views, which brought him into conflict with Dessau authorities. Ludwig Mies van der Rohe became the new director until the Nazi regime forced the school to close in 1933.

The Bauhaus had far-reaching influence. Its workshop products were widely reproduced, and widespread acceptance of functional, unornamented designs for objects of daily use owes much to Bauhaus precept and example. Bauhaus teaching methods and ideals were transmitted throughout the world by faculty and students. Today, nearly every art curriculum includes foundation courses in which, on the Bauhaus model, students learn about the fundamental elements of design. Among the best known of Bauhaus-inspired educational efforts was the achievement of Moholy-Nagy, who founded the New Bauhaus (later renamed the Institute of Design) in Chicago in 1937, the same year in which Gropius was appointed chairman of the Harvard School of Architecture. A year later Mies moved to Chicago to head the department of architecture at the Illinois Institute of Technology (then known as the Armour Institute), and eventually he designed its new campus.

International style was to be softened by elements of regionalism. Leading exponents of this school include Josef Paul Kleihues, Oswald Mathias Ungers, and the brothers Rob and Leon Krier.

Architectural developments in East Germany reflected the influence of Soviet ideological tenets and models. Buildings in the eastern region differ from those in western Germany in the immensity of their proportions. The major showpieces in eastern Berlin—the government buildings, apartment blocks, hotels, and public spaces along Unter den Linden, Marx-Engels-Platz, Alexanderplatz, and Karl-Marx-Allee, and the startlingly graceless Leipziger-Strasse—and their exaggerated decorations all testify to a propensity for sheer vastness. Later architecture under the communist regime is immediately recognizable not only by excessive dimensions, whether horizontal or vertical, but also by monotonously white facades seldom relieved by colour trimming. Except where ideological factors intruded (as in the destruction of the Berlin Palace), the East German government had a reasonable record for the preservation of historic buildings.

After unification the long-deserted Potsdamer Platz in the heart of Berlin, once a focus of Berlin's economic and administrative life, came alive with the construction of an array of public and private buildings by internationally renowned architects such as Renzo Piano, Helmut Jahn, and Richard Rogers. After somewhat acrimonious artistic and political debates, a Holocaust memorial designed by Peter Eisenman was opened in the area.

FILM

In contrast to the situation after World War I, when Germany helped set the pace in many newer forms of art and entertainment, most notably in the genre

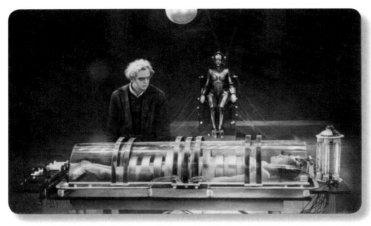

The inventor C.A. Rotwang (Rudolf Klein-Rogge) and his robotic invention (Brigitte Helm) in Fritz Lang's silent film classic Metropolis *(1927)*. From a private collection

work, as did German actors such as Marlene Dietrich, Paul Henreid, Peter Lorre, and Conrad Veidt.

After World War II the studios of the giant UFA (Universum-Film-Aktiengesellschaft) in Babelsberg (a suburb of Potsdam), the centre of German film production from 1917 to 1945, were in East German hands; the industry continued as a government-owned enterprise known as DEFA (Deutsche Film-Akademie), noted for animation, documentaries, and feature films, some of which achieved recognition at international film festivals. DEFA was privatized into six divisions in 1992, and its historical film stock has been preserved by the publicly owned DEFA Foundation.

In the 1960s West Germany's changing demographics, plus the encroachment of television, caused the collapse of its domestic film market. A group of young filmmakers, first organized at the Oberhausen Film Festival in 1962, established das neue Kino, or the New German Cinema. Relying on state subsidy to subsist, the members of the movement sought to examine Germany's unbewältige Vergangenheit, or "unassimilated past." The New German Cinema had little commercial success outside of Germany, but it still was internationally influential. The critical acclaim afforded directors such as Rainer Werner Fassbinder, Volcker Schlöndorff, Werner Herzog, Wim Wenders, Hans-Jürgen Syberberg, Wolfgang Petersen, and Percy

of motion pictures, both East and West Germany were slow in finding métiers of their own in the cinema in the early decades after World War II. Directors such as Fritz Lang, Ernst Lubitsch, F.W. Murnau, and G.W. Pabst, who had virtually defined cinematic art in the 1920s and early '30s, had no counterparts to rescue German film from the slough of mediocrity into which it had fallen as a result of the Third Reich. Leni Riefenstahl, one of Germany's leading filmmakers of the 1930s, was tapped by the Nazi regime to produce many of its propaganda films, including *Triumph des Willens* (1935; *Triumph of the Will*). Most noteworthy German filmmakers, such as Lang, Lubitsch, and Billy Wilder, relocated to Hollywood, where they enriched American cinema with their

Aldon helped reestablish West Germany as a serious filmmaking country, as did the work of actors such as Klaus Kinski, Bruno Ganz, and Hanna Schygulla. Women directors, such as Margarethe von Trotta, Helma Sanders-Brahms, and Doris Dörrie also came to prominence during the 1970s and '80s.

Germany's reunification in 1990 cut short attempts to forge a national cinematic identity in eastern Germany, though some notable productions marked the following decade, among them Tom Tykwer's *Lola rennt* (1998; *Run Lola Run*), Katja von Garnier's *Bandits*

(1996), Herzog's *Mein liebster Feind* (1999; *My Best Fiend*), and Wenders's *Buena Vista Social Club* (1999). Some noted German filmmakers also found significant success in the United States. Roland Emerich, for example, established himself in the action-adventure genre, and Wolfgang Petersen (*Das Boot*, 1982) became one of Hollywood's more noted practitioners of the thriller. Moreover, many of Hollywood's most prominent cinematographers, composers, and production artists have also hailed from Germany. Fatih Akin, a German director of Turkish descent, represented the next

Booths at a fall festival in Heidelberg, Germany © Heidelberger Kongress und Tourismus GmbH

generation in German filmmaking, and his films, which frequently drew on the immigrant experience, were favourably compared with those of Fassbinder.

ARTS FESTIVALS

The arts are celebrated with a proliferation of festivals in Germany on a scale scarcely equaled in any other country. Most major cities and scores of small towns and villages sponsor festivals that celebrate all genres of music, film, and the performing arts. Among the most renowned of these is the Bayreuth Festival, which celebrates the works of Richard Wagner. Founded by the composer himself in 1876, it is still under the direction of his descendants. The oldest German festival is the Passion play, first held in 1634 and now held every 10 years in Oberammergau in southern Bavaria to celebrate the town's deliverance from the plague.

Berlin alone has five major festivals: the Berliner Festspiele, a celebration of music, the performing arts, visual arts, and literature; the Berliner Jazzfest in November; the Berlin International Film Festival in February; the Theatertreffen Berlin ("Berlin Theatre Meeting"), featuring productions from throughout the German-speaking world; and the Karneval der Kulturen ("Carnival of Cultures"), a festival of world cultures. Munich has an opera festival in July and August, with emphasis on Richard Strauss. Festivals in Würzburg and Augsburg are dedicated to Mozart. Ansbach has a Bach festival, and Bonn has one celebrating Beethoven. Other noteworthy events include Documenta, an arts festival held every five years in Kassel that draws hundreds of thousands of visitors, the International May Festival in Wiesbaden, and the Festival of Contemporary Music in Donaueschingen. Expo 2000, Germany's first world's fair, was held in Hanover.

CULTURAL INSTITUTIONS

Germany has placed great importance on supporting the country's cultural, educational, and scientific resources. A prodigious number of organizations, maintained entirely or in part by public funds, is devoted to acquainting the international public with the culture, life, and language of the German peoples and familiarizing the German public with the culture and life of other countries. Cultural representation abroad is maintained in abundance with the advanced industrial countries of the West and with eastern Europe, but special emphasis is placed upon fostering educational and cultural ties with the world's less-developed countries. For them Germany not only has assumed a major role in lending reserves of technological skill and capital for developing resources, but it also has become a major centre for the education and training of students from these countries in the professions, the sciences, and technology.

Prominent among cultural groups is the Goethe-Institut Inter Nationes (formerly the Goethe Institut of Munich).

Founded in 1951, it has some 140 branches in more than 70 countries. It operates schools in Germany and abroad that offer instruction in the German language. It also maintains lending libraries and audiovisual centres, sponsors exhibits, film programs, musical and theatrical events, and lectures by prominent personalities.

MUSEUMS AND GALLERIES

Germany has some 2,000 museums of all descriptions, from those housing some of the world's great collections of painting and sculpture or of archaeological and scientific displays to those with exhibitions of minutiae, such as the playing-card museum in Stuttgart. Museums and galleries of great note include the museums of the Prussian Cultural Property Foundation in Berlin—i.e., the Pergamon Museum with its vast collection of Classical and Middle Eastern antiquities, located on the "Museum Island" in the River Spree, together with the Old (Altes) Museum, the New (Neues) Museum, the National Gallery (Nationalgalerie), and the Bode Museum—the Zwinger Museum and Picture Gallery (built by Gottfried Semper) in Dresden, the Bavarian State Picture Galleries and the Deutsches Museum in Munich, the Germanic National Museum in Nürnberg, the Roman-Germanic Central Museum in Mainz, the Senckenberg Museum of natural science in Frankfurt am Main, and the State Gallery in Stuttgart. Some museums are highly specialized, devoted to a single artist, school, or genre, but many combine natural science and fine arts. There are many ethnological museums, such as the Linden Museum in Stuttgart, the East German Gallery Museum in Regensburg, and the Ethnological Museum in Berlin-Dahlem. Important art treasures are scattered in the scores of smaller museums, libraries and archives, castles, cathedrals, churches, and monasteries throughout the country. The Berlin-Dahlem Botanical Garden and Botanical Museum, founded in the 17th century, is Germany's oldest botanical garden.

LIBRARIES

Among Germany's great libraries are the Bavarian State Library in Munich and the Berlin State Library. The German Library at Frankfurt am Main is the country's library of deposit and bibliographic centre. The Technical Library at Hannover is Germany's most important library for science and technology and for translations of works in the fields of science and engineering. The great university libraries at Heidelberg, Cologne, Göttingen, Leipzig, Tübingen, and Munich are complemented by scores of other good university libraries. A wealth of manuscripts, early printed works, and documents from the Middle Ages to the present are dispersed in smaller collections. The great research libraries are complemented by an extensive system of lending libraries operated by the states, the municipalities, the library associations of the Roman Catholic and

Evangelical churches, and other public associations and institutes. Virtually all citizens are within easy access of a library.

SPORTS AND RECREATION

Unity and disunity may be constant themes of German history, but in sports and physical culture Germans have long been well organized.

SPORTING CULTURE

In the early 19th century, coincident with the rise of nationalism, Friedrich Ludwig Jahn, considered the "father of gymnastics," founded the turnverein, a gymnastics club, and invented several of the disciplines that are now part of the Olympic gymnastics program. At the same time, Johann Christoph Friedrich GutsMuths initiated school programs that helped bring physical education to the forefront of German education. Ideals of health—Gesund—and athletic prowess became important components of the German conception of self. These ideals were later critical to the Nazi conception of the ideal German.

German athletes participated in the first modern Olympic Games in 1896 in Athens. In the aftermath of World War I, the country was not invited to the Olympic Games until the 1928 Winter Games in St. Moritz, Switzerland. However, Berlin was designated as the site for the 1936 Olympics in 1931, before the rise to power of Adolf Hitler, who transformed the Games into a stage to promote Nazi ideals, though this effort was thwarted somewhat by key victories by African American sprinter and long jumper Jesse Owens and other "non-Aryan" athletes. The 1936 Berlin Olympics also inaugurated the tradition of the Olympic torch relay, with the lighted torch carried from Olympia, Greece, to the Berlin stadium.

Nazi influence on German sports was not limited to the Olympics. German Max Schmeling, the world heavyweight boxing champion between 1930 and 1932, pulled a stunning upset of American Joe Louis in 1936 and quickly found himself an unwilling pawn of Nazi propaganda. Their rematch, won by Louis, generated enormous publicity and became the most politicized fight of the century.

Following partition, East and West German athletes competed on the same national team from 1956 to 1964. The two countries then split their teams for the next six Olympiads, joining the front lines of Cold War athletic competition. In 1972 Munich hosted the Summer Games, which were marred when Palestinian terrorists took hostage and killed 11 members of the Israeli team.

Germany's Olympic teams—East, West, and unified—have dominated many events, especially swimming. Indeed, in 1976 and 1980 East German female swimmers, including the famed Kornelia Ender, set more than 10 world records and captured 22 of the 26 gold medals. Among other renowned German Olympians are swimmers Kristin Otto, Michael Gross, and Franziska van Almsick, figure skater Katarina Witt, speed skaters Karin Enke and Christa Luding-Rothenburger, luger Georg Hackl, sprinter Armin Hary, canoer Birgit Fischer, and equestrians Hans Günter Winkler and Isabell Werth.

Football (soccer) is a passion for many Germans, and German teams excel at all levels of competition. The Bundesliga is among the world's most respected professional football leagues. The country's most famous international player was Franz Beckenbauer, a Bavarian who led his Bayern Munich club to three consecutive European Cup titles in the 1970s. Beckenbauer also was captain of the West German national team that won the 1974 World Cup, and he was the manager of the West German team that won the World Cup in 1990. In 2006 Germany hosted the World Cup. German tennis players Steffi Graf, Boris Becker, and Michael Stich also excelled on the international circuit, winning more than 25 major titles during the 1980s and '90s. Golfer Bernhard Langer won the Masters Tournament in 1985 and 1993, and Martin Kaymer captured the PGA Championship in 2010. The popularity of basketball grew considerably in the last part of the 20th century, and Germany began to produce world-class professional players such as Detlef Schrempf and Dirk Nowitzki.

The government of the Third Reich militarized many German sports, equating athletic and military excellence. In the period after World War II, organized sports suffered from this tainted association, but the devotion of Germans to health and fitness continued, and the West German government quickly made efforts to democratize sporting activities by emphasizing recreation and personal development over victory. Physical education is mandatory throughout the primary and secondary grades, and summertime camps devoted to outdoor recreation, especially swimming, hiking, and mountaineering, enjoy widespread popularity. Academic study of sports and sporting cultures has also flourished in Germany.

LEISURE ACTIVITIES

Leisure is a major pursuit, if not an industry, in German life. As did workers in most Western industrial countries, Germans once toiled under an unrestricted six-day workweek, often 10 hours a day with breaks only on Sundays and for major feasts and festivals. Added to these traditional feasts and festivals now are several secular holidays and three to six weeks or more of paid vacation time. Moreover, the German workweek is now 40 hours or less. As a result, Germans have more leisure time than workers of most Western countries. This abundance of leisure has become a national preoccupation, and the German Leisure Association conducts research on leisure activity and dispenses information and advice.

The German pattern of recreation is characterized by a duality of traditional and modern approaches. To a surprising

OKTOBERFEST

Revelers celebrate Oktoberfest in a beer hall in Munich, Germany. Joe Viesti/The Viesti Collection

Munich's annual Oktoberfest is held over a two-week period that ends on the first Sunday in October. The festival originated on October 12, 1810, in celebration of the marriage of the crown prince of Bavaria, who later became King Louis I, to Princess Therese von Sachsen-Hildburghausen. The festival concluded five days later with a horse race held in an open area that came to be called Theresienwiese ("Therese's green"). The following year the race was combined with a state agricultural fair, and in 1818 booths serving food and drink were introduced. By the late 20th century the booths had developed into large beer halls made of plywood, with interior balconies and bandstands. Each of the Munich brewers erects one of the temporary structures, with seating capacities of some 6,000. The mayor of Munich taps the first keg to open the festival. Total beer consumption during Oktoberfest is upwards of 1,430,000 gallons (65,000 hectolitres). The breweries are also represented in parades that feature beer wagons and floats along with people in folk costumes. Other entertainment includes games, amusement rides, music, and dancing. Oktoberfest draws more than six million people each year, many of them tourists.

A number of U.S. cities, particularly those with large German American populations, hold Oktoberfests modeled on the original in Munich. These popular celebrations, which feature beer and German food, are an attempt to reproduce the Bavarian sense of gemütlichkeit—cordiality.

extent in a country so highly industrialized, ancient feasts and practices are still observed on a wide scale in both Roman Catholic and Protestant areas, especially pre-Lenten celebrations known as Fasching in the southern regions or Karneval (carnival) in the Rhineland. In addition to the major religious festivals—Easter, Christmas, Whitsun (which are also national holidays), and, in Roman Catholic districts, Corpus Christi Day and Assumption—there are numerous local celebrations—wine, beer, harvest, hunting, and historical festivals—the so-called Volksfeste that are deeply rooted in German custom, the most notable being Munich's Oktoberfest, held each September.

Although the traditional observances continue unabated, Germans have adopted a wide range of more modern forms of recreation, amusement, and relaxation. Travel has become the favoured pastime of a majority of Germans. More than half of all adults take at least one annual trip for pleasure, and a great number take more than one. Many Germans now take both a winter and a summer vacation. Older persons often take a paid Kur at a spa to rest and recuperate, in addition to a holiday trip for pleasure. Germans spend more time and money on trips abroad than the citizens of any other country.

The weekend, a latecomer in Germany, has become firmly established. Private recreation typically includes spectator amusements and sports (especially football), active sports and physical exercise, automobile excursions, the pursuit of hobbies, visits with friends and family, and the long-favoured German pastime of walking or hiking.

It is estimated that about one-fifth of a household's income in Germany's western regions is spent on leisure expenses. Many institutions, including the government, local communities, schools, churches, and companies, encourage citizens to channel their free time into useful, rewarding, and healthful pursuits by providing physical facilities, impetus, and other prerequisites for all phases of public recreation. Leisure in Germany is now regarded—much like education and vocational training, decent housing, a job, good public transportation, health and disability insurance, and pensions—as an entitlement and a valuable adjunct of social policy.

In East Germany, leisure activity was arranged very differently. The state ideal was group leisure, group holidays, and group travel, often organized by the workplace or a youth organization. Cheap holiday facilities were available, especially along the resorts of the Baltic coast. Residents of East Germany were at liberty to travel privately to any of the Warsaw Pact countries and sometimes to Yugoslavia. It is worth noting that the fall of the communist bloc was precipitated in part by the large number of East Germans who, while visiting Hungary, crossed unimpeded into Austria when the Hungarian government opened its border with the West.

MEDIA AND PUBLISHING

Germany has robust domestic radio and television broadcasting systems. Germans are voracious readers of newspapers and periodicals, and the publishing industry remains comparatively strong.

BROADCASTING

Although German radio and television are not state-controlled, only public corporations were permitted to broadcast until the mid-1980s, when a dual system of public and commercial stations was established. Still, in 1986 the Federal Constitutional Court held that the public corporations comprised the "basic supply" of news and entertainment and commercial outlets were only a "supplementary supply." Licensing and control of public broadcasting is under the Federal Ministry of Post and Telecommunications. Support for public broadcasting is provided by fees paid by the owners of radios and television sets.

The public corporations enjoy great freedom in establishing their own broadcasting policies. Attempts to control these policies, which are often hostile to incumbent governments, have been repeatedly rebuffed; thus, in practice, German television, more than radio, enjoys remarkable latitude and independence in what it broadcasts.

Public radio and television are arranged along national and regional lines, with a number of regional corporations that offered two to four radio programming schedules combining to form one evening television offering, ARD (Arbeitsgemeinschaft der Öffentlich-Rechtlichen Rundfunkanstalten Deutschlands). This is complemented by a second television network, ZDF (Zweites Deutsches Fernsehen), which is based in Mainz. A third channel is operated by ARD but is organized and broadcast regionally, with special emphasis placed on local and regional events and school instruction, as well as on educational, informational, and fine arts programs. The uneven quality of entertainment in both radio and television is offset by the high-quality news coverage and political and social reporting that makes the German public one of the best-informed of any country.

Two radio stations—Deutschland Radio and Deutsche Welle—are publicly operated to provide a comprehensive German perspective of events; Deutsche Welle is beamed to Europe and overseas. There are also several regional public radio stations that provide localized programming and some 200 private radio stations that are regionally and locally focused.

By the early 21st century, cable and satellite television had achieved broad penetration throughout Germany. The cable and satellite networks offer extensive programming from public and commercial television in Germany and abroad. Germany switched its terrestrial television broadcast system from an analog signal to a digital one in 2008, and its satellite broadcast system changed to a digital signal in 2012. Digitization of the terrestrial signal greatly expanded the viewing options for the small percentage of homes that relied on an antenna to receive television broadcasts.

During the years of partition, viewers in East Germany could freely receive radio and television broadcasts from West Germany and from West Berlin, with the result that the public in East Germany kept current on news from the West. The broadcasting facilities in the former East Germany were reorganized along lines of the western states—i.e., each of the new states has its own regional stations.

THE PRESS

Freedom of the press is guaranteed under the Basic Law, and the economic state of Germany's several hundred newspapers and thousands of periodicals is enviably healthy. Most major cities support two or more daily newspapers, in addition to community periodicals, and few towns of any size are without their own daily newspaper. In the 21st century most German newspapers and periodicals published daily or weekly editions on the Internet, enabling access far beyond their traditional print circulation.

The press is free of government control, no newspaper is owned by a political party, and only about 10 percent of newspapers overtly support a political party, though most offer a distinctly political point of view. Laws restrict the total circulation of newspapers or magazines that can be controlled by one publisher or group. The Bundeskartellamt (Federal Cartel Office) oversees German industry (including the media) to ensure against a company abusing its dominant position within a particular industry. Although newspaper and periodical ownership cannot be the monopoly of any one ownership, Axel Springer Verlag AG controls a significant share of the market. Other major newspaper publishers, some of which also publish magazines and other periodicals, include Gruner+Jahr AG (a Bertelsmann company), Süddeutscher Verlag, Bauer Media Group, and Hubert Burda Media. The German Press Council, established in 1956, sets out guidelines and investigates complaints against the press.

A national press exists on one level in the form of *Süddeutsche Zeitung* (Munich), *Die Welt* (Berlin), and the *Frankfurter Allgemeine Zeitung*, together with regional newspapers (e.g., the *Stuttgarter Zeitung*, the *Westdeutsche Allgemeine Zeitung* (Essen), and the *Frankfurter Rundschau*), which also command international circulation and respect. Another level of the national press is represented by the universally circulated tabloid *Bild* (Hamburg), which has the largest readership of any paper and publishes several regional editions.

Berlin has many daily newspapers, including the liberal *Der Tagesspiegel*, the conservative *Berliner Morgenpost*, and the *Berliner Zeitung*, which had originally been published in East Germany. The *Berliner Zeitung* was acquired by western press interests after unification and swiftly gained recognition as the city's preeminent newspaper. Other leading newspapers of the former East Germany were also bought by western publishers.

The major edition of German newspapers, replete with politics and arts features, is published on Saturday. A lively Sunday press complements the daily newspapers, providing an overview, perspective, and interpretation of major news developments as well as political comment and artistic criticism; the most prestigious and influential of these is *Die Zeit* (Hamburg). Sunday counterparts of the major dailies, *Welt am Sonntag* and *Bild am Sonntag*, are run virtually as separate newspapers, competing with the other weeklies.

The genre of the Illustrierte (pictorial) dominates the German magazine market. Some of these popular weekly glossies, such as *Stern* and *Bunte*, carry features, including investigative reporting, of a high calibre; others, however, cater to an unquenchable public thirst for the escapades of celebrities, bizarre crime, the annals of gracious living, and sundry escapist topics. Apart from a wealth of specialized journals and quality business-oriented magazines, the role of high-prestige magazines of opinion is largely subsumed by the weighty weekend editions of the quality press.

A special niche is occupied by the weekly newsmagazine *Der Spiegel*, a journalistic power in its own right, which, since its founding in the period immediately after World War II, has shaped public opinion in Germany through its editorial posture as the skeptical, non-aligned observer and guardian of the public conscience. Exhaustive in its coverage and polemical in tone, it features thorough, critical investigations of events from both the past and the present.

PUBLISHING

Germany has some 2,000 publishing houses, and more than 90,000 titles reach the public each year, a production surpassed only by the United States. Germany traditionally was home to small and medium-size publishing houses. However, the Bertelsmann group, a multinational conglomerate based in Gütersloh, is now one of the world's largest publishers. Book publishing is not centred in a single city but is concentrated fairly evenly in Berlin, Hamburg, and the regional metropolises of Cologne, Frankfurt, Stuttgart, and Munich. Leipzig, prewar Germany's major publishing city, shared with East Berlin the major publishing houses of East Germany. Gotha in Thuringia is renowned for the production of maps and atlases. By law, book prices are fixed at the publisher level, a practice that tends to favour the smaller independent bookstores that are prevalent throughout Germany.

CHAPTER 6

GERMANY FROM ANCIENT TIMES TO 1250 CE

Germanic peoples occupied much of the present-day territory of Germany in ancient times. The Germanic peoples are those who spoke one of the Germanic languages, and they thus originated as a group with the so-called first sound shift (Grimm's law), which turned a Proto-Indo-European dialect into a new Proto-Germanic language within the Indo-European language family. The Proto-Indo-European consonants p, t, and k became the Proto-Germanic f, [thorn] (th), and x (h), and the Proto-Indo-European b, d, and g became Proto-Germanic p, t, and k. The historical context of the shift is difficult to identify because it is impossible to date it conclusively. Clearly the people who came to speak Proto-Germanic must have been isolated from other Indo-Europeans for some time, but it is not obvious which archaeological culture might represent the period of the shift. One possibility is the so-called Northern European Bronze Age, which flourished in northern Germany and Scandinavia between about 1700 and 450 BCE. Alternatives would be one of the early Iron Age cultures of the same region (e.g., Wessenstadt, 800–600 BCE or Jastorf, 600–300 BCE).

Evidence from archaeological finds and place-names suggests that, while early Germanic peoples probably occupied much of northern Germany during the Bronze and early Iron ages, peoples speaking Celtic languages occupied what is now southern Germany. This region, together with neighbouring parts of France and Switzerland, was the original homeland of the Celtic La Tène culture. About the time of the Roman expansion northward, in the first

Ancient Roman coin, c. 43 BCE, bearing the image of Julius Caesar. Hoberman Collection/Universal Images Group/Getty Images

centuries BCE and CE, Germanic groups were expanding southward into present-day southern Germany. The evidence suggests that the existing population was gradually Germanized rather than displaced by the Germanic peoples arriving from the north.

Solid historical information begins about 50 BCE when Julius Caesar's Gallic Wars brought the Romans into contact with Germanic as well as Celtic peoples. Caesar did cross the Rhine in 55 and 53 BCE, but the river formed the eastern boundary of the province of Gaul, which he created, and most Germanic tribes lived beyond it. Direct Roman attacks on Germanic tribes began again under Nero Claudius Drusus Germanicus, who pushed across the Rhine in 12–9 BCE, while other Roman forces assaulted Germanic tribes along the middle Danube (in modern Austria and Hungary). Fierce fighting in both areas, and the famous victory of the Germanic leader Arminius in the Teutoburg Forest in 9 CE (when three Roman legions were massacred), showed that conquering these tribes would require too much effort. The Roman frontier thus stabilized on the Rhine and Danube rivers, although sporadic campaigns (notably under Domitian in 83 and 88 CE) extended control over Frisia in the north and some lands between the Rhine and the upper Danube.

Both archaeology and Caesar's own account of his wars show that Germanic tribes then lived on both sides of the Rhine. In fact, broadly similar archaeological cultures from this period stretch across central Europe from the Rhine to the Vistula River (in modern Poland), and Germanic peoples probably dominated all these areas. Germanic cultures extended from Scandinavia to as far south as the Carpathians. These Germans led a largely settled agricultural existence. They practiced mixed farming, lived in wooden houses, did not have the potter's wheel, were nonliterate, and did not use money. The marshy lowlands of northern Europe have preserved otherwise perishable wooden objects, leather goods, and clothing and shed much light on the Germanic way of

ARMINIUS

The German tribal leader Arminius (born 18 BCE?—died 19 CE) inflicted a major defeat on Rome by destroying three legions under Publius Quinctilius Varus in the Teutoburg Forest (southeast of modern Bielefeld, Germany), late in the summer of 9 CE. This defeat severely checked the emperor Augustus's plans, the exact nature of which is uncertain, for the country between the Rhine and Elbe rivers.

Arminius was a chief of the Cherusci. In the service of the Romans he had obtained both citizenship and equestrian rank. Six years after the Teutoburg Forest Massacre, Germanicus Caesar engaged Arminius in battle, capturing his wife, Thusnelda, but in 16 CE Arminius skillfully survived a full-scale Roman attack. When Roman operations were suspended in 17, Arminius became involved in war with Maroboduus, king of the Marcomanni, and though successful he was subsequently murdered by his own people. The conception of Arminius as a German national hero reached its climax in the late 19th century. It could claim support from Tacitus's judgment of him as "unquestionably the liberator of Germany" (liberator haud dubie Germaniae); but it is clear that in Arminius's day a united "Germany" was not even an ideal.

life. These bogs were also used for ritual sacrifice and execution, and some 700 "bog people" have been recovered. Their remains are so well preserved that even dietary patterns can be established; the staple was a gruel made of many kinds of seeds and weeds.

Clear evidence of social differentiation appears in these cultures. Richly furnished burials (containing jewelry and sometimes weapons) have been uncovered in many areas, showing that a wealthy warrior elite was developing. Powerful chiefs became a standard feature of Germanic society, and archaeologists have uncovered the halls where they feasted their retainers, an activity described in the Anglo-Saxon poem *Beowulf*. This warrior elite followed the cult of a war god, such as Tyr (Tiu) or Odin (Wodan). The Roman historian Tacitus relates in the *Germania* that in 59 CE the Hermunduri, in fulfillment of their vows, sacrificed defeated Chatti to one of these gods. This elite was also the basis of political organization. The Germanic peoples comprised numerous tribes that were also united in leagues centred on the worship of particular cults. These cults were probably created by one locally dominant tribe and changed over time. Tribes belonging to such leagues came together for an annual festival, when weapons were laid aside. Apart from worship, these were also times for economic activity, social interaction, and settling disputes.

COEXISTENCE WITH ROME TO 350 CE

After Rome had established its frontiers, commercial and cultural contacts between Germanic peoples and the Roman Empire were as important as direct conflict. Although it was heavily fortified, the frontier was never a barrier to trade or travel. About 50 CE, tribes settled along the Rhine learned to use Roman money. Germanic graves—at least the richer ones—began to include Roman luxury imports such as fine pottery, glass, and metalwork. In return, raw materials, such as amber and leather, and many slaves went back across the frontier. Germanic tribesmen also served in Roman armies.

Border raiding was endemic, and periodically there were much larger disturbances. About 150 CE the Marcomanni, a Germanic tribe, moved south into the middle Danube region, and they even invaded Italy in 167. The emperor Marcus Aurelius and his son spent the next 20 years curbing their inroads, and archaeology shows that the wars were highly destructive. This migration was one manifestation of a broader problem, for between about 150 and 200 a whole series of Germanic groups moved south along the river valleys of central and eastern Europe. These migrations resulted in great violence along the entire frontier during the 3rd century. Parts of Gaul suffered greatly, and Goths, a Germanic people that originated in southern Scandinavia, ravaged the Danube region, even killing the emperor Decius in 251. Yet intensive campaigns brought the Germanic tribes back under control, so that by about 280 stability had returned to the Rhine and Danube. The Roman army and an alliance system involving, among others, Franks, Alemanni, and Goths maintained the frontier until about 370.

In the meantime the Germanic world was being transformed. For the balance of power in Europe, the most important development was the rise of larger and more cohesive Germanic political units, at least among the Germanic peoples living on the borders of the empire. This was largely a response to the military threat from Rome. Despite their occasional successes, more Germanic tribesmen than Romans had been killed in 3rd-century conflicts, and the Germanic peoples had learned that larger groups were more likely to survive. In the 4th century there were two powerful Germanic confederations: the Alemanni on the Rhine and the Goths on the Danube, both controlled by the military elite whose power over their fellow tribesmen continued to increase. Other contacts with the empire resulted in cultural borrowings. In the 3rd century Germanic peoples began to master the potter's wheel, and there is evidence of improved farming techniques; both were adopted from Rome. The empire was also partly responsible for Germanic groups' first steps toward literary culture. A written form of Gothic, the oldest literary Germanic language, was created about 350 by Ulfilas, a Roman-sponsored Arian

Christian missionary, in order to translate the Bible.

THE MIGRATION PERIOD

The situation was transformed by nomadic, non-Germanic Hunnish horsemen from the east who pushed Germanic peoples into the Roman Empire in several waves. First, in 376, Visigoths were admitted by the emperor Valens as foederati ("allies") to farm and defend the frontier. This procedure was not without precedent and was unusual only in the enormity of the group involved (traditionally estimated at about 80,000). The Romans were unprepared for such a large group, and their failure to accommodate the group and outright hostility toward the Visigoths led to confrontation. Two years later the Visigoths killed Valens, winning a famous victory at Adrianople (now Edirne, Turkey), though by 382 they had been subdued. Yet, as the Huns moved west, Rome's frontiers came under increasing pressure, and further large incursions (by Germanic as well as other peoples) occurred in 386, 395, 405, and 406. Some of the invaders were defeated, but Germanic Vandals and Suebi established themselves in Spain and later in North Africa, and the Visigoths exploited the disorder to rebel, especially after the election of Alaric as king. Marching to Italy, they demanded better terms, and, when these were not forthcoming, they sacked Rome on August 24, 410. Even though Rome was no longer capital of the empire, the sack was a profound shock for the people of the empire.

The Roman Empire nevertheless remained an important power in Europe, both militarily and economically. Hence Germanic groups on the run from the Huns were anxious to make peace; even the Visigoths accepted a settlement in Gaul in 418. Since Germanic peoples had no sense of either common interests or common identity, they could be played off against one another; thus the Vandals were savaged by the Visigoths between 416 and 418. Until about 450 fear of the Huns meant that the empire could, in moments of crisis, mobilize at least Visigoths, Burgundians (received into Gaul after being defeated by the Huns in 439), and Franks for its defense. Soon after Attila's death in 453, however, the Hun empire collapsed, and Rome lost this diplomatic weapon. It also suffered a progressive loss of revenue as territories were either occupied or—like Britain—abandoned by the imperial government. The balance thus swung further in the Germanic peoples' favour, and they eventually declared themselves independent. In the 470s a Visigothic kingdom emerged in southwestern Gaul and later gained control of most of the Iberian Peninsula. Meanwhile, a Burgundian kingdom arose in southeastern Gaul, and Clovis created a Frankish kingdom in the north. The Vandals already controlled North Africa and the Suebi part of Spain, and Gepid and Lombard kingdoms dominated the Danube. A band of Germans, led by Odoacer, deposed the last Roman emperor, Romulus Augustulus, in 476 and set up a kingdom in Italy. Ostrogoths freed by the collapse of the Hun empire struggled for a generation to find a new homeland. Their struggles sometimes brought them into conflict with the Eastern Empire, whose ruler, Zeno, sought to mitigate the situation by elevating the Ostrogothic king, Theodoric, to the office of patrician. When this solution failed, Zeno sent Theodoric against Odoacer. Theodoric ultimately defeated Odoacer and established a successful Ostrogothic kingdom in Italy that lasted from 493 to 555.

These Germanic successor states brought the Roman Empire in western Europe to an end. The empire could have resisted any of them singly, but the Hun invasions had pushed too many Germanic groups across the frontier too quickly. Battles, however, were the exception. More often the empire unwillingly, but peacefully, granted areas for settlement, and, as Rome became increasingly weaker, the local Roman provincial population looked to the newly settled Germanic peoples for protection. This period thus continued the transformation of the Germanic world. Because of the danger from Rome and the Huns, Germanic political units again increased in size. The new Germanic groups also fell under the influence of the Roman populations they came to rule. Literate, educated Romans enabled German kings systematically to raise taxation and expand their legal powers. The successor states to the Roman Empire were thus a fusion of Germanic military power and the administrative know-how of Roman provincial aristocrats. Transformation was complete in these regions when Germanic warrior and Roman provincial elites quickly intermarried, bringing into being a new aristocracy that was to shape medieval Europe.

Within the boundaries of present-day Germany, the Hunnish conquest drove Germanic peoples out of the region to the east of the Elbe and Saale rivers during the early 5th century. This area was subsequently settled by peoples speaking Slavic languages, and present-day eastern Germany remained Slavic for some seven centuries. To the west and south, Germanic peoples such as the eastern Franks, Frisians, Saxons, Thuringians, Alemanni, and Bavarians—all speaking West Germanic dialects—had merged Germanic and borrowed Roman cultural features. It was among these groups that a German language and ethnic identity would gradually develop during the Middle Ages.

MEROVINGIANS AND CAROLINGIANS

When the Western Roman Empire ended in 476, the Germanic tribes west of the Rhine were not politically united. The West Germanic tribes, however, spoke dialects of a common language and shared social and political traditions. These traditions had been influenced by centuries of contact with the Roman world, both as federated troops within the empire and as participants in the broader political and economic network that extended beyond the Roman frontier. In particular a strongly military structure of social organization, under the direction of commanders termed kings or dukes, had developed among the federated tribes within the empire and spread to tribes living outside the empire proper. Likewise, the Ostrogothic kings in Italy extended their influence over much of the Germanic world north of the Alps.

MEROVINGIAN GERMANY

The Franks, settled in Romanized Gaul and western Germany, rejected Ostrogothic leadership and began to expand their kingdom eastward. Clovis's eventual conversion to Catholic Christianity improved the position of the Franks in their new kingdom because it earned them the support of the Catholic population and hierarchy of late Roman Gaul. Clovis and his successors, particularly Theodebert I (reigned 534–548), brought much of what would later constitute Germany under Frankish control by conquering the Thuringians of central Germany and the Alemanni and Bavarians of the south. Generally, these heterogeneous groups were given a law code that included Frankish and local traditions and were governed by a duke of mixed Frankish and indigenous background who represented the Frankish king. In times of strong central rule, as under Dagobert I (629–639), this leadership could have real effect. When the Frankish realm was badly divided or embroiled in civil wars, however, local dukes enjoyed great autonomy. This was particularly true of the Bavarian Agilolfings, who were closely related to the Lombard royal family of Italy and who by the 8th century enjoyed virtual royal status. In the north the Frisians and Saxons remained independent of Frankish control into the 8th century, preserving their own political and social structures and remaining for the most part pagan. In areas under Frankish lordship, Christianity made considerable progress through the efforts of native Raetians in the Alpine regions, of wandering Irish missionaries, and of transplanted Frankish aristocrats who supported monastic foundations.

THE RISE OF THE CAROLINGIANS AND BONIFACE

By the end of the 7th century and the beginning of the 8th, Merovingian authority throughout the Frankish world had been seriously diminished by internal divisions among rival noble factions. Although the dynasty would retain possession of the crown until 751, it was effectively replaced by a rising power, the Carolingian family, which controlled the office of mayor of the palace. The Carolingians, or Pippinids as they are known in their early days, first rose to power in the second decade of the 7th century when they assisted Chlothar II in the overthrow of Queen Brunhild. Their leader, Pippin I, was rewarded with the office of mayor, and his descendants would use the office as a means to enhance their power. However, both the Merovingians and Carolingians faced the claims of rival aristocratic families, including the Agilolfings, who also held the office of mayor of the palace. The victory of Pippin II over the Agilolfing mayor at the battle of Tertry in 687 reunited the kingdom in the name of the Merovingian king Theuderic IV and signaled the rising power of the Carolingians. Pippin's son, Charles Martel, after a struggle with Pippin's widow, assumed his father's position and came to be the leading figure in the realm. His position was so secure that he was able to rule during the last three years of his life without a Merovingian king on the throne, and he also was able to divide the kingdom between his two sons as the Merovingians had traditionally done.

The early Carolingians consolidated control over the Frankish heartland and the duchies east of the Rhine, partly by supporting the missionary activities of churchmen who espoused Roman hierarchical forms of ecclesiastical organization that favoured political centralization; looser indigenous and Irish ecclesiastical structures meanwhile lost ground. Frankish penetration followed a pattern in which communities or churches were settled on land newly won from forest or marsh and granted them by their Carolingian protectors. Thus, from Frisia in the north to Bavaria in the south, religious, economic, and political penetration went hand in hand. A distinguished part

was played by Anglo-Saxon missionaries, who linked the Frankish world not only with the high culture of their homeland but also with Rome. One of the most prominent of these was St. Willibrord (c. 658–739), who worked as a missionary and Frankish agent among the Frisians and later the Thuringians. Of even greater significance was Willibrord's disciple St. Boniface (c. 675–754), the "apostle of Germany," who preached the Word to the pagan Germans and introduced religious reform to the Frankish church. Supported by Charles Martel, Boniface led missions into Franconia, Thuringia, and Bavaria, where he founded or restructured diocesan organization on a Roman model. In 742, with the support of the new mayors of the palace Pippin and Carloman, he played a large part in the first council of the new German church. By the time of his martyrdom at the hands of northern Frisians, all the continental Germanic peoples except the Saxons were well on the way toward integration into a Roman-Frankish ecclesiastical structure.

Boniface's missionary activities and religious reforms also influenced political developments in the Frankish kingdom. His close contact and frequent correspondence with the pope in Rome reinforced a developing trend in the Frankish world that involved the increasing devotion to St. Peter and his vicar. When Charles Martel's son and successor, Pippin, sought justification for his usurpation of the Frankish throne in 750, he appealed to Pope Zacharias, asking whether the person with the title or the power should be king. In the following year, Pippin assumed the throne and was crowned by the bishops of his realm, including, according to one account, the pope's representative in the Frankish kingdom, St. Boniface. Three years later, Pope Stephen II traveled to Pippin's kingdom to seek aid from the king against the Lombards. While there, Stephen strengthened the alliance with the Carolingians and Pippin's claim to the throne when he crowned Pippin and, according to some accounts, Pippin's sons Carloman and the future Charlemagne.

CHARLEMAGNE

Charlemagne built on the foundations laid by Boniface, Charles Martel, and Pippin. Contemporary writers were vastly impressed by Charlemagne's political campaigns to destroy the autonomy of Bavaria and his equally determined efforts against the Saxons. Under their Agilolfing dukes, who had at times led the opposition to the rising Carolingians, the Bavarians had developed an independent, southward-looking state that had close contacts with Lombard Italy and peaceful relations with the Avar kingdom to the east. Charlemagne's conquest of the Lombards in 774 left Bavaria isolated, and in 788 Charlemagne succeeded in deposing the last Agilolfing duke, Tassilo III, and replacing him with a trusted agent. Thereafter Charlemagne used Bavaria as the staging ground for a series of campaigns in 791, 795, and 796 that destroyed the Avar kingdom.

The subjugation of the north proved much more difficult than that of the south. In the wake of the missionaries, Frankish counts and other officials moved into northeastern Frisia, raising contingents for the royal host and doing the other business of secular government. As for the Rhineland, the richer it grew, the more necessary it became to protect its hinterland, Franconia (including present-day Hessen) and Thuringia, from Saxon raids. Because there was no natural barrier behind which to hold the Saxons, this was a difficult task.

Unlike the Bavarians, the Saxons were not politically united. Their independent edhelingi (nobles) lived on estates among forest clearings, dominating the frilingi (freemen), lazzi (half-free), and unfree members of Saxon society and leading raids into the rich Frankish kingdom. Thus each of Charlemagne's punitive expeditions, which began in 772 and lasted until 804, bit deeper into the heart of Saxony, leaving behind bitter memories of forced conversions, deportations, and massacres. These raids were inspired by religious as well as political zeal; with fire and sword, Charlemagne tried to break Saxon resistance both to Christianity and to Frankish dominance. Still, the decentralized nature of Saxon society made ultimate conquest extremely difficult. Whenever the Frankish army was occupied elsewhere, the Saxons could be counted on to revolt,

Bust of Emperor Charlemagne. Imagno/Hulton Archive/Getty Images

to slaughter Frankish officials and priests, and to raid as far westward as they could. Charlemagne in turn would punish the offending tribes, as he did when he executed 4,500 Saxons at Verden, and garrison the defense points abandoned by the Saxons. In time, resistance to the Franks gave the Saxons a kind of unity under the leadership of Widukind, who succeeded longer than any other leader in holding together a majority of chieftains in armed resistance to the Franks. Ultimately, internal feuding led to the capitulation even of Widukind. He surrendered, was baptized, and, like Tassilo, was imprisoned in a monastery for the remainder of his life. Despite this victory, it would take another 20 years before Saxony would be finally subdued.

Charlemagne's efforts were not limited to military repression, however. He also issued two edicts concerning the pacification and conversion of Saxony, which reveal the brutality of the process as well as its gradual success. The Capitulatio de Partibus Saxoniae (c. 785; "Capitulary for the Saxon Regions") was intended to force the submission of the Saxons to the Franks and to Christianity, imposing the death penalty for destruction of churches, refusal of baptism, and violating the Lenten fast. The Capitulare Saxonicum (797; "Saxon Capitulary"), although not necessarily abrogating the earlier decree, replaced the harsher measures of the earlier capitulary with conversion through less brutal methods. Moreover, Frankish churchmen and aristocrats loyal to Charlemagne were introduced to secure and pacify the region. Although the northern regions that enjoyed Danish support remained outside of Frankish control, most of Saxony gradually moved into the united Frankish realm and would become a great centre of political, cultural, and religious life in the 10th century.

THE EMERGENCE OF GERMANY

After his conquest of the German lands, Charlemagne administered the area like he did the rest of his kingdom, or empire (Reich): through his counts and bishops. He established his primary residence at Aachen (now in Germany), which was not far from the conquered territories, though his decision probably had more to do with the town's hot springs than with strategic planning. His son Louis I (Louis the Pious) remained involved in the affairs of the German, Danish, and Slavic lands, but his primary focus was on the regions of his empire where the Romance, or proto-Romance, language was spoken. In 817, however, he issued the Ordinatio Imperii, an edict that reorganized the empire and established the imperial succession. As part of the restructuring, Louis awarded his young son Louis II (Louis the German; 804–876) the government of Bavaria and the lands of the Carinthians, Bohemians, Avars, and Slavs. Becoming the king of Bavaria in 825, Louis the German gradually extended his power over all of Carolingian Germany.

THE KINGDOM OF LOUIS THE GERMAN

Louis the German's rise to power, however, was not a smooth one because internal turmoil plagued the Carolingian empire in the 830s and early 840s. Although he would ultimately rescue Louis the Pious on both occasions, the younger Louis was involved in revolts against his father in 830 and 833–834. In the final settlement of the succession, Louis the German's inheritance was restricted to Bavaria by his father, who had reconciled with his oldest son and the heir to the imperial throne, Lothar. After their father's death, the surviving sons of Louis fell into three years of civil war, which led to the division of the Carolingian empire. During these civil wars, Louis took side with his brother Charles the Bald and confirmed this alliance in the famous Oath of Strasbourg in 842 (an important political and linguistic document that contains versions of the Romance language and Old High German). The success of Charles and Louis against their older brother Lothar led to a formal end to the civil wars in the Treaty of Verdun in 843, which divided the realm among the three leaders and laid out the rough outlines of late medieval France and Germany. In this settlement, Louis received the eastern kingdom, which included the lands east of the Rhine River (Bavaria, Franconia, Saxony, Swabia, and Thuringia).

As ruler of the eastern Frankish kingdom, Louis faced the challenge of maintaining the unity of a very diverse kingdom as well as asserting his place in the wider Carolingian world and protecting the frontiers from invaders. Like his brothers, Louis sought to establish his preeminence in the old empire. On two occasions he invaded Charles the Bald's kingdom and on a third occasion supported the invasion of the kingdom by his son. Louis also invaded the territory of the heirs of Lothar and attempted to seize the imperial crown. Moreover, much of Louis's reign was taken up with campaigns against neighbouring Slavs. Although he faced attacks by the Slavs and Vikings and the challenge of powerful aristocratic families, Louis maintained stability and royal authority over the aristocracy as a result of his external focus. By 870 Louis's dominions reached almost the boundaries of medieval Germany. On the east they were bordered by the Elbe and the Bohemian mountains; on the west, beyond the Rhine, they included the districts afterward known as Alsace and Lorraine. Ecclesiastically, they included the provinces of Mainz, Trier, Cologne, Salzburg, and Bremen. Although the close kinship and rivalries of the descendants of Charlemagne still united the eastern and western Frankish lands, the eastern region was taking on the identity of Germany, and the west was emerging as France.

Louis's long reign provided a degree of unity and continuity for the peoples of his varied kingdom and also laid the foundation for developments in later medieval Germany. His appointment of his sons as subkings over regions of the kingdom foreshadowed the later

LOUIS THE GERMAN

The third son of the Carolingian emperor Louis I the Pious, Louis the German (born *c.* 804, Aquitaine?, France—died August 28, 876, Frankfurt) was assigned Bavaria at the partition of the empire in 817. Entrusted with the government of Bavaria in 825, he began his rule the following year. Louis took part in the revolts against his father (830–833) and joined his half brother, Charles the Bald, in opposing the claim of his brother, Lothar I, to imperial suzerainty over the whole empire after their father's death in 840. By the Treaty of Verdun (August 843), Charles, Lothar I, and Louis divided the western, middle, and eastern parts of the empire, respectively, between themselves. Louis received the territory of the Franconians, the Swabians, the Bavarians, and the Saxons, together with the Carolingian provinces to the east.

In 853 a group of nobles opposing Charles the Bald, then king of the West Franks, appealed to Louis for help; in 854 Louis sent his son Louis the Younger to Aquitaine, and in 858 went west himself to try to depose Charles; both expeditions failed. At the Peace of Coblenz (860) Louis renounced his claims to Charles's dominions.

When Lothar I died in 855, his lands were divided among his sons, one of whom, Lothar, received Lotharingia (Greater Lorraine). This Lothar had no legitimate children, and Louis the German and Charles the Bald agreed (865 and 867/868) on the partition of their nephew's dominions between themselves on his death. When Lothar died (869), however, Charles broke the agreements by annexing Lotharingia. Louis invaded Lotharingia (870), and the country was divided between Louis and Charles by the Treaty of Mersen (Meerssen), under which Louis received Friesland and an extremely large expansion of this territory west of the Rhine.

Louis in 865 and 872 divided his territories between his sons Carloman, Louis the Younger, and Charles III the Fat. Quarrels and discontent at the partitions led to revolts by one or another of the sons between 861 and 873.

Although Louis the German supported Frankish Catholic missions in Moravia, he could not maintain control in that area and lost a war that led to the founding of Greater Moravia, independent after 874.

Louis the German unsuccessfully sought the imperial dignity and the succession in Italy for his line after the death of Lothar I's son, the emperor Louis II; but though Louis II declared (874) in favour of Carloman, eldest son of Louis the German, as the next emperor (August 875), Charles the Bald had himself crowned by Pope John VIII after Louis II's death in August 875. Meanwhile, Louis the German unsuccessfully attempted to invade Charles's possessions in Lotharingia. At the time of his death, Louis the German was again preparing for war against Charles.

territorial dukes, and his support for and reliance on monasteries prefigured the policy of the Saxon dynasty in the 10th century. In good Carolingian tradition, he promoted missionary activity in concert with his military campaigns in the east. Louis also cultivated the German language and literature for the first time as a source of self-conscious cultural and political identity. Under his patronage the Gospels were translated into German dialects, and the first attempts at writing German poetry with Christian and traditional themes were undertaken.

After his death the kingdom was divided among his three sons according to Frankish tradition, but the deaths of two of them, in 880 and 882, restored its unity under Charles III (Charles the Fat). The ceaseless attacks by Danes, Saracens, and Magyars in the later 9th and 10th centuries, however, weakened the kingdom's cohesion and led to the creation of new kingdoms within the boundaries of the Carolingian realm. Incompetence in mounting effective resistance to invaders also led to revolts and civil wars, as for instance in 887 when Arnulf, an illegitimate son of Louis the German's son Carloman, led an army of Bavarians in a successful revolt against his uncle, Charles the Fat. Arnulf, however, was not equally successful in defending his eastern possessions. After his death in 899, the German kingdom came under the nominal rule of the last Carolingian king of Francia Orientalis, his young son, Louis IV (Louis the Child), and in the absence of strong military leadership it became the prey of the Magyar horsemen and other invaders from the east.

RISE OF THE DUCHIES

Because the Carolingians themselves were unable to provide effective defense for the whole kingdom, military command and the political and economic power necessary to support it necessarily devolved to local leaders whose regions were attacked. The inevitable result was the decentralization and decay of royal authority to the benefit of the regional dukes. Contrary to popular opinion, these dukes were not appointed by their peoples, nor were they descendants of the tribal chieftains of the postmigration period. The so-called Stammesherzogtümer (tribal duchies) were new political and, ultimately, social units. Their dukes were Carolingian counts, part of the international "imperial aristocracy" of the Carolingians, who organized defense on a local basis without questioning loyalty to the Carolingians. All the same, their initial success established them in the hearts of those whom they protected. In Saxony the Liudolfings, descendants of military commanders first established by Louis the German, achieved spectacular successes against the Slavs, Danes, and Magyars. In Franconia the Konradings rose to prominence over this largely Frankish region with the assistance of Arnulf but became largely independent during the minority of his son. Similarly, the Luitpoldings, originally named as Carolingian commanders, became dukes of Bavaria. Thuringia fell increasingly under the protection and lordship of the Liudolfings. In Swabia (Alemannia) several clans disputed control with one another and with regional ecclesiastical lords. Throughout the kingdom the only force for preserving unity remained the church, but the bishops approved the secularization of much monastic land to sustain troops who could counter the threat of external foes, thus further strengthening the power of the dukes.

The structural transformation of the "imperial aristocracy" into a local elite accompanied the emergence of an increasingly particularist, dynastically oriented aristocratic society that was bound together through ties of vassalage and in which local rulers exercised personal lordship over the free and half-free populations of the regions. This process did not advance as far in Germany as it did in France. Everywhere German society remained closer to older, regional varieties of social organization as well as to traditions of Carolingian government by ecclesiastical authorities and imperial deputies.

THE SAXON, SALIAN, AND HOHENSTAUFEN DYNASTIES

When in 911 Louis the Child, last of the East Frankish Carolingians, died without leaving a male heir, it seemed quite possible that his kingdom would break into pieces. In at least three of the duchies—Bavaria, Saxony, and Franconia—the ducal families were established in the leadership of their regions; in Swabia (Alemannia) two houses were still fighting for hegemony. Only the church, fearing for its endowments, had an obvious interest in the survival of the monarchy, its ancient protector. Against the growing authority of the dukes and the deep differences in dialect, customs, and social

structure among the tribal duchies there stood only the Carolingian tradition of kingship; but, with Charles III (Charles the Simple) as ruler of the West Frankish kingdom, its future was uncertain and not very hopeful. Only the Lotharingians put their faith in the ancient line and did homage to Charles, its sole reigning representative. The other component parts of the East Frankish kingdom did not follow suit.

THE 10TH AND 11TH CENTURIES

In the early 10th century, the Germanic peoples in the lands east of the Rhine and west of the Elbe and Saale rivers and the Bohemian Forest—as rudimentary and as thinly spread as their settlements were—had to face groups pressing in from farther east, especially the Magyars. The Saxons, headed by the Liudolfing duke Otto—who refused to be considered a candidate for the royal crown—were threatened by more enemies on their frontiers than any other tribe; Danes, Slavs, and Magyars simultaneously harassed their homeland. A king who commanded resources farther west, in Franconia, might therefore prove to be of help to Saxony. The Rhenish Franks, on the other hand, did not wish to abdicate from their position as the leading and kingmaking people, which gave them many material advantages.

CONRAD I

On November 10, 911, Saxon and Frankish leaders ended Carolingian rule

Germany in the 10th and 11th centuries.

in Germany when they met at Forchheim in Franconia to elect Conrad, duke of the Franks, as their king. The rejection of the Carolingian dynasty was motivated by the dynasty's inability to protect the kingdom from invaders and related internal political matters. Conrad of Franconia, elected by Franks and Saxons, was soon recognized also by Arnulf, duke of Bavaria, and by the Swabian clans. In descent, honours, and wealth, however, Conrad was no more than the equal of the dukes who had accepted him as king. To surmount them, to found a new royal house, and to acquire those wonder-working attributes that the Germans venerated in their rulers long after they had been converted to Christianity, he had yet to prove himself able, lucky, and successful.

In this period, political affairs became the monopoly of the German kings and a few score families of great magnates. The reason for this concentration of power was that, at the very foundation of the German kingdom, circumstances had long favoured those men whom birth, wealth, and military success had raised well above the ranks of the ordinary free members of their tribe. Their estates were cultivated in the main by half-free peasants—slaves who had risen or freemen who had sunk. The holdings of these dependents fell under the power of the lord to whom they owed service and obedience. Already they were tied to the lands on which they laboured and were dependent on their protectors for justice. For many reasons ordinary freemen tended generally to lose their independence and had to seek aid from their more fortunate and powerful neighbours; thus, they lost their standing in the assemblies of their tribe. Everywhere, except in Friesland and parts of Saxony, the nobles wedged themselves between king or duke and the rank and file. They alone could become prelates of the church, and they alone could compete for

the possession and enjoyment of political power. At the level below the dukes, the bulk of administrative authority, jurisdiction, and command in war lay with the margraves and counts, whose hold on their charges developed gradually into a hereditary right. The commended men and the half-free disappeared from the important functions of public life. In the local assemblies they came only to pay dues and to receive orders, justice, and penalties. Their political role was passive. Those lords whose protection was most worth having also had the largest throng of dependents and thus became more formidable to their enemies and to the remaining freemen. Lordship and vassalage were hereditary, and thus the horizon of the dependent classes narrowed until eventually the lord and his officials held all secular authority and power over their lives. Military strength, the possession of arms and horses, and tactical training in their use were decisive. Most dependent men were disarmed, and this became part of their degradation.

THE ACCESSION OF THE SAXONS

Conrad I was quite unequal to the situation in Germany. According to the beliefs of contemporaries, his failure meant that his house was luckless and lacked the prosperity-bringing virtues that belonged to true kingship. He also had no heir. On his deathbed in 918, he therefore proposed that the crown, which in 911 had remained with the Franks, should now pass to the leading man in Saxony, the Liudolfing Henry (later called the Fowler). Henry I was elected by the Saxons and Franks at Fritzlar, their ancient meeting place, in 919. With a monarch of their own ethnicity, the Saxons now took over the burden and the rewards of being the kingmaking people. The centre of gravity shifted to eastern Saxony, where the Liudolfing lands lay.

The transition of the crown from the Franks to the Saxons for a time enhanced the self-sufficiency of the southern German tribes. The Swabians had kept away from the Fritzlar election. The Bavarians believed that they had a better right to the Carolingian inheritance than the Saxons (who had been remote outsiders in the 9th century) and in 919 elected their own duke Arnulf as king. They, too, wanted to be the royal and kingmaking people. Henry I's regime rested in the main on his own position and family demesne in Saxony and on certain ancient royal seats in Franconia. His kingship was purely military. He hoped to win authority by waging successful frontier wars and to gain recognition through concessions rather than to insist on the sacred and priestlike status of the royal office that the church had built up in the 9th century. At his election he refused to be anointed and consecrated by the archbishop of Mainz. In settling with the Bavarians, he abandoned the policy of supporting the internal opposition that the clergy offered to Duke Arnulf, a plank to which Conrad had clung. To end Arnulf's rival kingship, Henry formally surrendered to him the most characteristic privilege and honour of the crown: the right to dispose of the region's bishoprics and abbeys. Arnulf's homage and friendship entailed no obligations to Henry, and the Bavarian duke pursued his own regional interests—peace with the Hungarians and expansion across the Alps—as long as he lived.

From these unpromising beginnings the Saxon dynasty not only found its way back to Carolingian traditions of government but soon got far better terms in its relations with the autonomous powers of the duchies, which had gained such a start on it. Nonetheless, the governing structures that it bequeathed to its Salian successors were self-contradictory; while seeking to overcome the princely aristocracies of the duchies by leaving them to themselves, the Saxon kings came to rely more and more, both for the inspiration and for the practice of government, on the prelates of the church, who were themselves recruited from the ranks of the same great families. They loaded bishoprics and abbeys with endowments and privileges and thus gradually turned the bishops and abbots into princes with interests not unlike those of their lay kinsmen. These weaknesses, however, lay concealed behind the personal ascendancy of an exceptionally tough and commanding set of rulers up to the middle of the 11th century. Thereafter the ambiguous system could not take the strain of the changes fermenting within German society and even less the attack on its values that came from without—from the reformed papacy.

The Liudolfing kings won military success, and with it they gained the respect for their personal authority that counted for so much at a time when the great followed only those whose star they trusted and who could reward services with the spoils of victory. In 925 Henry I brought Lotharingia (the region between the upper Meuse and Schelde rivers in the west and the Rhine River in the east that contained Charlemagne's capital Aachen) back to the East Frankish realm. Whoever had authority in that region could treat the neighbouring kingdom of the West Franks as a dependent. The young Saxon dynasty thus won for itself and its successors a hegemony over the west and the southwest that lasted at least until the mid-11th century. The Carolingian kings of France, as well as the great feudatories who sought to dominate if not to ruin them, became, in turn, petitioners to the German court during the reign of the Ottos. The kings of Burgundy—whose suzerainty lay over the valleys of the Saône and the Rhône, the western Alps, and Provence—fell under the virtual tutelage of the masters of Lotharingia. Rich in ancient towns, this region, once the homeland of the Carolingians, was more thickly populated and wealthier than the lands east of the Rhine. Lotharingian merchants controlled the slave trade from the Saxon marches to Córdoba.

THE EASTERN POLICY OF THE SAXONS

Greater prestige still and a claim to imperial hegemony fell to the Saxon rulers when they broke the impetus of the Hungarian (Magyar) invasions, against which the military resources and methods of western European society had almost wholly failed for several decades. In 933, after long preparations, Henry routed a Hungarian attack on Saxony and Thuringia. In 955 Otto I (Otto the Great; reigned 936–973), at the head of a force to which nearly all the duchies had sent mounted contingents, annihilated a great Hungarian army on the Lech River near Augsburg. The battle again vindicated the efficiency of the heavily armed man skilled in fighting on horseback.

With a Saxon dynasty on the throne, Saxon nobles gained office and power, with opportunities for conquest along the eastern river frontiers and marches of their homeland. Otto I implemented an eastern policy that aimed at getting more than slaves, loot, and tribute. Between 955 and 972 he founded and richly endowed an archbishopric at Magdeburg, which he intended to be the metropolis of a large missionary province among the Slavic Wends beyond the Elbe, who remained faithful to their traditional polytheistic religion. This would have brought their tribes under German control and exploitation in the long run, but the ruthless methods of the Saxon lay lords led to a rebellion that forced Otto to scale back his plans.

In the 10th century there was little or no German agricultural settlement beyond the Elbe. Far too much forested land remained available for clearing and colonization in western and southern

Germany. The Saxons attempted to secure their tenuous military victories in the region between the Elbe and Oder rivers by building and garrisoning forts. Beyond the Wends of Brandenburg and Lusatia, meanwhile, new Slavic powers rose; the Poles under Mieszko I and, to the south, the Czechs under the Přemyslids received missionaries from Magdeburg and Passau without falling permanently under the political and ecclesiastical domination of Saxons and Bavarians. The Wends, who had been subjugated by the Saxon margraves, resisted conversion to Christianity. They rebelled in 983 against the German military occupation, which collapsed along with the missionary bishoprics that had been founded at Oldenburg, Brandenburg, and Havelberg. Farther south the defenses of the Thuringian marches between the Saale and the middle Elbe remained in German hands, but only after a long and fierce struggle against Polish invaders early in the 11th century. The northern part of the frontier reverted to its position before Otto's trustees, Hermann Billung and Gero, had begun their wars. Missionary enterprises directed into Wendish territory from Bremen and Magdeburg achieved little before the 12th century.

The Saxon ruling class and margraves must bear the responsibility for the fiasco of eastward expansion in the 10th century. The prelates, too, saw their missions as means to found ecclesiastical empires of subject dioceses that would exact tribute from the conquered Wends. The Slavic tribes across the Elbe remained unconverted and implacable foes, a standing menace to the nearby churches. The wars also left a legacy of savagery on both sides, so that from about 1140 onward the colonization of conquered Slavic lands by German settlers became the common policy of both the church and the princes.

DUKES, COUNTS, AND ADVOCATES

Conrad I's and Henry I's kingships rested on the election by the tribal duchies' leaders and higher aristocracy. It was in the first place an arrangement between the Franks and the Saxons that the Bavarian and Swabian dukes recognized at a price by acts of personal homage, but the German kings, of whatever dynasty, had to live under Frankish law. After the death of Conrad I's brother Eberhard in 939, Otto I kept the Franconian dukedom vacant, and the Franconian counts henceforth stood under the immediate authority of the crown. In Saxony, too, Otto kept in his hands the dukedom of his ancestors, even though the beginning of the Billung line of dukes is traditionally dated to 936. The march-duchy of the Billungs, a bulwark raised against the Danes and the northern Slav tribes, gave the Billung family military command but did not give it authority over all the other Saxon princes.

In the south the Ottonians sought to turn the tribal duchies into royal lands and to supplant native dynasties with aliens and members of their own clan. When even that policy did not stop rebellions under the banner of tribal self-interest, the Ottonians began to break up the ancient Bavarian tribal land by carving out a new duchy in Carinthia where the Bavarian expansion southward had opened up new lands and sources of revenue. The first two members of the Rhine-Frankish Salian dynasty, Conrad II (reigned 1024–39) and Henry III (reigned alone 1039–56), also bestowed vacant duchies quite freely on their own kin and on men from outside the duchies. They competed against ducal power but could neither abolish nor replace it. In the 11th century, as before, the dukes held assemblies of their freemen and nobility, led the tribal army in war, and enforced peace.

The counts, who were the ordinary officers of justice in serious criminal cases, obeyed the ducal summons; but, for the most part, they received their "ban," the power to do blood justice, from the king himself. The lands and the customary rights attached to their office, and indeed the office itself, not only became hereditary but also came to be treated more and more as a patrimony to which they had an inherent right against all men, king and duke included. Even so, however, a good many lines died out, and their counties fell back into the king's hands. From Otto III's reign (983–1002) onward, kings often bestowed these counties on bishoprics and great abbeys rather than granting them again to lay magnates. The bishops, however, could not perform all the functions of the counts; in particular, their holy orders forbade them to pass judgments of blood. They often subinfeudated their countships, and they needed officials called advocates (Vögte; singular: Vogt) to take charge of the higher jurisdiction in the territories that their churches possessed by royal grant. In the 10th and 11th centuries these advocates had to be recruited from the aristocracy, the very class whose greed for hereditary office was to be checked, because ordinary freemen could not enforce severe sentences or defend the privileges of the church against armed intrusion. Ostensibly advocates and protectors of ecclesiastical possessions, the nobles were in fact anything but reliable servants of their ecclesiastical overlords and instead posed great danger for the bishoprics and abbeys.

Thus there arose in nearly all German lands, whether the ducal office survived or not, powerful lines of margraves, counts, and hereditary advocates who enriched themselves at the expense of the church (which meant also the crown) and in competition with one another. From the abler, more fortunate, and long-lived of these dynasties sprang the territorial princes of the later 12th and 13th centuries, absorbing and finally inheriting most of the rights of government.

The king was the personal overlord of all the great. His court was the seat of government, and it went with him on his long journeys. The German kings, even more than other medieval rulers, could make their authority respected in the far-flung regions of their kingdom only by traveling ceaselessly from duchy to duchy, from frontier to frontier. Wherever they stayed, their jurisdiction superseded the standing power of dukes, counts, and advocates, and they could collect the profits of local justice and wield some control over it. As they came into each region, they summoned its leaders to attend their solemn crown wearings, deliberated with them on the affairs of the kingdom and the locality, presided over pleas, granted privileges, and made war against peacemakers at home and enemies abroad.

THE PROMOTION OF THE GERMAN CHURCH

The royal revenues came from the king's demesne and from his share of the tributes that Poles, Czechs, Wends, and Danes paid whenever he could enforce his claims of overlordship. There were also profits from tolls and mints that had not yet been granted away. The king's demesne was his working capital. He and his household lived on its produce during their wanderings through the Reich, and he used its revenue to provide for his family, to found churches, and to reward faithful services done to him, especially in war. To swell his army, the king needed to add new vassals, and he inevitably had to grant land to some of them from his own demesne. Although the Salians inherited the remains of Ottonian wealth as an imperial demesne, they brought little of their own to make up for its diminution. The last Ottonian, Henry II (1002–24), and after him Conrad II, accordingly took to enfeoffing vassals with lands taken from the monasteries.

Since the beneficiaries were often already powerful and wealthy men in their own right, no class of freeborn, mounted warriors linked permanently with the crown resulted from the loyalties established and rewards granted during but one or two reigns. In any case, the lion's share of grants went to the German church.

From the Carolingians the German kings inherited their one and only institution of central government: the royal chapel, with the chancery that does not seem to have been distinct from it. Service there became a recognized avenue of promotion to the episcopate for highborn clerics. In the 11th century bishops and abbots conducted the affairs of the Reich much more than the lay lords, even in war. They were its habitual diplomats and ambassadors. Unlike Henry I, Otto I and his successors sought to free the prelates from all forms of subjection to the dukes. The king appointed most of them, and to him alone, as to one sent by God, they owed obedience.

Thus there arose beside the loose association of tribal duchies in the German kingdom a more compact and uniform body with a far greater vested interest in the Reich: the German church. By ancient Germanic custom, moreover, the founder of a church did not lose his estate in the endowment that he had made; he remained its proprietor and protecting lord. Still, the bishoprics and certain ancient abbeys, such as Sankt Gallen, Reichenau, Fulda, and Hersfeld, did not belong to the king; they were members of the kingdom, but he served only as their guardian. The greater churches therefore had to provide the rulers with mounted men, money, and free quarters. Gifts of royal demesne to found or to enrich bishoprics and convents were not really losses of land but pious reinvestments, as long as the crown controlled the appointments of bishops and abbots. The church did not merely receive grants of land, often uncultivated, to settle, develop, and make profitable; it was also given jurisdiction over its dependents. Nor did the kings stint the prelates in other regalian rights, such as mints, markets, and tolls. These grants broke up counties and to some extent even duchies, and that was their purpose: to disrupt the secular lords' jurisdictions that had escaped royal control.

This policy of fastening the church, a universal institution, into the Reich, with its well-defined frontiers, is usually associated with Otto I, but it gathered momentum only in the reigns of his successors. The policy reached a climax under Henry II, the founder of the see of Bamberg in the upper Main valley; nonetheless, Conrad II, though less generous with his grants, and his son Henry III continued it. Bishops and abbots became the competitors of lay princes in the formation of territories, a rivalry that more than any other was the fuel and substance of the ceaseless feuds—the smoldering internal wars in all the regions of Germany for many centuries. The welter and the confused mosaic of the political map of Germany until 1803 is the not-so-remote outcome of these 10th- and 11th-century grants and of the incompatible ambitions that they aroused.

THE OTTONIAN CONQUEST OF ITALY AND THE IMPERIAL CROWN

Otto first entered Italy in 951 and, according to some accounts, was already interested in securing the imperial crown. He campaigned in Italy at the request of Adelaide (Adelheid), the daughter of Rudolph II of Burgundy and widow of the king of Italy, who had been jailed by Berengar II, the king of Italy. Otto defeated Berengar, secured Adelaide's release, and then married her. His first Italian campaign was also motivated by political developments in Germany, including the competing ambitions in Italy of his son Liudolf, duke of Swabia, and Otto's brother Henry I, duke of Bavaria. Although he would be called back to Germany by a revolt in 953, Otto accomplished his primary goals during his first trip to Italy. He gained legitimate rights to govern in Italy as a result of his marriage, and securing his southern flanks guaranteed access to the pope. Moreover, after 951, expeditions into Italy were a matter for the whole Reich under the leadership of its ruler and no longer just expansion efforts by the southern German tribes. For the Saxon military class, too, the south was more tempting than the forests and swamps beyond the Elbe. With superior forces at their back, the German kings gained possession of the Lombard kingdom in Italy. There, too, their overlordship in the 10th and the 11th centuries came to rest on the bishoprics and a handful of great abbeys.

After Otto I's victory over the Magyars in 955, his hegemony in the West was indisputable. Indeed, he was hailed in traditional fashion as emperor (imperator) by his troops after the victory, which was seen as divine sanction for Otto's ascendant position by his contemporaries. Furthermore, according to one chronicler, the Saxon Widukind, he had already become emperor because he had subjected other peoples and enjoyed authority in more than one kingdom. But the right to confer the imperial crown, to raise a king to the higher rank of emperor, belonged to the papacy, which had crowned Charlemagne and most of his successors. The Carolingian order was still the model and something like a political ideal for all Western ruling families in the 10th century. Otto had measured himself against the political tasks that had faced his East Frankish

HOLY ROMAN EMPIRE

Traditionally believed to have been established by Charlemagne, who was crowned emperor by Pope Leo III in 800, the Holy Roman Empire lasted until the renunciation of the imperial title by Francis II in 1806. The reign of the German Otto I, who revived the imperial title after Carolingian decline, is also sometimes regarded as the beginning of the empire. The name Holy Roman Empire (not adopted until the reign of Frederick I Barbarossa) reflected Charlemagne's claim that his empire was the successor to the Roman Empire and that this temporal power was augmented by his status as God's principal vicar in the temporal realm (parallel to the pope's in the spiritual realm). The empire's core consisted of Germany, Austria, Bohemia, and Moravia. Switzerland, the Netherlands, and northern Italy sometimes formed part of it; France, Poland, Hungary, and Denmark were initially included, and Britain and Spain were nominal components. From the mid-11th century the emperors engaged in a great struggle with the papacy for dominance, and, particularly under the powerful Hohenstaufen dynasty (1138–1208, 1212–54), they fought with the popes over control of Italy. Rudolf I became the first Habsburg emperor in 1273, and from 1438 the Habsburg dynasty held the throne for centuries. Until 1356 the emperor was chosen by the German princes; thereafter he was formally elected by the electors. Outside their personal hereditary domains, emperors shared power with the imperial diet. During the Reformation the German princes largely defected to the Protestant camp, opposing the Catholic emperor. At the end of the Thirty Years' War, the Peace of Westphalia (1648) recognized the individual sovereignty of the empire's states; the empire thereafter became a loose federation of states and the title of emperor principally honorific. In the 18th century, issues of imperial succession resulted in the War of the Austrian Succession and the Seven Years' War. The greatly weakened empire was brought to an end by the victories of Napoleon.

predecessors and more or less mastered them. To be like Charlemagne, therefore, and to clothe his newly won position in a traditional and time-honoured dignity, he accepted the imperial crown and anointment from Pope John XII in Rome in 962. The substance of his empire was military power and success in war; but Christian and Roman ideas were woven round the Saxon's throne by the writers of his own and the next generation. Although the German kings as emperors did not legislate matters of doctrine and ritual, they became the political masters of the Roman church for nearly a century. The imperial crown enhanced their standing even among the nobles and knights who followed them to Italy and can hardly have understood or wanted all its outlandish associations. Not only the king but also the German bishops and lay lords thus entered into a permanent connection with an empire won on the way to Rome and bestowed by the papacy.

Otto I successfully revived the empire in the West on Carolingian precedents and secured Ottonian rule in Germany, but his greatest triumph may have come near the end of his reign when he secured both recognition from the Byzantine emperor and a marriage arrangement between his son, Otto II, and the Byzantine princess Theophano. In 973 Otto II succeeded his father as emperor. His attention, perhaps under his wife's influence, was drawn to Italy and the Mediterranean, and he campaigned in southern Italy with disastrous results, suffering a terrible defeat at the hands of Muslim armies. When Otto II

died in 983, his heir, Otto III, was only three years old, and a period of regency preceded a reign of great promise unfulfilled. Inheriting the traditions of both the Western and Eastern empires, the third Otto sought to revive the Christian Roman empire of Charlemagne and Constantine and planned a great capital in Rome. Otto's grand ambition is reflected in the appointment of Gerbert of Aurillac as pope, who took the name Sylvester II in imitation of Constantine's pope; in Otto's efforts to expand the empire and Christendom to the east; and in his discovery, with its apocalyptic overtones, of the tomb of Charlemagne in the year 1000. His premature death two years later, followed by that of Sylvester in 1003, ended this promising chapter of German history. His successor, Henry II, returned the imperial focus to Germany and contented himself with three brief Italian expeditions.

THE SALIANS, THE PAPACY, AND THE PRINCES, 1024–1125

During the reign of Conrad II (1024–39), the first Salian emperor, the kingdom of Burgundy fell finally under the overlordship of the German crown, and this tough and formidable emperor also renewed German authority in Italy. His son and successor, Henry III (1039–56), treated the empire as a mission that imposed on him the tasks of reforming the papacy and of preaching peace to his lay vassals. Without possessing any very significant new resources of power, he nevertheless lent his authority an exalted and strained theocratic complexion. Yet, under Henry, the last German ruler to maintain his hegemony in western Europe, the popes themselves seemed to become mere imperial bishops. He deposed three of them, and four Germans held the Holy See at his command; but lay opposition to the emperor in Germany and criticism of his control over the church were on the increase during the last years of his reign.

PAPAL REFORM AND THE GERMAN CHURCH

More than any other society in early medieval Europe, Germany was divided and torn by the revolutionary ideas and measures of the so-called Gregorian reform movement. Beginning with the pontificate of Leo IX (1048–54)—one of Henry III's nominees—the most determined and inspired spokesmen of ecclesiastical reform placed themselves at the service of the Holy See. Only a few years after Henry's death (1056), they agitated against lay authority in the church and issued a papal election decree that virtually eliminated imperial involvement. The ecclesiastical reformers sought to restore what they thought was the rightful order of the world and denied the notion of theocratic kingship. Priests, including bishops and abbots, who accepted their dignities from lay lords and emperors at a price, according to the reformers, committed the sin of simony (the buying and selling of church office). The reformers argued that earthly powers could

not rightly confer the gifts of the Holy Spirit and thus rejected the tradition of lay investiture. They believed, moreover, that true reforms could be brought about only by the exaltation of the papacy so that it commanded the obedience of all provincial metropolitans and was out of the reach of the emperor and the local aristocracy.

The endless repetition of the reformers' message in brilliant pamphlets and at clerical synods spread agitation in Italy, Burgundy, and Lotharingia—all parts of the empire. Their new program committed the leaders of the movement to a struggle for power because it struck at the very roots of the regime to which the German church had grown accustomed and on which the German kings relied. The vast wealth that Henry IV's predecessors had showered on the bishoprics and abbeys would, if the new teaching prevailed, escape his control and remain at the disposal of prelates whom he no longer appointed. Under Roman authority the churches were to be freed from most of the burdens of royal protection without losing any of its benefits. The most fiery spirits in Rome did not flinch from the consequences of their convictions. Their leader Hildebrand, later Pope Gregory VII (1073–85), was ready to risk a collision with the empire.

Henry IV was not yet six years old when his father died in 1056. The full impact of the Gregorian demands—coming shortly after a royal minority, a Saxon rising, and a conspiracy of the southern German princes—has often been regarded as the most disastrous moment in Germany's history during the Middle Ages. In fact, the German church had proved thoroughly unreliable as an inner bastion of the empire even before Rome struck. One of its leaders, Archbishop Anno of Cologne, kidnapped Henry in 1062 to gain control of both the young king and the regency, and another, Archbishop Adalbert of Bremen, exploited his influence over the young king by enriching his ecclesiastical possessions at imperial expense. In 1074 and 1075 Gregory proceeded against simony in Germany and humiliated the aristocratic episcopate by issuing summonses to Rome and sentences of suspension. These papal actions demoralized and shook the German hierarchy. The prelates' return to their customary support of the crown was not disinterested, nor wholehearted, nor unanimous.

THE DISCONTENT OF THE LAY PRINCES

Henry IV's minority also gave elbow-room to the ambitions and hatreds of the lay magnates. The feeble regency of his mother, the pious Agnes of Poitou, faltered before the throng of princes, who respected only authority and power greater than their own. The influence of the higher clergy at the court of Henry III and the renewed flow of grants to the church had estranged these princes from the empire. It is likely also that these eternally belligerent men lagged behind the prelates in the development of their agrarian resources. The prelates had a

vested interest in peace, and under royal protection they improved and enlarged their estates by turning forests into arable land and also by offering better terms to freemen in search of a lord. The bishops' market and toll privileges brought them revenues in money, which many of the lay princes lacked. So far, however, the princes' military power, their chief asset, had remained unchallenged. Now, for the first time, they also had to face rivals within their own sphere of action. Henry III and the young Henry IV began to rely on advisers and fighting men drawn from a lower tier of the social order—the poorer, freeborn nobility of Swabia and, above all, the class of unfree knights, known as ministeriales. These knights had first become important as administrators and soldiers on the estates of the church early in the 11th century. Their status and that of their fiefs were fixed by seignorial ordinances, and they could be relied on and commanded, unlike the free vassals of bishops and abbots. Beginning with Conrad II, the Salian kings used ministeriales to administer their demesne, as household officers at court, and as garrisons for their castles. They formed a small army, which the crown could mobilize without having to appeal to the lay princes, whose ill will and antipathy toward the government of the Reich grew apace with their exclusion from it.

Having come of age, Henry IV used petty southern German nobles and his ministeriales to recover some of the crown lands and rights that the lay princes and certain prelates had acquired during his minority, particularly in Saxony. His recovery operations went further, however, and a great belt of lands from the northern slopes of the Harz Mountains to the Thuringian Forest was secured and fortified under the supervision of his knights to form a royal territory, where the king and his court could reside. The southern German magnates were thus kept at a distance when Henry and his advisers struck at neighbouring Saxon princes such as Otto of Northeim and at the Billung family.

The storm broke in 1073. A group of Saxon nobles and prelates and the free peasantry of Eastphalia, who had borne the brunt of statute labour in the building of the royal strongholds, revolted against the regime of Henry's Frankish and Swabian officials. To overcome this startling combination and to save his fortresses, the king needed the military strength of the southern German princes Rudolf of Rheinfelden, duke of Swabia; Welf IV, duke (as Welf I) of Bavaria; and Berthold of Zähringen, duke of Carinthia. Suspicious and hostile at heart, they took the field for him only when the Eastphalian peasantry committed outrages that shocked aristocrats everywhere. Their forces enabled Henry to defeat the Saxon rebellion at Homburg near Langensalza in June 1075. But, when the life-and-death struggle with Rome opened only half a year later, the southern German malcontents deserted Henry and, together with the Saxons and a handful of bishops, entered into an alliance with Gregory VII. Few of them at this time were converted to papal reform doctrines, but Gregory's daring measures against the king gave them a chance to come to terms with one another and to justify a general revolt.

THE CIVIL WAR AGAINST HENRY IV

Although he intended to cooperate with Henry IV at the outset of his papacy, Gregory VII was drawn into a terrible conflict with the king because of Henry's refusal to obey papal commands. Emboldened by his success in 1075 against the Saxons, Henry took a firm stand against Gregory in disputes over the appointment of the archbishop of Milan and a number of Henry's advisers who had been excommunicated by the pope. At the synod of Worms in January 1076, Henry took the dramatic step of demanding that Gregory abdicate, and the German bishops renounced their allegiance to the pope. At his Lenten synod the following month, Gregory absolved all men from their oaths to Henry and solemnly excommunicated and deposed the king. The situation quickly became desperate for Henry, who both lost much support and faced a reinvigorated revolt. In October Gregory's legates and leaders of the German opposition assembled at Tribur (modern Trebur, Germany) to decide the future of the king, who by this point had been abandoned by his last adherents. Gregory was then invited to attend a meeting at Augsburg the following February to mediate the situation. Henry hastened to meet Gregory at Canossa before the pope reached Augsburg, however, and appealed to him as a penitent sinner. Gregory had little choice but to forgive his rival and lifted the excommunication in January 1077. Despite Gregory's reconciliation with Henry, the princes elected Rudolf of Rheinfelden king at a gathering in Forchheim in March.

The civil war that now broke out lasted almost 20 years. A majority of the bishops, most of Rhenish Franconia (the Salian homeland), and some important Bavarian and Swabian vassals sided with Henry. He thus held a geographically central position that separated his southern German from his Saxon enemies, who could not unite long enough to destroy him. With the death in battle of Rudolf of Rheinfelden in 1080 and the demise of another antiking, Hermann of Salm, in 1088, the war in Germany degenerated into a number of local conflicts over the possession of bishoprics and abbeys. Henry was also successful in the larger struggle with Gregory, invading Italy and forcing the pope from Rome in 1084. At that time, Henry elevated Wibert of Ravenna to the papal throne as the antipope Clement III, who then crowned Henry emperor.

The situation remained in flux throughout the rest of Henry's reign. In 1093 Henry was nearly toppled by a revolt led by his son Conrad, and a revived papacy under Urban II challenged the legitimacy of Clement. In 1098 the tide turned again when Henry appointed his other son, Henry, as his heir and relations with the bishops and papacy improved. Ultimately, however, Henry's reign was doomed to failure by one final revolt. Even his apparent triumph at Canossa was tempered by his loss of status as a divinely appointed ruler.

Throughout these years the crown, the churches, and the lay lords had to enfeoff more and more ministeriales in order to raise mounted warriors for their forces. Though this recruitment and frequent devastations strained the fortunes of many nobles, they recouped their losses by extorting fiefs from neighbouring bishoprics and abbeys. The divided German church thus bore the brunt of the costs of civil war, and it needed peace almost at any price.

HENRY V

The Salian dynasty and the rights for which it fought were saved because Henry IV's son and heir himself seized the leadership of a last rising against his father (1105). This maneuver enabled Henry V (1106–25) to continue the struggle for the crown's prerogative over the empire's churches against the demands of the papacy. As the struggle continued, the princes became the arbiters and held the balance between their overlord and the pope. In 1122, acting as intermediaries and on behalf of the Reich, they reached the agreement known as the Concordat of Worms with the Holy See and its German spokesman, Archbishop Adalbert of Mainz, the bitter personal enemy of Henry V. By then, however, the

Henry V. Hulton Archive/Getty Images

French kings were achieving forms of government and concentrations of military and economic strength that the older and larger empire lacked. The papacy had dimmed the empire's prestige and decreased the emperor's power, and Rome became the true home of universalistic causes. When Pope Urban II preached the First Crusade in 1095, Henry IV, cut off and surrounded by enemies, was living obscurely in a corner of northern Italy. The Holy See, by its great appeal to the militant lay nobility of western Europe, thus won the initiative over the empire. At this critical moment the Reich also lost control in the Italian bishoprics and towns just when their population, trade, and industrial production were expanding quickly. Germany did not even benefit indirectly from the Crusaders' triumphs, although some of their leaders (e.g., Godfrey of Bouillon and Robert II of Flanders) were vassals of the emperor. The civil wars renewed for a time the relative isolation of the central German regions.

Internally, the crown had saved something of the indispensable means of government in the control over the church; but it was a bare minimum, and its future was problematic. The ecclesiastical princes henceforth held only their

princes had for the most part defeated efforts to restore royal rights in Saxony and to stem the swollen jurisdictions and territorial powers of the aristocracy elsewhere.

When Henry V, the last Salian, died childless in 1125, Germany was no longer the most effective political force in Europe. The brilliant conquest states of the Normans in England and Sicily and the patient, step-by-step labours of the

temporal lands as imperial fiefs, for which they owed personal and material services. As feudatories of the empire, they came to represent the same interests toward it as did the lay princes; at least, their sense of a special obligation tended to weaken. The king's jurisdiction continued to exist alongside and in competition with that of the local powers. The great tribal duchies survived as areas of separate customary law. Each developed differently, and the crown could not impose its rights on all alike or change the existing social order. The most tenacious defenders of this legal autonomy had been the Saxons; but it also prevailed in Swabia, where distinct territorial lordships grew fast.

The Gregorian reform movement therefore aggravated the age-old contradictions in Germany's early medieval constitution, but its monastic culture and its intellectual interests were anything but barren. Both sides fought with new literary weapons over public opinion in cathedrals and cloisters and perhaps also in the castles of the lay aristocracy. In their hard-hitting polemical writings they attempted to expound the fundamental theological, historical, and legal truths of their cause. The agitation did something to disturb the cultural self-sufficiency of the German laity. It drove many of the southern German nobles to maintain direct connections with the Holy See, and, whether they wanted to or not, they had to fall in with the aspirations of the religious leaders. The reform movement of the 11th and 12th centuries, it might almost be said, very nearly completed the

conversion of Germany that had begun five centuries before.

GERMANY AND THE HOHENSTAUFEN, 1125–1250

The nearest kinsmen of Henry V were his Hohenstaufen nephews—Frederick, duke of Swabia, and his younger brother Conrad—the sons of Henry's sister Agnes and Frederick, the first Hohenstaufen duke of Swabia. Some form of election had always been necessary to succeed to the crown, but, before the great civil war, nearness to the royal blood had been honoured whenever a dynasty failed in the direct line. By 1125, however, the princes, guided by Archbishop Adalbert of Mainz, no longer respected blood right. Affinity with Henry V was no recommendation to them, and hereditary succession seemed to lower the authority they vested in the government of the Reich. Instead of Frederick, they chose the duke of Saxony, Lothar of Supplinburg (reigned as King Lothar III in 1125–37 and as Emperor Lothar II in 1133–37). Like the Hohenstaufens, he had risen through a lucky marriage and continuous combat into the first rank of dynasts; but, unlike them, he had served the cause of the Saxon opposition to the Salians.

DYNASTIC COMPETITION, 1125–52

With the enormous Northeim and Brunonian inheritances behind him, Lothar II could humble the Hohenstaufen brothers after marrying his only daughter and heiress to a Welf, Henry the Proud, in 1134. Even without this dazzling alliance, the Welfs—already dukes of Bavaria and possessors of vast demesnes, countships, and ecclesiastical advocacies there, in Saxony, and in Swabia—were somewhat better off than their Hohenstaufen rivals. On the death of Lothar in 1137, however, the fears of the church and a few princes turned against the Welfs. Instead of Henry the Proud, who now held the duchies of Saxony and Bavaria and the Mathildine lands in Italy, they chose as their ruler Conrad (reigned 1138–52), who had been Lothar's unsuccessful Hohenstaufen opponent.

The battle against the Welfs, which Conrad III put foremost on his political program, was abandoned with his death in 1152, when an election once again decided the succession and the political situation in Germany for the next 30 years. This time the princes chose Frederick I (reigned as king in 1152–90 and emperor in 1155–90), the son of Conrad's elder brother Frederick and the Welf princess Judith. Selected in part because of his connections with important families in Germany, Frederick (known as Frederick Barbarossa, "Redbeard") was careful to maintain good relations with them and made concessions to his powerful Welf cousin Henry the Lion. In 1156 the duchy of Bavaria, which Conrad had tried to wrest from the Welfs, was restored to Henry the Lion, already undisputed duke of Saxony. Henry II Jasomirgott, the Babenberg margrave of Austria who was

Henry the Lion's rival for Bavaria, had to be compensated with a charter that raised his margravate into a duchy and gave him judicial suzerainty over an even wider area. Taken out of the Lion's duchy, it was to be held as an imperial fief that might descend both to sons and daughters. A perpetual principality, it served as a model for the aspirations of many other lay princes.

COLONIZATION OF THE EAST

The history of Germany in the 12th and 13th centuries is one of ceaseless expansion. A conquering and colonizing movement burst across the river frontiers into the swamps and forests from Holstein to Silesia and overwhelmed the Slavic Wendish tribes between the Elbe and the Oder. Every force in German society took part: the princes, the prelates, new religious orders, knights, townsmen, and peasant settlers. Agrarian conditions in the older German lands seem to have favoured large-scale emigration. With a rising population, there was much experience in drainage and wood clearing but a diminishing fund of spare land to be developed in the west. Excessive subdivision of holdings impoverished tenants and did not suit the interests of their lords. Sometimes also, seignorial oppression is said to have driven peasants to desert their masters' estates. They certainly found a better return for their labour in the colonial east: personal freedom, secure and hereditary leasehold tenures at moderate rents, and, in many places, quittance from services and the jurisdiction of the seignorial advocate.

The colonists brought with them a disciplined routine of husbandry, an efficient plow, and orderly methods in siting and laying out their villages. Very soon, even the Slavic rulers of Bohemia (now in the Czech Republic) and Silesia (now in Poland) were competing for immigrants. First and foremost, however, the princes of the Saxon and Thuringian marches sought to attract settlers for the lands that they had conquered and the towns that they had founded to open up communications and trade routes. The older regions of the Reich, moreover, had not only peasants but also men of the knightly class to spare—soldiers who needed fiefs and lordships to uphold their rank. Both could be gained beyond the Elbe under the leadership of successful princes. The Germanized east thus became the home of fair-sized principalities in the 13th century, while all along the Rhine River valley the rights of government were scattered over smaller and less compact territories. The Ascanian dynasty, for instance, which under Albert I (Albert the Bear) began to advance into Brandenburg, by 1250 not only ruled over a broad belt of land up to the Oder River but, having already established its control on the Oder's eastern banks, was ready for further advances. Farther south the Wettin margraves of Meissen busied themselves with settlements and town foundations in Lusatia.

For a time Henry the Lion, as duke of Saxony (1142–80), overshadowed all these rising powers, and the Welf profited as much by the ruthless use of his resources against weaker competitors as by his own efforts in Mecklenburg. As his was the only protection worth having in northeastern Germany, the newly established Baltic bishoprics were at his mercy, and he alone could attract the traders of Gotland to frequent the young port town of Lübeck, which he extorted from one of his vassals in 1158.

The Reich, too, possessed demesnes in the east, notably the Egerland, Vogtland, and Pleissnerland in the Thuringian march. The Hohenstaufen kings therefore took some part in opening up these regions. They, too, founded towns and monasteries on their thickly wooded lands and established their ministeriales as burgraves and advocates over them. But in this, as in many other things, they only competed with the princes. They did not and could not control the eastward movement as a whole.

HOHENSTAUFEN POLICY IN ITALY

In the other great field of German expansion in the 12th century—Lombardy and central Italy—the emperors and their military following alone counted. Indeed, from the very start of his reign, Frederick Barbarossa sought to recover and exploit regalian and imperial rights over the growing Lombard city communes and the rest of Italy. The connection between the

German crown, the empire, and dominion over Italy has sometimes been regarded as a disaster for Germany and the ever-increasing concern of the Hohenstaufen dynasty with the south as its most tragic phase. Although Frederick's policy was opportunistic, it was motivated by political necessity and personal inclination. Having bought off the Welfs, reconciled other great families with yet more concessions, and lastly endowed his own cousin, Conrad III's son Frederick, with Hohenstaufen demesnes in Swabia, he had to try to mobilize their goodwill toward the empire while it lasted. He now aimed to set up a regime of imperial officials and captains who were to exact dues and to control jurisdiction that the communes had usurped from the failing grasp of their bishops. In 1158, as part of this plan, Frederick made his second Italian expedition and conquered Milan, the preeminent city in Lombardy. This was followed by an assembly and the publication of the Roncaglia decrees, which defined royal rights and attempted to establish Frederick's authority in Italy.

For the Hohenstaufen ministeriales the rule of their masters in northern and central Italy provided a career. Because they could be deployed continuously, they became the backbone of the imperial occupation. A handful of minor dynasts also served Frederick for many years in the powerful and profitable commands that he established. The German bishops and certain abbots still had to supply men and money, and some of them threw themselves wholeheartedly into the war:

for instance, Rainald of Dassel and Philip of Heinsberg, archbishops of Cologne from 1159 to 1167 and from 1167 to 1191, respectively, as archchancellors for Italy, had a vested interest in it. The support of the lay princes, conversely, was fitful and sporadic. Even at critical moments they could not be counted on, unless they individually agreed to serve or to send their much-needed contingents for a season. The refusal of the greatest of them, Henry the Lion, in 1176 brought about the emperor's defeat at the Battle of Legnano and spoiled many years' efforts in Lombardy.

THE FALL OF HENRY THE LION

Forced to retreat before the papacy and the Lombard League after the Battle of Legnano, Frederick cooled toward his Welf cousin, whom he could justly blame for some of his setbacks. Hitherto, the enemies of Henry—the princes, bishops, and magnates of Saxony—had been unable to gain a hearing against him at the emperor's court days. By 1178, however, the emperor was ready to help them. Outlawed (1180), beaten in the field, and deserted by his vassals, Henry had to surrender and go into exile in 1182. His duchies and fiefs were forfeited to the empire.

His fall left a throng of middling princes face to face with an emperor whose prestige, despite reverses, stood high and whose resources had greatly increased since the beginning of his reign. The princes were nonetheless the chief and ultimate beneficiaries of the events of 1180. The final judgment by which Henry the Lion lost his honours was not founded on tribal law but on feudal law. The princes who condemned him regarded themselves as the first feudatories of the empire, and they decided on the redistribution of his possessions among themselves. During the 12th century the tribal duchies of the Ottonian period finally disintegrated. Within their ancient boundaries not only bishops but also lay lords succeeded in eluding the authority of the dukes. In their large immunities, bishops and nonducal nobles themselves wielded ducal powers. To enforce the imperial peace laws became both their ambition and their justification. Everywhere the greater lay dynasties and even some bishops tried to acquire a ducal or an equivalent title that would enable them to consolidate their scattered jurisdictions and, if possible, to force lesser free lords to attend their pleas.

These highest magnates had interests in common, and they closed their ranks not only against threats from above but also against fellow nobles who had been less successful in amassing wealth, counties, and advocacies and who did not possess the superior jurisdiction of a duke, a margrave, a count palatine, or a landgrave. They and they alone were now called princes of the empire. To lend a certain cohesion to their varied rights, they were willing to surrender their house lands to the empire and receive them back again as a princely fief. For the emperor it was theoretically an advantage that men so powerful in their own right should owe their chief dignity and most valued privileges to his grant. It opened the possibility of escheats (reversions to the property of the emperor), for in feudal law the rules of inheritance were stricter than in folk right. In Germany, however, the political misfortunes of rulers succeeded, by and large, in ensuring that ancient caste feeling and notions of inalienable right conquered the principles of feudal law. By 1216 it was established that the emperor could neither abolish principalities nor create princes at random.

The "heirs" of Henry the Lion had to fight a ceaseless battle to establish and maintain themselves. In Bavaria the Wittelsbachs had received the vacant duchy, but they were not recognized as superiors by the dukes of Styria or by the dukes of Andechs-Meran. In Saxony the archbishop of Cologne was enfeoffed with Henry the Lion's ducal office and with all his rights in Westphalia, while an Ascanian prince, Bernard of Anhalt, received the eastern half of Henry's duchy. Neither Bernard nor the archbishop, however, could make much out of their dukedoms, except in the regions where they already had lands and local jurisdictions. All over the empire these and regalian rights, such as mints, fairs, tolls, and the right of granting safe-conducts, were the substance of princely power. To possess them as widely as possible became the first goal of the abler bishops and lay lords.

HOHENSTAUFEN COOPERATION AND CONFLICT WITH THE PAPACY, 1152–1215

Frederick's interest in Italy stemmed not only from his difficulties in Germany but also from his desire to obtain imperial coronation at the hands of the pope, who alone could bestow this dignity. Frederick enjoyed good relations with the papacy early in his reign, and in 1153 he and Pope Eugenius III signed a treaty acknowledging each other's rights, though the pontiff died before he could crown Frederick emperor. That task fell to Adrian IV in 1155, whom Frederick had restored to the papal throne after suppressing the revolt of Arnold of Brescia and the people of Rome. Good relations would not last between the two, however. Neither side upheld the terms of the treaty of 1153, and in 1157 open conflict erupted in the so-called incident at Besançon, wherein Adrian declared that Frederick had received the empire as a beneficium, or fief, from the pope, provoking the emperor and his advisers. Adrian apologized for the use of the term, explaining it meant "favour," but only after relations between the emperor and pope had become embittered. The incident at Besançon was the first of a series of controversies between the papacy and Frederick and the Hohenstaufen line.

The attempt to establish a direct imperial regime in Italy in 1159 antagonized the papacy once again and led to a new struggle with Rome, the ally of the Lombard communes. Political and territorial rather than ecclesiastical interests were at stake; but the popes could only fight as heads of the universal church, defending its liberty against a race of persecutors, and they had to employ their characteristic weapons—excommunication, propaganda, and intrigue. Nonetheless, the German bishops stood by Frederick and, for the most part, followed him in maintaining a prolonged schism against Pope Alexander III. Unsuccessful in Lombardy, the Hohenstaufen shifted the centre of their ambitions after 1177 to Tuscany, Spoleto, and the Romagna. This redoubled the fears and the resentment of the popes, particularly after Frederick's death while Crusading in 1189, when his son and chosen successor, Henry VI (reigned 1190–97), became the legitimate claimant to the Sicilian kingdom through his wife Constance, the sole surviving heiress.

With their backs to the wall, the popes had to make what use they could out of any opposition to the Hohenstaufen. Their chance came in 1197 when Henry VI died prematurely, leaving a three-year-old son, Frederick, to succeed him. To escape the chaos of a minority regime, the bulk of the German princes and bishops in 1198 elected the boy's uncle Philip of Swabia; but an opposition faction in the lower Rhenish region, led by the archbishop of Cologne and financed by Richard I of England, raised an antiking in Otto IV, a younger son of Henry the Lion. Concerned with preserving traditional papal rights regarding the imperial succession and territorial holdings in Italy as well as with the interests of his ward, Frederick, Pope Innocent III involved himself in the electoral dispute. Territorial interests in the Romagna tempted the papacy to exploit the weaknesses of the empire's constitution, the uncertainties of electoral custom, and the lack of strict legal norms in Germany. During the war for the crown, much hard-won demesne and useful rights over the church had to be sacrificed by the rivals to bribe their supporters.

FREDERICK II AND THE PRINCES

Henry's son Frederick II entered Germany in 1212 to advance his claim to Otto IV's throne and secured the crown in 1215. Despite promises to divide his inheritance, he kept the kingdom of Sicily and the empire together, and thus he also became locked in the inevitable life-and-death struggle with the papacy. The Hohenstaufen demesne in Swabia, Franconia, and Alsace and on the middle Rhine was still very considerable, and Frederick even recovered certain fiefs and advocacies that had been lost during the earlier civil wars. Their administration was improved, and they provided valuable forces for his Italian wars. The great peace legislation of 1235, moreover, showed that the emperor had not become a mere competitor in the race for territorial gain. But, except for brief intervals, the princes and bishops were left free to fight for the future of their lands against one another and against the intractable lesser lords who refused to accept

their domination. The charters that Frederick had to grant to the ecclesiastical princes (the so-called Confoederatio cum Principibus Ecclesiasticis, 1220) and later to all territorial lords (Constitutio, or Statutum in Favorem Principum, 1232) gave them written guarantees against the activities of royal demesne officials and limited the development of imperial towns at the expense of episcopal territories. But the charters were not always observed, and until 1250 the crown remained formidable in southern Germany, despite the antikings Henry Raspe and William of Holland, whose election by the Rhenish archbishops in Germany in 1246 and 1247, respectively, was engineered by the papacy.

THE EMPIRE AFTER THE HOHENSTAUFEN CATASTROPHE

Frederick II died in 1250, in the midst of his struggle against Pope Innocent IV. His son Conrad IV left the north the next year to fight for his father's Italian possessions. William of Holland, antiking from 1247 to 1256, was thus without a rival in an indifferent Germany that had lost interest in its rulers. The bishops' cities and the towns, many of them founded on royal demesne, could not be subjugated. Their economic power challenged the age-old aristocratic order in German society, and, deprived of royal protection, they banded together to defend their autonomy. Within the nobility each rank tended to acquire some of the personal rights of its betters. The Hohenstaufen breakdown after 1250 left a gap in Swabia that no rising territorial power was able to fill. Countless petty lords and imperial ministeriales of the southwest succeeded in holding their seigniories as immediate vassals of the empire. Their independent territories often survived for centuries.

The ministeriales elsewhere, too, ceased to be the dependable servants that they once had been. Many free nobles voluntarily joined their ranks, and the knights thus assimilated the rights of the free aristocracy. They became the governing class of the territorial principalities, the standing councillors of their masters, whose household offices and local justice they monopolized and held in fee for many generations. Without the consent of this territorial nobility, the princes could neither tax nor legislate. Even the less important ministeriales, who only administered manors for their lords, became entrenched as hereditary bailiffs, keeping surplus produce for themselves and usurping seignorial dues, so that it paid the owners to commute the labour services of their villeins into money rents and to lease out those portions of the demesne that the unfree peasants had cultivated for them. Even then, however, the hereditary officials could not be easily dislodged. Finally, the ambitions of the princes themselves did not aim above the patrimonial policies of the past. They were acquisitive and attempted to build up their territories by usurpation, inheritance, marriage treaties, and escheats. They also tried, where possible, to administer their lands with officials whom they could depose at will. Yet they did so not to found sovereign states but chiefly to provide for their families. Again and again, they divided their dominions among sons, who, in turn, founded cadet lines and set them up on a fraction of the principality.

By 1250 there was thus no really effective central authority left in Germany. The prince-bishoprics had become fiercely contested prizes between neighbouring dynasties, themselves often vassals of the bishopric. But constant feuds, disorder, and insecurity did not, by any means, frustrate the immense energies of the Germans in the 13th century. Eastward expansion continued under the leadership of the princes and, above all, of the Knights of the Teutonic Order. Their advance into Prussia went hand in hand with the opening up of the Baltic by the merchants of Lübeck. It is possible that three centuries of complete security from foreign invasion made it unnecessary for the German aristocracy to learn the virtues of political self-discipline and subordination. Still, it would be a great mistake to judge Hohenstaufen Germany solely by its failure to achieve political and administrative unity.

CHAPTER 7

GERMANY FROM 1250 TO 1493

T he death of Frederick II in 1250 and of his son Conrad IV in 1254 heralded the end of Hohenstaufen power in Germany and in the conjoint kingdoms of Naples and Sicily. The rise of the houses of Habsburg and Luxembourg presaged the assumption of authority by regional princes as the German monarchy entered a period of decline.

THE EXTINCTION OF THE HOHENSTAUFEN DYNASTY

Conrad's infant son Conradin, heir to Naples and Sicily, remained in Germany under the guardianship of his Bavarian mother. His uncle Manfred seized the reins of government in both Italian kingdoms and in 1258 formally supplanted Conradin by engineering his own coronation in Palermo. Manfred's defiance of papal claims to suzerainty over the kingdoms impelled the French-born Pope Urban IV to grant them to Charles of Anjou, brother of Louis IX of France. Papal taxation of the French clergy and loans from Florentine bankers enabled Charles to raise a large mercenary army for an expedition to Italy. Manfred, deserted by his barons, was defeated and slain near Benevento in 1266. Conradin then rallied his German supporters and led them across the Alps. But Conradin's financial resources were inadequate; unpaid troops deserted, and his depleted following was routed by Charles near Tagliacozzo (1268). Conradin was captured as he fled toward Rome, convicted of lèse-majesté (a form of treason), and beheaded in the public square at Naples.

THE GREAT INTERREGNUM

In Germany the death of Frederick II ushered in the Great Interregnum (1250–73), a period of internal confusion and political disorder. The antikings Henry Raspe (landgrave of Thuringia, 1246–47) and William of Holland (ruled 1247–56) were elected by the leading ecclesiastical princes at the behest of the papacy. William's title was recognized initially only in the lower Rhineland, but his marriage to Elizabeth of Brunswick in 1252 ensured his acceptance by the interrelated princely dynasties of northern Germany. The death of the Hohenstaufen Conrad IV left William without a rival in Germany. His growing strength and independence enabled him to escape from the tutelage of his ecclesiastical electors and to devote himself to purely dynastic policies. He pursued his feud with Margaret, countess of Flanders, over their conflicting territorial claims in Zeeland at the mouth of the Rhine. He renewed the attempts of his dynasty to obtain complete mastery of the Zuider Zee by thrusting eastward into Friesland; he died at the hands of the Frisians in 1256.

Pope Alexander IV forbade the election of a Hohenstaufen but interfered no further with the succession. Hence the initiative was taken by a small group of influential German princes, lay and ecclesiastical, acting out of self-interest. None desired the election of a ruler powerful enough to threaten their growing independence as territorial princes; nor did they single out a German candidate, who might prove to be as uncontrollable as William. Archbishop Conrad of Cologne approached Richard, earl of Cornwall, brother of Henry III of England. Richard's gifts and assurances of future favour bought him the votes of the archbishops of Cologne and Mainz, the count palatine of the Rhine, and Otakar II of Bohemia. He was formally elected in 1257 and crowned king at Aachen (Aix-la-Chapelle). Three months after Richard's election, Alfonso X of Castile, who aspired to the empire in order to strengthen his foothold in Italy, was chosen in similar fashion by the archbishop of Trier, the duke of Saxony, the margrave of Brandenburg, and the duplicitous Otakar.

The candidates were distracted by the turbulence of the aristocracy in their countries—Richard paid four fleeting visits to Germany; Alfonso failed to appear at all. Each appealed to the papacy for confirmation of his election. Their claims were summarized in Urban IV's bull *Qui coelum* (1263), which assumed that the exclusive right of election lay with the seven leading princes involved in the double election of 1257.

THE RISE OF THE HABSBURGS AND LUXEMBOURGS

When Richard died in 1272, the electoral princes were spurred into action by Pope Gregory X, who desired the election of a German monarch sympathetic toward a Crusade for the recovery of the Holy

Land. The princes sought a candidate who was strong enough to lead, but not so strong as to assert his independence. The tense relationship that existed between the princes and subsequent kings led to an alternating series of dynasties that left the monarchy in a greatly weakened state.

RUDOLF OF HABSBURG

The princes, dreading an overly powerful king, rejected the advances of Philip III of France and Otakar. In 1273 they chose instead Rudolf of Habsburg, a minor count of Swabia who lacked the strength to regain the crown domains the electors had usurped during the Great Interregnum. Papal diplomacy persuaded Alfonso X to abandon his pretensions to the throne; but Otakar denounced the election on the grounds that the duke of Bavaria had voted as lay elector in his stead. Rudolf I allied himself with the Wittelsbach family of Bavaria and with other envious neighbours of Otakar, who was defeated and slain in 1278. The duchies of Austria and Styria, overrun by Otakar during the Interregnum, were declared vacant and conferred jointly on Rudolf's sons Albert and Rudolf in 1282. These acquisitions placed the Habsburgs in the first rank of the German territorial princes and lent impetus to a gradual shift in the political centre of gravity from the Rhineland to eastern and southern Germany. The growing Habsburg power, however, disquieted the electoral princes, who frustrated the king's attempts to secure the election of his elder son Albert in 1287 and of his younger son Rudolf in 1290.

ADOLF OF NASSAU

On the death of Rudolf I in 1291, the electors averted the danger of a hereditary Habsburg monarchy by choosing Count Adolf of Nassau as his successor. Adolf, possessing only a small patrimony to the south of the river Lahn, strengthened himself financially by promising military aid to and receiving subsidies from both sides in the then current Anglo-French war. He took possession of Meissen when the cadet branch of the Wettin dynasty died out, and he used his foreign subsidies to purchase Thuringia in 1295. He was thus able to adopt a more independent attitude toward his electors. On June 23, 1298, five of the electors pronounced Adolf unfit to rule and deposed him; on the following day they elected Albert of Austria in his stead. Albert marched westward from Austria at the head of a large army, and, in a battle at Göllheim, Adolf was slain and his supporters fled.

ALBERT I OF HABSBURG

By restoring the Habsburg Albert I (ruled 1298–1308) to the kingship, the electors placed themselves in jeopardy. The new ruler, backed by the ample resources of his Austrian dominions, was more powerful and unscrupulous than his predecessor. The electors regarded his treaty of friendship with Philip IV of

France (1299) as a move to enlist French support for the election of his son Rudolf as his successor in Germany. In 1300 his attempt to seize Holland and Zeeland as a vacant fief of the empire was rightly interpreted by the electors as an effort to establish Habsburg influence on the lower Rhine. The four prince-electors of the Rhineland (the archbishops of Mainz, Trier, and Cologne and the count palatine) conspired to depose Albert. But Albert wrecked the design by decisive military action in 1301–02, and he sealed his victory over the electors by obtaining confirmation in 1303 of his election from Pope Boniface VIII in return for an unprecedented oath of fealty and obedience to the papacy. Albert subsequently renewed Adolf's claims to Meissen and Thuringia, but his authority there was still disputed when he was assassinated in 1308. Albert had temporarily tamed the electoral princes, placated the papacy, and renounced intervention in Italy; but this policy foundered at his death, and the electors were given a fresh opportunity to reassert their influence over the German monarchy.

HENRY VII OF LUXEMBOURG

The princes, released from Albert's heavy hand, sought a servant, not a master. Archbishop Baldwin of Trier sponsored the candidacy of his brother, Count Henry of Luxembourg, who was elected at Frankfurt am Main in 1308 as Henry VII. The house of Luxembourg (Luxemburg)

was not a major territorial power, and Henry lost no time in exploiting his new status to extend its possessions. Under his direction the Diet of Frankfurt (1310) closed the long-disputed question of the Bohemian succession by awarding the kingdom, with the consent of the Bohemian estates, to Henry's son John. Thus, in common with the Habsburgs, the main weight of Luxembourg interests gravitated eastward. But Henry, unlike his Habsburg predecessors, dreamed of a restoration of the ancient authority of the empire in Italy. His Italian expedition (1310–13) opened brilliantly, and in 1312 he was crowned Holy Roman emperor at Rome. The old fear of German domination, however, stiffened the resistance of the Italian states. Pope Clement V was alarmed by Henry's preparations to invade the kingdom of Naples, a papal fief, and threatened excommunication. A renewed collision of empire and papacy seemed imminent when Henry died in 1313.

THE GROWTH OF TERRITORIALISM UNDER THE PRINCES

The decline of Hohenstaufen influence in Germany, the Great Interregnum, and the rapid alternation of dynasties on the German throne created favourable conditions for the territorial princes, lay and spiritual, to gain power. Frederick II had purchased the support of the princes with lavish grants of crown lands, chiefly

Illustration of Henry VII in the fight between Visconti and Torriani. DEA Picture Library/De Agostini/ Getty Images

in the Rhineland and Thuringia; in 1220 he procured the cooperation of the ecclesiastical princes in the election of his son Henry as king and eventual heir to the empire by renouncing his regalian rights of building castles, issuing coinage, and imposing tolls on merchandise in their territories. Henry himself had extended similar concessions to the lay princes in 1231.

Thereafter the direct action of royal authority was virtually precluded in the princely domains. The princes were at liberty to multiply castles and toll stations, establish mints, exploit mineral deposits, and settle all judicial cases except those transferred on appeal to the court of the emperor. The machinery of administration under the prince and his council (Hofrat) was, nevertheless, still rudimentary. Public taxation was intermittent and restricted to emergency occasions, and it was subject to the consent of the three estates of the principality (clergy, nobles, townspeople), which were consulted separately by the prince. The estates grasped the opportunity to ventilate their grievances and to press their advice upon the prince. The emerging territorial state was thus under the dual government of the prince and the estates, and its development was to be heavily influenced by a shifting balance of power between them.

CONSTITUTIONAL CONFLICTS IN THE 14TH CENTURY

The death of Henry VII led to a disputed election and a civil war in Germany. The electors' impulse to choose another lesser count as king was checked by the houses of Habsburg and Luxembourg, which pressured the prince-electors to choose between their candidates. The pro-Habsburg majority elected Frederick the Handsome, duke of Austria. The minority withdrew their support from Henry VII's son John and transferred it to a more formidable candidate, the Bavarian duke Louis of Wittelsbach, who had recently broken an Austrian invasion of his duchy.

Electoral custom did not yet acknowledge the majority principle. The papacy, which had claimed the right to adjudicate disputed elections since 1201, was vacant. Hence the two claimants settled their differences by the sword. In 1322 Louis defeated and captured his rival at Mühldorf, but his triumph in Germany merely raised the curtain on a long and bitter dispute with the papacy.

Pope John XXII, guided by canon law and precedent, affirmed that Louis might not legally rule until confirmed by the papacy; thus the disputed election of 1314 and the absence of papal approbation invalidated Louis's royal title and his right to govern. Louis contended, however, that election by a majority conferred a legitimate title and administrative power and did not require papal confirmation. His defiance of the pope exposed him to excommunication in 1324 and to the procedures of canon law, whereby he was required to submit entirely to the papal terms before absolution could be granted. Louis warned the electors that their rights were endangered by the subjection of the elections to papal confirmation. Six electors responded in the Declaration of Rhens (1338), proclaiming as an ancient custom of the empire that election by a majority was valid and that the king-elect assumed his administrative power immediately, without the intervention of papal approbation. Under Louis's direction the declaration was repeated at the subsequent Diet of Frankfurt as an imperial law, and offenders against it were declared guilty of lèse-majesté.

John XXII and his successors were unyielding. In 1343 Pope Clement VI made diplomatic overtures to Charles of Luxembourg, heir to the Bohemian throne, with the object of procuring his election to the German kingship in Louis's stead. The electors, led by Baldwin of Luxembourg, the archbishop of Trier, began to desert Louis one by one. The pope thereupon urged a new election. Charles assured the pope secretly that he would await papal confirmation of his forthcoming election before exercising governmental power in the Italian possessions of the empire, but, despite intense pressure by Clement, he would accept no such restriction with regard to Germany. In 1346 only two electors remained faithful to Louis: his son Louis of Brandenburg and his kinsman Rudolf, count palatine of the Rhine. The other five assembled at Rhens on July 11 and elected Charles under the title of Charles IV. The new king was spared a lengthy conflict with his rival, who died of a stroke in 1347. Shortly after his accession to the throne, however, the kingdom faced one of the greatest epidemics of all time, the Black Death (caused by bubonic and pneumonic plague), which killed perhaps one-third of the population, caused a labour shortage, and left the survivors shaken.

CHARLES IV AND THE GOLDEN BULL

Charles IV (ruled 1346–78) readily perceived that disputed elections exploding into civil war had been a standing malady of the German body politic since 1198 and that the stability of the German monarchy depended largely upon the degree of cooperation achieved with the territorial princes, more especially with the prince-electors. In 1355 on his return from his imperial coronation as Holy Roman emperor, he promulgated, with the consent of the German assembly of estates, or diet (1356), a basic constitutional document, known as the Golden Bull. Charles's double objective was to minimize areas of dispute in future elections and to strengthen his ties with the electors. Unanimity among the electoral princes had always been difficult to attain; hence the validity of election by majority vote, a principle already set forth in the Declaration of Rhens, was reaffirmed. The territories of the lay electors were declared indivisible and heritable only by the eldest son. Thus, partitions of land by family agreement and consequent uncertainty concerning the holder of the electoral vote were eliminated. In conformity with ancient custom, the archbishop of Mainz was to convene the electors and to request them to name their favoured candidate. He was to announce his own choice after the other electors had given their vote verbally so that he could cast the deciding vote in the event of a tie. The election was to be held in Frankfurt am Main, the royal coronation in Aachen.

The membership of the electoral body was fixed at the traditional number of seven: the archbishops of Mainz, Cologne, and Trier, the count palatine of the Rhine, the king of Bohemia, the margrave of Brandenburg, and the duke of Saxony. When the throne was vacant, the count palatine would be regent in southern Germany and the duke of Saxony in the north; thus the long-standing papal claim to govern the empire during a vacancy was tacitly rejected. The question of papal confirmation of elections was ignored; neither Charles nor his electors were prepared to yield, but an open affirmation of their position would have been ill received by the papacy, which had played a leading role in Charles's election.

The Golden Bull consolidated and extended the territorial power of the electors. Their right to construct castles, issue coinage, and impose tolls was confirmed. They could judge without appeal. Conspiracy or rebellion against them was deemed high treason. They were to meet the ruler once yearly as supreme advisory council on affairs of state. The formation of city leagues against them was specifically prohibited. On the basis of these enactments, the Golden Bull has been called the Magna Carta of German particularism. The electors in their capacity as territorial lords were its chief beneficiaries; the rest of the princes were envious and strove thenceforth to acquire an equally large measure of territorial sovereignty.

Rudolf IV of Austria ordered his chancery to fabricate a series of imperial charters, including two from Julius Caesar and Nero, as evidence of his virtual independence of the empire. Charles IV submitted them for examination to the Italian humanist Petrarch, who declared the charters spurious. Rudolf took up arms and was bought off by the recognition of his claim to Tirol in 1364.

The election of Charles's son Wenceslas (Wenzel) as king in 1376 (two years before Charles's death) was a striking example of the emperor's skill in securing the cooperation of the electors for his dynastic purposes. The election of an emperor's son as king of the Romans during the father's lifetime had not occurred since 1237; the prince-electors, in their anxiety to prevent any single dynasty from strengthening its grip on the succession, had checked all subsequent attempts. But unprecedented gifts, concessions, and a renewed prohibition of city leagues by Charles overcame the opposition of the electors. Pope Gregory XI had previously announced that the election would be invalid without papal confirmation. Charles, in concert with the electors, speeded the election and subsequent coronation of his son and then submitted an antedated request for confirmation to the pope, who countered these devious tactics by delaying confirmation; it was still under consideration at Gregory's death in 1378. The decline of the papacy during the Great Schism (Western Schism; 1378–1417) precluded the vigorous assertion of its right of confirmation, which became a mere formality and was subsequently tacitly abandoned.

DECLINE OF THE GERMAN MONARCHY

Charles IV's power was based primarily upon the territorial possessions of the house of Luxembourg, which he greatly extended by the purchase of the electorate of Brandenburg (1373). The German

GOLDEN BULL OF EMPEROR CHARLES IV

The Golden Bull, the constitution for the Holy Roman Empire promulgated in 1356 by the emperor Charles IV, was intended to eliminate papal interference in German political affairs and to recognize the importance of the princes, especially the electors, of the empire. Its name, like that of other "golden bulls," derived from its authentication with a golden seal (Latin: *bulla*).

Returning to Germany in July 1355 after his coronation as emperor in Rome, Charles IV summoned the princes to deliberations at Nürnberg, which resulted in the promulgation of the first 23 chapters of the Golden Bull on January 10, 1356; the concluding 8 chapters were added after further negotiation with the princes in Metz on December 25, 1356. The purpose was to place the election of the German ruler firmly in the hands of the seven electors and to ensure that the candidate elected by the majority should succeed without dispute. That the electoral college consisted of three ecclesiastical and four lay princes had been established since 1273, but it was not always clear who these seven were. Therefore, the Saxon vote was now attached to the Wittenberg (not the Lauenburg) branch of the Saxon dynasty; the vote was given to the count Palatine (not to the duke of Bavaria); and the special position of Bohemia, of which Charles himself was king, was expressly recognized. In addition Charles established succession by primogeniture, attached the electoral vote to the possession of certain lands, and decreed that these territories should never be divided. The candidate elected by the majority was regarded as unanimously elected and entitled to exercise his royal rights immediately. Thus the pope's claim to examine rival candidates and to approve the election was ignored. Also, by instituting the duke of Saxony and the count Palatine as regents during the vacancy, the Golden Bull excluded the pope's claim to act as vicar.

These results were achieved only by concessions to the electoral princes, who were given sovereign rights, including tallage and coinage, in their principalities. Appeals by their subjects were severely curtailed; conspiracies against them incurred the penalties of treason. Moreover, the efforts of cities to ensure autonomous development were repressed, with serious and long-lasting consequences for the future of the German middle classes. In theory, these privileges were confined to the seven electors; in practice, all the princes quickly adopted them.

monarchy was a source of dignity and influence, but in terms of land and revenue it was outweighed by Charles's hereditary domains in the east and northeast. The Golden Bull, replete with privileges to the electors, attacked none of the fundamental problems of the monarchy: dwindling crown lands, slender revenues, and the lack of an army and of an expert bureaucracy.

The financial problem was acute and long-standing. The succession of disputed elections between 1198 and 1257 had compelled the various claimants to purchase support by grants of royal land and revenues; the attempt by Rudolf of Habsburg to recover possession of crown lands alienated since 1245 had been opposed by his electors, who were unwilling to set an example by surrendering their own considerable acquisitions. At every election the votes of the princes had been secured by the grant or pledge of royal rights and property; thus, every king began his reign with a financial millstone round his neck and could attain freedom of action only by the possession or acquisition of extensive dynastic territories. The system of pledging crown lands led to the permanent loss of this land and its revenues and to the enrichment of the princes at the expense of the emperor. The imperial cities (Reichsstädte) had been heavily taxed by Rudolf, and, before his acquisition of Austria, they had furnished the bulk of his revenue. His less provident successors had pledged them in a few cases to the local territorial princes and had thus lost

the right of taxation. Charles IV carefully cultivated his dynastic revenues from Bohemia, but he lavishly expended crown assets in Germany to expand his family possessions. His financial exploitation of the cities for purely dynastic purposes naturally stiffened their resistance to taxation. By 1400 the annual revenues from all the German crown possessions averaged only 30,000 florins.

The enforcement of the public peace, a taproot of royal power in other countries, had long since slipped from the hands of the German monarchs. The German monarchy possessed no executive officials comparable to the English sheriff or justice of the peace, and it was diverted from its guardianship of law and order by recurrent conflicts with the papacy and by its absorption in purely dynastic matters. Consequently, the proclamation and enforcement of the peace fell into the hands of regional associations of cities and of the individual territorial princes. Thus the monarchy was prevented from using its function as defender of the public peace as an entering wedge to invade the jurisdiction of the municipalities and the territorial lords.

In sum, the German rulers were being gradually deprived of their triple role as feudal suzerain, defender of the church, and keeper of the peace. The sweeping privileges granted to the princes in 1220 and 1231 had undermined the monarch's position as feudal suzerain. The rulers' bitter struggles with the papacy cast doubt on their credibility as protectors of the church. They allowed their powers as guardians of the public peace to slip into the hands of others.

THE CONTINUED ASCENDANCY OF THE PRINCES

By Charles IV's death in 1378, the division of Germany into numerous loosely defined territorial principalities had reached an advanced stage.

SOUTHERN GERMANY

In southern Germany the dissolution of the Hohenstaufen duchy of Swabia gave territorial predominance to the Habsburgs, whose original possessions were scattered across Alsace, Breisgau, the Vorarlberg, and Tirol. Rudolf's acquisition of the provinces of Austria and Styria in 1282 had more than doubled the Habsburg patrimony and established its centre of gravity in southeastern Germany. The Habsburg's rivals and neighbours to the north, the counts of Württemberg, had combined with the Swabian nobles to foil the attempt of Rudolf to revive the defunct duchy of Swabia for one of his sons. (The counts, insatiably acquisitive and the inveterate enemies of the cities of the region, were finally raised to ducal status in 1495.) The margraves of Baden were chiefly preoccupied with the southward expansion of their territory on the upper Rhine at the expense of the independent small nobles and cities of Swabia.

These three large entities contained lesser lordships, which were in constant danger of absorption by marriage, purchase, or feud. Bavaria, granted to the house of Wittelsbach as a duchy in 1180, was strengthened by the acquisition of the Palatinate in 1214; but subsequent testamentary partition restricted this important gain to the Upper Palatinate.

CENTRAL GERMANY

In central Germany the margraves of Meissen of the Wettin dynasty thrust steadily eastward and received the electorate of Saxony in 1423, when the Ascanian line of electors died out; in the west they obtained Thuringia (1263) and clung to it tenaciously despite repeated royal attempts to oust them by claiming it as a vacant fief. The landgraves of Hesse, though surrounded by powerful neighbours, contrived to make modest territorial gains at the expense of the Wettin dynasty and the archbishops of Mainz. East and south of Hesse, the Rhine-Main region was a land of great ecclesiastical princes: the archbishops of Mainz, Trier, and Cologne; the bishops of Speyer, Worms, Würzburg, and Bamberg; and the wealthy abbots of Fulda and Lorsch. It abounded in counts of the second rank, dominated by a great secular prince, the count palatine of the Rhine. The area contained four electorates and was therefore of crucial political importance.

NORTHERN GERMANY

In northern Germany the dukes of Brunswick dissipated their strength by frequent divisions of their territory among heirs. Farther east the powerful duchy of Saxony was also split by partition between the Wittenberg and Lauenburg branches; the Wittenberg line was formally granted an electoral vote by the Golden Bull of 1356. The strength of the duchy lay in the military and commercial qualities of its predominantly free population. But the vigour of its eastward expansion into the Slav lands beyond the Elbe tended to diminish its involvement in the internal politics of the Reich. As in central Germany, large areas of northern Germany were held by ecclesiastical princes, including the archbishops of Bremen and Magdeburg and the bishops of Utrecht, Münster, and Osnabrück. During the 13th and 14th centuries the major trading cities of the north, including Münster, Bremen, Hamburg, and Lübeck, joined together to form the powerful Hanseatic League, which was a powerful economic and political force not only in northern Germany but in most of the lands surrounding the North and Baltic seas.

EASTERN GERMANY

In eastern Germany the duchy of Mecklenburg, Germanized by a steady stream of immigrants, was drawn deeply into Scandinavian affairs and in 1363 provided Sweden with a new royal dynasty in the person of Albert of Mecklenburg. The electorate of Brandenburg, purchased by Charles IV and bequeathed to his second son, Sigismund, was dominated by a disorderly and rapacious nobility. Sigismund granted this dubious asset in 1415 to his faithful ally Frederick, burgrave of Nürnberg. The kingdom of Bohemia remained the durable territorial core of the Luxembourg dominions, and its silver mines at Kuttenberg (now Kutná Hora, in the Czech Republic), under German supervision, vastly increased crown revenues. The Czech population increasingly resented the economic and cultural influence of the German minority, and this created antagonisms profoundly disturbing to the monarchy.

CONTINUED DISPERSEMENT OF TERRITORY

Inside the various territories the consolidation of princely authority was far from complete. The principalities were often ragged in outline and territorially dispersed because of the accidents of inheritance, grant, partition, and conquest. Everywhere lesser nobles disputed the power of the prince and formed associations in defense of their rights and fiefs. In the ecclesiastical princedoms the ascendancy of an archbishop or a bishop was contested by the cathedral chapter, which had become a preserve of the nobility. The self-governing cities fought to protect their chartered liberties and drew together in formidable leagues to resist princely encroachment. Thus the princes, in trying to enforce their authority, tended to consolidate the opposition and to excite potential or open hostility.

In this crucial struggle the great secular potentates undermined their own strength by persisting in the Germanic custom of dividing their territory among their sons instead of transmitting it intact to the eldest. By 1378 the Bavarian lands of the house of Wittelsbach were shared between three grandsons of Louis IV. In 1379 the wide possessions of the Habsburgs were partitioned by family agreement between Albert III and his younger brother Leopold.

The ecclesiastical princes, vowed to celibacy and elected by their cathedral chapters, could not hand on their lands to descendants. Still, their policies and aspirations were not much different from those of the secular princes, and most of them managed to install their relatives in rich canonries and prebends.

INTERNAL STRIFE AMONG CITIES AND PRINCES

The electors had voted for Wenceslas reluctantly during Charles IV's reign, fearful that the monarchy might become a perquisite of the house of Luxembourg. Most of the other princes shared their concern over the continued ascendancy of the dynasty.

WENCESLAS

Wenceslas (ruled 1378–1400) inherited a variety of problems, which grew after his father's statesmanlike hand had been removed. Wenceslas's habitual indolence and drunkenness, which increased as he grew older, excited the indignation of his critics. His prolonged periods of residence in Bohemia betrayed his lack of interest in German affairs and allowed the continuous friction between princes, cities, and nobility to develop into open warfare.

The collision of princes and cities was prompted by vital issues of long standing. The flight of the rural population from servile tenures on the land to the free air of the cities aggravated the population losses from the Black Death and further reduced the labour force and the revenues of territorial lords. Others who stayed on the land accepted the protection and jurisdiction of the neighbouring city as "external" citizens (Ausbürger, or Pfahlbürger) and thus withdrew themselves and their land from seignorial control. Only the most powerful cities (e.g., Nürnberg, Rothenburg) were able to extend their extramural territory to a substantial degree by force, but all strove to expand the area of their jurisdiction at the expense of local lords, partly to prevent village industries from competing with the city guilds.

A second major issue was the insistence of territorial lords on imposing tolls on city merchandise in transit through their possessions. In theory, tolls on road and river traffic were exacted in return for the protection of merchants and their goods, but the multiplication of toll stations hampered trade and provoked innumerable disputes, which often culminated in the seizure of merchants and merchandise by exigent lords.

The third and immediate cause of the crisis lay in the financial policy of Wenceslas himself. His Bohemian revenues, though large, were strained by the great sums payable to the electors in return for his elevation to the kingship. Hence he attempted to tap the resources of the imperial cities by demanding heavy taxes, and he threatened to mortgage recalcitrant cities to the neighbouring princes, their chief enemies.

On July 4, 1376, an alliance of 14 imperial cities of Swabia was formed under the leadership of Ulm and Constance for mutual protection against unjust taxes and seizure from the empire. The Swabian League counted 40 members by 1385 and was linked with similar coalitions in Alsace, the Rhineland, and Saxony. Wenceslas's initial hostility to the league faded as its membership increased, and in 1387 he gave it his verbal and unofficial recognition. He feared offending the territorial princes by extending full recognition; further, a clause of the Golden Bull had declared all city leagues to be illegal. Thus he temporized and awaited the outcome of the approaching trial of strength between cities and princes. On August 28, 1388, the princes of Swabia and Franconia routed the largely mercenary forces of the Swabian League at Döffingen, near Stuttgart. The stipendiaries of the Rhenish League were put to flight by the count palatine Rupert II near Worms on November 6.

The cities triumphantly withstood the ensuing siege operations, but their economy was injured by the forays, ambuscades, and blockades instituted by the princes. The protracted campaigns also exhausted the financial resources of the princes. When Wenceslas intervened in 1389, both parties were ready for peace. At the Diet of Eger (May 2) he ordered them to desist and declared the city leagues to be dissolved. The contestants complied. The princes were satisfied with the prospective disbandment of the cities, and the cities feared the consequences of further resistance, but neither side relished Wenceslas's opportunism. The princes disliked his political flirtation with the cities, and the cities resented his final championship of the cause of the princes.

Wenceslas's early gestures of support for the cities rankled the electors, who in 1384 and 1387 discussed the advisability of replacing him with an imperial vicar or regent. Wenceslas, however, learned of the plan and conveyed his opposition, while the electors were unable to unite on their choice of a regent. Some electors turned to a more drastic solution—Wenceslas's deposition. In 1394 Rupert II and Archbishop Frederick of Cologne considered the election of Richard II of England but failed to win the support of their electoral colleagues. In the following year, however, Wenceslas's elevation of Gian Galeazzo Visconti, imperial vicar of Milan, to the status of duke was assailed as a dismemberment of the empire and enabled the electors to act as the indignant defenders of the integrity of the Reich against a wasteful and profligate king. Wenceslas attempted to conciliate the princes by appointing his younger brother Sigismund as German regent in 1396. But the Milanese issue enabled Rupert and Frederick to enlist the support of the archbishops of Mainz and Trier for their proposed deposition of Wenceslas. The death of Rupert in 1398 occasioned some delay, but at length the electors compiled a lengthy series of charges against the king, and in September 1399 they openly proclaimed their intention of deposing him.

At this critical stage further proceedings were temporarily checked by serious differences concerning the choice of Wenceslas's successor. The favoured candidate of the Rhenish electors was the count palatine, Rupert III, who was himself an elector. However, another elector, Duke Rudolf of Saxony, and a powerful group of northern German princes contended that the electors could not raise one of their own members to the kingship. The Golden Bull had declared otherwise, but Rudolf held his ground and declined to participate in the subsequent proceedings. On June 4, 1400, the four Rhenish electors invited Wenceslas to Oberlahnstein to consider measures for the reform of the empire and threatened to release themselves from their oath of allegiance if he failed to appear. The king's efforts to rally support for his cause were utterly fruitless, and he decided to stay in Bohemia. On August 20 Archbishop John of Mainz, on behalf of the four electors, publicly proclaimed the deposition of Wenceslas as an unfit and useless king and freed his German subjects from their allegiance to him. On the following day the three archbishops elected Rupert in Wenceslas's stead. Rupert's consent to his election was presumed to furnish the necessary majority required by the Golden Bull.

RUPERT

Rupert (ruled 1400–10) lacked the skill and resources necessary to revive the drooping power of the German monarchy. His title was not beyond dispute while Wenceslas lived, and the territorial princes and cities were therefore slow to acknowledge him. Pope Boniface IX, maintaining that only a pope might legally depose a German monarch, withheld his approbation of Rupert. An expedition against Wenceslas in 1401 failed before the walls of Prague. Rupert then embarked upon an Italian expedition (1401–02), hoping to obtain the imperial crown from the pope and thus dispel the cloud of uncertainty that hung over his title. The enterprise was crippled by lack of financial means, Boniface's conditions were exorbitant, and Rupert returned to Germany without the coveted imperial coronation. Fortunately, he had little to fear from Wenceslas, who was fully occupied in protecting his Bohemian throne from the machinations of his ambitious younger brother Sigismund. Far more dangerous was the degeneration of Rupert's relations with the Rhenish electors. In 1405 he offended Archbishop John of Mainz by refusing him military aid in his war against Hesse and Brunswick. Consequently the archbishop united all the enemies of Hesse and Brunswick in the League of Marbach, which included 18 imperial cities. Rupert contended that coalitions of cities were prohibited by the Golden Bull, and he denounced the league as illegal. The dispute was arrested by the mediation of the archbishop of Cologne, but the memory rankled. Rupert's prospects darkened still further in 1408, when he lent his support to Pope Gregory XII against the cardinals who wished to summon a general council to end the Great Schism in the church. The archbishops of Mainz and Cologne and the vast majority of the German prelates favoured the conciliar solution and strongly approved the policy of the cardinals. Wenceslas shrewdly followed suit and in return received assurances from the cardinals that the future general council would recognize him as German king. The powerful proconciliar party in the German church proceeded to agitate openly for the restoration of Wenceslas to the throne. The threat of civil war, however, was averted by Rupert's death on May 18, 1410.

SIGISMUND

On the death of Rupert, the movement for the reinstatement of Wenceslas immediately lost headway. The Rhenish electors, having deposed Wenceslas 10 years previously on grounds of his unfitness, could not reelect him without admitting their inconsistency. Nonetheless, the house of Luxembourg was powerful and would assuredly throw its full weight against any non-Luxembourg candidate to the German throne. The four electors agreed on the expediency of selecting Rupert's successor from the Luxembourg dynasty but disagreed on the choice of candidate. The count palatine and the archbishop of Trier elected Wenceslas's brilliant but unreliable brother, Sigismund, at Frankfurt on September 20, 1410. Eleven days later, the archbishops of Cologne and Mainz elected Wenceslas's turbulent and treacherous cousin, Jobst of Moravia. Jobst died in the next year, and Wenceslas agreed to accept Sigismund on condition that he himself retained the title of German king. But Sigismund ignored the reservation and assumed the disputed title. Wenceslas's protests were greeted with indifference in Germany and quickly died away. A second election of Sigismund at Frankfurt (July 21, 1411) gave him an ample majority and removed all doubt concerning the validity of the previous election.

Sigismund was energetic, versatile, and intelligent; but long experience never blunted his rashness in rushing into new projects, and his financial incapacity never ceased to astonish his contemporaries. His pursuit of personal power and dynastic possessions was unceasing and unscrupulous. His kingdom of Hungary and his later acquisition, Bohemia, were his primary concerns, and the interests in Germany were constantly set aside in their favour. The disastrous reigns of his predecessors, Wenceslas and Rupert, had emphasized Germany's basic problems: the weakness of the monarchy, the friction between princes and cities, and the unchecked growth of lawlessness and disorder. During his long reign (1410–37) Sigismund appeared less and less frequently in Germany and did little to correct these evils.

THE HUSSITE CONTROVERSY

Sigismund's prolonged absences were caused in great part by the explosive Hussite controversy in Bohemia. The Czech church in Bohemia had long retained a marked individuality and much autonomy in its liturgy. This independent temper in ecclesiastical affairs was being slowly fused in the late 14th century with a rising sentiment of nationality among the Czechs. The upsurge of feeling took the negative form of a growing resentment of the German minority, which dominated the towns by virtue of its economic power and cultural influence. The luxury and immorality of the Bohemian clergy were castigated by a series of religious reformers such as Conrad of Waldhauser, Thomas of Štítný, John Milíč of Kroměříž (Kremsier), and Matthew of Janov. The teachings of Conrad and Milíč had a strongly puritanical tinge; in opposition to the wealthy sacramental

church with its external means of grace, they held up the ideal of the primitive church in a condition of apostolic poverty and the exclusive authority of the Bible as the foundation stone of faith and belief. These movements met and intermingled in the person of Jan Hus.

JAN HUS

A graduate in divinity of the University of Prague, Hus was appointed incumbent of the Bethlehem Chapel in Prague in 1402 and immediately attracted wide attention with his sermons, which were delivered in Czech in accordance with the foundation charter of the chapel. In 1403 he strongly defended a number of extracts from the religious writings of the Englishman John Wycliffe calling for church reform. Czech opinion in the university solidly supported Hus, but the more numerous German masters carried the day, and the teaching of the controversial extracts was forbidden. Similarly, when Pope Gregory XII's cardinals rebelled against the pope and demanded a general council to terminate the schism in the papacy in 1408, the Czech members of the university aligned themselves with the cardinals, while the Germans stood with the pope. On matters of general policy, the masters of the university voted by "nations," of which there were four: Bohemian, Bavarian, Saxon, and Polish, the last consisting in fact largely of Germans. Thus the Germans controlled three votes, the Czechs only one. When King Wenceslas reversed the proportion by decree, the German masters and students seceded to found their own university at Leipzig, and the mutual enmity deepened.

In 1410 Hus was excommunicated by Archbishop Zbyněk of Prague but refused to appear at the papal court for judgment and continued to preach. Two years later he protested against the sale of indulgences and was placed under papal sentence of excommunication. The city of Prague was subjected to a papal interdict. Hus left the capital at Wenceslas's request but preached throughout the land and vastly enlarged his following. From the lower Czech clergy who popularized Hus's doctrines, the masses learned that the German minority were intruders and foes of Bohemia and of the true religion. Lesser nobles who had lost their lands by mortgage or purchase to the prosperous German burghers of the cities were readily converted. The more self-interested members of the upper nobility were attracted by Hus's proposed reduction of the Czech church to apostolic poverty, which would bring the rich territorial possessions of the higher clergy within their grasp.

The rising ferment in Bohemia disquieted the heir apparent, Sigismund, and he intervened with the suggestion that Hus should expound and justify his opinions to the Council of Constance (1414–18), recently convened to heal the schism in the papacy. Hus accepted, and Sigismund furnished him with a comprehensive safe-conduct. The conciliar commission that examined Hus focused the debate on two issues: the unauthorized Bohemian practice of extending communion in both kinds (bread and wine) to the laity and the points of agreement between Wycliffe and Hus. Hus declined to retract his Wycliffite opinions until they were refuted by Holy Writ, and thus he defied the authority of the council in matters of doctrine. He was arrested on November 28, 1414, and died at the stake on July 6, 1415. Sigismund's protests against the breach of his safe-conduct were silenced by the argument that excommunicates automatically lost imperial protection.

THE HUSSITE WARS

The death of Hus enshrined him at once as a martyr and a national hero in the memory of his followers among the Czechs. They raised a storm of denunciation against Sigismund and expressed their resentment by widespread attacks on orthodox priests and churches. The Catholics retaliated in kind, and Bohemia was in a state of civil war when the death of Wenceslas (August 16, 1419) brought Sigismund to the tottering throne. The new king's talent for conciliation and compromise was useless in the heated religious atmosphere. Pope Martin V urged him on against the Hussites and promised him imperial coronation as his reward. At his prompting, Sigismund raised a motley host in Germany and launched it into Bohemia under the

The Hussite Wars. © Fine Art Images/SuperStock

banner of a papal Crusade (March 1, 1420). But the invaders were thrown back from the walls of Prague, and on July 7, 1421, Sigismund was declared deposed by the Bohemian assembly of estates. The shock of defeat forced Sigismund to attempt a fuller mobilization of German resources. Under the traditional system, princes and cities had been allowed to fix at their own discretion the quota of men provided by each when a royal campaign was in prospect. Naturally, both estates used their discretionary power to reduce contributions to a minimum. In 1422, however, Sigismund himself fixed the strength of the contingents demanded from the individual princes and cities throughout Germany. The response was disappointing. In 1426 the king raised his requirements, but to no effect. Hence the yearly campaigns against the Hussites were waged largely by mercenary armies. To meet the rising costs, the Diet of Frankfurt was persuaded in 1427 to vote a general tax, the so-called Common Penny. But there was little enthusiasm in Germany for the Crusade; massive evasions of payment occurred, and the strength of local feeling hampered the coercion of defaulters.

In 1429–30 the irrepressible Hussites swept through Saxony, Thuringia, and Franconia in a destructive foray. Sigismund, exploiting the general alarm, reverted to the older system and demanded contingents from each prince and city. The response improved, and a large army invaded Bohemia, only to meet complete disaster in 1431 at Taus (now Domažlice, in the Czech Republic). It was evident that the veteran Hussites could not be crushed by force. Sigismund therefore welcomed the opportunity to transfer the problem of reconciling the Hussites with the church to the Council of Basel (1431–49). The Hussite extremists, the Taborites, were inflexible. They condemned the hierarchical system of church government and affirmed the priesthood of all true believers. Hence the council conducted its long and arduous negotiations with the majority party among the Hussites—the Calixtines, or Utraquists, who were prepared to accept the grant of communion in both kinds as a basis of settlement. The Utraquist nobles annihilated the protesting Taborites at the Battle of Lipany (May 30, 1434) and made peace with the council by the Compact of Iglau (July 5, 1436), which conceded them communion in both kinds and reunited them with the Roman Catholic Church. The Utraquist nobles extracted far better terms from Sigismund as the price of their recognition. He agreed to accept the guidance of Czech councillors in governmental affairs, to admit only Czechs to public office, to grant an amnesty for all offenses committed since the death of Wenceslas, and to allow the Czechs a large measure of autonomy in their civil and religious life. It is unlikely that the slippery Sigismund intended to honour these pledges, but they cleared the way for his triumphant return to Prague in August 1436.

In Germany the Hussite threat had clearly revealed the inadequacies of the existing financial and military systems, but the incentive to press Sigismund's reforms to a successful conclusion faded when the Hussite peril was scotched by negotiation. The general apathy was demonstrated in 1434, when Sigismund proposed to the princes a land peace embracing the whole of Germany. The abolition of private wars and feuds by such a peace was undeniably a paramount necessity. The princes themselves, however, were among the chief offenders against law and order, and their nominal approval of the plan deceived no one. Sigismund himself, increasingly absorbed in crucial negotiations with the Hussites, did not persevere, and the project gathered dust in the imperial archives. The impulse he gave to the cause of reform did not, however, fade entirely, though Sigismund did not live to see the sequel. His death on December 9, 1437, terminated the tenure of the German throne by the house of Luxembourg and opened the door of opportunity to the Habsburg dynasty.

THE HABSBURGS AND THE IMPERIAL OFFICE

In the absence of a male heir, Sigismund had named his son-in-law Albert of Habsburg, duke of Austria, as his successor. As with previous kings, the princely electors attempted to assert their influence, but they would have far more luck with Albert's son, Frederick.

ALBERT II

Albert was able and vigorous, and the union of the territories of the two dynasties enabled him to exert considerable leverage in German politics. Albert declared his neutrality in the current dispute between Pope Eugenius IV and the Council of Basel on the subject of conciliar sovereignty and thereby evaded an issue on which the electors were strongly divided; thus, on March 18, 1438, he was unanimously elected at Frankfurt. The electors attempted to elicit from the new king an understanding that he would grant privileges to his subjects only with their advice and consent. They also submitted a project for the division of Germany into four new administrative units (Kreise) in which the enforcement of the land peace would be entrusted to captains of princely rank. Albert judged that the princes were seeking to enlarge their power and influence under the guise of introducing reforms for the common good. The German cities also doubted the impartiality of the princes as custodians of law and order. Both proposals were therefore stillborn. The king hastened from Frankfurt to defend his kingdom of Hungary, endangered by Turkish raids on Siebenbürgen (part of Transylvania, now in Romania). The campaign was brought to a premature close by the death of the king on October 27, 1439.

FREDERICK III

Albert II had left only an infant son, and the leadership of the house of Habsburg passed to his cousin Frederick, duke of Styria. Inside the electoral college the duke was vigorously supported by his brother-in-law Frederick of Saxony and was elected unanimously on February 2, 1440. The choice of Frederick tightened the hold of the Habsburgs on the German kingship. It also brought to the throne a ruler who, absorbed in dynastic concerns and in astrology, had no more than a passing interest in Germany. Under the absentee government of Frederick III, the feuds among the princes and the collisions between the princes and the cities developed into savage wars accompanied by widespread ravaging and pillage. All paid lip service to the need for peace; but who was to enforce it? Was it to be enforced by the monarchy, which lacked power and executive machinery? Was it to be enforced in the courts of the princes, whose judicial impartiality was suspect? Were complaints against the princes to be heard and decided in the king's court (Hofgericht)? Or must they be adjudicated by the council (Hofrat) of the prince concerned? The right to enforce peace effectively was a major source of power to the holder; hence the struggle between Frederick and the princes was long, bitter, and inconclusive.

These issues were brought to a head by the rapid westward progress of the Ottoman Turks after their victory at Varna on the Black Sea in 1444 and their definitive conquest of Serbia in 1459. The Habsburg kingdom of Hungary and Frederick III's own duchy of Styria lay in the path of the invaders. In 1453 the fall of Constantinople extinguished the Eastern Empire and aroused fears in Germany that the Western (i.e., Holy Roman) Empire would meet the same fate. The king used the opportunity to demand financial aid against the Turks from the diet, the German assembly of estates. Under the leadership of the princes, the diet reminded him that Germany's capacity for defense was weakened by the current internal anarchy. In 1455 six electors proposed to the king the establishment of an imperial court of justice in which all three estates (electors, princes, and cities) should be represented. Frederick dismissed the scheme as an attempted invasion of his authority and stubbornly maintained his disapproval in a series of stormy interviews.

In time an increasing number of princes became convinced that reform would make no significant progress until Frederick was removed. As early as 1460 the Wittelsbach princes urged his deposition in favour of George of Poděbrady, the able and resourceful king of Bohemia. To check the danger, Frederick began to dole out reforms with a sparing hand. In 1464 he consented to make the court of the treasury (Kammergericht) independent of his person, to staff it with representatives of the three estates, and to extend its jurisdiction into fields other than financial. It was the acquisition of Austria in 1463 on the death of his brother Albert that finally proved his undoing. The unruly Austrian nobility early took the measure of Frederick and thereafter disregarded his authority. On the east and south the duchy was imminently threatened by the expanding kingdom of Hungary under its land-hungry ruler Matthias Corvinus. The southern borders of the Habsburg lands were also ravaged by the Turks. Frederick's continuing irresolution and passivity encouraged Matthias Corvinus, who had already seized a portion of Bohemia, to launch a campaign against Austria. The Austrian nobility made no move against him, and Vienna fell to him in 1485. Frederick fled to Germany and made pitiful appeals for help to the princes. His misfortune provided the party of reform with a long-awaited opportunity. Led by Berthold von Henneberg, the able and resolute archbishop of Mainz, they pressed the aging and afflicted Frederick to relinquish the kingship in favour of his son Maximilian. Solaced somewhat by the assurance of a Habsburg succession, he gave a reluctant acquiescence, and Maximilian was elected on February 16, 1486. Frederick retained the title of emperor, held since his imperial coronation at Rome in 1452—the last imperial coronation held in the Holy See. But he played no part in the government of Germany, and his death on August 19, 1493, passed almost unnoticed.

Frederick III. Hulton Archive/Getty Images

DEVELOPMENTS IN THE INDIVIDUAL STATES TO ABOUT 1500

In the various principalities the outcome of the struggle between the territorial princes and the assemblies of estates (Landstände) was not fully decided by 1500. The vigour of the conflict arose partly out of the contrasting conceptions of government held by the protagonists. The secular princes looked upon their lands as private possessions that could be divided by agreement among their sons and drew little distinction between their private and their public revenues. The three estates regarded themselves as the corporate representatives of the whole territorial community and maintained that actions by a prince affecting their interests and privileges should be subject to their consent. They therefore opposed the partition of the territory by family pact among the princes' sons. The inadvisability of breaking up the principalities into petty territorial lordships was at length conceded by the more prudent princes. By 1500 the rulers of Bavaria, Brandenburg, Saxony, and Württemberg had accepted the principles of territorial indivisibility and primogeniture.

THE PRINCES AND THE LANDSTÄNDE

In financial matters the imposition of extraordinary taxes (Notbeden) remained the crucial issue between the princes and the estates. The mounting cost of war and administration outstripped the ordinary revenues of the ruler, plunged him deeply into debt, and compelled him to seek financial aid from the estates with increasing frequency. In the absence of a clear distinction between public and private revenue, the estates often contended that the deficit was a private debt of the prince and disclaimed responsibility. Needy princes were thus forced to buy temporary solvency by concessions that later shackled them in their dealings with the estates. The estates regarded the Notbede strictly as an occasional emergency tax and insisted that it should be reasonable in amount. Indeed, the estates of Bavaria and Brunswick extracted from their respective princes in the course of the 14th century a formal recognition of their right of armed resistance to extortionate taxation. Similarly, any prince who broke his agreements with the estates was subject to the right of resistance. Thus the aims of these territorial assemblies were mixed. They sought to preserve the privileges of the three orders, to restrain the power of the prince, and to limit taxation. They were, however, also actively interested in good government, and the more enlightened rulers usually issued their ordinances only after consultation with the estates.

The princes proceeded against these powerful and often turbulent bodies with great caution. They persistently demanded that territorial assemblies convene only at the summons of the prince. They discountenanced the widespread conviction that absentees from the assembly were not bound to pay the taxes that it voted. In consequence, the peasants, who were not represented except in the Swiss cantons, Baden, Friesland, and Tirol, remained in the grasp of the princes' tax collectors. In these directions the princes had generally made notable advances by 1500, but in the vital matter of the Notbede they were still obliged to bargain with the estates as equals. They had nowhere attained their ultimate objective: to transform the tax into a regular imposition voted automatically by the estates on demand.

Beyond the confines of the assemblies of estates, the attempts of the princes to curb their overmighty subjects aroused vigorous resistance. The noble vassals, proud and unruly, readily combined against any prince who sought to tamper with their liberties. Wise rulers deflected the nobles' energies into useful channels by employing them as stipendiaries. Hence even the most powerful princes—the Habsburgs in Austria and the Hohenzollerns in Brandenburg—proceeded circumspectly, and the difficult task of bringing the nobility to heel was far from completed in 1500. The cities of the princely territories defended their independence no less stubbornly. The princes revoked their charters, influenced municipal elections, and forbade the cities to associate in self-defense. The struggle was most intense in the north and east, where the Hohenzollern dynasty of Brandenburg emerged as the chief foe of municipal freedom. In 1442 the elector Frederick II ("Iron Tooth") crushed a federation of Brandenburg cities and deprived its leader, Berlin, of its most valued privileges. In the Franconian possessions of the dynasty, Albert Achilles of Hohenzollern waged a destructive war (1449–50) against a city league headed by Nürnberg. He suffered a resounding defeat in a pitched battle near Pillenreuth in 1450. The elector John Cicero took up

the battle 38 years later, when the cities of the Altmark in west Brandenburg refused to pay an excise tax on beer voted by the assembly of estates. He discomfited the cities in the ensuing "Beer War" and radically revised their constitutions to his own advantage. On the other hand, the great cities of southern Germany, enriched by the Italian trade, were more than a match for the local princes: the Wittelsbach dukes of Bavaria were decisively worsted by Regensburg in 1488.

THE GROWTH OF CENTRAL GOVERNMENTS

Between 1300 and 1500 the organs of central government in the territorial states became more specialized and diversified. The parent body was the advisory council (Hofrat) of high nobles and ecclesiastics, whom the prince consulted at his discretion. Its business was not differentiated, and there was no division of labour among the councillors. It met at the summons of the prince and did not convene at regular intervals. Its membership was not fixed, and some advisers did not attend except at special invitation. Others were regional councillors who attended the prince only when he appeared in their locality. A body so unspecialized and fluctuating was ill-adapted to cope with the increasingly complex problems of central government. Hence in the 14th and 15th centuries a professional element of "daily" or permanent councillors was introduced. They

University of Heidelberg. Alexander Hassenstein/Digital Vision/Getty Images

were usually legists, trained in Italy or in the newly founded universities of Prague (1364), Vienna (1365), Heidelberg (1386), Rostock (1419), and Tübingen (1477). They were well versed in Roman law, which, with its centralizing and authoritative precepts, provided a congenial climate for the growth of the powers of the territorial princes everywhere save in Saxony, Schleswig, and Holstein, where the ancient customary codes were deeply rooted.

Financial administration, which required specialized skills, was placed under the direction of a separate department of government, the treasury (Hofkammer). An inner ring of favoured advisers, the privy council (Geheimrat), was also instituted to counsel the prince on affairs of state. The besetting weakness of the new administrative structure was financial. Few princes followed the example of the Hohenzollern dynasty in drawing up an annual budget and requiring financial officials to submit regular accounts to the government. On the positive side, chanceries gradually created a common German language, which Luther later used to spread his message.

GERMAN SOCIETY, ECONOMY, AND CULTURE IN THE 14TH AND 15TH CENTURIES

Despite the impressive advance of trade and industry in the later Middle Ages, German society was still sustained chiefly by agriculture. Of an estimated population of 12 million in 1500, only 1.5 million resided in cities and towns. Still, the expansion of trade and growth of professional guilds would have a profound effect on German culture.

TRANSFORMATION OF RURAL LIFE

In the 15th century agriculture exhibited strong regional differences in organization. The more recently settled areas of the north and east were characterized by great farms and extensive estates that produced a surplus of grain for export through the Baltic ports. The south and west was a region of denser population, thickly sown with small villages and the "dwarf" estates of the lesser nobility. In the northeast the great landlords, headed by the Knights of the Teutonic Order, tightened their control over the originally free tenants, denied them freedom of movement, and ultimately bound them to the soil as serfs. In the south the heavy urban demand for grain chiefly benefited the larger peasant proprietors, who sold their surplus production in the nearest town and used their gains to acquire more land. The lesser peasantry, with their smaller holdings, practiced chiefly subsistence farming, produced no surplus, and therefore failed to benefit from the buoyant urban demand. The frequent division of the patrimony among heirs often reduced it to uneconomically small fragments and encouraged an exodus to the cities. On the other hand, landless day labourers who survived the Black Death in the mid-14th century were able to command higher wages for their services.

In southern Germany the strain of transition in rural society was heightened by the policies of the landlords, both lay and ecclesiastical. Confronted by labour shortages and rising costs, many landlords attempted to recoup their losses at the expense of their tenants. By means of ordinances passed in the manorial courts, they denied to the peasantry their traditional right of access to commons, woods, and streams. Further, they revived their demands for the performance of obsolete labour services and enforced the collection of the extraordinary taxes on behalf of the prince. The peasants protested and appealed to custom, but their sole legal recourse was to the manorial court, where their objections were silenced or ignored. Ecclesiastical landlords were especially efficient, and peasant discontent assumed a strong anticlerical tinge and gave rise to the localized disturbances in Gotha (1391), Bregenz (1407), Rottweil (1420), and Worms (1421). Disturbances recurred with increasing frequency in the course of the 15th century on the upper Rhine, in Alsace, and in the Black Forest. In 1458 a cattle tax imposed by the archbishop of Salzburg kindled a peasant insurrection, which spread to Styria, Carinthia, and Carniola. In Alsace the malcontents adopted as the symbol of revolt the Bundschuh, the wooden shoe usually worn by the peasants. They also formulated a series of specific demands, which included the abolition of the hated manorial courts and the reduction of feudal dues and public taxes to a trifling annual amount. On these fundamental points there was little room for compromise, and the outbreaks were stifled by the heavy hand of established authority. But the rigours of repression added fuel to peasant discontent, which finally burst forth in the great uprising of 1524–25.

THE NOBILITY

The lesser nobility included two distinct elements. The imperial knights (Reichsritter) held their estates as tenants in chief of the crown. The provincial nobility (Landesadel) had lost direct contact with the crown and were being compelled by degrees to acknowledge the suzerainty of the local prince. The imperial knights had been extensively employed by the Hohenstaufen emperors in military and administrative

capacities and were chiefly concentrated in the former Hohenstaufen possessions in Swabia, Franconia, Alsace, and the Rhineland. With the extinction of the Hohenstaufen dynasty, they lost their function and rewards as a nobility of service. The revenues from their small estates sank in purchasing power as prices rose. Caste prejudice prevented them from seeking an alternative role in trade or industry. Resentful of the decline in their fortunes and fiercely independent, they clung grimly to their remaining privileges: exemption from imperial taxes and the right to indulge in private war. They stubbornly resisted the persistent attempts of the princes to reduce them to subject status, and in Trier and Württemberg especially they were given valuable aid by the provincial nobles. For purposes of defense or aggression, the imperial and provincial knights combined freely in powerful regional leagues, usually directed against the local princes or cities. In the course of their chronic feuds with the cities, many knights became mere highwaymen. Many others, who had been forced to sell their estates or who were encumbered with debts, took service in Germany or Italy as mercenaries (Soldritter). In eastern Germany the knights, though equally unruly, were far more affluent. The knightly estate (Rittergut) was larger and produced a profitable surplus for export. The provincial knights sat in the assembly of estates, and taxation by the prince required their consent. They were therefore well-entrenched against the encroachments of princely power.

URBAN LIFE

Urban society in 15th-century Germany was concentrated in some 3,000 cities and towns. About 2,800 of the total were extremely small, with populations varying from 100 to 1,000. Of the remainder, no more than 15 cities contained more than 10,000 inhabitants. In this restricted group three were preeminent. Cologne reached its peak in the 13th century with a population of 60,000 but sank to 40,000 by 1500 following epidemics, internal disputes, and expulsions. In 1500 Augsburg was the most populous German city, with a resident population of 50,000. Third place was held by fast-growing Nürnberg, which counted 30,000 souls. The social unity of the citizen body had been most marked in the 13th century, when the guilds joined the dominant patrician families (Geschlechter) in wresting the right to form independent city councils (Stadtrat) from the lords of the cities. In the 14th century the guild masters, methodically excluded from the councils by the patrician oligarchy, broke into open revolt in Speyer (1327), Strassburg (now Strasbourg; 1332), Nürnberg (1348), and elsewhere. In its economic aspect the ensuing conflict embodied an attempt by the guildsmen as industrial producers to free urban industry from the tight control exercised by the merchant patriciate. By 1500 the guilds almost everywhere had gained varying degrees of representation in the city council.

In the meantime the guilds themselves had become increasingly oligarchic and exclusive as the established masters restricted the entry of new members in order to reduce competition. The ascent of journeymen and apprentices to the rank of master was obstructed by the imposition of excessive fees, and in many guilds membership became virtually hereditary. In consequence, the journeymen began to associate in fraternities of their own to press their demands for higher wages and a shorter working day. The masters denounced the fraternities as illegal, compiled blacklists of leading agitators, and formed intercity associations to enforce low wage rates. The day labourers and casual workers outside the guild structure had no protective organization and suffered heavily in periods of economic depression. The surviving tax records of the German cities, though not wholly reliable guides, nevertheless suggest wide extremes of wealth and poverty. In late 15th-century Augsburg 2,985 of a total of 4,485 households (66 percent) were recorded on the tax rolls as exempt from taxation on the ground of insufficient means. At the other extreme stood the enterprising and prosperous business dynasties of the Fuggers and the Welsers. Not all wealthy citizens lacked public spirit, however, and hospitals, almshouses, and charitable foundations multiplied within the city walls. The spreading problem of mendicancy was combated by stringent legislation against able-bodied beggars in Esslingen (1384), Brunswick (1400), Vienna (1442), Cologne (1446), and Nürnberg (1447).

THE DECLINE OF THE CHURCH

The vigour and assertiveness of secular society in Germany were exercised increasingly at the expense of the clergy and the church. Among the upper clergy more than 100 archbishops, bishops, and abbots were temporal rulers. The prelates were usually sons of the nobility and did not allow election to church office to interfere with their aristocratic ardour for war and territorial acquisition. They were expert in the accumulation of benefices and were notoriously lax in the performance of their spiritual duties. Their influence was freely used to advance their kinsmen and partisans among the greater and lesser nobles, who dominated the cathedral chapters and ruled the abbeys. The monasteries were filled with monks and nuns who were distinguishable from the lay aristocracy only by a nominal celibacy. Among the secular princes, the rulers of Austria, Brandenburg, and Saxony wrested a right of appointment to a fixed number of bishoprics and lesser church offices from the papacy, which had been gravely weakened by the schism and the conciliar movement of the 15th century. All lay and ecclesiastical princes imposed heavy extraordinary taxes on the clergy. The steady invasion of the church by secular interests was also exemplified by the moral and material condition of the lower clergy. The Black Death of 1348–50 had decimated the ranks of the more dedicated priests, who ministered to their plague-stricken flocks instead of seeking safety by flight. The new recruits who rushed into holy orders were often self-seeking and spiritually unqualified. As the inflow continued, the problem of clerical unemployment and inadequate stipends attained greater proportions. Many were compelled by need to accept ill-paid livings. Others obtained no benefice at all and lived precariously as chantry priests or as itinerant chaplains. Their moral and intellectual defects were bitterly assailed by church reformers and by an increasingly well-informed laity. Many pious Christians, especially in the cities, began to turn away from the priesthood in their search for spiritual comfort and to seek relief in mysticism or in lay associations practicing a simple, undogmatic form of Christianity.

TRADE AND INDUSTRY

The most impressive achievements of the German economy between 1200 and 1500 lay in trade and industry. German trade benefited from the Hundred Years' War between France and England, which diverted northbound Mediterranean merchandise from the customary Rhône valley route to the eastern Alpine passes; from the fierce internal warfare between the Italian city-states, which weakened their supremacy in long-distance trade;

HANSEATIC LEAGUE

The Hanseatic League (from German *Hanse*, "association") was founded in the late medieval period by northern German towns and merchant communities to protect their trading interests. The league dominated commercial activity in northern Europe from the 13th to the 15th century. It protected transport of goods by quelling pirates and brigands and fostered safe navigation by building lighthouses. Most important, it sought to organize and control trade by winning commercial privileges and monopolies and by establishing trading bases overseas. In extreme cases its members resorted to warfare, as when they raised an armed force that defeated the Danes in 1368 and confirmed the league's supremacy in the Baltic Sea. Over 150 towns were at some point associated with the league, including Bremen, Hamburg, and Lübeck.

and from the rapid economic development of "colonial" eastern Europe between the Baltic and the Danube. The northern German trade was chiefly based on staple commodities such as grain, fish, salt, and metals; but the southern German merchants, in their capacity as middlemen between Italy and the rest of Europe, had taken the lead by 1500. They combined trade and industry in the great Ravensburg Trading Company (1380–1530), which produced and exported Swabian linen and laid the foundation of the fortunes of the Höchstetter, Herwart, Adler, Tucher, and Imhof families. The most important independent concern was that of the Fuggers, whose founder, Hans Fugger, began his career as a linen weaver in Augsburg. The Fuggers' accumulated profits provided capital for moneylending and banking, which they conducted with the aid of business techniques borrowed from the more advanced Italians.

The wealth and prosperity of Germany, which Machiavelli remarked on in 1512, stood in sharp contrast to its political and military weakness, a disparity that contributed significantly to a profound sense of malaise and discontent on the eve of the Reformation.

CULTURAL LIFE

In the absence of a strong centralized monarchy to act as a focus, German culture continued to be regional in character and widely diffused. The mysticism of Meister Eckhart, Johann Tauler, and Heinrich Suso, which commanded all men to look for the kingdom of God within themselves, flourished chiefly in the cities of the Rhineland, where lack of diligent pastoral care forced Christians to call upon their own inner resources. In the same region social and moral satire attained an urgent and vivid realism.

Sebastian Brant (1458–1521), born at Strassburg, spared no class in his epic on human stupidity, the *Narrenschiff* (*Ship of Fools*). But it was in the thriving cities of southern Germany, as yet little affected by Italian humanism, that late Gothic culture reached magnificent heights in art, architecture, and sculpture. Albrecht Dürer, born in Nürnberg in 1471, challenged his generation with his evocative engraving "Melancolia I," in which a brooding figure with closed wings sits idly amid a chaos of scientific instruments and meditates on the futility of human endeavour. In architecture the hierarchical elaboration of the late Gothic style maintained its ascendancy and even made a notable conquest in Italy with the construction of the great cathedral of Milan, begun in 1387. The sculptured carvings of Tilman Riemenschneider (c. 1460–1531) in the chapels and cathedrals of Würzburg and other Franconian cities revealed the anxiety, the deep piety, and the religious sensibility of Christian men engaged upon a spiritual pilgrimage that was to continue through the Reformation and beyond. His work was the pinnacle of a great flowering of sculpture, one of the greatest in German history.

CHAPTER 8

GERMANY FROM 1493 TO 1871

From the late 15th to the late 19th century, Germany underwent a remarkable transformation. Religious and political conflicts reshaped the balance of power in Europe, and Prussia asserted dominance over the other Germanic territories. The rise of Napoleon marked the end of the Holy Roman Empire, but his fall would result in the eventual unification of Germany.

REFORM AND REFORMATION, 1493–1555

The reign of Maximilian I (1493–1519) was dominated by the interplay of three issues of decisive importance to the future of the Holy Roman Empire: the rise of the Austrian house of Habsburg to international prominence, the urgent need to reform the empire's governing institutions, and the beginnings of the religious and social movement known as the Reformation.

THE EMPIRE IN 1493

The accession of the dynamic and imaginative Maximilian to the German throne aroused in many Germans, and in particular among humanists, expectations of a time when the old imperial idea—the vision of the empire as the political expression of a united Christendom in which the emperor, as God's deputy, rules over a universal realm of peace and order—might become a reality. Since the extinction of the Hohenstaufen dynasty in 1254, imperial authority had been in disarray; as weak emperors had become absorbed in struggles against foreign and domestic, secular and ecclesiastical rivals, real power in the empire had moved toward the governments of territorial states and independent cities. From their first appearance on the historical scene (briefly from 1273 to 1308, then from 1438 in a nearly unbroken line until the dissolution of the empire in 1806), Habsburg rulers had fostered imperial unity. But they had been notably unsuccessful in creating agencies for its attainment, partly because they were assiduously working to build up a power base for their own house. This, in turn, brought them into conflict with European antagonists, chiefly France. The long reign of Maximilian's father, Frederick III (1440–93), was regarded by nationalists as lamentable in its inattention to the problems pressing on the empire. The solutions proposed for them were subsumed under the name of "reform," a highly charged word that acquired enormous additional force in the 15th century when the conciliar movement and its lay and clerical proponents exerted pressure for religious renewal. Maximilian's arrival on the throne thus generated a surge of anticipation, expressed in an outpouring of agendas for restructuring what was then coming to be called the "Holy Roman Empire of the German Nation."

IMPERIAL REFORM

Inevitably, perhaps, Maximilian's performance with regard to the empire disappointed, but he was successful in significantly extending the dynastic might of his family. He took over the duchy of Tirol with its vast mining resources. Ambitious marriage alliances spread Habsburg entitlements west and east: in 1496 Maximilian's son Philip wed Joan, the daughter of the king and queen of Spain, thus linking Habsburg Austria to Spain and the Netherlands (the future Charles V was born of this union in 1500); and in 1516 Maximilian's grandson Ferdinand was betrothed to the heiress of Hungary and Bohemia. These connections, however, only escalated Maximilian's internal and external problems. In foreign politics his ventures ended, for the most part, in calamities for the empire. Switzerland was lost in 1499, several Italian campaigns were repulsed, and an attempt against the duchy of Burgundy brought the hostility of France and led to the fall of Milan. Even the imperial crown eluded Maximilian: his advance on Rome for this purpose was halted, and he had to be content with the self-bestowed title of Roman emperor-elect.

These reverses strengthened a reform party among leading members of the empire's estates (Stände); especially prominent was their spokesman, the archbishop-elector of Mainz, Berthold von Henneberg. Given the long rivalry between emperor and estates, it goes without saying that their respective plans for reforming the empire diverged on crucial points of direction and control. The estates, acting from their—to them entirely legitimate—sense of the prerogatives of particularism, favoured a central administration responsive to them; the emperor, to the contrary, insisted on organs subservient to him, modeled on bureaucratic agencies recently established in Burgundy and Austria and shored up by the authority-enhancing principles of Roman law.

At the imperial diet held in the city of Worms in 1495, the estates, whose members had begun to see themselves as the authentic representatives of the whole country, prevailed. The four reform measures adopted on this occasion were in large part intended to limit the emperor's powers. An "Eternal Peace" outlawed private feuds, with steps taken, and agreed to by the emperor, to implement this pacification. An Imperial Chamber Court functioned as supreme tribunal for the empire, most of its judges being named by the estates. An empirewide tax, the "Common Penny," was imposed, the collection of which fell to the estates. To these measures was added, in 1500, an Imperial Governing Council to monitor, under the domination of the electors, the empire's foreign policy. Maximilian was able to impede the operation of this body (it was reestablished in 1521), but overall the emperor's reform objectives had come to nothing.

The historical judgment of this failure has swung widely, on one hand between scorn for Maximilian's imperial "fantasies"—for whose realization a reorganized Germany was to furnish the means—and respect for his grasp of the country's perilous geopolitical situation, and on the other hand between sympathy for the estates' single-minded pursuit of the imperatives of regional state building and disdain for the parochialism of their political vision. Most historians have found Maximilian's actions distorted by a brand of romantic idealism. (In all seriousness he proposed to Bayezid II that Turks and Christians should settle their differences by the rules of the tournament; he also cherished for a time the hope of becoming pope as well as emperor.) What is clear is that the reform effort so briskly launched at the beginning of his reign resulted in permanent confrontation between sovereign and estates, a posture in which neither party could outmaneuver the other and every matter of policy required tenacious negotiation. In light of this permanent tug of war, the notion of a universal realm ruled by a "German" emperor does seem fantastic, though it never lost its ideological force. No one in the empire possessed plenary authority, but real power was shifting to territorial rulers and their bureaucratic agents and to the magistrates of larger cities. This shift was to be of the greatest importance in determining the direction in which the Reformation established itself in Germany.

THE REFORMATION

The Reformation presents the historian with an acute instance of the general problem of scholarly interpretation—namely, whether events are shaped primarily by individuals or by the net of historical circumstances enmeshing them. The phenomenon that became the Protestant Reformation is unthinkable without the sense of mission and compelling personality of Martin Luther. But in social and intellectual conditions less conducive to drastic change, Luther's voice would have gone unheard and his actions been forgotten. Among the preconditions—which are the deeper causes of the Reformation—the following stand out: (1) Everyone agreed that the Roman Catholic church was in need of correction. The lack of spirituality in high places, the blatant fiscalism, of which the unrestrained hawking of indulgences—the actual trigger of the Reformation—was a galling example, and the embroilment in political affairs all were symptoms of corruption long overdue for purgation. While the church continued to be accepted as the only legitimate mediator of divine grace, denunciations of its abuses, perceived or actual, became more strident in the decades before 1517. (2) A subtle change, moreover, had been occurring in people's religious needs and expectations, leading to demands for a more personal experience of the divine. Failing to meet this aspiration, the church was widely, if diffusely, rebuked for its unresponsiveness. (3) More focused criticism came from the Christian humanists, an influential group of scholars bent on restoring the fundamental texts of Western Christianity. Led by Desiderius Erasmus, the most renowned biblical scholar of the time, these men held the Catholic church up to the spiritual ideals for which it claimed to stand and, finding it wanting, set the principle of Evangelicalism against the church's secularized ambitions. (4) Still more fatefully, by 1500 the church had come under attack from European rulers whose administrative, legal, and financial hegemony could not be completed in their respective states without domination of the ecclesiastical sector. In the empire, as elsewhere, the trend in ecclesiastical politics was toward state churches (Landeskirchen), in which governments, using "reform" as a pretext, gradually gained, while church authorities lost, a large measure of control over clerical properties, personnel, and functions. The Reformation was the culmination of this process, which, in the empire, took place in nearly all princely territories and in most independent cities, where governments brought the administration of the church under political direction. (5) In Germany this development was facilitated by an ancient feudal custom entitling a landlord to extend "protection" to churches located on his estates. Over this "owner's church" (Eigenkirche) he enjoyed the right of patronage, allowing him to appoint incumbents and manage properties. In the course of extending their sovereignty, territorial princes took over this right to patronage and fashioned of it the legal basis on which, in the Reformation, they assumed full control over the administration of the church. (6) In every segment of German society, but particularly among the poor, voices were being raised against injustice and exploitation. Wide disparities in income and discriminatory laws in cities as well as the deteriorating standard of living of small peasants and agricultural labourers caused riots and uprisings, which by the early 1500s had become endemic.

These, then, were the forces driving events toward a crisis. In the first decade of the 16th century they coalesced into a powerful surge of religious, social, and political agitation, for which "reform" (of church and society) was the code word. Ironically, Luther, who was to channel this agitation into the Reformation, had, until his emergence as a national figure in the 1520s, nothing to do with it. For him one issue alone mattered: the imperative of faith. His personal path to the Reformation was an inner search for religious truth, to which his conscience was his guide.

When he wrote his *Ninety-five Theses* against indulgences in October 1517, Luther was an Augustinian friar, a preacher in the Saxon city of Wittenberg, and a theology professor at the university founded there in 1502 by the elector of Saxony, Frederick III, called "the Wise." His ambitious father had pushed him toward a career in law, but in 1505 the fervently devout Martin entered a monastic house. His order, that of the Augustinian eremites, was a strict reform congregation dedicated to prayer, study, and the ascetic life. Deeply troubled by the question of justification—of how a human being, a sinner, may be justified (saved) in God's sight—Luther found no comfort in monastic routine and turned

to an exploration of the sources of Christian doctrine, notably St. Paul and St. Augustine. His intellectual promise having been recognized, he was sent by his order to study theology at Erfurt and Wittenberg. He was awarded a doctorate in 1512 and commenced his teaching of the Bible in Wittenberg that same year. According to his own account, it was during his close reading of Paul's Epistle to the Romans, while preparing to give a course of lectures on that text, that he discovered what struck him as the solution to the problem posed by the huge gap between human sin and divine grace. Justification is not earned as a reward for human effort through good works (a position Luther now attributed to a misguided and misguiding Roman church). To the contrary, human beings are justified without any merit of their own by God's freely given and prevenient (i.e., coming before any worthy human deeds) grace, through faith, which is a gift of God. This is the meaning Luther found in the crucial passage in Romans 1:17: "For in it [i.e., the Gospel] the righteousness of God is revealed through faith for faith: as it is written, 'He who through faith is righteous shall live.'" "Righteousness"—*justitia* in Latin—does not refer, Luther believed, to God's activity as judge but to the justifying righteous condition he effects in the human sinner, a condition expressing itself as faith. The momentous consequences of this theological insight, which Luther appears to have taken as a unique discovery but which had in fact been espoused by a score of theologians before him, were not then apparent to him. They asserted themselves powerfully, however, once he began to lecture and preach on the—for him—paramount themes of salvation by faith alone (*sola fide*) and exclusive reliance on scripture (*sola scriptura*). It was the indulgence controversy of October 1517 that brought it all into the open.

Few other issues could so clearly have exposed the gulf that separated this ardent friar from an urbane and pragmatic church. The indulgence offered in Saxony in 1517 had its origin in two purely financial arrangements. First, Popes Julius II and Leo X needed funds for rebuilding St. Peter's Basilica in Rome; second, Bishop Albert of Hohenzollern, forced to buy papal dispensations in order to gain the archbishoprics of Mainz and Halberstadt, agreed to promote indulgences in his domains, half the income from which was to go to Rome, the other half to him and his bankers. For Luther, the issue turned not so much on the outrageous venality of this deal as on the indulgence itself. Truly contrite sinners do not desire relief through an indulgence (which is a remission of the penance, or temporal punishment, that the sinner would otherwise owe following absolution); they crave penance. This is the gist of Luther's argument in the *Ninety-five Theses*, which he sent to his ecclesiastical superiors to persuade them to abandon the indulgence sale. (The story that he nailed a copy of the theses to the door of the Castle Church in Wittenberg may be the invention of a later time.)

Luther intended no defiance with this action. He intervened as a priest on behalf of his flock and as a conscientious theologian against a corrupting church. But the public reaction to the theses (he had written them in Latin, but they were soon translated and printed) made it evident that he had touched a nerve. Encouraged by expressions of support and goaded by opponents, Luther became more outspoken, harsher in his criticism of the church, and more focused in his attacks on the papacy. By 1520 he was well on his way to becoming the spokesman for Germany's grievances against Rome. A pamphlet he published that year, *Address to the Christian Nobility of the German Nation*, urged the empire's secular rulers to reform a church that would not set its own house in order. Popes and prelates are not sacrosanct, he argued; they may be brought to justice. As every Christian can read the Bible for himself, papal claims to interpretive authority are a vain boast. Luther prodded the German princes to consider the state of the church and to reform it for the sake of the faith. In this way Luther drew out, albeit reluctantly, the full consequences of his principle of "salvation by faith alone." No church was needed to act as God's agent; grace was available without mediation. No priest, not even the pope, has special powers, for, so Luther argued, all human beings are priests, made so by their faith. It is scarcely surprising that a bull of excommunication against him (*Exsurge domine*) issued from Rome in June 1520.

IMPERIAL ELECTION OF 1519 AND THE DIET OF WORMS

At any other time the Lutheran matter would probably have ended there. But 1521 was no ordinary moment in the empire's history. When he died in 1519, Maximilian had not succeeded in having his grandson and heir, Charles, designated his successor. King of Castile and Aragon since 1516 and suzerain also over Habsburg lands in the Netherlands, Naples, and central and eastern Europe—not to mention the Spanish possessions in the New World—Charles posed a formidable problem for the electors. Should they choose a man whose vast resources might well empower him to centralize authority in the empire when this would limit their hard-won autonomy? Should they elect a prince whose international commitments would entangle Germany in European conflicts? The only other viable candidate was the king of France, Francis I, who recognized in the rapidly growing Habsburg ascendancy a serious threat to his own power. But, though Francis made tempting promises, the electors, in the end, opted for Charles—not, however, without drawing from him a 36-point "electoral capitulation" in which he swore to uphold the estates' prerogatives. In making this choice, the electors strove to secure their own privileges, but the German public tended to see in the new monarch a fulfillment of national aspirations—mistakenly, as it turned out, but giving rise, at the time, to patriotic expressions of hopes for a brighter future.

Coinciding with these events in the political realm and gaining resonance from them, the Lutheran matter was inevitably drawn into the political vortex, thereby acquiring the features of a national cause.

Delayed by disturbances in his Spanish domains, Charles reached Germany late in 1520. He was crowned king in Aachen, assuming at the same time the title of Roman emperor-elect. He then proceeded to Worms, where he was to meet with the German estates in early 1521. By then no other issue counted as much on the agenda as the Lutheran affair. Acting out of what appears to be a blend of conviction and political expediency, the estates' leaders, prompted by Frederick the Wise, the elector of Saxony, demanded that the Diet of Worms reopen Luther's case by allowing the excommunicated friar to speak before the estates. Unable to resist, the emperor issued a safe-conduct, and Luther traveled to Worms, treated on his way to such extravagant public acclaim that he must have felt like a national hero. On April 17 and 18 he stood before the emperor and representatives of the estates. He refused to revoke his views on justification and other points of theology, reiterated his denial of ultimate authority to pope and church councils, and—when pressed—asserted the principle of individual responsibility in matters of faith:

> As long as my conscience is held captive by the words of God, I cannot and will not revoke anything, for it is dangerous, and a great

peril to salvation, to act against conscience. God help me. Amen.

These words, and all else that transpired, were broadcast to the country in scores of pamphlets in which Luther was cast in the role of the man sent by God to cleanse the German church. While an imperial edict condemned his teachings and placed him and his adherents under the ban, Luther himself was offered a refuge in the Wartburg, Frederick the Wise's castle in the Thuringian Forest. There, fretting over his enforced absence from events, he turned to the translation of the New Testament, while the movement, of which he was now the acknowledged head, gained momentum.

Analysis of what happened at Worms reveals the first signs of what was to become a fateful split in the self-perception of this movement. The estates saw it as a means of promoting ecclesiastical reform; on questions of faith, they were willing to compromise. Luther, on the contrary, tolerated no distinction between points of faith and aspects of church practice, and on his understanding of the former he stood rock-solid. He and his political patrons were thus pursuing different ends; for the present, however, his support in official circles was, for whatever reason, substantial.

Luther's hold on the general public was even more impressive than his hold on the political leadership. Historians are not unanimous in explaining how this friar from the German east, utterly obscure only five years earlier, could have gained such a following by 1521 that few governments would enforce the ban against him, knowing that they would face strong resistance if they tried to do so. It is not clear whether the general population, still largely illiterate, understood the doctrine of faith alone well enough to make it the object of informed choice. More likely, the German populace took Luther not as the preeminently religious prophet he was but saw in him their best hope of achieving an amelioration of the many troubles vexing them in their respective stations, not only in religion but also, and perhaps mainly, in their social condition. Against these conditions, the products of deeply rooted legal and institutional structures, Luther—or so people seem to have understood him—raised the standard of Evangelical morality: all things were to be judged by scripture and God's law.

Scholars have often pointed out that this view is less attributable to the Wittenberg reformer than to another theologian and preacher then beginning to be active in the Swiss city of Zürich, Huldrych Zwingli. Luther explicitly rejected the use of the—to him purely spiritual—New Testament as a norm for social reform. But Zwingli affirmed it. On the other hand, Luther's vehemence and forceful rhetoric were so compelling that, rightly or wrongly, his name came to be fused with the general hope of improvement in human affairs. His partisans, proficient in their use of the media of print and woodcut illustration, helped shape this conviction by furnishing propaganda for a strong popular drive toward Lutheranism. This drive from below, further nourished by traditional anticlerical sentiments, was met from above by the eagerness of territorial and urban governments to utilize Lutheran ideas as legitimation for the extension of political control over the church. Thus, by the mid-1520s a number of German cities and states had formally turned Lutheran, meaning that they had severed their legal and administrative ties to Rome and its prelates and were building new ecclesiastical institutions and framing new doctrines.

THE REVOLUTION OF 1525

The events of the revolutionary years 1524–25 impelled Lutheran rulers to establish centrally controlled church organizations. In their own time and often since then, these events were labeled a "peasant rebellion"; but modern scholarship has made it clear that the insurrection was far more than a series of uprisings by rural bands. The tens of thousands of peasants drawn into the movement, some of them massed in major military actions, were a symptom of the general unrest that had gripped Germany since the middle of the 15th century. Both peasants and city dwellers resented the concentration of land and economic and political power in the hands of the landed nobility and wealthy merchants, as well as the burden of the tributes, taxes, and forced labour that these elites exacted. The growth of the population heightened

these resentments by causing a shortage of available land, particularly in the south, and driving up prices and rents. The particular demands pressed in the 1520s—mitigation of fiscal and labour burdens imposed on peasants by their lords, autonomy for village communes, and relief from high taxes—had been voiced before.

New were the linkage of these demands with the grievances of restive urban groups also protesting exploitation and disenfranchisement and their formulation as an agenda of social reform on the principle of Christian communitarianism. This ideological redirection of old patterns of resistance could not have occurred without the impetus of the Reformation, specifically the incendiary preaching in towns and villages of Evangelical pastors who presented Lutheran and Zwinglian ideas as solutions to the problems at hand. The clearest evidence of the Reformation's impact on the shaping of what some modern scholars call "the revolution of the common man" are the Twelve Articles drawn up for the Swabian peasantry by an Evangelical cleric and associate of Zwingli's. Article 3 of this document asserts, "The Bible proves that we are free, and we want to be free," while another article claims for every congregation the right to choose its minister; these articles are a strong indication of how vital the principle of Biblicism had become to people preeminently concerned with worldly life.

In the regions involved—Franconia, Swabia, the Upper Rhine and Alsace,

Thuringia, and Tirol—large forces of peasants attacked castles, monasteries, and some cities. News of these actions encouraged discontented urban groups to rise against their oligarchic town governments, and for a while it looked as though a united revolutionary front of ordinary—i.e., nonprivileged—people might be forged. Manifestos and lists of articles abounded; there was talk everywhere of judging things by "God's law" (meaning the Gospel), and some groups even laid plans for a "Christian association" across regional and urban-rural lines. But before long the forces of the propertied won the upper hand, and the insurrectionaries were put down with the ferocity customary in those days. The war's final stage was dominated by Thomas Müntzer, a visionary theologian with a message of social deliverance for and by the poor. The defeat of his forces at Frankenhausen in May 1525 marked the final victory of the old order over the would-be new dispensation.

Luther was heavily implicated in this turnabout. Realizing that his words and deeds had served to encourage popular action against rulers, he sought to separate himself drastically from the movement, going so far as to urge the rulers' soldiers to "cut [the peasants] down, hit them, choke them wherever you can." His brush with revolution confirmed Luther in the rigorous segregation he made between "two realms," the worldly and the spiritual, the respective laws and ideals of which must not be confounded, as, he claimed, the revolutionaries had

done. The Gospel, he said, cannot be used as a standard for governing in the world, which has its own rules and ways of justice, many of them, he acknowledged, unfair and blameworthy. Luther's separation of worldly and Evangelical values, soon made binding law by Lutheran governments, brought an abrupt end to the early phase of the Reformation, during which events seemed to many to be moving toward a sweeping transformation of social, as well as religious, structures. At the same time, Lutheran governments read 1525 as a lesson on the need to control subjects, concluding that preaching in particular, and religious behaviour generally, must be controlled. To accomplish this purpose, new laws and bureaucracies were set up everywhere.

LUTHERAN CHURCH ORGANIZATION AND CONFESSIONALIZATION

The 1525 revolution was but one of several upheavals worrying German rulers. Three years earlier a group of imperial knights led by Franz von Sickingen had declared a feud against the archbishop of Trier, claiming to derive from scripture their right to despoil Roman Catholic prelates. The ensuing "Knights' War" was quickly crushed. But about the same time a disturbance broke out in Wittenberg where, during Luther's exile in the Wartburg, a group of reforming spiritualist activists forced the city council to abolish many traditional Catholic practices. Upset by this rash move, Luther intervened to reverse it. But this incident and the knights' attack caused consternation among the heads of government, who feared loss of control. Their anxiety was deepened by the spread from Switzerland in the mid-1520s of Anabaptism, a radical religious movement whose most distinctive tenet was adult baptism. The events of 1525 thus strengthened a growing resolution that firm structures and clear doctrines were needed to reassert authority in a situation of drift.

The foreign entanglements of the Habsburgs, champions of Catholicism in Germany, helped free Lutheran states to act on this resolution. Far from seeing to the execution of the 1521 edict against Luther, Charles V left his brother Ferdinand in charge of imperial affairs and departed from Germany after the Worms diet to deal with the many problems besetting his far-flung interests. The most perilous of these was the war with France, which implicated the emperor in a constantly shifting balance of alliances with other powers and in a seesaw of military actions in which sometimes Charles had the upper hand and sometimes Francis I did. Charles's victory at the Battle of Pavia in 1525 led to the formation of a coalition against him (the so-called "Holy League of Cognac"), intended to forestall Habsburg hegemony in Europe (a scenario to be replayed many times in the following two centuries). In 1526, therefore, Charles was in no position to dictate to the German estates on the Lutheran matter. Within a year, however, the situation turned in

his favour. Spanish troops captured and plundered Rome in 1527, and by 1529 Charles was dominant once more, though it had become clear that neither warring party could bring the other to its knees. At the same time a potentially fatal danger loomed in the east where the Turks, under Süleyman I (the Magnificent), began to aim their path of conquest at the Balkans and Hungary. The death of King Louis II at the Battle of Mohács in 1526 put Ferdinand in line for the Bohemian and Hungarian crowns, thereby exposing the already overextended Habsburgs on a new front. By 1529 the Turks were moving toward Buda (now part of Budapest), which they captured in September of that year, and Vienna. Facing these perils, Charles concluded peace with France, sealing his triumph in the west with his coronation as emperor at Bologna, Italy. He then returned to Germany.

These events formed the larger political context in which Lutheran church organization took place. Forced to solicit military aid from the estates in 1526, Ferdinand postponed implementation of the Worms edict, accepting a declaration by the Diet of Speyer of that year to the effect that every estate "will, with its subjects, act, live, and govern in matters touching the Worms edict in a way each can justify before God and his Imperial Majesty." This declaration gave Lutheran rulers the signal to proceed with their intended legal, administrative, financial, and liturgical reforms, and the years following 1526 saw the construction in every Lutheran territory of what amounted to a state church, headed by the ruling prince.

In 1529 this process was interrupted when, following the emperor's military successes, Ferdinand demanded at a diet, also held in Speyer, that, pending a general council to decide the religious issue, Lutherans and other religious dissenters should end their separation. (It was the "protest" of a number of princes and cities against this abrogation of the earlier Speyer decree that attached to the followers of Luther and other Reformation theologians the name "Protestants.") By then Protestants were no longer a united party. Luther and Zwingli had met at Marburg in 1529 in an attempt to iron out differences, but they could not agree on the question of Christ's real presence in the Eucharist. While a few Lutheran princes prepared for military action, a compromise-minded group led by the humanist Philipp Melanchthon, who dreaded the prospect of fragmentation within Protestantism, drew up a moderate outline of Lutheran positions. These were presented for discussion at the Diet of Augsburg in 1530, which was attended by the emperor. The Augsburg Confession, which became a fundamental statement of Lutheran belief, assumed that reconciliation with the Catholics was still possible. This view was shared by Charles, who was pushing the pope toward the summoning of a general council to mend the religious split. Negotiations among theologians and politicians, however, came to nothing, and the end result was that, with the Augsburg Confession rejected by

Catholic theologians, Lutheranism was outlawed again. The militant Protestant faction, led by Philip, landgrave of Hesse, now established a formal organization of resistance, the Schmalkaldic League (1531), and the empire moved toward armed conflict as Lutherans became not just a political party but a military force as well.

About this time much more rigid standards of religious orthodoxy and conformity were imposed. This development has been called "confessionalization," a concept used by some historians to define developments in the empire during the mid-16th century. Confessionalization completed the process, under way since the late Middle Ages, of meshing religious and church politics with the objectives of the state. Central to this process was the institution of a territorial religion that was based on an authorized declaration of doctrines (a "Confession") binding on all subjects and implemented by an established church responsible to the ruler (or, in city states, to the magistrates). Tending toward exclusiveness and therefore intolerance, this system contributed to the warlike turn taken by events after 1530. More important in the long run, confessionalism promoted a social drive, also long under way, toward the inculcation of discipline and order in public and private as well as in religious and civic affairs. Through catechisms, schooling, family and welfare legislation, norms for work, and standards for personal life, state and church attempted to restructure society in accordance with the goals of what has since been called the Protestant temperament. Success was slow in coming and never more than partial. But there is no doubt that, through the confessional process, Protestantism left a deep imprint on the German character.

RELIGIOUS WAR AND THE PEACE OF AUGSBURG

After the diet of 1530, Charles left Germany for more than a decade, occupied with troubles in the Mediterranean, the Netherlands, and, once again, France. In 1535 he campaigned against Tunis to subdue the Barbary pirates who, as a naval arm of the Ottomans and as corsairs and privateers, had been making navigation unsafe. Renewed war with France was temporarily halted in 1538 by a treaty meant to last 10 years, but in 1542 France struck again, along with several European allies, including the duke of Gelderland and Cleves (or Kleve), whose lands were claimed by Charles as part of his Burgundian inheritance. The emperor's conquest of this duchy in 1543, which considerably broadened his power base, and the peace he concluded with France in 1544 (the Peace of Crépy), followed by an armistice in 1545 with the Ottoman Empire, left him free at last to deal decisively with the German Protestants.

The emperor's policy toward religious deviants was guided by his concept of empire. The universal realm over which he hoped to reign faced external and internal threats; its desired unity and order were assaulted by infidels from without and by national rivalries and heresy from within. He had dealt with the first and second threats; now he turned his attention to the third. Protestantism had spread rapidly in Germany. More than a religion, it was, by the 1540s, a full-fledged political movement with a growing military capacity. The number of Protestant territories had recently grown to include, among others, Brandenburg, the Palatinate, Albertine Saxony, and the bishoprics of Cologne, Münster, Osnabrück, Naumburg, and Merseburg. In Philip of Hesse the Lutherans had an able political strategist. At least provisionally, pending the settlement of all religious issues by a general council, the Protestants had won grudging recognition of their right to exist. Such a council was actually summoned by Pope Paul III—though only upon repeated prodding by the emperor—but there were few signs that the Protestant states would submit. In 1545, therefore, Charles decided on war. He found a pretext in the capture, by Lutheran princes, of the duke of Braunschweig-Wolfenbüttel, a Catholic who had tried to reconquer the lands from which he had been expelled by his Lutheran subjects. Claiming that this capture violated imperial law, Charles opened the conflict in 1546, in which he was joined by Maurice, duke of Saxony, an ambitious Lutheran prince to whom Charles had secretly promised the Saxon electorship. The ensuing war fell into two phases, the first of which saw the emperor victorious at the Battle of Mühlberg, in

PEACE OF AUGSBURG

The Peace of Augsburg was the first permanent legal basis for the existence of Lutheranism as well as Catholicism in Germany. It was promulgated on September 25, 1555, by the Diet of the Holy Roman Empire assembled earlier that year at Augsburg. The emperor Charles V's provisional ruling on the religious question, the Augsburg Interim of 1548, had been overthrown in 1552 by the revolt of the Protestant elector Maurice of Saxony and his allies. In the ensuing negotiations at Passau (summer 1552), even the Catholic princes had called for a lasting peace, for fear that otherwise the religious controversy would never be settled. The emperor, however, was unwilling to recognize the religious division in Western Christendom as permanent and granted a peace only until the next imperial Diet.

The Diet, which opened at Augsburg on February 5, 1555, was proclaimed by Charles V, but, not wishing to take part in the inevitable religious compromises, he refused to attend the proceedings and empowered his brother Ferdinand (the future emperor Ferdinand I) to settle all questions.

The Diet determined that in the future no ruler in the empire should make war against another on religious grounds and that this peace should remain operative until the churches were peacefully reunited. Only two churches were recognized, the Roman Catholic and the adherents of the Augsburg Confession—i.e., the Lutherans. Moreover, in each territory of the empire, only one church was to be recognized, the religion of the ruler's choice being thus made obligatory for his subjects. Any who adhered to the other church could sell his property and migrate to a territory where that denomination was recognized. The free imperial cities, which had lost their religious homogeneity a few years earlier, were exceptions to the general ruling. Lutheran and Catholic citizens in these cities remained free to exercise their religion as they pleased. The same freedom was furthermore extended to Lutheran knights and to towns and other communities that had for some time been practicing their religion in the lands of ecclesiastical princes of the empire. This last concession provoked vehement Catholic opposition, and Ferdinand circumvented the difficulty by deciding the matter on his own authority and including the clause in a separate article.

Ecclesiastical lands taken by Lutheran rulers from Catholic prelates who were not immediate vassals of the emperor were to remain with the Lutherans if continuous possession could be proved from the time of the Treaty of Passau (August 2, 1552), but, to ensure the permanence of the remaining ecclesiastical territories, the Catholics gained the condition that in the future any ecclesiastical prince who became Protestant should renounce his office, lands, and revenues. Because the Lutherans would not accept this ecclesiastical reservation and the Catholics would not yield, Ferdinand incorporated the clause on his own authority with a note that agreement had not been reached on it. In fact, Lutherans were in many cases able to nullify its effect.

The wish for a lasting settlement was so strong that the compromise peace, which satisfied no one completely and had many loopholes, was accepted. In spite of its shortcomings, the Peace of Augsburg saved the empire from serious internal conflicts for more than 50 years. It also strengthened the power of the territorial ruler. Germany thus emerged from the 16th century as a religiously divided country.

1547. Capitalizing on this strong position, Charles in 1548 forced the estates to accept an Interim, a temporary religious settlement on the emperor's terms. It was the political concessions Charles demanded from the estates, however—concessions that would have permanently limited their autonomy—that led to a resumption of war. Among the Protestants the lead was now taken by Maurice of Saxony, who had abandoned the emperor and had obtained material support from the new French king, Henry II, for fighting on the Protestant side. The resulting "Princes' War" was brief (1552–53) and inconclusive, and in 1555 a peace was signed at an imperial diet held, again, in Augsburg.

The Peace of Augsburg closed one epoch of German history and opened another. It decided the religious issue but did so in a way bound to occasion future problems. It reinforced the princes' authority over their territories but failed to settle their relations with the emperor. Most important, it legalized Lutheranism, laying down the rule, later epitomized in the phrase *cuius regio, eius religio* ("he who governs the territory decides its religion"), that each ruler in the empire—i.e., each prince or city government—could opt for either the Roman Catholic or the Lutheran religion (*jus reformandi*) and that this choice was binding on everyone under that ruler's jurisdiction. Only one faith could legitimately exist in a given state, and that faith had to be the ruler's and could be only Catholicism or Lutheranism; Calvinism, Zwinglianism, and Anabaptism were excluded. A subject unwilling to live by this choice was free to emigrate and take his belongings with him (a provision considered liberal at the time). Confiscated church properties could be kept by the governments that had taken them. An Ecclesiastical Reservation prevented ruling prelates from converting their lands along with them. These terms make it clear that the real winners of the war, and of the entire Reformation period, were the territorial princes, whose authority and power, which now encompassed the church, were greatly increased. As for the emperor, he abdicated in frustration and retired to a monastery in Spain, leaving his Spanish and Burgundian crowns to his son Philip and the empire and the Habsburg lands in central Europe to his brother Ferdinand. These two men, as Philip II and Ferdinand I, strong-minded Catholics both, were to play prominent roles in the period of Counter-Reformation and confessionalism that dominated Europe after 1555.

THE CONFESSIONAL AGE, 1555–1648

The changes that resulted from state building and the Reformation yielded little real benefit for ordinary people. Historians agree that the later 16th century was, for many, a time of economic hardship and social stress. Rapid increase in population (the European population rose by more than half between 1500 and 1700) and, secondarily, the influx of precious metals from the New World were the main causes of an inflationary trend that spanned the entire century and reached painful stages in Germany in the 1590s and early 1600s. Grain prices were especially affected, with the result that an ever smaller share of the ordinary person's budget was available for the purchase of other products. This had several effects, which, at least in outline, are well documented. The quality of nutrition for all but the wealthiest became much worse than it had been in the late Middle Ages, when meat consumption was at an all-time high. Illness and epidemic disease were frequent as the nutritional deficiency was aggravated by a series of bad harvests, perhaps caused by unusually severe winters in the decades after 1560.

GERMAN SOCIETY IN THE LATER 1500S

Cities and towns suffered loss of income as the market for their manufactured wares declined. In consequence, municipal guilds lost ground, not only economically but also politically, as their participation in urban policy making was curtailed. There were exceptions to this trend. Craftsmen specializing in the manufacture of luxury cloths and arms found lucrative markets at princely courts; but overall the position of artisans declined. Journeymen could no longer anticipate becoming masters. Artisans employed in traditional handiwork felt the pressure of the putting-out system favoured by merchant capitalists, whereby much

production was moved from the town, where artisanal guilds protected their members, to the countryside, where merchants could hire cheaper labour. Division of labour increased, gradually transforming self-employed craftsmen into dependent workers.

In the agricultural sector, high grain prices and rising land values improved the lot of peasant proprietors, but the greatest beneficiaries were landowning nobles and urban patricians with investments in agriculture. Society was polarized by these developments. A minority of rich peasants lived amid struggling smallholders hard-pressed by feudal lords who maximized their profits by increasing labour and tax burdens (the period has been called a "second serfdom"), and in the cities an upper crust of wealthy merchants and landed aristocrats faced a proletariat, whole sections of which were pauperized by the end of the century. The populous cities, once the glory of Germany, began to play a smaller role, as economic troubles and the centralizing policies of territorial princes decreased their prosperity and sapped their political strength.

The highly visible contrast between rich and poor and the animosity of the weak against the powerful created tensions among groups and classes. Political and economic power was more concentrated than ever before. Its new centres in Germany were the splendid courts of secular and ecclesiastical princes, whence it was distributed to favoured groups: the nobility, rising in importance again but finding its function limited to the service of rulers, and the upper bourgeoisie, shifting its loyalty from guild hall to palace. For ordinary people, administrative centralization and politically sanctioned Reformation had the effect of imposing more rigid control over their lives. A host of mandates flowed from centres of government, seeking to promote an ethic of order, productivity, and morality by shaping working and domestic activities as well as private habits and attitudes. These inroads caused resentment, and there is evidence of widespread resistance, most of it passive. Under these circumstances, the Evangelical Reformation seems to have made but slight impact on the populace at large, whose effective religion continued to be a mixture of traditional Christianity and folk magic.

Most people were worse off near the end of the 16th century than at its beginning. The lot of women, in particular, had deteriorated. About 1500 many German women had been at work in numerous urban occupations. But a century later they had been crowded out of all but the most demeaning trades as economic pressures, reinforcing ancient prejudices, eliminated them wherever they offered competition to male craftsmen. In this light, it is not surprising that the period from the 1580s to the 1620s also witnessed a surge of persecutions for witchcraft in Germany (mainly in the southwest and Bavaria). As elsewhere, the witch craze in the empire seems to have been a reaction to the strains of a time of troubles, the actual causes of which, fairly

clear now to historians, were hidden from contemporaries.

RELIGION AND POLITICS, 1555–1618

Four forces contended for supremacy in the Holy Roman Empire in the aftermath of the Peace of Augsburg. Lutherans—that is to say, Lutheran estates and governments—sought to extend the rights they had won in 1555 to parts of Germany that were still Roman Catholic. Calvinists, having been excluded from the Augsburg settlement, strove for recognition and made major territorial gains in the 1560s and '70s. Adherents of the old faith, invigorated by the Catholic Reformation issuing from Spain and Rome, attempted to turn back the Protestant advance by making common cause with strong governments. Habsburg emperors tried to serve the Catholic cause by weakening Protestant princes wherever possible and by holding the line against Protestantism in their dynastic lands. Political conflicts were constant under these circumstances and wars frequent, since the empire's institutions were powerless to neutralize or channel these competing endeavours. Maximilian II (from 1564), Rudolf II (from 1576), and Matthias (from 1612), though ardent Catholics, were preoccupied with the intertwined problems of retaining the loyalty of their dynastic lands and securing the eastern borders against the Turks. They had, in any case, been stripped of the ability to maintain order in the empire, as the Augsburg terms had placed public security under the supervision of the empire's administrative districts, which were controlled by the estates. The period leading up to the Thirty Years' War was therefore one of more or less constant strife in nearly all parts of the empire.

The second half of the 16th century introduced two new agents of change to this scene. The Catholic Reformation, operating mainly through the Council of Trent (1545–63) and the Jesuits (Society of Jesus), brought about major changes in Roman Catholicism. Trent produced authoritative definitions of dogma for the first time in the long history of the church; declared tradition to be, with the Bible, a source of revelation; reaffirmed the sacraments as mediators of grace; declared the church to be a hierarchical institution headed by the pope (against Luther's formulation of the "priesthood of all believers"); and issued a large number of reform mandates to meet, at last, the age-old charges of laxness and corruption. After the 1560s the Catholic Reformation's chief energies went to the implementation of the Trent decrees. Most effective in this endeavour were the Jesuits, a militant order founded by Ignatius of Loyola in 1534, pledged to strict obedience to the pope and to acting as the church's instrument for regaining ground lost to Protestantism. Germany was a major area of Jesuit activity; the order settled in Cologne in 1544 and later in Vienna, Ingolstadt, and Prague. In close collaboration with Catholic rulers, often as their confessors, the Jesuits embodied the activist phase of Catholic reform that is known as the Catholic Reformation.

On the Protestant side, this activism was represented by the Calvinists, who made so forceful an impact on German society in these decades that some historians have called their appearance a "Second Reformation." The Palatine electorate went Calvinist when its ruler converted; later the "Reformed" creed (as its partisans named it, denying to other Protestant denominations the claim to have truly reformed the faith) established itself, among other places, in the electorates of Brandenburg and (for a time) Saxony, the territories of Hesse-Kassel, Nassau, Durlach, and Anhalt, and the cities of Bremen, Emden, and Münster. Unlike Genevan Calvinism, the Reformed religion in Germany coexisted easily with the autocratic territorial church. Calvinist German princes, for their part, saw the faith as a far more aggressive theological and political weapon with which to wage the struggle for Protestant supremacy in the empire. Calvinist theology, with its emphasis on action in the world and its association of success with sanctification, even with election, was well suited, in the use made of it by German state churches, to act as an aggressive creed of social discipline. Calvinism also inspired the formation of militant parties pressing for its recognition as a legitimate religion under the *cuius regio, eius religio* ("whose region, his religion") rule, which had been formulated in the Peace of Augsburg.

With the religious situation thus more inflamed than ever and the confessional and political issues inextricably intertwined, any incident might have triggered renewed conflict, which—given the competition for power in Europe among the Habsburg dynasties, France, England, and the Netherlands—was likely to lead to a general war. A series of incidents moved events toward the brink. In 1582 the archbishop-elector of Cologne, having converted to Calvinism, challenged the Ecclesiastical Reservation of the 1555 Augsburg treaty by holding on to his title, thus threatening to give the majority vote in the College of Electors to the Protestants. In the "Cologne War" of 1583 he was expelled by Spanish troops, and Duke Ernst of Bavaria was chosen as his successor. Throughout the 1590s the incorporation of church properties by Protestant governments was a cause of litigation before the empire's courts, as Roman Catholic authorities sought to compel the return of everything confiscated since 1555; Protestant states, in turn, made support for the emperor's war against the Turks dependent on further concessions.

The Habsburgs, meanwhile, were hampered in their advancement of the Roman Catholic cause by the growing mental incapacity of Rudolf II; indeed, much of the direction of affairs was transferred to his brother Matthias, who eventually succeeded him in 1612. A more serious undermining of Habsburg imperial power occurred in the dynastic lands. Rigorous Catholic reform occasioned peasant uprisings in Austria and resistance by nobles in Hungary and Bohemia (where Calvinism had made inroads among the ruling classes). In Hungary a nationalist party under Bocskay István forged an alliance with Lutheran princes and obtained support from the Turks. In Bohemia in 1609 the estates extracted from the emperor a guarantee of religious freedom, the so-called Letter of Majesty.

At about the same time, the city of Donauwörth was occupied by Bavarian troops, since the emperor had empowered Duke Maximilian of Bavaria to "protect" the Roman Catholic minority there. Seeing this "Donauwörth incident" as a straw in the wind, Lutheran and Calvinist rulers formed a Protestant Union (1608), the answer to which was the Catholic League (1609), headed by Maximilian, the most resolute Catholic prince in the empire. Each party organized an army and allied itself with foreign powers, the Protestants with France and Bohemia, the Catholics with Spain. In this way the German struggle was both militarized and internationalized.

General war nearly broke out in 1609–10 over the Jülich-Cleves succession crisis. When the Roman Catholic ruler of these counties, which formed the strategically most important block of territories on the lower Rhine, died without an heir, two Protestant claimants occupied his lands, aided not only by the German Protestant Union but also by France and England; they were, however, militantly opposed by Spain and the emperor. The assassination of Henry IV of France, who had been about to launch an invasion in support of the Protestant claimants, defused the crisis in 1610.

Peace was preserved, although not for long. The Bohemian situation finally precipitated the war. Because neither Rudolf II nor Matthias had left legitimate heirs, the governance of the Habsburg dynastic lands fell to Archduke Ferdinand of Styria (later Emperor Ferdinand II), a ruthless counterreformer who reduced the religious liberties granted to Bohemians under the Letter of Majesty. In response, the Bohemian estates in May 1618 mounted a protest in Hradčany (the Prague Castle district), which prompted a militant faction of deputies to throw two imperial councillors from a castle window (defenestration being a traditional Bohemian gesture of defiance). In response to this event, which came to be known as the Defenestration of Prague, Ferdinand now prepared military action, while the Bohemian estates elected a Calvinist, Frederick V of the Palatinate, to be their king. As the alliances fell into place on each side, the stage was set for the sequence of large-scale military actions that constituted the Thirty Years' War.

THE THIRTY YEARS' WAR AND THE PEACE OF WESTPHALIA

The Bohemian problem was resolved swiftly. Two Roman Catholic armies, the emperor's and the League's, converged on the kingdom, routing Frederick at the White Mountain in November 1620 and replacing the regime of the estates in Bohemia with a system of "confessional absolutism" based on rigid Catholic conformity and political authoritarianism.

At the same time, the Palatinate was conquered by Spanish and Bavarian troops, and the electoral title was transferred to Maximilian of Bavaria in 1623. In the Palatinate, too, the Counter-Reformation sought to bring Protestantism to an end. As the war spread into Hesse and Westphalia and as Spain resumed its attack on the Netherlands, Catholic forces seemed near triumph. This prospect, however, renewed the old fear, as in the time of Charles V, of Habsburg hegemony; an anti-Habsburg alliance was therefore forged by France (where Cardinal Richelieu took charge of affairs in 1624), England (whose ruler, James I, was father-in-law to the deposed Frederick V), the Netherlands, and Denmark (whose Protestant king, Christian IV, had extensive territorial interests in northern Germany, now threatened by Catholic armies). In 1625 Christian IV commenced hostilities. He was opposed by a

much-enlarged imperial force under the war's most flamboyant figure, Albrecht von Wallenstein, a military entrepreneur with a gift for mobilizing troops and supplying them through ruthless plundering. Wallenstein's plan was to wreck Dutch and English commerce in the Baltic by subduing all of northern Germany and by dislodging the Swedish king, Gustav II Adolf, from Prussia (taken in the course of Sweden's war against Poland).

By 1628 much of this objective was realized. Christian IV had been decisively defeated in 1626 in the Battle of Lutter am Barenberge and forced to make peace in 1629. To crown these successes, Ferdinand II issued in March of that year the Edict of Restitution, by which Protestant rulers were to restore to the church more than 500 bishoprics, monasteries, abbeys, and other ecclesiastical properties secularized since 1552.

Engraving depicting the Sack of Magdeburg during the Thirty Years' War. Fotosearch/Archive Photos/Getty Images

But this impressive strengthening of the sovereign's power in the empire brought his foreign and domestic enemies together once more, the latter including now not only Protestants but also Roman Catholic estates concerned about their liberties. Subsidized by the Dutch and French and allied with Saxony, Sweden entered the conflict in 1630, winning commanding victories at Breitenfeld (1631) and Lützen (1632) but suffering defeat at Nördlingen in 1634. This phase of the war was marked by unprecedented brutality; for example, in 1631, imperial troops massacred two-thirds of the population of Magdeburg, a city of 20,000 that had withstood a long siege.

A way out of the long conflict appeared in 1635 when Saxony, Brandenburg, and other Protestant states seeking to end foreign intervention joined the emperor in the Peace of Prague, which included the revocation of the Edict of Restitution. But in the war's final phase, France, seeking to forestall Spanish preponderance on the Continent, offered large subsidies to Sweden and to German princes to enable them to fight on. Combined Swedish-French campaigns commenced in 1638, and a decade later foreign armies operated as far south as Bavaria, while the French held Lorraine and Alsace, which was important to France to prevent construction of a Spanish land bridge from the Netherlands to Italy.

By then most belligerents were exhausted. Several German princes had quit the war. Since 1644, representatives of the powers had been talking about terms, although military operations continued in hopes of improving bargaining positions. In 1648, finally, treaties were signed in Münster and Osnabrück (both in Westphalia) by agents of the emperor, the German states, Sweden, and France as well as between Spain and the Netherlands. Fighting continued for some years—France and Spain did not conclude peace until 1659—but the war was at last winding down. The Peace of Westphalia brought territorial gains to Sweden and France, awarded an electoral seat to Bavaria, and secured for Protestant rulers the church properties they had confiscated, based on the status quo of 1624. More important, it brought Calvinists into the religious settlement and established the independence of the Netherlands from Spain and of Switzerland from the empire. Most significant of all, it guaranteed the nearly unlimited territorial sovereignty of German princes, bringing to an end the last effort (until the 19th century) to centralize power in the empire. In this way the Peace of Westphalia sealed the fragmentation of the Holy Roman Empire into hundreds of autonomous political entities, most of them small. At the same time, it brought to an end the last major conflict in continental Europe in which religion was a central issue; indeed, the war itself had demonstrated that reason of state was a stronger determinant of policy than faith. In declaring the religious situation fixed as of 1624, the treaty mandated that, if a prince converted, his land no longer converted with him.

Religious pluralism and—albeit grudgingly—coexistence were now the norm.

The war's social and economic cost is difficult to gauge, modern scholarship having greatly modified original claims of vast human losses and near-total economic ruin. Nonetheless, in the most embattled realms, such as Württemberg, more than 50 percent of the people died or disappeared; elsewhere, the loss was less severe. Most historians agree that an overall population decline of 15 to 20 percent (from about 20 million to 16 or 17 million) occurred during the war and the ensuing epidemics. In addition, historians agree that in theatres of war rural impoverishment and displacement of people were widespread, while economic regression happened nearly everywhere. For German society overall, the war was a traumatic experience; it is rivaled in the national consciousness only by World War II as a time of unmitigated disaster.

To gain perspective on these calamities, their wider European aspects must be considered. Wars, uprisings, and political turmoil had occurred in many countries during the first half of the 17th century. The Fronde—a series of civil wars in France between 1648 and 1653 whose goal, at least in part, was to halt the growing power of royal government—and the Civil Wars in England (1642 to 1651) are only the most famous of these disturbances. Turmoil had occurred also in Catalonia, Portugal, Naples, Ireland, Scotland, Sweden, and Russia. Historians have referred to these events, including the numerous local manifestations of the Thirty Years' War, as parts of a general crisis in the fabric of European society, the causes of which range from a worsening of the climate (Little Ice Age) to plagues, often spread by the armies roaming Europe almost continuously at that time. But the most destabilizing factor burdening society was the centralizing monarchy with its expanding bureaucracy, extravagant courts, swollen armies, and incessant wars, all of them supported by heavy taxation. No social group, or estate, was unaffected by the effort of monarchs to alter in their favour traditional ways of distributing power and wealth. Resentment of this and of its social cost was widespread; hence the proliferation and the scale of rebellions.

TERRITORIAL STATES IN THE AGE OF ABSOLUTISM

The empire was an awkward structure. German historians of an older, nationalistic generation deplored the fact that the empire lacked the attributes of a Great Power and lamented its victimization by more unified foreign states. Such critics always quote the 17th-century legal scholar Samuel von Pufendorf, who called the empire a "monstrosity," and interpret this term as a value judgment rather than an expression indicating the inapplicability of standard categories of political classification. Recent scholars have been more appreciative of the post-1648 empire as a loose-jointed but not ineffective constitutional edifice within which could coexist 300 large and small

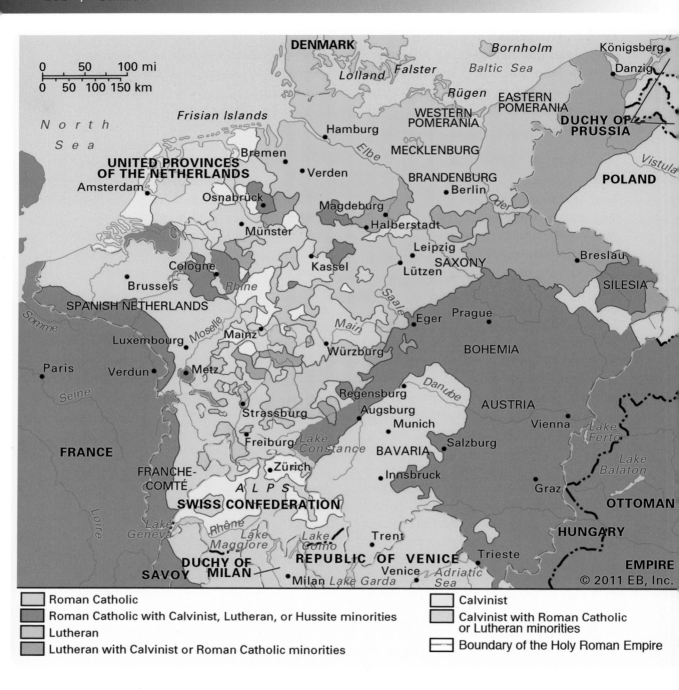

The range of confessions in Germany, 1650, as a result of the Thirty Years' War.

secular and ecclesiastical principalities, 51 imperial (i.e., independent within the empire) cities, and nearly 2,000 imperial counts and knights, each of whom possessed the same territorial sovereignty as an elector or a duke.

THE EMPIRE AFTER WESTPHALIA

The empire proved a working federation for the varied interests of these distinct sovereign entities, some of them large and powerful (such as Saxony, whose electors were also kings of Poland from 1697 to 1763, or Brandenburg, whose prince was also king of Prussia) and some laughably tiny (such as the Abbey of Baindt in Swabia, a fully independent territory of a few hundred acres inhabited by 29 nuns and governed by a princess-abbess). The empire's administrative organs, especially the districts (Kreise), protected the small and weak from the predatory aims of the strong. Because most constituent members were vulnerable, there was no general inclination, despite disunity among the estates on matters of taxation and religious parity, to break the frame that guarded the status quo. The emperor's suzerainty over the entire realm went unchallenged, but virtually no real power adhered to his title, executive authority having been thoroughly particularized between 1555 and 1648. To prevent a resurgence of imperial power, princes formed alliances among themselves, such as the League of the Rhine (Rheinbund), tied in 1658 to France

and Sweden. In the princely territories authority fell increasingly to the princes (though Württemberg and Mecklenburg were exceptions), while territorial estates dwindled in political importance. In each of the empire's constituent units, estates served mainly to uphold established hierarchies and traditions, as did the empire as a whole. It was an inherently conservative system.

THE CONSOLIDATION OF BRANDENBURG-PRUSSIA AND AUSTRIA

Against an overall tendency among the empire's constituent units to keep things as they were, the larger territories pursued an insistent policy of dynastic and personal aggrandizement. A number of factors favoured state building in the post-1618 era. General economic exhaustion made central direction of, and active intervention in, commerce and production seem to be the only way out of stagnation. War taxes, raised to a steep level during the French wars of the 1670s, greatly increased the financial might of rulers, who came to control an unprecedented share of society's wealth by preparing for and engaging in military conflict. Because territorial assemblies opposed this siphoning process—whose proceeds, augmented by subsidies from abroad, served mostly to create standing armies and a supporting state apparatus—rulers attempted to reduce even further the estates' role in policy making. The nobility, growing economically dependent on princely service, adapted itself to an essentially ancillary function at court and in the military. In society at large, the view gained ground that the country's welfare was safest with the ruler—a view vigorously promoted by official propaganda. Two of the empire's territories, Brandenburg-Prussia and Austria, profited above all others from these developments.

For historians over the years, the story of Brandenburg-Prussia has exemplified the triumph of political skill and audacity over unfavourable conditions. Sparsely populated and deficient in resources, Brandenburg in 1648 held sovereignty over a patchwork of scattered territories. Its ruler, Frederick William (1640–88), later known as the "Great Elector," faced the problem of integrating and defending widely separated possessions, which included the duchy of Prussia, inherited in 1619 but remaining under Polish suzerainty and geographically separated from the electorate of Brandenburg; the counties of Cleves, Mark, and Ravensberg in the Rhineland and Westphalia regions, gained in 1614, also distant from Brandenburg and not contiguous with each other; and eastern Pomerania and various small lands and bishoprics acquired in the Treaty of 1648. Through nimble diplomatic maneuvering, such as changing sides several times between Sweden and Poland and between France and the emperor, he augmented and solidified his realm and his authority within it; moreover, he won

direct rule over Prussia as its duke and acquired the important episcopal territory of Magdeburg.

Frederick William's instrument in the attainment of these and subsequent prizes was the army, a permanent force of 30,000 disciplined professionals, the adequate financial support of which dictated every aspect of his government. Large revenues from taxes required a flourishing economy, the stimulation and direction of which by mercantilist principles was a main undertaking. Economic growth was further accelerated late in the Great Elector's reign by the influx of nearly 20,000 skilled Huguenot refugees following the revocation of the Edict of Nantes by Louis XIV in 1685 and by the resettlement of Dutch colonists. A territorywide system of state administration undergirded this economic and fiscal effort and resulted in the creation of a professional bureaucracy that permitted the Great Elector to govern essentially without estate participation. The landowning nobility supported their prince in exchange for the freedom to exploit their peasants as they saw fit. In these ways Frederick William laid the foundation for what was to become an autocratically ruled state, enabled by its strong economy, tightly run administration, efficient fiscal organization, and powerful army to play a prominent role in the empire's and Europe's affairs.

The Great Elector's efforts were rewarded in 1701 when his successor, Frederick III (1688–1713), obtained from the emperor (who needed the

Brandenburg army for the impending War of the Spanish Succession) the right to style himself Frederick I, King in Prussia (Prussian rulers renumbered themselves upon bestowal of the royal title). The title of king, recognized internationally upon the conclusion of the war in 1713, was of considerable importance to Brandenburg in its competition with Saxony, whose ruler had become king of Poland in 1697, for preeminence in northern Germany. But it was Frederick's son, Frederick William I (1713–40), who perfected the combination of statist structure, productive energy, and ethical drive that came to be identified with modern Prussia. Known as the "soldier-king," Frederick William built his standing army into a force of more than 80,000 men. Although Prussia was only the 13th most populous country in Europe, it had the continent's fourth largest army (after those of France, Russia, and Austria), a superbly drilled and equipped force that served mainly defensive purposes. Only peasants and journeymen served in the ranks, while the middle classes were safe from the draft but obliged to quarter soldiers in their homes. A huge war chest obviated foreign subsidies, and reliable revenues, more than 70 percent of which went to the army, provided ample support.

For the state to continue to draw high taxes without ruining land and people, the country's level of wealth had to be raised. Frederick William therefore pursued an aggressive policy (known as cameralism) of stimulating agriculture and manufacturing while reducing unnecessary expenditures; even his court was stripped of many of its royal trappings. Export bans preserved raw materials, and sumptuary laws limited indulgence in luxuries. Town governments were subordinated to royal commissioners, whose powers included supervision of urban production. A work ethos suffused society from the top; the king's ascetic Calvinism, which dictated to him a life of hard work and personal engagement, was spread to his Lutheran subjects by a Pietist clergy who instilled in their flocks habits of intense labour, frugal living, and dutiful subservience to the state.

Organizationally, Frederick William completed the centralizing process begun by the Great Elector, its capstone being the General Directory, set up in 1723. Tied to regional and local organs by a network of commissioners, this supreme body of state policy and administration directed industry, trade, finance, internal affairs, and military matters in all the state's territories. Upper-level bureaucrats came entirely from the nobility, as did the army's officer corps; in this way nobles were bound more closely than ever to the state. Ruling, not merely reigning, over the entire edifice was the king-elector in his "cabinet," a small circle of close advisers and trusted secretaries. So successful were these measures in lifting the state to influence and prestige that by 1740 Prussia counted as a full-fledged member of Europe's concert of Great Powers.

In Austria the ruling Habsburg house's lasting conflict with France and the Ottoman Empire dominated all questions of statecraft. With their powers as emperors greatly diminished, Leopold I (1658–1705), his son Joseph I (1705–11), and Joseph's brother Charles VI (1711–40) bent all their efforts to the consolidation of their dynastic and crown lands in central and eastern Europe. Although they failed to achieve Prussian-style streamlining, they raised Austria to the rank of a major state. The Habsburgs' conglomeration of territories included the Austrian lands (the duchies of Austria, Styria, Carinthia, and Krain [in present-day Slovenia] and the county of Tirol), the Bohemian provinces (kingdoms of Bohemia and Moravia [both now in the Czech Republic] and of Silesia [in present-day Poland]), the kingdom of Hungary, and—after 1714, following the War of the Spanish Succession—the southern Netherlands (including Brabant and Flanders [both now in Belgium] and the duchy of Luxembourg [now divided between Belgium and Luxembourg]) and the duchy of Milan (in Italy).

These disparate lands were held together only by the Habsburg monarchy, but the monarchs were distracted from the task of integrating them. They were preoccupied by imperial concerns and by dynastic complications, notably the succession question. Until the reforms of Maria Theresa's reign (1740–80), Austrian administration never became effective. Finances were especially muddled, because tax administration remained with the estates of the various territories, along with control over other sources of revenue. The army of 100,000 men,

though the third largest in Europe, was barely adequate for the defense of so large and scattered a realm. A supreme war council and a central financial chamber overlapped with special commissions created by the emperor's privy council, which also handled military and fiscal affairs. Nonetheless, the realm held together.

The prospect of a succession without a male heir, however, presented the severest test to the realm's cohesion. It became the chief enterprise of Charles VI to persuade the estates of his territories to accept an order of succession, known as the "Pragmatic Sanction," by which the Habsburg lands were declared indivisible and Charles's oldest daughter, Maria Theresa, was to inherit them. The other European powers assented, because splitting the Habsburg complex would have thrown the European balance into disarray and played into the hands of France; the Sanction was proclaimed a basic law in 1713. By then Austria had met successfully a series of Turkish incursions from the east and French invasions in the west.

THE AGE OF LOUIS XIV

For the empire as a whole, the half century following the Peace of Westphalia was almost entirely shaped by the dominant political figure of the time, King Louis XIV of France. The response of the empire and its members to the aggressive undertakings of this monarch, whose aim from his assumption of power in 1661 to his death in 1715 it was to make France the mightiest state in Europe, was largely reactive. Only in its struggles against Louis's ally in the east, the Ottoman Turks, did the empire show some initiative. After a Polish relief army had helped imperial, Bavarian, and Saxon troops to lift a three months' Turkish siege of Vienna in 1683 in the Battle of Kahlenberg, imperial armies took the offensive, winning battles at Ofen (1686), Mohács (1687), and, most notably, Zenta (1697). In the Treaty of Carlowitz (1699), Austria gained parts of Hungary, Transylvania (now in Romania), Slavonia (now in Croatia), and Croatia, all formerly occupied by the Turks. The eastern wars resumed in the early and mid-18th century, but the Turks were never again a threat to Europe, since Russia became the chief bulwark against Ottoman expansionism.

Matters were different on the empire's western and southern fronts. The overriding political question in Europe in the second half of the 17th century was the future of Spain and its vast holdings in the southern Netherlands, Italy, and the Americas because it was expected that the Spanish Habsburg line would die out with the feeble Charles II. Contenders for the Spanish inheritance were the Habsburg emperor, Leopold I, husband of a younger Spanish princess, and Louis XIV. The French monarch, son of the eldest daughter of Philip III, had further strengthened his claim to the Spanish throne in 1659 when, in accordance with the Peace of the Pyrenees, which had ended the long conflict between Spain and France, he had married Marie-Thérèse, daughter of Philip IV of Spain.

While waiting for the Spanish throne to become vacant, Louis pursued an aggressive expansionist policy. He pushed his forces toward Germany to make the Rhine River France's new eastern border. In 1667 he occupied Flanders and in 1670 Lorraine; in 1672 he attacked Cleves and invaded the United Provinces of the Netherlands, his main antagonist in the wars that followed. In 1679 he began to penetrate Alsace, occupying the imperial city of Strassburg (now Strasbourg) in 1681. Lacking the military power to bring the whole empire to its knees, Louis resorted to the lure of money; at one time or another almost every German state was in his pocket, either serving as ally or remaining neutral. Though not incapable of acting on national impulses, German princes—the Great Elector being a case in point—always served territorial interests first. This prevented the emperor, himself at times allied with Louis, from forging a solid front against France.

Leadership of the anti-France coalition passed to the Dutch Republic. William of Orange, as stadtholder of Holland and captain general of the United Provinces, emerged as the most determined opponent of French aggression. Upon becoming king of England in 1689, he changed the direction of English politics, which had been pro-French under the last Stuart king. The threat of a French universal monarchy arose dramatically as the death of the last Habsburg in Spain approached and

Louis's plans for a French claim on the entire Spanish inheritance swung into place. When the Spanish king died in 1700, he left all of his realm, including his American colonies, to Louis's grandson, Philip, duc d'Anjou, thus dramatically shifting the balance of European power in France's favour. Against this a Grand Alliance took shape (it was formally concluded in 1701), consisting of the empire (except Bavaria and the electorate of Cologne), the Netherlands, England, Sweden, Brandenburg-Prussia, and Savoy (Portugal also eventually joined the alliance). Its aim was to restore the European balance to the status of 1648 and 1659 by ejecting Louis from his conquests and by splitting the Spanish empire. From 1701 to 1714, France, with a few minor allies, fought the Grand Alliance in the War of the Spanish Succession. Despite a number of major battles, including Blenheim (1704), Ramillies (1706), Oudenarde (1708), and Malplaquet (1709), neither side was able to win a decisive victory (though the Alliance did seem to be prevailing). The death of the emperor Joseph I in 1711 placed his brother Charles, who had been proclaimed the Spanish king, on the imperial throne as Charles VI (1711–40). This raised the spectre of a Habsburg reunion of the Holy Roman and Spanish empires—a situation no more agreeable to European powers than the prospect of French hegemony. Thus, the alliance was severed and the war began to wind down.

Peace negotiations began in 1712, resulting in a number of treaties, signed at Utrecht and Rastatt in 1713–14. The Spanish empire was partitioned, with the Spanish Netherlands, Milan, Naples, and Sicily going to Austria and Spain itself coming under the rule of Philip V of Bourbon, a grandson of Louis XIV. The alliance's original aim, to prevent French hegemony, had been achieved, though in the follow-up War of the Polish Succession (1733–35) France acquired control of Lorraine. Austria profited substantially in territorial terms, and a few other German rulers profited as well, albeit less so. As for the empire itself, it had gained no real benefit from more than half a century of intermittent warfare.

German society, however, was deeply affected. Economic stagnation and slow demographic recovery after the Thirty Years' War made Germany dependent on governmental intervention as a means of stimulating recovery. As centres of economic vitality, the princely courts, attended by an international nobility, exposed Germany to a variety of cultural innovations that originated in other, more prosperous European countries.

Baroque art—the preeminent expression of monarchical power and of Roman Catholic resurgence after the Reformation—came from Spain and Italy, opera from Italy, and polite language and manners from France. The style of this period took French patterns as its model, from elaborately coded court ceremonials to dress, social conventions, food, and conversation. French absolutism not only became the political model, however scaled down, for the governance of all states in the empire, but every German prince and princeling imitated the lavish display with which Louis XIV created his aura of majesty and outshone his rivals. This started up a lively domestic market in luxuries, not to mention splendid works of architecture and decoration. But the cost of these luxuries was prohibitive (in 1719 the Palatine court consumed 50 percent of the territory's revenues) and represented an enormous burden on the people, especially when added to the cost of large armies and proliferating bureaucracies. Not only did this conspicuous consumption widen the social division between the court-oriented elite and the bulk of the urban and rural population, but the preference for foreign cultural products also inhibited creative impulses at home.

In the second half of the 17th century, German energies were to a large extent still focused on religion. The confessional pluralism legitimized by the settlement of 1648 encouraged emphasis on theological distinctions, exacerbating the move toward religious orthodoxy under way in each denomination since the 16th century. The one genuinely German product of this religious preoccupation was Pietism, a movement within Lutheranism that opposed rigid dogmatism and promoted instead a subjective, mystical devoutness and an emphasis on a pious life guided by love of one's neighbour as well as of God. Influenced by English Puritanism, Pietism was shaped in its theology by Philipp Jakob Spener (1635–1705) and in its organization by his disciple August Hermann Francke

(1663–1727), who established a centre for its promulgation in Halle. There he founded schools, orphanages, medical facilities, and a printing house for publishing cheap Bibles and devotional works, which made Pietism a widely influential program of Evangelical activism. The intensely emotional and mystical flavour of Pietist poetry is preserved in the cantata texts set to music by Johann Sebastian Bach, in whose deeply spiritual church music Protestant chorale singing, another indigenous German product, reached its apogee.

THE CONTEST BETWEEN PRUSSIA AND AUSTRIA

In 1740 the death of the Habsburg emperor Charles VI without a male heir unleashed the most embittered conflict in Germany since the wars of Louis XIV. The question of the succession to the Austrian throne had occupied statesmen for decades. Rival claimants disputed the right—by the terms of the Pragmatic Sanction (1713)—of Charles's daughter Maria Theresa to succeed; France supported them, its aim being, as before, the fragmentation of the Habsburg state. But it was the new Prussian king, Frederick II (1740–86), who began the conflict. To understand what follows, the modern reader should remember that few observers, even in the enlightened 18th century, disputed a ruler's right to do what he wished with his state. Dynastic aggrandizement, territorial expansion, prestige, honour, power, and princely glory were legitimate grounds for war and sound reasons for demanding the sacrifices necessary to wage it. The only position from which to oppose this arrogation was the Christian ethic, but to do so had proved futile when last tried by Erasmus and Sir Thomas More in the 16th century. No checks—philosophical, moral, or political—therefore restrained kings from indulging their taste for conquests.

Soon after assuming power, Frederick reversed his father's cautious policy of building and hoarding, rather than deploying, Brandenburg-Prussia's military potential. He attacked Silesia, a province in the kingdom of Bohemia and thus part of the Habsburg monarchy, which Prussia had long desired for its populousness, mineral resources, and advanced economy. In exchange for an Austrian cession of Silesia, he offered to accept the Pragmatic Sanction (formally recognized by his predecessor in the 1728 Treaty of Berlin) and support the candidacy of Maria Theresa's husband, Francis Stephen, as emperor. But the resolute woman who now headed the Austrian Habsburgs (1740–80) decided to defend the integrity of her realm, and the War of the Austrian Succession (1740–48; including the Silesian Wars between Prussia and Austria) began in 1740. Austria was helped only by a Hungarian army, though initial financial support came from England. Prussia was joined by Bavaria and Saxony in the empire as well as by France and Spain. The Prussian armies, though greatly outnumbered by Austria's forces, revealed themselves as by far the best as well as the best-led. The Treaties of Dresden (1745) and Aix-la-Chapelle (1748) confirmed the Prussian conquest of Silesia. During the succeeding Seven Years' War (1756–63), Prussian forces occupied Saxony, which had allied itself with Austria. In the Treaty of Hubertusburg of 1763, Prussia kept Silesia but could not hold on to Saxony.

In a sense, the War of the Austrian Succession was another of the many internal struggles over the constitutional balance in the empire in which territorial states opposed imperial authority. But it was also part of an international struggle, with France and England fighting out their rivalry in western and southern Europe, North America, and India. In this way it prefigured the worldwide Seven Years' War, except that the latter followed the "diplomatic revolution" in which England switched its support from Austria to Prussia and France allied itself with its traditional foe, Austria. (A part of this agreement was the marriage, in 1770, of the Austrian princess Marie-Antoinette to the future Louis XVI.) The real significance of the Seven Years' War lay in the Treaty of Paris of 1763, which concluded for a time the maritime and colonial conflict between France and England.

After these wars Prussia—which had increased in size and immeasurably in prestige—and Austria dominated German affairs in a condition of tension usually called "the German dualism," meaning that each had become so powerful that only the other could keep it in some sort of check. The monarchs of both realms carried out important internal reforms. Guided by her interior minister, Count Friedrich Wilhelm Haugwitz, Maria Theresa streamlined the Austrian administrative structure on the Prussian model, thus drawing together, to the extent possible, the multiethnic and polyglot regions of the vast Habsburg empire. The remaining powers of the estates were curtailed everywhere and centralization institutionalized in absolutist fashion but without attaining the full integration of the Prussian system. Maria Theresa's son, Joseph II (1765–90), completed this program of modernization.

In Prussia, Frederick II further tightened his control of all aspects of public life in his far-flung kingdom. However, in accordance with his personal commitment to rational tolerance and free-thinking skepticism, he also undertook extensive legal reforms. He virtually abolished judicial torture, lifted some of the tax burden from the poorest of his subjects, established religious tolerance as a policy of his state, and encouraged scientific and scholarly activity in the Prussian Academy of the Sciences. Like his father, he was a vigorous promoter of economic development. His taste for French Enlightenment thought and his own prolific creativity in letters and music lent his reign the flavour of an era shaped by a philosopher-king, albeit one with the instincts of a ruthless power politician. His successes in war and peace earned him a place as national hero as well as the title "the Great."

THE RISE OF PRUSSIA AND THE NAPOLEONIC ERA

Germany in the middle of the 18th century was a country that had been drifting in the backwaters of European politics for more than a hundred years. The decisive roles in the affairs of the Continent were played by those great powers—such as France, England, and Spain—whose economic resources and commercial connections provided a solid foundation for their military might. The German states, on the other hand, floundered in a morass of provincialism and particularism. All the forces that had contributed to the rise of powerful national monarchies west of the Rhine were lacking in the east. In the Holy Roman Empire the central government was losing rather than gaining strength, the princes were enlarging their authority at the expense of the crown, and business initiative was being discouraged by the lack of political unity and by the remoteness of the major trade routes.

Political power increasingly fell to small regional governments controlled by aristocratic overlords, ecclesiastical dignitaries, or municipal oligarchs. The history of Germany between the Thirty Years' War and the French Revolution is largely the sum total of the histories of dozens upon dozens of small political units, each enjoying virtually full rights of sovereignty. The rulers of these gingerbread principalities, copying the example of the royal court of France or Austria, built costly imitations of the palaces of

Versailles and Schönbrunn, which today are the delight of tourists but which were once the curse of an impoverished peasantry. The tradition of princely authority, an instrument of national greatness in western Europe, encouraged divisiveness in Germany. The country's petty rulers legislated at will, levied taxes, concluded alliances, and waged wars against each other and against the emperor. Policies pursued in Munich, Stuttgart, Dresden, or Darmstadt reflected policies originating in Paris, Vienna, London, or Madrid but had no goal beyond the promotion of particularistic interests.

Political institutions designed theoretically to express the will of the nation continued to function, yet they had become empty shells. The Holy Roman emperor was still elected in accordance with a time-honoured ritual that proclaimed him to be the successor of Caesar and Augustus (indeed, the German word for emperor, Kaiser, was derived from Caesar). The splendid coronation ceremony in Frankfurt am Main, however, could not disguise the fact that the office conferred on its holder little more than prestige. Since all the emperors in this period except Charles VII were Habsburgs by birth or marriage, they enjoyed an authority that had to be respected. But that authority rested not on the prerogative of the imperial crown but on the possession of hereditary lands stretching from Antwerp in the west to Debrecen in the east. The sovereigns of the Holy Roman Empire, in other words, were able to play an important role in German affairs by virtue of their non-German resources. And, since, apart from Austria, Germany was not the main source of their strength, Germany was not the main object of their concern. The emperors tended to regard the dignity bestowed upon them as a means of furthering the interests of their dynastic holdings. The Imperial Diet meeting in Regensburg had also become an instrument for the promotion of particularistic advantage rather than national welfare. It continued in theory to express the will of the estates of the realm meeting in solemn deliberation. In fact it had degenerated into a debating society without authority or influence. The princes had ceased to attend the sessions, so that only diplomatic representatives were left to discuss questions for which they were powerless to provide answers. The other central institutions of the empire, such as the imperial cameral tribunal in Wetzlar, languished in indolence. Constitutionally and politically, Germany circa 1760 resembled Poland in that a once vigorous and proud state had become weakened by internal conflict to the point that it invited the intervention of its more powerful neighbours.

What saved Germany from the fate of Poland was the ability of one of the member states to defend the empire against aggression. For 200 years Austria acted as the bulwark of central Europe against French expansion. Its possessions, forming a chain of protective bases extending between the North Sea and the Danube, had time and again borne the brunt of attacks by French armies. The frontiers of France kept moving closer to the Rhine, but the Holy Roman Empire was at least spared the tragedy of partition that befell the Polish state. It was partly in recognition of the vital role that the Habsburgs played in the defense of Germany that the electors chose them as emperors with such regularity. The Austrian monarchy, moreover, endowed with resources comparable to those of the western nations, was able to pursue a policy of political rationalization with greater success than most of the principalities. The rulers in Vienna succeeded in improving the administration, strengthening the economy, and centralizing the government. Until the middle of the 18th century, Austria remained the only Great Power east of the Rhine.

FURTHER RISE OF PRUSSIA AND THE HOHENZOLLERNS

The emergence of the Hohenzollerns of Prussia as rivals of the Habsburgs and the beginning of the Austro-Prussian dualism created the possibility of reversing the process of civic decentralization that had prevailed in Germany since the late Middle Ages. The interests of the territorial princes of the Holy Roman Empire inclined them toward a policy of particularism, while the government of Austria, with its Flemish, Italian, Slavic, and Magyar territories, could not perforce become the instrument of German unification. Prussia, on the other hand, was militarily strong enough and

ethnically homogeneous enough to make national consolidation the main object of statecraft. Still, in the 18th century, no Prussian ruler thought in national terms. The intention of Frederick II (Frederick the Great) and of his successors Frederick William II and Frederick William III was to pursue dynastic rather than national objectives. Like the lesser princes of Germany, all they sought was to maintain and enlarge their authority against the claim of imperial supremacy. Far from wanting to end the disunity of Germany, they hoped to prolong and exploit it. The patriotic Prussophile historians, who a hundred years later argued that what Bismarck had achieved was the consummation of what Frederick had sought, were letting the present distort their understanding of the past. In fact, the greatest of the Hohenzollerns had remained as indifferent to the glaring political weaknesses of his nation as to its great cultural achievements. His attitude toward the constitutional system of the Holy Roman Empire was similar to that of the self-seeking princelings who were his neighbours and from whom he was distinguishable only by talent and power. He may have scorned their sybaritic way of life, but politically he wanted what they wanted—namely, the freedom to seek the advantage of his dynasty without regard for the interests of Germany as a whole.

His preoccupation with the welfare of his state rather than with that of his nation is apparent in the strategy by which he tried to check Habsburg ambitions after the Seven Years' War

(1756–63). During the first half of his reign he had relied primarily on military force to advance his dynastic interests at the expense of the Habsburgs. In the second half he preferred to employ the weapons of diplomacy to achieve the same end. In 1777 the ruling dynasty of Bavaria came to an end with the death of Maximilian Joseph. The elector of the Palatinate, the Wittelsbach Charles Theodore, now became ruler over the Wittelsbach territory of Bavaria as well. Without legitimate heirs and without affection for his newly acquired eastern possessions, he agreed to a plan proposed by Emperor Joseph II to cede part of the Bavarian lands to Austria. But any increase in the strength of the Habsburgs was unacceptable to Frederick the Great. With the tacit approval of most of the princes of the empire, he declared war against Austria in 1778, hoping that other states within and outside central Europe would join him. In this expectation he was disappointed. Expecting an easy success, Joseph also became discouraged by the difficulties that he encountered. The War of the Bavarian Succession dragged on from the summer of 1778 to the spring of 1779, with neither side enhancing its reputation for military prowess. There was much marching back and forth, while hungry soldiers scrounged for food in what came to be called the "Potato War." The upshot was the Treaty of Teschen (May 1779), by which the Austrian government abandoned all claims to Bavarian territory except for a small strip along the Inn River. The conflict had brought Frederick no significant military victories, but he had succeeded in frustrating Habsburg ambition.

Joseph II, however, was a stubborn adversary. In 1785 he once again advanced a plan for the acquisition of Wittelsbach lands, this time on an even more ambitious scale. He suggested to Charles Theodore nothing less than an outright exchange of the Austrian Netherlands for all of Bavaria. The emperor, in other words, proposed to surrender his distant possessions on the North Sea, which were difficult to defend, for a territory that was contiguous and a population that was assimilable. The scheme went far beyond that which Prussia had defeated seven years before, and Frederick opposed it with equal determination. He hoped to enlist the diplomatic aid of France and Russia against what he regarded as an attempt to upset the balance of power in central Europe. But, more than that, he succeeded in forming the Fürstenbund (League of Princes), which 17 of the more important rulers in Germany joined. The members pledged themselves to maintain the fundamental law of the empire and to defend the possessions of the governments included within its boundaries. The growing opposition to the absorption of Bavaria by Austria persuaded Joseph that the risks inherent in his plan outweighed its advantages. The proposed exchange of territories was dropped, and Frederick could celebrate yet another triumph of his statecraft, the last of an illustrious career. But the association of princes that he founded did not survive its author. Its sole purpose had been the prevention of Habsburg hegemony. Once the danger had passed, it lost the only justification for its existence. Those nationalists who later maintained that it foreshadowed the creation of the German Empire misunderstood its origins and objectives. It was never more than a weapon in the struggle for the preservation of a decentralized form of government in Germany.

The Hohenzollerns' subordination of national to dynastic interests was even more apparent in the partitions of Poland. Frederick the Great was the chief architect of the First Partition, that of 1772, by which the ill-starred kingdom lost about one-fifth of its inhabitants and one-fourth of its territory to Prussia, Russia, and Austria. His successor, Frederick William II, helped to complete the destruction of the Polish state by the partitions of 1793 (between Prussia and Russia) and 1795 (between Prussia, Russia, and Austria). The result was bound to be an enhancement of Prussia's role in Europe but also a diminution of its focus on Germany. The Hohenzollerns willingly embarked on a course that would in time have transformed their kingdom into a binational state comparable to the Habsburg empire. The German population in the old provinces would have been counterbalanced by the Slavic population in the new; the Protestant faith of the Brandenburgers and Prussians would have had to share its influence with the Roman Catholicism of the Poles; the capital city of Berlin would have found a competitor in the capital city of Warsaw. In short, the centre of gravity of the state would have shifted eastward, away from the problems and interests of the Holy Roman Empire. Yet the rulers of Prussia did not shrink from a policy that was likely to have such far-reaching consequences. They never contemplated sacrificing the advantage that their state would gain from an enlargement of its resources in order to assume the role of unifiers of their nation. Such a political attitude would have been an anachronism during the age of princely absolutism in Germany. It was not design but accident that before long led to the abandonment by Prussia of most of its Polish possessions and that thereby allowed it to play a leading role in the affairs of Germany.

THE CULTURAL SCENE

Whereas in England the great literary epoch of Queen Elizabeth I had coincided with commercial and naval expansion, and in France the golden age of Classicism had added lustre to the military glory of Louis XIV, German arts and letters flourished amid tiny principalities and somnolent towns that could only envy the powerful national monarchies west of the Rhine. In France and England public opinion could exert a significant influence on government, and the debate over issues of state and society was conducted with a vigour that reflected its importance, but in the autocratic states of Germany the debate was bound to remain purely theoretical. No Voltaires, Rousseaus, or Burkes were likely to emerge out of such an environment. The thinkers of Germany tended to emphasize introspection and spirituality. Culture became an escape from the narrow world of princely absolutism. Intellectual energies that could not reform the community fought to emancipate the individual through self-purification and self-perfection.

This was the background of German idealism, a philosophical movement seeking to establish a foundation for ethics and aesthetics beyond the realm of empirical knowledge. Proceeding from principles articulated by Immanuel Kant, it attempted to prove that there was a realm of experience lying beyond the categories of scientific investigation: the realm of the good, the true, and the beautiful. There were realities of the spirit and the mind, in other words, that were inaccessible to the practicality of the British empiricists or the intellectualism of the French rationalists. The disciples of idealism hoped to transcend the barriers created by nation, class, and religion. They spoke in the name of humanity as a whole, which manifested its underlying harmony through the infinite variety of its political, social, and theological categories. Gotthold Ephraim Lessing pleaded for religious toleration on the basis of a common system of ethical values to which all men of goodwill could subscribe. Johann Gottfried Herder preached that the unique character and meaning of each culture contributed to the richness of common humanity that defied state boundaries. Johann Joachim

Winckelmann idealized the Classical ideal of beauty that he found in Greek art as an eternal standard, immune to the vicissitudes of time and history. These were views that offered an escape from the narrowness of everyday life. Kant, Lessing, Herder, and Winckelmann all believed in the necessity of changing institutions, but they were convinced that the place to begin was the individual's moral consciousness. This gave thought in Germany a metaphysical coloration that distinguished it from the more robust pragmatism of philosophy in the west. It was during the second half of the 18th century that the Germans began to consider their country "the land of thinkers and poets."

The literary revival of the age displayed the same quality of introspective idealism as the philosophical movement. Johann Wolfgang von Goethe, the greatest genius of German letters, willingly accepted the existing system of civic and social values. He regarded the disunity of his nation as an expression of its historic character and defended the authority of the petty princes as an instrument of good government. He urged his countrymen to seek greatness not in collective action but in individual perfectibility. After a period of youthful rebellion against traditional canons of literary propriety, he turned to a Classicism in which a serene acceptance of life harmonized with his own sympathy for the established order. Friedrich Schiller, a man of more turbulent temperament, resented political injustice and weakness. In his plays and

STURM UND DRANG

The German Sturm und Drang ("Storm and Stress") literary movement of the late 18th century exalted nature, feeling, and human individualism and sought to overthrow the Enlightenment cult of Rationalism. Johann Wolfgang von Goethe and Friedrich Schiller began their careers as prominent members of the movement.

The exponents of the Sturm und Drang were profoundly influenced by the thought of Jean-Jacques Rousseau and Johann Georg Hamann, who held that the basic verities of existence were to be apprehended through faith and the experience of the senses. The young writers also were influenced by the works of the English poet Edward Young, the pseudo-epic poetry of James Macpherson's "Ossian," and the recently translated works of Shakespeare.

Sturm und Drang was intimately associated with the young Goethe. While a student at Strasbourg, he made the acquaintance of Johann Gottfried von Herder, a former pupil of Hamann, who interested him in Gothic architecture, German folk songs, and Shakespeare. Inspired by Herder's ideas, Goethe embarked upon a period of extraordinary creativity. In 1773 he published a play based upon the 16th-century German knight, *Götz von Berlichingen,* and collaborated with Herder and others on the pamphlet "Von deutscher Art und Kunst," which was a kind of manifesto for the Sturm und Drang. His novel *Die Leiden des jungen Werthers* (1774; *The Sorrows of Young Werther*), which epitomized the spirit of the movement, made him world famous and inspired a host of imitators.

The dramatic literature of the Sturm und Drang was its most characteristic product. Indeed, the very name of the movement was borrowed from a play by Friedrich von Klinger, who had been inspired by the desire to present on the stage figures of Shakespearean grandeur, subordinating structural considerations to character and rejecting the conventions of French Neoclassicism, which had been imported by the critic Johann Christop von Gottsched. With the production of *Die Räuber* (1781; *The Robbers*) by Schiller, the drama of the Sturm und Drang entered a new phase.

Self-discipline was not a tenet of the Sturm und Drang, and the movement soon exhausted itself. Its two most gifted representatives, Goethe and Schiller, went on to produce great works that formed the body and soul of German classical literature.

poems there are occasional outbursts of indignation and appeals for reform. Yet there is also a pessimistic mood of resignation induced by the burden of civic ineffectualness that history had imposed on his people. Ultimately, he, too, sought refuge from the world in the poet's private vision. The Sturm und Drang ("Storm and Stress") was a movement of literary innovation through which a group of young writers in the last decades of the 18th century sought to throw off the yoke of accepted standards of composition, but it remained confined to problems of prosody and taste and reluctant to confront political and social issues directly.

The cultural achievements could not alter the harsh realities of national fragmentation and princely autocracy. They supported, however, the ideals of rational reform and social progress that the Enlightenment had introduced throughout the Continent. In Germany as elsewhere the 18th century became the age when the monarchical principle advanced the loftiest justification of its claim to power. The authority of the prince, so the argument went, was to be exercised not for his private advantage or gratification but for the greatness of his state and the welfare of his people. His power had to be unrestricted so that his benevolence might be unlimited. Absolute government was the only effective instrument for achieving the general good. Impressed by the scientific discoveries and material advances that they saw about them, Europeans began to believe that the prejudices and injustices that had plagued society would gradually disappear before the steady march of reason.

ENLIGHTENED REFORM AND BENEVOLENT DESPOTISM

The main source of enlightened reform was to be the crown, but many well-intentioned people of means and education also began to apply a new standard of conduct in their dealings with their fellow man. This change in attitude was apparent in the decline of religious resentments and discriminations. Never before had the relationship between Roman Catholics and Protestants among the well-to-do classes of central Europe been as free of rancour as on the eve of the French Revolution. It was at this time also that Jews first began to emerge from the isolation to which a deep-seated intolerance had consigned them. The idea of assimilation held out to them the prospect of escape from the ghetto on the condition that they identify themselves in thought, speech, and attitude with the Christian society in which they lived. That prospect was to attract the Jewish minority in Germany more and more during the next 150 years. Religious toleration, however, was not the only article of faith of the Enlightenment. Its vision of a happier future included the reformation of education, the abolition of poverty, the alleviation of sickness, and the elimination of injustice. Men of goodwill established schools, founded orphanages, built hospitals, improved farming methods, modernized industrial techniques, and tried to raise the standard of living of the masses. While the hopes of the enlightened reformers of the 18th century far outstripped their accomplishments, the practical results of their efforts should not be underestimated.

According to the doctrines of benevolent despotism, however, the chief instrumentality for the improvement of society was not private philanthropy but government action. The state had the primary responsibility for preparing the way for the golden age that, in the opinion of many intellectuals, awaited humankind. The extent to which official policy conformed to rationalist theory depended,

JUNKERS

The Junkers ("country squires") were the landowning aristocracy of Prussia and eastern Germany. Under the German Empire (1871–1918) and the Weimar Republic (1919–33) they exercised substantial political power. Otto von Bismarck himself, the imperial chancellor during 1871–90, was of Junker stock and at first was regarded as representing its interests. Politically, Junkers stood for extreme conservatism, support of the monarchy and military tradition, and protectionist policies for agriculture. The German Conservative Party in the Reichstag, or Imperial Assembly, and the extraparliamentary Agrarian League represented Junker interests throughout the imperial era. Because the Junkers staffed the Prussian army, which had brought about Germany's unification, they were accorded great influence, particularly in Prussia, where a highly illiberal constitution remained in force (1850–1918). During the Weimar period, Junkers were continuously hostile to the republic, the collapse of which contributed to the rise of Adolf Hitler.

in central Europe as elsewhere, on the personality and ability of the ruler. Both of the leading powers of the Holy Roman Empire followed the teachings of benevolent despotism but with substantially different results. The emperor Joseph II, a well-meaning though doctrinaire reformer, attempted to initiate a revolution from above against the opposition of powerful forces that continued to cling to tradition. In the course of a single decade he tried to centralize the government of his far-flung domains, reduce the influence of the church, introduce religious toleration, and ease the burden of serfdom. His uncompromising program of innovation, however, alienated the landed aristocracy, whose support was essential for the effective operation of the government. The emperor encountered mounting unrest, which did not end until his death in 1790, and the subsequent abandonment of most of the reforms that

he had promulgated. Frederick the Great was more successful as an enlightened autocrat, but only because he was more cautious. His reorganization of the government was not as drastic, his belief in religious toleration remained less profound, and his assistance to the peasants did not go beyond a prohibition against the absorption of their holdings by the nobility. He invited settlers to cultivate reclaimed lands, and he encouraged entrepreneurs to increase the industrial capacity of Prussia. Among his most important accomplishments, although it was not completed until after his death, was the Prussian Civil Code, which defined the principles and practices of an absolute government and a corporative society. Yet Frederick was also convinced that the Prussian landed noblemen, the Junkers, were the backbone of the state, and he continued accordingly to uphold the alliance between crown and aristocracy on which his kingdom had been built.

The achievements of benevolent despotism among the minor states of the Holy Roman Empire varied considerably. Some princes employed their inherited authority in a serious effort to improve the lot of their subjects. Charles Frederick of Baden, for example, devoted himself to the improvement of education in his margravate, and he even abolished serfdom, although manorial obligations remained. Charles Augustus of Saxe-Weimar-Eisenach was a hardworking administrator of his small Thuringian principality, whose capital, Weimar, he transformed into the cultural centre of Germany. Charles Eugene of Württemberg, on the other hand, led a life of profligacy and licentiousness in defiance of protests by the estates of the duchy. Frederick II of Hesse-Kassel was another princely prodigal whose love of pleasure impoverished his subjects and forced his soldiers into mercenary service for England. The record of enlightened autocracy in central Europe was as uneven as in western Europe. Yet the ideas of the Enlightenment even at their best were unable to transform the basis of political life in the Holy Roman Empire. They could palliate, reform, and improve, but they could not alter a system of particularistic sovereignty and absolutistic authority resting on a hierarchical structure of society. They could not become an instrument of national consolidation or representative government. Only some great creative disruption of existing civic institutions could break through the crust of habit and tradition sanctified by history. Germany lacked the internal preconditions for a process of political reconstruction. The galvanizing forces of rejuvenation and regeneration were to come from the outside.

THE FRENCH REVOLUTIONARY AND NAPOLEONIC ERA

In transforming the Bourbon kingdom into a constitutional state, the French Revolution aroused intense excitement east of the Rhine. Most German intellectuals were at first in sympathy with the new order in France, hoping that the defeat of royal absolutism in western Europe would lead to its decline in central Europe as well. The princes, on the other hand, were from the outset fearful of the Revolution, which they regarded as a serious danger, for the example of unpunished insubordination by the French might encourage demands for reform among the Germans. The result was a growing hostility between the government in Paris and the rulers of the Holy Roman Empire, which led in the spring of 1792 to the outbreak of the War of the First Coalition (1792–97), the first phase of the French Revolutionary and Napoleonic wars. The immediate occasion of the conflict was a quarrel over the rights of German princes with holdings in France and over the propagandistic activities of French émigrés in Germany. But the underlying cause was the clash of two incompatible principles of authority

Napoleon Bonaparte. DEA/G. Dagli Orti/De Agostini/Getty Images

divided by profound differences regarding the nature of political and social justice. The course of hostilities soon revealed that the civic ideals and military power of Revolutionary France were more than a match for the decrepit Holy Roman Empire. After 1793 France occupied the German lands on the left bank of the Rhine, and for the next 20 years their inhabitants were governed from Paris. Yet there is no evidence that they were dissatisfied with French rule or at least no evidence that they strongly opposed it. Devoid of a sense of national identity and accustomed to submission to authority, they accepted their new status with the same equanimity with which they had regarded a succession to the throne or a change in the dynasty.

The Prussians, moreover, discouraged by defeats in the west and eager for Polish spoils in the east, concluded a separate peace at Basel in 1795 by which they in effect recognized the French acquisition of the Rhineland. The Austrians held out two years longer, but the brilliant successes of the young Napoleon Bonaparte forced them to accept the loss of the left bank in the Treaty of Campo Formio (October 17, 1797).

END OF THE HOLY ROMAN EMPIRE

The peace proved short-lived, however, for at the end of 1798 a new coalition directed against France was formed (the War of the Second Coalition, 1798–1802). This time Prussia remained neutral. Frederick William III, a conscientious and modest but ineffectual ruler, was notable for private morality rather than political skill. The government in Berlin drifted back and forth, dabbling in minor economic and administrative reforms without significantly improving the structure of the state. A decade of neutrality was frittered away while the army commanders rested on the laurels of Frederick the Great. Austria, on the other hand, played the same leading role in the War of the Second Coalition that it did in the War of the First Coalition, with the same unfortunate result. The French victories at Marengo (June 14, 1800) and Hohenlinden (December 3, 1800) forced Emperor Francis II to agree to the Treaty of Lunéville (February 9, 1801), which confirmed the cession of the Rhineland. More than that, those rulers who lost their possessions on the left bank under the terms of the peace were to receive compensation elsewhere in the empire. In order to carry out this redistribution of territory, the Imperial Diet entrusted a committee of princes, the Reichsdeputation, with the task of drawing a new map of Germany. France, however, exercised the major influence over its deliberations. Napoleon had resolved to utilize the settlement of territorial claims to fundamentally alter the structure of the Holy Roman Empire. The result was that the Final Recess (Hauptschluss) of the Reichsdeputation of February 1803 marked the end of the old order in Germany. In their attempt to establish a chain of satellite states east of the Rhine, the French diplomats brought about the elimination of the smallest and least viable of the political components of Germany. They thereby also furthered the process of national consolidation, since the fragmentation of civic authority in the empire had been a mainstay of particularism. That Napoleon did not intend to encourage unity among his neighbours goes without saying. Yet he unwittingly prepared the way for a process of centralization in Germany that helped to frustrate his own plans for the future aggrandizement of France.

The chief victims of the Final Recess were the free cities, the imperial knights, and the ecclesiastical territories. They fell by the dozens. Too weak to be useful allies of Napoleon, they were destroyed by the ambition of their French conquerors and by the greed of their German neighbours. They could still boast of their ancient history as sovereign members of the Holy Roman Empire, but their continued existence had become incompatible with effective government in Germany. The principal heirs to their holdings were the larger secondary states. To be sure, Napoleon could not keep Austria and Prussia from making some gains in the general scramble for territory that they had helped make possible. But he worked to aggrandize those German rulers, most of them in the south, who were strong enough to be valuable vassals but not strong enough to be potential threats. Bavaria, Württemberg, Baden, Hesse-Darmstadt, and Nassau were the big winners in the competition for booty that had been the main object of the negotiations. Napoleon's strategy had been in the classic tradition of French diplomacy, the tradition of Richelieu and Mazarin. The princes had been pitted against the emperor to enhance the role that Paris could play in the affairs of the German states. Yet the German princes did not resent being used as pawns in a political game to promote the interests of a foreign power. Whatever objections they raised against the settlement of 1803 were based on expediency and opportunism. The most serious indictment of the old order was that in the hour of its imminent collapse none of the rulers attempted to defend it in the name of the general welfare of Germany.

The Final Recess was the next to last act in the fall of the Holy Roman Empire. The end came three years later. In 1805 Austria joined the third coalition of Great Powers determined to reduce the preponderance of France (resulting in the War of the Third Coalition, 1805–07). The outcome of this war was even more disastrous than those of the wars of the first and second coalitions. Napoleon forced the main Habsburg army in Germany to surrender at Ulm (October 17, 1805); then he descended on Vienna, occupying the proud capital of his enemy; and finally he inflicted a crushing defeat (December 2, 1805) on the combined Russian and Austrian armies at Austerlitz in Moravia (now in the Czech Republic). Before the year was out, Francis II was forced to sign the humiliating Treaty of Pressburg (December 26), which ended the dominant role his dynasty had played in the affairs of Germany. He had to surrender his possessions in western Germany to Württemberg and Baden, and the province of Tirol to Bavaria. Napoleon's strategy of playing princely against imperial ambitions had proved a brilliant success. The rulers of the secondary states in the south had supported him in the war against Austria, and in the peace that ensued they were richly rewarded. Not only did they share in the booty seized from the Habsburgs, but they also were permitted to absorb the remaining free cities, petty principalities, and ecclesiastical territories. Finally, asserting the rights of full sovereignty, the rulers of Bavaria and Württemberg assumed the title of king, while the rulers of Baden and Hesse-Darmstadt contented themselves with the more modest rank of grand duke. The last vestiges of the imperial constitution had now been destroyed, and Germany was ready for a new form of political organization reflecting power relationships created by the force of arms.

In the summer of 1806, 16 of the secondary states, encouraged and prodded by Paris, announced that they were forming a separate association to be known as the Confederation of the Rhine. Archbishop Karl Theodor von Dalberg was to preside over the new union as the "prince primate," while future deliberations among the members were to establish a college of kings and a college of princes as common legislative bodies. There was even talk of a "fundamental statute" that would serve as the constitution of a rejuvenated Germany. Yet all these brave plans were never more than a facade for the harsh reality of alien hegemony in Germany. Napoleon was proclaimed the "protector" of the Confederation of the Rhine, and a permanent alliance between the member states and the French Empire obliged the former to maintain substantial military forces for the purpose of mutual defense. There could be no doubt whose interests these troops would serve. The secondary rulers of Germany were expected to pay a handsome tribute to Paris for their newly acquired sham sovereignty. On August 1 the confederated states proclaimed their secession from the empire, and a week later, on August 6, 1806, Francis II announced that he was laying down the imperial crown. The Holy Roman Empire thus came officially to an end after a history of a thousand years.

PERIOD OF FRENCH HEGEMONY IN GERMANY

The long conflict between emperors and princes in Germany had concluded with the triumph of the latter. Yet the victors soon discovered that, instead of achieving independence, they had merely exchanged one master for another. Indeed, they were more subordinate now to the wishes of Paris than they had been to those of Vienna. Napoleon gradually induced or forced all the states of Germany except Austria and Prussia, 36 states in all, to join the confederation. The inclusion of the two leading powers of central Europe might have proved troublesome for him or even dangerous. The participation of the secondary states, on the other hand, provided him with reliable mercenaries who owed him too much and feared him too much to oppose his wishes. He was free to do as he liked in the region between the Rhine and the Elbe rivers. In order to enforce his embargo on Continental trade with England, he annexed the entire coastline along the North Sea, including much of the electorate of Hanover, a dependency of Britain, Napoleon's archenemy. When that was not enough, he added Lübeck on the Baltic to the French Empire. He carved out the kingdom of Westphalia, consisting mainly of the remainder of Hanover and conquered Prussian territory, for his brother Jérôme and the grand duchy of Berg, incorporating additional Prussian territories, for his brother-in-law Joachim Murat. He was the undisputed master of all of western Germany.

After the formation of the Confederation of the Rhine, there was only one state in central Europe that had not yet been forced to submit to France. But the leaders of Prussia hesitated and wavered in their policy until they lost the opportunity of profiting from the War of the Third Coalition. Had they joined Austria and Russia against Napoleon, they might have kept him from gaining hegemony over Germany. Or had they become the allies of Napoleon, they might have established a sphere of influence in the region north of the Main River. As it was, they waited until they fell between two stools. They finally declared war against the French in October 1806, after Austria had been forced to surrender, Russia had decided to retreat, and the secondary states had become the vassals of Paris. Yet public opinion in the Prussian capital remained confident that the army of Frederick the Great would prove a match for the conqueror of Europe. The result of such self-deception was a military disaster of unparalleled magnitude. In the two simultaneous battles of Jena and Auerstädt (October 14, 1806), the Prussian armies were completely routed, and the road to Berlin lay open before the French invaders. The city was occupied on October 27.

More disastrous than the military defeat, however, was the moral collapse of a state that had taught its citizens that obedience to authority was the supreme political virtue. The civilian population never thought of offering resistance to the advancing enemy. Even many army officers were so disheartened by Napoleon's success that they surrendered one fortified position after another without a fight. Frederick William III had to pay a terrible price for the policy of his ancestors, who had built efficient government at the expense of civic initiative. He tried to hold out in East Prussia, hoping that the Russian armies, which were still at war with Napoleon, would help him regain the rest of his kingdom. But when in July 1807 Alexander I concluded peace with France at Tilsit, the unfortunate Frederick William had no choice but to follow suit. The treaty that he was forced to sign was a catastrophe. Prussia lost almost half its territory and population, including most of the Polish possessions in the east as well as all the territories west of the Elbe River. Subsequent agreements, moreover, imposed a heavy indemnity, a military occupation, and a reduction in the size of the army. The proud monarchy of Frederick the Great had been reduced to a secondary state in Germany.

Central Europe remained under the dominant influence of France for more than a decade. That influence was at first limited and indirect, then pervasive and overpowering. Yet it was during this period of alien preponderance that Germany for the first time felt the stirrings of liberalism and nationalism. The regions that had become part of the French Empire experienced firsthand the advantages of efficient centralized government in which equality before the law and freedom of opportunity were accepted principles. Those states that retained a pseudo-independence as satellites of Napoleon, moreover, sought to imitate the example of their master, partly in order to gain his favour, partly in order to emulate his success, but most importantly in order to integrate the new territories that they had so suddenly acquired. One government after another began to remove religious restrictions, relax economic barriers, eliminate servile obligations, and centralize administrative functions. Above all, constitutional rule and popular representation ceased to seem Utopian to men of property and education who had witnessed the stirring events of the years since 1789. The French hegemony also led to the birth of nationalism in Germany. For one thing, the

achievement of political unity became a distinct possibility, once the territorial fragmentation of the Holy Roman Empire had come to an end. Furthermore, the presence of foreign occupiers—arrogant, overbearing, and avaricious—aroused among Germans a sense of nationality that they had never felt in the tranquil days of the old order. Finally, all who admired or envied the triumphs of Napoleon had an example of the great deeds that the love of fatherland could inspire. The ideal of cosmopolitan individualism that had been generally accepted in the 18th century began to give way before a growing consciousness of national identity. Yet the emergence of the concepts of constitutional freedom and national unity not through indigenous developments but rather in response to foreign domination influenced the form that these concepts assumed in Germany.

Every German state felt the influence of the new principles of government and economy that the period of French hegemony had introduced, but nowhere was that influence more consequential than in Prussia. For only in the hour of deepest humiliation did the Hohenzollern kingdom finally make an effort to adapt its structure to the changing political and social conditions that it had stubbornly ignored during its years of greatness. Between 1806 and 1813 the statesmen in Berlin initiated a revolution from above to transform a rigid despotism into a popular monarchy supported by the loyalty of a free citizenry. Out of the disasters of Jena and Tilsit emerged a group of gifted reformers who sought to regenerate their country. The leading figures in this movement for civic reconstruction were the civil servants Karl, Freiherr (baron) vom Stein, and Karl August, Fürst (prince) von Hardenberg, along with the military commanders Gerhard von Scharnhorst and August, Graf (count) Neidhardt von Gneisenau. Among their most important achievements was the abolition of serfdom, a measure designed to create citizens out of human beasts of burden. Yet, while the reforms gave the peasant personal freedom, they failed to provide him with economic independence. Most of the land remained in the hands of the aristocracy, which therefore continued to dominate the countryside politically as well as socially. More successful was the law establishing municipal self-government. Thereafter the cities of the kingdom were to be administered by officials chosen not by the central bureaucracy but by the propertied inhabitants of the cities themselves. The autonomy of the cities, it was hoped, would help train a politically conscious and active middle class. The most effective reforms, however, were those introduced in the armed forces. After the officers who had shown themselves incompetent during the war were dismissed or retired, the high command carried out a thorough reorganization of the military system. Discipline became more humane, promotion was to be based on merit rather than aristocratic connections, the method of recruitment was improved, and the training in tactics was modernized. Most important, the army's

leaders sought to instill in the soldiers a new spirit rooted in inner conviction rather than unquestioning obedience. Defeat had changed Prussia from a garrison state into a centre of political and intellectual ferment.

Patriotic sentiments became increasingly widespread in Germany as the burden of French domination grew progressively heavier. The financial sacrifices that Napoleon demanded reinforced the personal resentments aroused by his ruthless statecraft. Before long a network of secret organizations had sprung up in the German states seeking the expulsion of the foreign invaders. Yet it would be a mistake to think that all Germans regarded the hegemony of France as an unmitigated evil. There were, in fact, wide differences of opinion among them. The rulers of the secondary states and their supporters in the army and the bureaucracy saw Napoleon as the instrument of their new importance. Many reformers in the south—the Bavarian statesman Maximilian Joseph, Graf (count) von Montgelas, for example—believed that only French influence had made possible the modernization of government in Germany. Some men of letters (writers, journalists, and professors) continued to argue, moreover, that the political disunity of Germany was a natural result of its historical experience and reflected its essential character. Even among those who opposed French domination, there was no agreement regarding the future political structure of the nation. Many of them dreamed of a liberal and united fatherland that would take its place among the Great Powers of Europe. Others preferred a loose association of governments, similar to the Confederation of the Rhine, that could safeguard the interests of the secondary states against Prussia and Austria. Still others hoped for a complete restoration of the old order in which they had grown up and to which they longed to return. And then there were the broad masses of the population of the German states, exploited, illiterate, and uninformed. They remained by and large indifferent to the crosscurrents of political thought, seeking nothing more than an improvement in their standard of living and the preservation of their way of life. Germany was beginning to move toward new civic and social norms, but the transformation of political attitudes was gradual and intermittent.

The slow spread of the ideals of unity and freedom became apparent during the first serious effort to throw off the yoke of foreign domination in the German states. The Austrian government concluded in 1809 that Napoleon's recent reverses in Spain presaged a general uprising against French hegemony on the Continent. The result was an ill-fated attempt at a war of liberation, in which the Habsburg troops challenged Napoleon for the fourth time, only to go down in defeat once again. Appeals from Vienna to the people of Germany found little response except in Tirol and among a few nationalist hotspurs in the north. The princes refused to risk French wrath until they could be sure of ultimate victory, while their subjects refused to rise against French oppression without princely approval. The result was that the war in central Europe, unlike the one in the Iberian Peninsula, was waged primarily by regular forces rather than by guerrilla bands. Archduke Charles gained important successes for the Austrian army at Aspern and Essling (May 21–22, 1809), an indication that the strategic mastery of the French was drawing to a close. But at Wagram (July 5–6) Napoleon was able to work the last of his military miracles. Vienna had to sue for peace once more, the Treaty of Schönbrunn (October 14) ceding Salzburg to Bavaria, West Galicia to the grand duchy of Warsaw, and the Adriatic coastland to France. The defeat finally persuaded the emperor, who had exchanged the title Francis II of the Holy Roman Empire for Francis I of the Austrian Empire, that resistance would be as futile in the future as it had been in the past. He therefore adopted a policy of collaboration with France, signaled by the marriage of his daughter Marie-Louise to Napoleon. Germany continued to languish in the grip of foreign domination.

THE WARS OF LIBERATION

A new struggle for liberation opened three years later with the defeat of Napoleon's grande armée in Russia. As the Russian armies began to cross western frontiers in December 1812, the crucial question became what reception they would find among the rulers and the inhabitants of central Europe. The first state to cut its ties to Paris was Prussia. It was not the king, however, but one of his generals, Johann, Graf (count) Yorck von Wartenburg, who decided on his own initiative to cooperate with the Russians. Only hesitatingly and fearfully did Frederick William III then agree in February 1813 to a war against France, although many Prussians greeted the outbreak of the conflict with enthusiasm. The other rulers of the German states refused initially to follow the Prussian example. The members of the Confederation of the Rhine were still convinced of Napoleon's invincibility, while Austria preferred to see the combatants exhaust each other until it could play the role of mediator and arbiter. The foreign minister in Vienna, Klemens, Fürst (prince) von Metternich, was afraid that the hegemony of France in central Europe might be replaced by that of Russia. He tried, therefore, to pursue a strategy of armed neutrality, hoping that he could persuade the opposing sides to accept a compromise that would maintain an equilibrium between Alexander I and Napoleon. This plan failed because of the obstinacy of the latter, who feared that concessions in foreign affairs would weaken his control over internal politics in France. The upshot was that in August 1813 Austria entered the conflict on the side of Russia and Prussia, and the balance of military power shifted in favour of the anti-French coalition. The faith of the secondary states in Napoleon's star began to weaken, and Bavaria became the first member to secede from the Confederation of the Rhine (October 8). One great allied victory would now suffice to bring all of Germany into the struggle against France.

That victory came on October 19, 1813, at the Battle of Leipzig. After four days of bitter fighting, the French army was forced to retreat, and its domination of central Europe was finally at an end. Before the year was out, Napoleon had withdrawn across the Rhine. Of all his conquests in Germany, only the left bank was still under the effective control of Paris. The Confederation of the Rhine promptly collapsed, as its members rushed to go over to the winning side before it was too late. The Rhineland was also reconquered early in 1814, after the allies had launched their invasion of France. In the course of the spring, the capture of Paris, the restoration of the Bourbons, and the conclusion of peace in the first Treaty of Paris (May 30) ended the Wars of Liberation except for the episode of the Hundred Days, when Napoleon briefly returned to power and was ultimately beaten at Waterloo. The western frontier of the German states was to remain essentially the same as at the time of the initial outbreak of hostilities more than 20 years previously. New state boundaries within Germany would still have to be determined, to be sure, and the problem of a new political organization of the nation awaited the victorious statesmen, but the period of foreign hegemony was over at last. The rulers of the German states, relying partly on the forces of innovation, partly on those of tradition, had succeeded in freeing themselves from alien domination. Now they had to decide what use they would make of their freedom. Would they create a new polity of unity and liberty, which many reformers demanded, or would they reestablish the old order of absolutism and particularism, which the conservatives advocated? As the statesmen began to gather in Vienna in the fall of 1814 to restore peace to a continent ravaged by two decades of war, they pondered the problem of devising an enduring form of government for Germany.

RESULTS OF THE CONGRESS OF VIENNA

The men who, in the nine months from September 1814 to June 1815, redrew the map of Europe were diplomats of the old school. Francis I and the prince von Metternich of Austria, Frederick William III and the prince von Hardenberg of Prussia, Alexander I of Russia, Viscount Castlereagh of England, Talleyrand of France, and the representatives of the secondary states were all intellectual heirs of the 18th century. They feared the principles of the French Revolution, they scorned the theories of democratic government, and they opposed the doctrines of national self-determination. But they recognized that the boundaries and governments of 1789 could not be restored without modification or compromise. There had been too many changes in attitudes and loyalties that the rigid dogmas of legitimism were powerless to undo.

The task before the peacemakers was thus the establishment of a sound balance between necessary reform and valid tradition capable of preserving the tranquillity that Europe desperately needed. The decisions regarding Germany reached during the deliberations in Vienna followed a middle course between innovation and reaction, avoiding extreme fragmentation as well as rigid centralization. The Confederation of the Rhine was not maintained, but neither was the Holy Roman Empire restored. Although the reforms introduced during the period of foreign domination were partly revoked, the practices of enlightened despotism were not entirely reestablished. Despite the complaints of unbending legitimists and the dire predictions of disappointed reformers, the peacemakers succeeded in creating a new political order in Germany that endured for half a century. The long years of war and unrest that had convulsed Europe during the era of the French Revolution and Napoleon were followed by even longer years of stability and tranquillity.

The Germany that emerged in 1815 from the Congress of Vienna included 39 states ranging in size from the two Great Powers, Austria and Prussia, through the minor kingdoms of Bavaria, Württemberg, Saxony, and Hanover; through smaller duchies such as Baden, Nassau, Oldenburg, and Hesse-Darmstadt; through tiny principalities such as Schaumburg-Lippe, Schwarzburg-Sondershausen, and Reuss-Schleiz-Gera; to the free cities of Hamburg, Bremen,

Lübeck, and Frankfurt am Main. The new boundaries in Germany bore little resemblance to the bewildering territorial mosaic that had been maintained under the Holy Roman Empire, but there were still many fragments, subdivisions, enclaves, and exclaves, too many for the taste of ardent nationalists. Yet the overall pattern of state frontiers represented a significant improvement over the chaotic patchwork of sovereignties and jurisdictions that had characterized the old order. The peacemakers not only created more integrated and viable political entities but also altered the role that these entities were to play in the affairs of the nation. Without design or even awareness on the part of Frederick William III, his kingdom of Prussia assumed a pivotal position in Germany. The victorious powers, on guard against a revival of French aggression, decided to make Prussia the defender of the western boundary of Germany. The Rhineland and Westphalia, including the Ruhr district that would develop into the greatest industrial centre on the Continent, became Prussian provinces. More than that, the king agreed at the urging of Alexander I to cede the bulk of his Polish possessions to Russia in return for a substantial part of Saxony. Prussia, which at the end of the 18th century had been in the process of becoming a binational state, was thrust back into Germany and given a strategic position on both frontiers of the nation. The centre of gravity of Austria, on the

other hand, shifted eastward. Francis I had decided to abandon the historic role of his state as protector of the Holy Roman Empire against the French for the sake of greater geographic compactness and military defensibility. The possessions in southern and western Germany were surrendered along with the Austrian Netherlands in return for Venetian territory on the Adriatic. The Habsburg empire thus became less German in composition and outlook as its focus shifted in the direction of Italy and eastern Europe. The consequences of this territorial rearrangement were to be far-reaching.

METTERNICH AND THE UNIFICATION OF GERMANY

In place of the Holy Roman Empire, the peacemakers of the Congress of Vienna had established a new organization of German states, the German Confederation. This was a loose political association in which most of the rights of sovereignty remained in the hands of the member governments. There was no central executive or judiciary, only a federal Diet meeting in Frankfurt am Main to consider common legislation. The delegates who participated in its deliberations were representatives appointed by and responsible to the rulers whom they served. The confederation was in theory empowered to adopt measures strengthening the political and economic bonds of the nation. In fact it remained a stronghold of particularism, unwilling to sacrifice local autonomy in order to establish centralized authority. It was designed essentially to defend the interests of the secondary states and the Habsburgs. The former, jealously guarding the independence and importance they had gained during the period of French hegemony, were opposed to any reform that might limit their sovereignty. The latter believed that only a decentralized form of political union in Germany would give them enough freedom of action to pursue their non-German objectives. The confederation was thus from the outset an ally of localism and traditionalism. To the nationalists, whose hopes had risen so high during the Wars of Liberation, it seemed to be an instrument of blind reaction. Yet the truth is that the confederal system established in 1815 accurately reflected the slow development of civic consciousness and economic integration in Germany. The militant reformers who demanded the centralization of government were a vocal but small minority. The lower classes accepted the territorial and constitutional decisions of the Congress of Vienna without a murmur of protest. The weakness of the peace settlement was not its failure to embody present realities but its inability to adjust to future changes. What had been a reasonable adaptation to the political needs of an agrarian and rural society became a hopeless anachronism 50 years later in the age of factories and railroads. This was the fatal flaw in the German Confederation.

REFORM AND REACTION

Yet the reform movement that had begun under the impact of the French hegemony did not end with the downfall of Napoleon. It continued to exert influence over affairs of state for another few years, before the forces of authoritarianism and particularism crushed it. That influence was strongest in southern Germany, where the political example of western Europe had made the deepest impression. There many civil servants, court officials, army officers, and even aristocratic landowners came to believe that the future of the state depended on its readiness to reform civic institutions in accordance with liberal theories. In the years following Waterloo, one government in the south after another promulgated a constitution: Bavaria and Baden in 1818, Württemberg in 1819, and Hesse-Darmstadt in 1820. These constitutions established representative assemblies, elected by the propertied citizens, whose assent was required for the enactment of legislation. Their purpose was not only to win for the crown the support of the educated classes of society but also to engender a sense of unity in a heterogeneous population that still had diverse allegiances and traditions.

To the north there were also persistent echoes of the reform movement. The followers of the baron vom Stein were still influential in the councils of state, and Frederick William III of Prussia at first seriously considered ways of fulfilling the promise he had made in 1815 to establish constitutional government. Economic reformers succeeded in enacting the Prussian Customs Law of 1818, which united all the Prussian territories into a customs union free of internal economic barriers; this later formed the nucleus of a national customs union. The agitation for political reorganization, however, was loudest among university students, who formed patriotic groups known as Burschenschaften. They demanded the abandonment of the confederal system, the establishment of greater unity, and the achievement of national power. Gathering in 1817 at the Wartburg, the castle near Eisenach where Luther had once taken refuge, they listened to veiled denunciations of the existing order and consigned to flames various symbols of traditional authority. The rulers of Germany began to stir uneasily at this bold display of defiance of the established order.

The chief strategist of the forces hostile to reform was Metternich. Not only did he reject the teachings of liberalism and nationalism in principle, but also, as the leading statesman of the Habsburg empire, he recognized that the establishment of centralized authority in Germany (which still included Austria) would seriously impede the policies his government was pursuing in Hungary, Italy, and the Balkans. When on March 23, 1819, an unbalanced student, Karl Ludwig Sand, assassinated the conservative playwright and publicist August von Kotzebue, Vienna persuaded the princes of the German Confederation that they were facing a dangerous attempt to overthrow the established order in the German states. The result was a series of repressive measures called the Carlsbad Decrees, which the federal Diet adopted on September 20, 1819. General censorship was introduced, and the Burschenschaften were outlawed. This first major success of the conservative counteroffensive had an important effect on the struggle within the state governments between the advocates and the opponents of reform. In Prussia the liberal members of the ministry were forced to resign, and the plan to promulgate a constitution for the kingdom was rejected. This shift to the right by Berlin encouraged authoritarian tendencies among the secondary states of the north, which soon abandoned their own constitutional projects. By the end of 1820 the reform movement, which had begun some 15 years before, came to a complete halt. It had succeeded in altering the political and economic structure of society, but it had been unable to establish a tradition of liberal government and national loyalty in Germany. The forces of particularism and legitimism, deriving their chief support from the landowning nobility and the conservative peasantry, remained strong. The foundation of bourgeois civic consciousness and material prosperity on which England and France had built their representative institutions was still relatively weak beyond the Rhine. The ideas of political reform had arisen in Germany not from the experience of revolution and social transformation but rather as imitations of foreign examples and in reaction against foreign oppression.

The established order was once again threatened briefly in the wake of the July Revolution of 1830 in France. The news that there had been a successful insurrection against the Bourbons in Paris had an electrifying effect throughout the Continent. In Germany there were sympathetic uprisings in some of the secondary states of the north. The rulers of Brunswick, Saxony, Hanover, and Hesse-Kassel, seeking to forestall more extreme demands, agreed to promulgate liberal constitutions. A mass meeting of southern radicals at Hambach Castle in the Palatinate (May 1832), moreover, called for national unification, republican government, and popular sovereignty. A group of militant students even launched a foolhardy attempt to seize the city of Frankfurt am Main, dissolve the federal Diet, and proclaim a German republic. The effect of such harebrained schemes was predictable. As the princes of the German Confederation gradually recovered from their initial fear of the revolutionary movement, they opposed with increasing vigour plans to alter the existing system of government. Again Metternich led the effort to crush liberalism and nationalism. Under his direction the federal Diet adopted additional repressive measures reinforcing the position of the crown in state politics, limiting the power of the legislature, restricting the right of assembly, enlarging the authority of the police, and intensifying censorship. Within a few years the

opposition had been subdued, and the German Confederation could continue to vegetate in its cozy provincialism. Not until the middle years of the century did a new and more violent outburst of civil disaffection shake the foundations of the political structure that the Congress of Vienna had erected.

EVOLUTION OF PARTIES AND IDEOLOGIES

Although the critics of the established order could be defeated, they could not be silenced. The struggle between the supporters and the adversaries of the existing form of government led to the emergence of a rudimentary party system in the German Confederation. In the legislative assemblies of the secondary states, the proponents of reform began to meet, plan, organize, and propagandize. The defenders of legitimism were thereby forced in turn to concert their strategy and to publicize their program. Even in Prussia and Austria, where there were as yet no constitutions or parliaments, political criticism could be expressed obliquely through clubs, meetings, newspapers, pamphlets, and petitions. The result was the gradual development of amorphous civic associations held together by common convictions regarding politics and society. These primitive groupings were only the raw material out of which disciplined political parties slowly developed in the course of the century. They still lacked the cohesive ideologies and the institutional means to disseminate them that characterize a fully mature system of parliamentary politics. Yet they became the means by which disaffected groups in the community could express their opposition to the established order. They also reflected the transformation in civic attitudes that had occurred since the age of enlightened despotism. There were now men in the German states who refused to submit without question to princely authority and to seek freedom only in the inner recesses of the soul. The social and economic changes resulting from the beginnings of industrialization transformed the system and organization of politics.

The most important opponents of legitimism and particularism were the liberals, or moderates. Deriving their support primarily from industrialists, merchants, financiers, mine owners, railroad developers, civil servants, professionals, and university professors, they represented the opposition of the well-to-do and educated bourgeoisie to a form of government in which an aristocracy of birth rather than of talent predominated. Their political principles favoured a monarchical system of authority, but the crown was to share its powers with a parliament elected by the men of property. Influence in public affairs should be accessible to all male citizens who had demonstrated through the acquisition of wealth and education that they were capable of exercising the franchise intelligently. While the liberals resented the inherited privileges of the nobility, they also feared the proletariat. The

man who lived in poverty and ignorance, they reasoned, was ripe for demagoguery and insurrection. The path of civic wisdom was therefore the happy medium between royal absolutism and mob rule, a medium that had been established in Britain by the Reform Bill of 1832 and in France by the regime of Louis-Philippe. In economics, most, although by no means all, liberals advocated a policy of unrestrained competition by which wealth would become the reward of business acumen rather than the perquisite of corporative privilege. Guild monopolies, government regulations, and rules reserving landed estates for the nobility were to be abolished as violations of the freedom of enterprise that alone could ensure the well-being of all society. The liberals favoured the transformation of the German Confederation into a national monarchy in which the states' rights would be curtailed but not destroyed by a central government and a federal parliament.

To the liberals' left stood the democrats, or radicals, whose following was made up largely of small businessmen, petty shopkeepers, skilled workers, independent farmers, teachers, journalists, lawyers, and physicians. While the divisions between liberals and democrats were often indistinct and the two groups often worked together, democrats looked with scorn on the golden mean between autocracy and anarchy that the liberals sought. They preferred an egalitarian form of authority in which not parliamentary plutocracy but popular sovereignty would be the underlying principle of government. Their supporters drew inspiration from the French Revolution rather than from British parliamentary reforms. Their ideal of democracy was the Jacobin republic of 1793, an instrument that could shape the energies and aspirations of the people into a disciplined force for political and social reform. The spokesmen for this ideal could not openly demand the overthrow of monarchical institutions without risking imprisonment. Yet, while they were forced to accept the crown as a political institution, they nevertheless sought to transfer its power to a parliament elected by universal male suffrage. The masses would thereby become the ultimate arbiter of politics. The democrats were also willing to accept government regulation of business activity as a means of improving the economic position of the lower classes, although their belief in the sanctity of private property was as firm as that of the liberals. In their advocacy of national unification, however, they were less solicitous about royal prerogatives and state rights. While not as influential as the moderates, the radicals remained an important source of opposition to the established order.

Growing criticism of the restored political order forced conservatives to define their ideological position more precisely. The old theories of monarchy by divine right or despotic benevolence offered little protection against the assaults of liberalism and democracy. The defenders of legitimism, who came mostly from the landed nobility, the court aristocracy, the officer corps, the upper bureaucracy, and the established church, therefore began to advance new arguments based on conservative assumptions about the nature of man and society. The relationship between the individual and government, so the reasoning went, cannot be determined by paper constitutions founded on a doctrinaire individualism. Human actions are motivated not solely by rational considerations but by habit, feeling, instinct, and tradition as well. The impractical theories of visionary reformers fail to take into account the historic forces of organic development by which the past and the present shape the future. To assert that all men are equal is to ignore the differences in rights and duties that result from differences in birth, class, background, education, and tradition. The dogmas of constitutional authority and parliamentary government are merely a facade behind which a self-seeking bourgeoisie seeks to disguise its lust for power. An enduring form of government can be built only on the traditional institutions of society: the throne, the church, the nobility, and the army. Only a system of authority legitimated by law and history can protect the worker against exploitation, the believer against godlessness, and the citizen against revolution. According to these tenets, the political institutions of the German Confederation were valid because they represented fundamental ideals deeply embedded in the spirit of the nation.

ECONOMIC CHANGES AND THE ZOLLVEREIN

The struggle of parties and ideologies during the restoration of the old order reflected the beginning of important changes in the structure of the economy and the community. In the long run, the most significant of these changes was the gradual emergence of large-scale industry in Germany. Mechanization, introduced in textile mills and coal mines, spread to other branches of manufacture and influenced the entire economic life of the nation. The transportation network improved with the construction of railroads, steamships, and better roads and canals. Banking institutions and private investors began to transfer their funds from government bonds and commercial ventures to manufacturing enterprises. Factory and railroad owners, financiers, and stockbrokers gradually formed a new upper middle class whose wealth derived primarily from industrial activity and whose growing economic importance encouraged its members to demand greater political influence. Skilled handicraftsmen, who had constituted the bulk of the urban working class, could not compete successfully with the factories. Because rural population grew faster than rural employment following the Congress of Vienna, population began to shift from country to city, although a majority of the inhabitants of the German Confederation continued to live in rural communities. Many of the migrants from the countryside took jobs as factory labourers in the cities.

Agriculture went through as difficult a period of reorganization and rationalization as industry. Peasant emancipation in Prussia allowed the Junkers east of the Elbe River to enlarge their lands by absorbing the holdings of small farmers. The former serfs now formed a propertyless rural proletariat who cultivated the aristocratic landowners' large estates. The result was the continuing economic, social, and political domination of the village by the nobility in the eastern provinces of Prussia. The squirearchy entrenched in Pomerania, Brandenburg, Silesia, and East Prussia controlled agriculture, commanded the army, directed the bureaucracy, and influenced the court. It constituted a powerful force for conservatism and particularism.

West of the Elbe the basic problem was not landlessness but overpopulation. The aristocracy along the Rhine and the Danube was often willing to give the peasantry possession of the soil in return for a substantial payment. The farmer was thereby saddled with heavy financial obligations. Many small farmers tried to escape poverty by emigrating to the New World; those who remained faced rapid population growth and often had to subdivide small holdings among their children until they yielded no profit. Civil discontent mounted among impoverished villagers who lacked employment in industry.

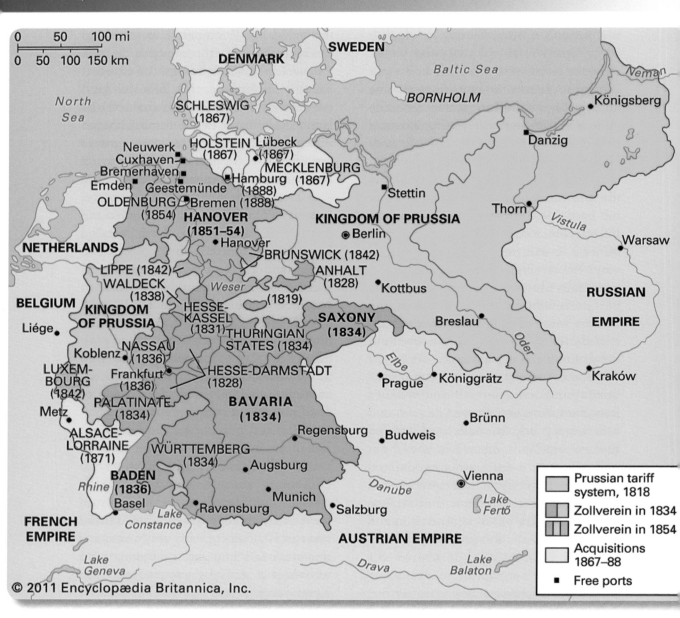

The growth of the German Zollverein.

The system of authority in the German Confederation was thus being undermined by the struggle of artisans against industrial mechanization, by the disaffection of peasants hungry for land, and above all by the criticism of businessmen constrained by the policies of unresponsive governments. Industrialists and financiers had to overcome the barriers created by a variety of monetary systems, commercial regulations, excise taxes, and state boundaries. It is little wonder that the bourgeoisie of Germany turned increasingly to the teachings of liberalism and nationalism. Yet the established order did make a major attempt to meet the needs of the business community. Before long, several of the more important secondary governments concluded agreements with Prussia by which a sizable free trade area was established in the heart of Germany.

In 1834 the Zollverein, or Customs Union, including most of the states of the German Confederation, came into existence. With the accession of several more states by 1842, only Austria and the northwest coastland remained aloof. The industrialists of the Habsburg empire, who wanted their products protected against outside competition, felt that the tariffs of the new association were too low for their needs, whereas the merchants and bankers of the coastal region, who depended on foreign trade, thought they were too high. Yet for some 25 million Germans the Zollverein meant in effect the achievement of commercial unification without the aid of political unification. Prussia, meanwhile, acquired a powerful new weapon in the struggle against Austria for the dominant position in Germany. Still, although the Zollverein helped meet the demands of some businessmen for economic consolidation,

it could not surmount all the material disadvantages of a particularistic form of government. People of means and education continued to grumble about the confederal system under which they lived, while the masses became increasingly restless under the pressure of social and economic dislocation.

THE REVOLUTIONS OF 1848–49

The hard times that swept over the Continent in the late 1840s transformed widespread popular discontent in the German Confederation into a full-blown revolution. After the middle of the decade, a severe economic depression halted industrial expansion and aggravated urban unemployment. At the same time, serious crop failures led to a major famine in the area from Ireland to Russian Poland. In the German states, the hungry 1840s drove the lower classes, which had long been suffering from the economic effects of industrial and agricultural rationalization, to the point of open rebellion. There were sporadic hunger riots and violent disturbances in several of the states, but the signal for a concerted uprising did not come until early in 1848 with the exciting news that the regime of the bourgeois king Louis-Philippe had been overthrown by an insurrection in Paris (February 22–24). The result was a series of sympathetic revolutions against the governments of the German Confederation, most of them mild but a few, as in the case of the fighting in Berlin, bitter and bloody.

When on March 13 Metternich, the proud symbol of the established order, was forced to resign his position in the Austrian cabinet, the princes hastened to make peace with the opposition in order to forestall republican and socialist experiments like those in France. Prominent liberals were appointed to the state ministries, and civic reforms were introduced to safeguard the rights of the citizens and the powers of the legislature. But even more important was the attempt to achieve political unification through a national assembly representing all of Germany. Elections were held soon after the spring uprising had subsided, and on May 18 the Frankfurt National Assembly met in Frankfurt am Main to prepare the constitution for a free and united fatherland. Its convocation represented the realization of the hopes that nationalists had cherished for more than a generation. Within the space of a few weeks, those who had fought against the particularistic system of the restoration for so long suddenly found themselves empowered with a popular mandate to rebuild the foundations of political and social life in Germany. It was an intoxicating moment.

Once the spring uprising was over, the parties and classes that had participated in it began to quarrel about the nature of the new order that was to take the place of the old. There were, first of all, sharp differences between the liberals and the democrats. While the former had comfortable majorities in most of the state legislatures as well as in the Frankfurt parliament, the latter continued to plead, agitate, and conspire for a more radical course of action. There were also bitter disputes over the form that national unification should assume. The Grossdeutsch ("great German") movement maintained that Austria, the state whose rulers had worn the crown of the Holy Roman Empire for 400 years, should play a leading role in the united fatherland. The Kleindeutsch ("little German") party, on the other hand, argued that the Habsburgs had too many Slavic, Magyar, and Italian interests to work single-mindedly for the greatness of Germany, that Austria should therefore be excluded from a unified Germany, and that the natural leader of the nation was Prussia, whose political vigour and geographic position would provide efficient government and military security for Germany. Finally, there was a basic conflict between poor and marginalized social groups, many of whom wanted protection against mechanized production and rural impoverishment, and the business interests who sought to use their new political influence to promote economic growth and freedom of enterprise. Popular support for the revolution, which had made the defeat of legitimism during the March days possible, began to dwindle with the realization that the liberals would do no more to solve the problems of the masses than the conservatives had done. While the Frankfurt parliament was debating the constitution under which Germany would be governed, its following diminished and its authority declined. The forces of the right, recovering from the demoralization of their initial defeat, began to regain confidence in their own power and legitimacy.

Their first major conservative victory came in Austria, where the young emperor Francis Joseph found an able successor to Metternich in his prime minister, Felix, Fürst (prince) zu Schwarzenberg. In the summer of 1848 the Habsburg armies crushed the uprising in Bohemia and checked the insurrection in Italy. By the end of October they had subjugated Vienna itself, the centre of the revolutionary movement, and now only Hungary was still in arms against the imperial government. At the same time, in Prussia the irresolute Frederick William IV had been gradually persuaded by the conservatives to embark on a course of piecemeal reaction. Early in December he dissolved the constituent assembly that had been meeting in Berlin, unilaterally promulgated his own constitution for the kingdom—which combined conservative and liberal elements—and proceeded little by little to reassert the prerogatives of the crown. Among the secondary states there was also a noticeable shift to the right, as particularist princes and legitimist aristocrats began to recover their courage.

By the time the Frankfurt parliament completed its deliberations in the spring of 1849, the revolution was everywhere at ebb tide. The constitution that the National Assembly had drafted called for a federal union headed by a hereditary emperor with powers limited by a popularly elected legislature. Since the Austrian government had already indicated that it would oppose the establishment of a federal government in Germany, the imperial crown was offered to the king of Prussia. Frederick William IV refused a crown whose source he deplored and whose authority seemed too restricted. This rejection of political consolidation under a liberal constitution destroyed the last chance of the revolutionary movement for success. The moderates, admitting failure, went home to mourn the defeat of their hopes and labours. The radicals, on the other hand, sought to attain their objectives by inciting a new wave of insurrections. Their appeals for a mass uprising, however, were answered mostly by visionary intellectuals, enthusiastic students, radical politicians, and professional revolutionaries. The lower classes remained by and large indifferent. There was sporadic violence, especially in the southwest, but troops loyal to princely authority had little difficulty in defeating the insurrection. By the summer of 1849 the revolution, which had begun a year earlier amid such extravagant expectations, was completely crushed.

THE 1850S: YEARS OF POLITICAL REACTION AND ECONOMIC GROWTH

The attempt to achieve national unification through liberal reform was followed by an attempt to achieve it through conservative statesmanship. Frederick William IV had refused to accept an imperial crown vitiated by parliamentary government, but he was willing to become the head of a national federation in which the royal prerogative remained unimpaired. While the Austrian armies were still engaged in the campaign against the revolution in Hungary, Prussia began to exert diplomatic pressure on the smaller German states to join in the formation of a new federal league known as the Prussian Union. If Frederick William IV had acted with enough determination, he might have been able to reach his goal before Francis Joseph could intervene effectively in the affairs of Germany. But he allowed his opportunity to slip away. Though he succeeded through threats and promises in persuading most of the princes to accept his proposals, no irrevocable commitments had been made by the time the Hungarians were defeated in August 1849. Vienna could now proceed to woo the governments, which had in most cases submitted to Prussia only out of weakness and fear. Basically they remained opposed to sacrificing their sovereignty to Prussia. When Schwarzenberg suggested the reestablishment of the old federal Diet, he won the support of many rulers who had agreed to follow Berlin against their will. The nation was now divided into two camps, the Prussian Union on one side and the revived German Confederation on the other. It was only a question of time before they would clash. When both Austria and Prussia decided to intervene in Hesse-Kassel, where there was a conflict between the supporters and the opponents of the prince, Germany stood on the brink of civil war. But Frederick William IV decided at the last moment to back down. His fear overcame his pride, especially after Nicholas I of Russia indicated that he supported Vienna in the controversy. By the Punctation of Olmütz of November 29, 1850, the Prussians agreed to the restoration of the German Confederation, and the old order was fully reestablished in all its weakness and inadequacy.

The years that followed were a period of unmitigated reaction. Those who had dared to defy royal authority were forced to pay the penalty of harassment, exile, imprisonment, or even death. Many of the political concessions made earlier, under the pressure of popular turmoil, were now restricted or abrogated. In Austria, for example, the constitution that had been promulgated in 1849 was revoked, and legitimism, centralization, and clericalism became the guiding principles of government. In Prussia the constitution granted by the king remained in force, but its democratic potential was reduced through the introduction of a complicated electoral system by which the ballots were weighted according to the income of the voters. The consequence was that well-to-do conservatives controlled the legislature. The secondary states returned to the policies of legitimism and particularism that they had pursued before the revolution. In Frankfurt am Main, where the federal Diet now resumed its sessions, diplomats continued to guard the prerogatives of princely authority and state sovereignty. The restoration of the confederal system also served the interests of the Habsburgs, who stood at the pinnacle of their prestige as the saviours of the established order. In Berlin, on the other hand, the prevailing mood was one of confusion and discouragement. The king, increasingly gloomy and withdrawn, came under the influence of ultraconservative advisers who preached legitimism in politics and orthodoxy in religion. The government, smarting under the humiliation suffered at the hands of Austria, was as timid in foreign affairs as it was oppressive in domestic matters. The people, tired of insurrection and cowed by repression, were politically apathetic. The German Confederation as a whole, rigid and unyielding, remained during these last years of its existence blind to the need for reform that the revolution had made clear.

Yet the 1850s, so politically barren, were economically momentous, for it was during this period that the great breakthrough of industrial capitalism occurred in Germany. The national energies, frustrated in the effort to achieve civic reform, turned to the attainment of material progress. The victory of the reaction was followed by an economic expansion as the business community began to recover from its fear of mob violence and social upheaval. The influx of gold from America and Australia, moreover, generated an inflationary tendency, which in turn encouraged a speculative boom. Not only did the value of industrial production and foreign trade in the Zollverein more than double in the course of the

decade, but also new investment banks based on the joint-stock principle were founded to provide venture capital for factories and railroads. The bubble burst in 1857 in a financial crash that affected the entire Continent. For many investors the price of overoptimism and speculation was misfortune and bankruptcy. Yet Germany had now crossed the dividing line between a preindustrial and an industrial economy. Although the rural population still outnumbered the urban, the tendency toward industrialization and urbanization had become irreversible. And this in turn had a profound effect on the direction of politics. As wealth continued to shift from farming to manufacturing, from the country to the city, and from the aristocracy to the bourgeoisie, the pressure for a redistribution of political power also gained strength. While the reactionaries were solemnly proclaiming the sanctity of traditional institutions, economic change was undermining the foundation of those institutions. By the end of the decade, a new struggle between the forces of liberalism and conservatism was in the making.

THE 1860S: THE TRIUMPHS OF BISMARCK

The revival of the movement for liberal reform and national unification at the end of the 1850s came to be known as the "new era." Its coming was heralded by scattered but distinct indications that the days of the reaction were numbered. In 1859 the defeat of Austria in the war against France and Piedmont had a profound effect on the German states. For one thing, the maintenance of the authoritarian regime in Vienna depended on respect for its military strength. Now that the Habsburg armies had shown themselves to be vulnerable, popular unrest in the empire began to increase. Since autocracy was no longer an effective principle of government, Francis Joseph decided to experiment with a parliamentary form of authority. On October 20, 1860, he promulgated a constitution (the October Diploma) for his domains, setting up a bicameral legislature with an electoral system favouring the bourgeoisie, and Austria ceased to be an absolutist state. The beginnings of political unification in Italy, moreover, aroused hope and envy north of the Alps. If the Italians could overcome the obstacles of conservatism and particularism, why not the Germans? National sentiment in Germany, dormant since the revolution, suddenly awoke. Patriotic organizations like the Nationalverein (National Union) and the Reformverein (Reform Union) initiated agitation for a new federal union, the former advocating Prussian and the latter Austrian leadership. Liberal writers and politicians began to advance plans for the reform of the German Confederation. Some of the states, detecting a shift in public opinion, decided to change their course accordingly. Here and there the conservative ministers of the reaction were retired or dismissed, and statesmen with more moderate views took their place.

The most significant portent of a new age in politics, however, appeared in Prussia. In 1857 Frederick William IV, crushed by memories of the mass insurrections and diplomatic defeats that he had been forced to endure, suffered a series of incapacitating strokes. A year later his brother became regent, and the government in Berlin immediately began altering the direction of its policy. Prince William, although a man of conservative inclination, had little sympathy with the mystical visions and pious dogmas prevailing at the court during the period of reaction. He dismissed Frederick William's cabinet, announced a program of cautious reform in Prussian as well as German affairs, and won a popular endorsement of his course in elections that gave the liberals control of the legislature. After a long period of discouragement, the advocates of civic reconstruction could once again look to the future with hope and expectation.

Yet there was an important difference between the political attitude of the liberals in 1858–59 and that of 1848–49. Some liberals came to feel during the new era that they had owed their defeat 10 years before to an excess of idealism and exuberance. The fatal mistake of the revolution, they reasoned, had been the assumption that enthusiasm and selflessness could be translated into power and substituted for statesmanship. Now a more calculating policy, one of Realpolitik, must be adopted. Not theory and rhetoric but negotiation and compromise would lead to the attainment of unity and freedom. The liberals therefore pursued at first a strategy of conciliation, anxious not to frighten the established order into blind resistance against all reform. In Prussia, for example, they waited patiently for the regent to move against the forces of disunity and oppression, confident that if they only gave him enough time he would obtain for them by royal authority what they could not seize through revolutionary violence. Yet it gradually became apparent that their hopes would not be realized. Prince William, who in 1861 became king in his own right, was a moderate conservative but a conservative nevertheless. As the advocates of reform grew increasingly restless, the more militant among them formed the Fortschrittspartei (Progressive Party), which sought to hasten the enactment of liberal legislation by exerting pressure on the government. The monarch, afraid that he was being pushed farther to the left than he wanted to go, became more adamant and uncompromising. Sooner or later a conflict between crown and parliament was bound to arise.

It came in connection with the question of army reform, although, if that issue had not developed, there would undoubtedly have been another. The king wanted to strengthen the armed forces by increasing the number of line regiments and decreasing the size of the popular militia. The necessary budget increase, under the constitution, required legislative approval. The legislature, reluctant to enhance the power of the conservative officer corps, demanded a modification of the plan. The king refused, convinced that the politicians were attempting to gain control of the army, which he considered subject only to royal authority. The legislature responded by withholding approval of the budget. A complete deadlock ensued. In the spring of 1862 the liberal ministers who had been appointed under the regency were dismissed, and a conservative cabinet took office. But the new leaders of the government were as unsuccessful as the old in resolving the crisis. William I (commonly known as Kaiser Wilhelm after becoming emperor in 1871) began to think about abdicating in favour of his son, who was believed to have political views close to those of the parliamentary opposition. He was persuaded, however, to consider first the possibility of naming a new ministry led by Otto von Bismarck, then Prussian ambassador to Paris. There was a momentous interview between the monarch and the envoy, as a result of which the former abandoned all thought of retirement and the latter became head of a cabinet pledged to continue the struggle against the legislature. The battle between crown and parliament, which the liberals had been on the point of winning, was now to be waged without regard for constitutional provisions concerning the budget. On September 23, 1862, the nation was startled by the news that a statesman with a reputation for unyielding conservatism had become the prime minister of Prussia. It meant that the established order, having successfully defended its interests against the forces of reform after 1815 and after 1848, was determined to fight to the bitter end against the new challenge to its predominance.

The constitutional conflict in the Hohenzollern kingdom continued for another four years. The legislature refused to approve the budget until its wishes concerning military reform had been met. Bismarck's government, after carrying out the controversial reorganization of the army, continued to collect taxes and disburse funds without regard for parliamentary authorization. The liberals condemned the prime minister as a violator of the constitution, while the prime minister denounced the liberals and maintained the government's right to act autonomously, since the constitution did not specify a procedure in the event that the legislature failed to approve a budget. Although the electorate remained on the side of the opposition, the cabinet declared that it would not be swayed by party politics or parliamentary majorities. The broad masses of the population, it maintained, were still loyal to the crown. And so the struggle went on without prospect of alleviation or resolution. There were even dark prophecies of a violent uprising against a regime that was so indifferent to its constitutional obligations. Yet in fact Bismarck was not blind to the need for a reconciliation between crown and bourgeoisie. Despite his reputation as a fire-eating legitimist, he had a supple mind and recognized

that the political principles of Frederick the Great could not solve the problems facing William I. He hoped, therefore, for an eventual reconciliation between the government and the legislature, but a reconciliation in which the prerogative of the monarch and the influence of the nobility would remain undiminished.

What Bismarck sought in essence was an alteration in the form of government to create parliamentary institutions that would not undermine monarchical authority. The middle class wanted to end the domination of the traditional forces in society, he calculated, but it also wanted to achieve national unification in Germany. Here was the key to a solution of the constitutional conflict. Unity could be used to restrict freedom; nationalism could become the means of taming liberalism. Bismarck had concluded that the political integration of Germany was, in the long run, inevitable. If the established order did not effect it, the reformers, democrats, and revolutionaries would. Thus, it was in the interest of conservatism to take the task of centralization in hand, bring it to a successful conclusion, and create a new system of authority compatible with the preservation of royal and aristocratic dominance. Such a policy would make possible a compromise between crown and bourgeoisie by which the latter obtained the benefits of national consolidation while the former retained the advantages of political domination. The achievement of national unification by military means would have the further advantage of reconciling the bourgeoisie

OTTO VON BISMARCK

The Prussian statesman Otto von Bismarck (born Otto Eduard Leopold, April 1, 1815, Schönhausen, Altmark, Prussia—died July 30, 1898, Friedrichsruh, near Hamburg) founded the German Empire in 1871 and served as its chancellor for 19 years. Born into the Prussian land-owning elite, Bismarck (the name by which he is best known is derived from his highest noble title, prince von Bismarck) studied law and was elected to the Prussian Diet in 1849. In 1851 he was appointed Prussian representative to the federal Diet in Frankfurt. After serving as ambassador to Russia (1859–62) and France (1862), he became prime minister and foreign minister of Prussia (1862–71). When he took office, Prussia was widely considered the weakest of the five European powers, but under his leadership Prussia won a war against Denmark in 1864, the Seven Weeks' War (1866), and the Franco-Prussian War (1870–71). Through these wars he achieved his goal of political unification of a Prussian-dominated German Empire. Once the empire was established, he became its chancellor. The "Iron Chancellor" skillfully preserved the peace in Europe through alliances against France. Domestically, he introduced administrative and economic reforms but sought to preserve the status quo, opposing the Social Democratic Party and the Catholic church. When Bismarck left office in 1890, the map of Europe had been changed immeasurably. However, the German Empire, his greatest achievement, survived him by only 20 years because he had failed to create an internally unified people.

with a strong military. Through this strategy the prime minister hoped to end the constitutional conflict.

THE DEFEAT OF AUSTRIA

The international situation was favourable to an aggressive program of unification in the German Confederation. Since its defeat in the Crimean War (1853–56), Russia had ceased to play a decisive role in the affairs of the Continent. Britain remained preoccupied with the problems of domestic reform. And Napoleon III was not unwilling to see a civil war east of the Rhine that he might eventually use to enlarge the boundaries of France.

Bismarck could thus prepare for a struggle against Austria without the imminent danger of foreign intervention that had faced Frederick William IV. His first great opportunity came in connection with the duchies of Schleswig and Holstein, which were ruled by the king of Denmark but which were politically and ethnically tied to Germany. When the government in Copenhagen sought to make Schleswig an integral part of the Danish state in 1863, nationalist sentiment in Germany was outraged. William I proposed to Francis Joseph that the two leading powers of the German Confederation should occupy the duchies in order to prevent the violation of an international agreement that had guaranteed their autonomy. Afraid to let the Prussians act on their own, the emperor agreed, and in 1864 the brief German-Danish War demonstrated the strength of the reorganized Prussian army. Danish hopes for foreign assistance proved illusory, and by the Peace of Vienna (October 30) the duchies became the joint possession of Prussia and Austria.

The easy victory of the allies, however, was only the prelude to a bitter conflict between them. Vienna would have liked to see Schleswig-Holstein become an independent secondary state in the German Confederation, committed to a policy of particularism. Berlin, on the other hand, hoped for the outright annexation of the duchies or at least the indirect control of their government. Even more important than the disposition of the spoils of war, however, was the mounting rivalry between the two Great Powers for hegemony in Germany. In 1865 their differences were papered over by the Convention of Gastein, which placed Schleswig under Prussian and Holstein under Austrian administration but which also reaffirmed the joint sovereignty of the two governments over the duchies. Still, this was only a temporary solution, and before long the danger of civil war in the German Confederation began to grow once again.

In the course of the spring of 1866 both sides stepped up their preparations for a military solution to the Austro-Prussian rivalry. Bismarck concluded an alliance with Italy by which

the Italians were to receive Venetia as a reward for participating in a war against the Habsburg empire. He also sought to gain the support of public opinion in the German Confederation by introducing a motion in the federal Diet for the convocation of a national parliament elected by equal manhood suffrage. The Austrians in the meantime secured a promise of French neutrality in the event of hostilities and tried to win the adherence of the secondary states in the impending struggle. The last desperate attempts to preserve peace collapsed in June. Vienna announced that it would submit the question of the duchies to the federal Diet. Berlin, condemning this step as a violation of the Convention of Gastein, ordered its troops in Schleswig to expel the Austrians from Holstein. Francis Joseph in reply called on the other states of the confederation to mobilize their armies against the Prussian threat to domestic tranquillity, and Germany trembled on the verge of civil war. The only question now was the position of the secondary states. Most of them lined up behind Austria, which they regarded as the defender of their independence against the ambitions of Berlin. Bismarck's attempt to enlist the aid of the national movement by advocating reform of the confederal system thus failed. It alarmed the particularists without propitiating the centralists. Public opinion remained frightened and confused, distrusting one side and fearing the other. The future of the nation was decided not by popular insurrections or parliamentary deliberations but by the force of arms.

The Seven Weeks' War between Prussia and Austria (June–August 1866) produced a diplomatic revolution in Europe, destroying the balance of power that had been established 50 years before by the Congress of Vienna. Yet this momentous alteration in the international equilibrium was accomplished so swiftly that foreign diplomats had barely begun to grasp its implications before the struggle for hegemony in Germany ended. The Prussian armies had a brilliant strategist in Helmuth von Moltke and a deadly weapon in the breech-loading needle gun. The Austrian high command, on the other hand, became irresolute and demoralized before a decisive encounter had even taken place. The Prussians succeeded in dividing and defeating the forces of the secondary states, and on July 3 they routed the Habsburg troops as well at the Battle of Königgrätz (Sadowa). The war was thus decided within a few weeks after its outbreak. Bismarck, refusing to be dazzled by the brilliance of the victory, urged the swift conclusion of an honourable peace. Not only did he feel that the preservation of a strong Austria was essential for the maintenance of stability on the Continent, but he also feared that a prolongation of hostilities would enable Napoleon III to intervene in the affairs of Germany. By the preliminary Peace of Nikolsburg (July 26) and the definitive Treaty of Prague (August 23), Francis Joseph was permitted to retain all of his possessions except Venetia, which had been promised to the Italians. There was to be no occupation and only a modest indemnity. The emperor had to acquiesce, however, in the Prussian annexation of Hanover, Nassau, Hesse-Kassel, Schleswig-Holstein, and Frankfurt am Main, in the dissolution of the German Confederation, and in the formation under Prussian leadership of a new federal union north of the Main River. The contest between Berlin and Vienna that had determined the history of the German states for more than a century was now over.

BISMARCK'S NATIONAL POLICIES: THE RESTRICTION OF LIBERALISM

Bismarck's triumph in the military struggle led directly to his victory in the constitutional conflict. Before the outbreak of hostilities, he had tried to reach an understanding with the liberal opposition, but the liberals hesitated to make peace with a statesman who had so flagrantly violated the fundamental law of the kingdom. The defeat of Austria changed all that. While the war was still in progress, general elections resulted in important gains for the right. Many voters, elated over the successes of the Prussian armies, expressed their confidence in the government by supporting its adherents at the polls. Some of the ultraconservatives hoped that the cabinet would now capitalize on its triumph by suspending the constitution and establishing an authoritarian regime. Yet the prime minister recognized that such reactionary schemes would prove futile in the long run. What he wanted was not the suppression of liberalism but an accommodation with it. As soon as peace was concluded, he introduced in the legislature a bill of indemnity granting the government retroactive approval for its operation without a legal budget. The consequence, as Bismarck had foreseen, was a split in the ranks of his adversaries. Those who argued that there could be no compromise on the principle of constitutional government rejected the indemnity bill, but many more moderate liberals, who eventually formed the National Liberal Party, decided to accept the settlement offered by the prime minister. Their reasoning was that an obstinate resistance against the cabinet would only condemn them to sterile dogmatism, whereas a willingness to accept what could not be prevented would enable them to influence official policy in the direction of greater freedom. With the support of these moderate liberals, on September 3, 1866, the legislature approved the Bill of Indemnity, 230 to 75. By dividing the forces of reform and weakening their sense of purpose, Bismarck won as important a success in domestic affairs as the victory on the field of battle.

The prime minister had long believed that the achievement of unity could appease liberal demands for political freedom. The success of the Prussian armies provided him with an opportunity to test this assumption. Once Austria had been subdued, he cajoled and bullied the secondary governments north of the Main River into joining Berlin in the establishment of the North German Confederation. It was the union of a giant and 21 pygmies, for, with its annexation of Hanover, the second largest North German state, as well as other secondary states in the wake of the Seven Weeks' War, Prussia constituted about four-fifths of the territory and population of the confederation. Executive authority was vested in a hereditary presidency occupied by the kings of Prussia, who were to govern with the assistance of a chancellor responsible only to them. The legislature comprised the Federal Council, or Bundesrat, whose members were appointed by the state governments, and a lower house, the Imperial Diet, or Reichstag, elected by equal manhood suffrage. Since Prussia had 17 votes out of 43 in the Bundesrat, it could easily control the proceedings with the support of a few of its satellites among the small principalities. Although the Reichstag could theoretically exercise considerable influence over legislation by granting or withholding its approval, parliamentary authority and party initiative were weak and untested, and Bismarck had little difficulty in piecing together a workable majority for his program by a strategy of divide and rule. His support came largely from a combination of moderate liberals and moderate conservatives who shared a willingness to compromise to achieve pragmatic goals. The federal constitution provided no bill of rights, no ministerial responsibility, and no civilian supervision over military affairs. But it made possible the creation of a national currency and uniform weights, measures, commercial practices, industrial laws, and financial regulations. In short, by satisfying the long-frustrated demands of middle-class Germans for economic and legal unity, the constitution helped reconcile them to the defeat of their hopes for greater political freedom.

FRANCO-GERMAN CONFLICT AND THE NEW GERMAN REICH

The Seven Weeks' War, by creating the North German Confederation, a powerful new state in the heart of central Europe, abruptly altered the system of international relations on the Continent. Every government now had to reexamine its diplomatic and military position. No nation, however, was affected by the victory of the Prussian armies as directly as France. Emperor Napoleon III had encouraged hostilities between Austria and Prussia on the assumption that both combatants would emerge from the struggle exhausted and that the Second Empire of France could then expand eastward against little resistance. The outcome of the war revealed how shortsighted such calculations had been. Instead of profiting from the conflict between Francis Joseph and William I, Paris suddenly confronted a strong and united German state that presented a serious threat to French interests. The French government was bound to regard this turn of events with suspicion and hostility. It sought to mitigate its discomfiture by seeking compensation in the Rhineland, Luxembourg, or Belgium. But Berlin succeeded in frustrating these plans, and the conviction began to grow in France that sooner or later a struggle with Germany would be unavoidable. The prospect of a new armed conflict was not unwelcome to Bismarck. He wanted to see national unification consummated by the entry of the southern states into the North German Confederation. Yet public opinion south of the Main River remained distrustful. Only a common patriotic struggle against foreign aggression might overcome the reluctance of the south to unite politically with the north. Thus in Berlin as well as in Paris there were reasons for seeking a test of strength. The immediate occasion came in the spring of 1870 with the candidacy of Prince Leopold, a relative of William I, for the throne of Spain, a prospect that appeared to threaten French national security. Bismarck cleverly exploited the ensuing controversy to provoke the French into initiating hostilities in such a way as to inflame German patriotic indignation.

When France learned of Leopold's acceptance of the offer of the Spanish crown, there were wild protests in Paris and an immediate demand that Leopold be ordered to withdraw. On July 12 his father renounced the Spanish candidature on his behalf. This was not enough for the French government; it insisted that William I, as head of the Hohenzollern family, should promise that the candidature would never be renewed.

This demand was presented to William at Ems by the French ambassador. Though William refused to give a promise, he dismissed the ambassador in a friendly enough way. But when the Ems telegram, a report of the encounter, reached Bismarck, he shortened it for publication to imply that the French ambassador had insulted William and that the king had refused to see the French ambassador again. The French used the king's supposed refusal as an excuse to declare war on Prussia on July 19.

Bismarck's calculation that a struggle waged ostensibly against the aggression of Napoleon III would overcome particularism south of the Main River proved correct. The southern states joined the north in the Franco-Prussian War, and the brotherhood of arms brought a sense of unity that was soon enhanced by the intoxication of victory. The German troops won one battle after another in hard fighting along the frontier, until on September 2 they forced a large French army, headed by the emperor himself, to surrender at Sedan. The result was the establishment of a republican government in France, which continued to wage the struggle in the name of the old revolutionary ideals of 1793. The generalship of Moltke and the might of the German armies, however, were too much for the fierce determination of the new regime. Paris capitulated on January 28, 1871, after a long and bitter siege, and on May 10 the Treaty of Frankfurt brought the war officially to a close. The Third Republic had to cede Alsace-Lorraine to Germany, pay an indemnity of five billion francs, and accept an army of occupation. It was a peace designed to crush a dangerous rival. The work of national unification in Germany, in the meantime, was successfully completed even before hostilities had ended. Bismarck had entered into negotiations with the southern states soon after the outbreak of war, determined to use patriotic fervour as an instrument for achieving political consolidation. The enthusiasm aroused in Germany by the victory over France proved too much for the defenders of particularism. On January 18, while Prussian guns bombarded Paris, William I was proclaimed emperor of a united nation at military headquarters in Versailles. The governments south of the Main River joined the North German Confederation to form a powerful new Reich under the Hohenzollerns. Within a single lifetime, Germany had completed the transition from cosmopolitanism to nationalism, from serfdom to industrialization, from division to union, from weakness to dominance, from the Holy Roman Empire to the German Empire.

CHAPTER 9

GERMANY FROM 1871 TO THE MODERN ERA

The German Empire was founded on January 18, 1871, in the aftermath of three successful wars by the North German state of Prussia. Within a seven-year period Denmark, the Habsburg monarchy, and France were vanquished in short, decisive conflicts. The empire was forged not as the result of the outpouring of nationalist feeling from the masses but through traditional cabinet diplomacy and agreement by the leaders of the states in the North German Confederation, led by Prussia, with the hereditary rulers of Bavaria, Baden, Hesse-Darmstadt, and Württemberg. Prussia, occupying more than three-fifths of the area of Germany and having approximately three-fifths of the population, remained the dominant force in the nation until the empire's demise at the end of another war in 1918.

THE GERMAN EMPIRE, 1871–1914

At its birth Germany occupied an area of 208,825 square miles (540,854 square km) and had a population of more than 41 million, which was to grow to 67 million by 1914. The religious makeup was 63 percent Protestant, 36 percent Roman Catholic, and 1 percent Jewish. The country was ethnically homogeneous apart from a modest-sized Polish minority and smaller Danish, French, and Sorbian populations. Approximately 67 percent lived in villages and the remainder in towns and cities. Literacy was close to universal because of compulsory education laws dating to the 1820s and '30s.

DOMESTIC CONCERNS

From its origins in 1871, the empire was governed under the constitution designed four years earlier by Otto von Bismarck, the Prussian prime minister, for the North German Confederation. This constitution reflected the predominantly rural nature of Germany in 1867 and the authoritarian proclivities of Bismarck, who was a member of the Junker landowning elite. There were two houses: the Reichstag, to represent the people, and the Bundesrat, to represent the 25 states. The former comprised 397 members elected by universal manhood suffrage and a secret ballot. The constituencies established in 1867 and 1871 were never altered to reflect population shifts, and rural areas thus retained a vastly disproportionate share of power as urbanization progressed. In theory the Reichstag's ability to reject any bill seemed to make it an important reservoir of power; in practice, however, the power of the lower house was circumscribed by the government's reliance on indirect taxes and by the parliament's willingness to approve the military budget every seven (after 1893, every five) years. Most legislative proposals were submitted to the Bundesrat first and to the Reichstag only if they were approved by the upper house. Although members of the Reichstag could question the chancellor about his policies, the legislative bodies were rarely consulted about the conduct of foreign affairs. Imperial ministers were chosen by and were responsible to the emperor rather than to the legislature.

A problem that was to plague the empire throughout its existence was the disparity between the Prussian and imperial political systems. In Prussia the lower house was elected under a restricted three-class suffrage system, an electoral law that allowed the richest 15 percent of the male population to choose approximately 85 percent of the delegates. A conservative majority was always assured in Prussia, whereas the universal manhood suffrage resulted in increasing majorities for the political centre and left-wing parties in the imperial parliament. William I was both German emperor (1871–88) and king of Prussia (1861–88). Apart from two brief instances the imperial chancellor was simultaneously prime minister of Prussia. Thus, the executives had to seek majorities from two separate legislatures elected by radically different franchises. A further problem was that government ministers were generally selected from the civil service or the military. They often had little experience with parliamentary government or foreign affairs.

The constitution had been designed by Bismarck to give the chancellor and monarch primary decision-making power. Universal manhood suffrage had been proposed because of Bismarck's belief that the rural population would vote for either the Conservative or Free Conservative parties. (Female suffrage had not been proposed because politics was considered a male preserve at the time.) The Progressives, a left-wing liberal party, were expected to do poorly in the two-thirds of Germany that was rural in 1867. Bismarck had not counted on new parties such as the Centre Party, a Roman Catholic confessional party, or the Social Democratic Party (Sozialdemokratische Partei Deutschlands; SPD), both of which began participating in imperial and Prussian elections in the early 1870s. The Centre generally received 20–25 percent of the total vote in all elections. The SPD grew from 2 seats in the first imperial election to 35 by 1890, when the SPD actually gained a plurality of votes. Bismarck termed the Centre and SPD along with the Progressives Reichsfeinde ("enemies of the empire") because he believed that each sought in its own way to change the fundamental conservative political character of the empire.

Beginning in 1871, he launched the Kulturkampf ("cultural struggle"), a campaign in concert with German liberals against political Catholicism. Bismarck's aim was clearly to destroy the Centre Party. Liberals saw the Roman Catholic Church as politically reactionary and feared the appeal of a clerical party to the more than one-third of Germans who professed Roman Catholicism. Both Bismarck and the liberals doubted the loyalty of the Catholic population to the Prussian-centred and, therefore, primarily Protestant country. In Prussia the minister of ecclesiastical affairs and education, Adalbert Falk, introduced a series of bills establishing civil marriage, limiting the movement of the clergy, and dissolving religious orders. All church appointments were to be approved by the state. As a result hundreds of parishes and several bishoprics were left without incumbents. Clerical civil servants were purged from the Prussian administration.

The Kulturkampf failed to achieve its goals and, if anything, convinced the Roman Catholic minority that their fear of persecution was real and that a confessional party to represent their interests was essential. By the late 1870s Bismarck abandoned the battle as a failure. He now launched a campaign against the SPD in concert with the two conservative parties and many National Liberals. Fearing the potential of the Social Democrats in a rapidly industrializing Germany, Bismarck found a majority to outlaw the party from 1878 to 1890, although constitutionally it could not be forbidden to participate in elections. Party offices and newspapers were closed down and meetings prohibited. Many socialists fled to Switzerland and sought to keep the party alive in exile. During the 1880s Bismarck also sought to win the workers away from socialism by introducing legislation granting them modest pensions, accident insurance, and a national system of medical coverage. Like the Kulturkampf, the campaign against the SPD was a failure, and, when the 1890 elections showed enormous gains for the Reichsfeinde, Bismarck began to consider having the German princes reconvene,

KULTURKAMPF

The Kulturkampf ("culture struggle") was the bitter struggle (c. 1871–87) on the part of the German chancellor Otto von Bismarck to subject the Roman Catholic Church to state controls. The term came into use in 1873, when the scientist and Prussian liberal statesman Rudolf Virchow declared that the battle with the Roman Catholics was assuming "the character of a great struggle in the interest of humanity."

Bismarck, a staunch Protestant, never fully trusted the loyalty of the Roman Catholics within his newly created German Empire and became concerned by the Vatican Council's proclamation of 1870 concerning papal infallibility. The Roman Catholics, who were represented politically by the Centre Party, distrusted the predominance of Protestant Prussia within the empire and often opposed Bismarck's policies.

The conflict began in July 1871, when Bismarck, supported by the liberals, abolished the Roman Catholic bureau in the Prussian Ministry of Culture (i.e., ministry of education and ecclesiastical affairs) and in November forbade priests from voicing political opinions from the pulpit. In March 1872 all religious schools became subject to state inspection; in June all religious teachers were excluded from state schools, and the Jesuit order was dissolved in Germany; and in December diplomatic relations with the Vatican were severed. In 1873 the May Laws, promulgated by the Prussian minister of culture, Adalbert Falk, placed strict state controls over religious training and even over ecclesiastical appointments within the church. The climax of the struggle came in 1875, when civil marriage was made obligatory throughout Germany. Dioceses that failed to comply with state regulations were cut off from state aid, and noncompliant clergy were exiled.

Roman Catholics, however, strongly resisted Bismarck's measures and opposed him effectively in the German parliament, where they doubled their representation in the 1874 elections. Bismarck, a pragmatist, decided to retreat. He conceded that many of the measures were excessive and served only to strengthen the resistance of the Centre Party, whose support he needed for his new thrust against the Social Democrats. The advent of a new pope in 1878 eased compromise. By 1887, when Leo XIII declared the conflict over, most of the anti-Catholic legislation had been repealed or reduced in severity. The struggle had the consequence of assuring state control over education and public records, but it also alienated a generation of Roman Catholics from German national life.

as in 1867, to draw up a new constitution. The new emperor, William II, saw no reason to begin his reign (1888–1918) with a potential bloodbath and asked for the 74-year-old chancellor's resignation. Thus, Bismarck, the architect of German unity, left the scene in a humiliating fashion, believing that his creation was fatally flawed. Indeed, his policy of supporting rapid social and economic modernization while avoiding any reform of the authoritarian political system did lead to an atmosphere of persistent crisis.

THE ECONOMY, 1870–90

The empire was founded toward the end of two decades of rapid economic expansion, during which the German states surpassed France in steel production and railway building. By 1914 Germany was an industrial giant second only to the United States. After the establishment of the North German Confederation (1867), the impediments to economic growth were quickly removed. The usury laws and fetters on internal migration disappeared. A uniform currency based on gold was adopted by Bismarck and his National Liberal allies. An imperial central bank was created, and the tough regulations hindering the formation of joint-stock corporations fell by the wayside. Combined with the euphoria over unification, these changes led to an unprecedented boom between 1870 and 1873. The Gründerjahre ("founders' years"), as the years after unification were called, saw 857 new companies founded with a capital of 1.4 billion talers—more new companies and investment in the private sector than in the previous 20 years. Dividends reached an astounding 12.4 percent. The railway system almost doubled in size between 1865 and 1875. Tens of thousands of Germans invested in stock for the first time to demonstrate both their patriotism and their faith in the future of the new German Empire.

These halcyon years came to an abrupt end with the onset of a worldwide depression in 1873. The prices for agricultural and industrial goods fell precipitously; for six successive years the net national product declined. A sharp decline in profits and investment opportunities persisted until the mid-1890s. About 20 percent of the recently founded corporations went bankrupt.

In agriculture, the deeply indebted Junker elite now faced severe competition as surplus American and Russian grain flooded the German market. Among the more immediate consequences of the crash was a burst of emigration from the depressed provinces of rural Prussia. During the 1870s some 600,000 people departed for North and South America; this number more than doubled in the 1880s. As a result of the depression, social and economic questions increasingly preoccupied the Reichstag, while constitutional and political issues were put on the back burner.

It would be incorrect to draw the conclusion that the economy remained in the doldrums for an entire generation. While the 1870s and early 1890s were depressed periods, the 1880s saw significant recovery in industry, if not in agriculture. The British, who had paid scant attention to Germany's emergence as an industrial power, began to respect their competitor during this decade.

In adjusting to the depression of the 1870s, Germany's leaders chose to return to a regulated economy after a generation of increasingly free trade. The hallmark of the new age was concentration; Germany became the land of big industry, big agriculture, big banks, and big government. The two areas in which the trend toward a controlled economy was most evident were tariff policy and the formation of cartels. Cartel agreements, which were sanctioned by the state, apportioned markets, set standards for manufactured goods, and fixed prices. It is not coincidental that Germany, where the guild system prevailed into the 19th century, should have given birth to the cartel. Cartels arose rapidly in the steel, coal, glass, cement, potash, and chemical industries. Between 1882 and 1895 the total number of business enterprises grew by 4.6 percent, but the number employing more than 50 workers grew by 90 percent.

In 1878–79 Bismarck initiated a significant change in German economic policy in conjunction with his new alliance with the two conservative parties at the expense of the National Liberals. Protective import tariffs were introduced on iron and the major agricultural grains; the latter were raised in 1885 and again in 1887. This departure from liberal economic policy addressed complaints from industrialists, estate owners, and peasants about the terrible impact the depression was having on their respective incomes. Only Britain held out against the protectionist tide that swept Europe in the

1880s. Bismarck's shift, nevertheless, had serious political implications. It signified his opposition to any further evolution in the direction of political democracy. The grain tariffs provided the Junker estate owners of Prussia, who constituted the main opposition to full political emancipation, with subventions that insulated them somewhat from the international market. Thus, the landed elite, major industrialists, the military, and the higher civil service formed an alliance to forestall the rise of social democracy, prevent further political liberalization, and make sure that the uncertainties of the market did not weaken the elites.

FOREIGN POLICY, 1870–90

Until his resignation in 1890, Bismarck had a relatively free hand in the conduct of foreign policy. After three successful wars, he saw his task as promoting peace and gaining time so that a powerful German Empire in the middle of Europe would come to be accepted as natural rather than as an interloper. The Prussian victories had led to great insecurity among the Continental powers, who now reformed their armies in imitation of Germany and maneuvered for defensive alliances so they would not find themselves isolated in the event of war. Bismarck's two areas of concern were the Balkans—where the disintegration of the Turkish Ottoman Empire could easily lead to conflict between Habsburg-ruled Austria-Hungary and Russia—and France, which desired revenge against

0   50   100   150 mi
0   100   200 km

NORTH SEA
DENMARK
SWEDEN
BALTIC SEA
SCHLESWIG
Bornholm
Königsberg
HOLSTEIN
Danzig
EAST PRUSHA
Lübeck
LAUENBURG
WEST POMERANIA   PRUSSIA
Frisian Islands
Hamburg
Stettin
Bremen
Elbe
Berlin
HANOVER
Hanover
BRANDENBURG   Oder
POSEN
Vistula
Warsaw
NETHERLANDS
Rhine
WESTPHALIA
PROVINCE OF SAXONY
RUSSIAN EMPIRE
Essen
Leipzig
Dresden
SILESIA
BELGIUM
Cologne
Breslau
ELECTORATE OF HESSE
THURINGIAN STATES
KINGDOM OF SAXONY
RHINE PROVINCE
NASSAU
REUSS
Prague
LUX.
Frankfurt
Trier
AUSTRO-HUNGARIAN EMPIRE
BAVARIA
LORRAINE
Stuttgart
Danube
BADEN
WÜRTTEMBERG
FRANCE
Munich
ALSACE
HOHENZOLLERN
SWITZERLAND
Lake Constance

1. Anhalt
2. Brunswick
3. Grand Duchy of Hesse
4. Lippe-Detmold
5. Mecklenburg-Schwerin
6. Mecklenburg-Strelitz
7. Oldenburg
8. Palatinate (to Bavaria)
9. Schaumburg-Lippe
10. Waldeck

Kingdom of Prussia, 1866
German Empire, 1871–1918

© 2011 Encyclopædia Britannica, Inc.

The German Empire, 1871–1918.

the German victors. Each might spark a general European conflagration that would inevitably involve Germany.

Bismarck's most important diplomatic objective was to prevent France from allying itself with either Austria-Hungary or Russia to create a coalition of enemies in both the east and the west. In 1873 he negotiated the Three Emperors' League with Russia and Austria-Hungary. The league collapsed in the mid-1870s when rebellion broke out in Turkey's Slavic provinces. In 1877 Russia declared war on Turkey, leading both Britain and

Austria-Hungary to express serious concern about Russia's expansionist war aims. When Russia forced Turkey to cede considerable territory in the Treaty of San Stefano, Bismarck called for an international conference to reconsider the peace treaty and to forestall another military conflict. At the Congress of Berlin in 1878, Bismarck played the role of honest broker among the powers. Russia reluctantly accepted more modest territorial gains, and tensions dissipated.

But a conflagration had barely been avoided. Soon after the conference, Bismarck negotiated an alliance with Austria-Hungary (1879), which remained in effect through World War I. While Bismarck did not intend to do so, he had tied the fate of the youthful German Empire to the aged multinational empire that faced continuous problems from its many ethnic minorities. The chancellor had clearly opted for the Dual Monarchy over Russia should a war break out. The alliance gave him leverage in Vienna, and he steadfastly used it to prevent a war over the Balkans. He chose Austria-Hungary because he feared that its dissolution would lead to Russian hegemony over the empire's Polish, Czech, and other Slavic provinces. In addition, seven million Austro-German Catholics might seek admission to the German Empire, leading to a strengthening of the hated Centre Party.

Having a solid ally, Bismarck demonstrated his virtuosity by negotiating a revived Three Emperors' League in 1881. He now had influence in St. Petersburg as well as in Vienna to prevent a conflict over the Balkans. In 1882 Italy, fearing French hostility, joined the Dual Alliance with Austria-Hungary, making it into the Triple Alliance. On the surface Bismarck had triumphed. France had no allies for a war of revenge, and the alliance with both Austria-Hungary and Russia gave him influence with the two major adversaries in the Balkans.

The transient nature of this artistry soon became apparent. A crisis in Bulgaria inflamed Russo-Austrian relations, leading to the breakup of the revived league. Once again a war was avoided with Bismarck's intervention, but Austria-Hungary and Russia could no longer patch up their differences. Bismarck negotiated a separate Reinsurance Treaty with the Russian tsar in 1887. Nevertheless, France and Russia began courting each other before Bismarck left office.

Between 1870 and 1890 Bismarck earned the respect of European leaders for his pacific policies. Apart from a few colonial additions in the mid-1880s, Germany under his guidance acted as a satiated power. The question remained whether this burgeoning industrial power led by the Junker and industrial elites would continue this policy while the other Western powers carved out world empires.

POLITICS, 1890–1914

The political structure established by Bismarck in 1867 remained with scant change until the empire's demise in 1918. Leo, Graf (count) von Caprivi, Bismarck's successor, was a political neophyte, having spent his entire career in the military. Given the disjuncture between the Prussian and German political systems, Caprivi, surprisingly, sought to work with the parties of the centre and left, Bismarck's Reichsfeinde. With their support, he reduced the grain tariffs and negotiated long-term trade treaties with Russia, the Dual Monarchy, and Romania. Food prices fell as a result, and industry flourished. National wealth rose rapidly, as did the standard of living of the industrial labour force. The Junker elite were outraged at Caprivi's willingness to sacrifice their interests on behalf of industry and labour. Utilizing their political power in Prussia and their access to the emperor, they were able to force his resignation in 1894, making his chancellorship the shortest before the war. After his resignation, the former general wrote to a friend:

In regard to the "Junker agrarians" I see only evil, and it appears to me that a revolution by the agrarians is not impossible and for the moment more dangerous than a Social Democratic revolution.

Succeeding chancellors learned from Caprivi's fall that opposition to the landed elite was fraught with peril. Bernhard, Fürst (prince) von Bülow, chancellor from 1900 to 1909, abandoned Caprivi's trade policy and resurrected the alliance of the agrarian and industrial elites.

As Germany entered the 20th century, its economy was the most dynamic in Europe, but its authoritarian political system was marked by paralysis. With each election, the increasingly urban electorate returned Social Democrats in growing numbers. By 1890 the Social Democrats (who had adopted a Marxist program of revolution at their Erfurt congress in 1891) received more votes than any other party, although four other parties won more seats. By 1912 they had more voters supporting them than the next two largest parties combined. Both the Centre and Social Democrats were able to create parties with a mass base in German society. The Conservatives, National Liberals, and Progressives were more traditional parties, led by notables who were ill at ease in the world of populist politics. All three declined relatively, especially the Conservatives, who, despite flirting with anti-Semitism after 1893 by becoming a Christian party, fell to less than 15 percent of the vote by 1912. Many contemporary observers thought that a major crisis was impending between the recalcitrant elites and the increasing number of Germans who desired political emancipation similar to that of Britain and France.

While the Liberals and Conservatives declined in the Reichstag, new single-issue extraparliamentary interest groups gained adherents. For the most part organizations such as the Pan-German League, the Navy League, the Farmers League, and the Colonial League were authoritarian in their politics and aggressively expansionist in foreign policy. Their constituencies were overwhelmingly middle-class and educated (except for the Farmers League), and they sought to influence the decision-making process both directly, by impressing the ministers with their strength, and indirectly, by supporting parties that adhered to their goals. Given the wealth and high status of their membership (professors were highly visible as leaders), they were unusually effective in publicizing their goals. One of the striking characteristics of the empire was the support it received from the educated strata of the population, despite (or perhaps because of) its elitist constitution.

In the last election during the empire (1912), the Social Democrats scored a great victory, capturing 34.8 percent of the vote and 110 seats. On the local level they had begun to cooperate with the Progressives and occasionally with the Centre Party. Southern states such as Württemberg were moving toward full parliamentary government, and Alsace-Lorraine was given a surprising degree of self-government. Thus, there were some indications that the empire was evolving into a representative democracy. On the other hand, the states of Saxony and Hamburg adopted even more restrictive franchises than Prussia in the years before World War I. Above all, Prussia and its Junker, military, and bureaucratic elites, supported by much of the professoriat, stood firm in opposition to any substantial democratization of the Prussian electoral system, which was a

key to political reform in the Reich. It is not at all clear, therefore, how German politics might have evolved if war had not come in 1914. Some historians have viewed the outbreak of war in that year as an attempt by these elites to shore up their sagging position with a successful war and annexations, as Bismarck had done in the 1860s when the authoritarian Prussian state was besieged by a liberal opposition.

THE ECONOMY, 1890–1914

The speed of Germany's advance to industrial maturity after 1890 was breathtaking. The years from 1895 to 1907 witnessed a doubling of the number of workers engaged in machine building, from slightly more than one-half million to well over a million. An immediate consequence of expanding industrial employment was a sharp drop in emigration; from an average of 130,000 people per year in the 1880s, the outflow dropped to 20,000 per year in the mid-1890s. The surplus population continued to leave Prussia's eastern provinces, but the destination was the growing and multiplying factories of Berlin and the Ruhr rather than the Americas. Earlier British fears of German competition were now fully justified. While Britain produced about twice as much steel as Germany during the early 1870s, Germany's steel production exceeded Britain's in 1893, and by 1914 Germany was producing more than twice as much steel as Britain. Moreover, only one-third of German exports in 1873 were finished goods; the portion rose to 63 percent by 1913. Germany came to dominate all the major Continental markets except France.

The focus of national wealth as well as population shifted to the urban industrial sector by 1900. Only 40 percent of Germans lived in rural areas by 1910, a drop from 67 percent at the birth of the empire. Cities of more than 100,000 inhabitants accounted for one-fifth of the population in 1914, compared to one-twentieth at the time of unification. The application of intensive agricultural techniques led to a doubling in the value of all farm products despite a sharp decline in the rural population. Industry accounted for 60 percent of the gross national product in 1913.

The German working class grew rapidly in the late 19th and the early 20th century. Total union membership reached 3.7 million in 1912, of which 2.5 million were affiliated with the socialist unions. Bismarck's social welfare legislation covered some 13.2 million workers by 1911. Although German employers were extremely authoritarian and hostile to collective bargaining, the labour force did make significant economic gains. Between 1867 and 1913 the average number of hours worked per year declined by 14 percent. Nearly every study of real income shows a rapid rise until 1902 and then a modest increase yearly thereafter. National income per capita rose from 352 marks to 728 during the life of the empire. Despite these advances, industrial workers lacked full political rights, which led

a large number of them, including many Roman Catholic workers, to vote for the revolutionary socialist party.

While industrialization was rapid, it occurred only in certain sectors of the economy; other areas were only marginally affected. Some two million Germans persisted in traditional artisanal enterprises even as the nation became an industrial colossus. While Germany was characterized by large Junker estates and cartels, it was also the nation of dwarf-sized farms (60 percent of farmers owned less than five acres) and small workshops. German factories were larger and more modern than their British and French counterparts, but the preindustrial sector was more backward. During depressions those in the traditional trades often turned to anti-Semitism as an ideology that was portrayed as both patriotic and anticapitalist.

FOREIGN POLICY, 1890–1914

Bismarck's successors rapidly abandoned his foreign policy. The Reinsurance Treaty of 1887 with Russia was dropped, leaving Germany more firmly tied to the Dual Monarchy and Russia free to conclude an alliance with France in 1894. Within four years Friedrich von Holstein, a councillor in the political division of the foreign office, had weakened Germany's influence in the Balkans and allowed France to end its isolation. German overtures to Britain remained ineffective.

In 1895 the brilliant young sociologist Max Weber gave an inaugural

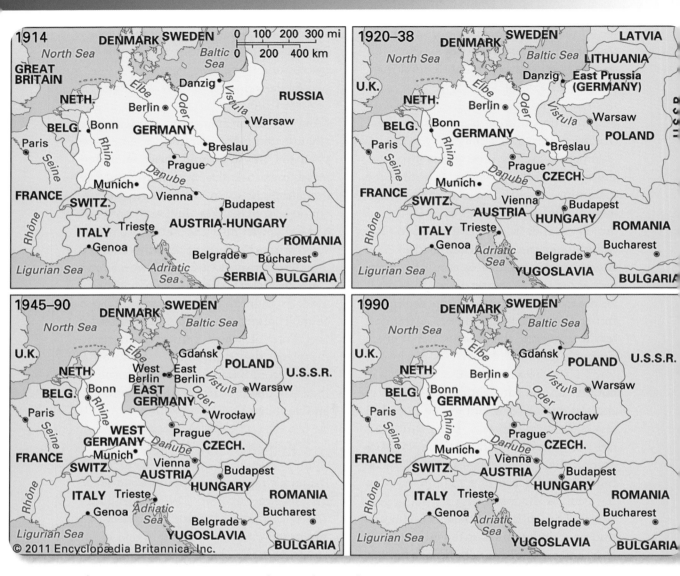

Changes in Germany's territory and internal status from 1914 to 1990.

lecture in Freiburg in which he pointed out that, while Germany was establishing a nation-state belatedly, the other powers had been founding world empires in Africa and Asia. Weber admonished his audience that Germany had to follow suit or become another Switzerland. Weber's contemporaries needed little convincing. From 1897 to 1912 William II, with his politically astute naval adviser, Alfred von Tirpitz, sought to make Germany a global power. Germany's naval power went from being negligible to being second only to Britain's in little more than a decade. Nor did Germany build a navy simply to defend its coastline; rather, the new battleships were capable of challenging the other naval powers on the oceans. Tirpitz was a master of publicity, able to win much of the commercial and industrial middle class for his vision of a mighty empire, whose shipping lanes would be guarded by his fleet. The fleet was also expected to make the monarchy more popular and stem the growth of the left-wing parties. Germany's efforts to build a global empire proved to be a colossal failure. Germany came on the imperial scene late, when the choicest territories had already been occupied. Togo, Cameroon, part of New Guinea, a few Pacific islands, and east-central and southwestern Africa—all territories of limited economic value—hardly seemed to justify the enormous expenditures on the navy. Moreover, Tirpitz's plans alienated Britain. Germany already had the most powerful army in the world when it fastened on becoming a great naval power. The British found this threatening and negotiated an alliance with Japan in 1902 and another one with France in 1904. In 1907 Britain settled its differences with Russia, and the Triple Entente (including France) was established. Germany now found itself surrounded by three major powers allied against it.

The more established powers found Germany meddling everywhere. This behaviour was particularly striking because it followed two decades of Bismarck's policy of avoiding conflict. The Japanese objected to Germany's involvement in China in the 1890s. Russia watched as German power and influence grew in Turkey, its hereditary enemy. The French, of course, still harboured dreams of undoing their defeat in 1870. With Britain also alienated, Bismarck's nightmare of a coalition against the young upstart empire had become a reality. Twice Germany's rulers sought to break up the alliance that was forming against it. In 1905 and 1911 Germany created crises over the French penetration of Morocco. In each case the British and Russians stood firm, and, even though Germany gained concessions, the Triple Entente remained solid. At home, the political system that Bismarck had created was in serious trouble, in part because neither his successors nor the unstable young emperor, William II, shared the master politician's gifts, in part because Bismarck's social world no longer existed. It became increasingly difficult to govern with a democratically elected Reichstag and a Prussian parliament that represented a conservative plutocracy.

In 1912 the chancellor, Theobald von Bethmann Hollweg, and his ministers reassessed the decade and a half of efforts to achieve global power and judged them a failure. The army, which had not been expanded since 1894, once again became the pride of the regime. Eastern Europe and the Balkans were now considered the most likely areas for German economic and political penetration. Since Italy had become unreliable, Austria-Hungary was the only ally to be counted on in the event of war. Any threat to the stability of the Dual Monarchy could leave Germany totally isolated.

The assassination of the Austrian heir to the throne, Archduke Francis Ferdinand, by a Bosnian Serb in June 1914 augured poorly for the future of Austria-Hungary unless it showed resolve in dealing with the provocation. William II and Bethmann Hollweg urged strong measures against Serbia and reasserted their unconditional loyalty if war should eventuate. With Russia rapidly recovering from its defeat by Japan in 1905 and Austria-Hungary increasingly threatened by the national aspirations of its minorities, time appeared to be on the side of the Triple Entente. Thus, if war was inevitable, the sooner it came, the better. A localized conflict between Austria-Hungary and Serbia with a quick victory for the former would be desirable. If Russia chose to intervene to help its Slavic brother, Serbia, then a general European conflict would ensue. This was acceptable to the German government both because of its pessimism about the long-term strength of the Central Powers (i.e., the German Empire and Austria-Hungary) and because the civilian population could be expected to rally to the war effort if tsarist Russia appeared to bear much of the responsibility.

WORLD WAR I

During the first days of World War I, many Germans experienced a sense of bonding that had eluded them since the founding of the empire. Differences of class, religion, and politics seemed to disappear as Germans flocked to their city centres to show their enthusiastic support for the impending conflict. Overwhelmingly, the parties, including the Social Democrats, voted for war credits. The euphoria of the early days masked Germany's dangerous situation. The Triple Entente commanded the seas, had more than twice the population of Germany and Austria-Hungary, and had access to the world's natural resources through their empires and close contact with the United States. Germany was immediately blockaded and had to rely on its own resources and those of Austria-Hungary and contiguous non-belligerents such as the Netherlands, Denmark, and Switzerland. The Central Powers did have interior lines of transit, which was valuable in a two-front war. They also had a unified command structure—in contrast to the Triple Entente powers, whose rivalries resulted in three different wars being fought simultaneously with little coordination.

General Alfred von Schlieffen, chief of the German general staff from 1891 to 1906, had recognized Germany's vulnerability in a two-front war and seen the best hope in an overwhelming attack against France through Belgium. If all went according to plan, France's eastern industrial region would be occupied in six to eight weeks and Paris itself surrounded. The slow-moving Russians would occupy Prussia's eastern rural provinces, facing

U-BOAT

The destruction of enemy shipping by German U-boats (an abbreviation of *Unterseeboot* or "undersea boat") was a spectacular feature of both World Wars I and II.

WORLD WAR I

Germany was the first country to employ submarines in war as substitutes for surface commerce raiders. At the outset of World War I, German U-boats, though numbering only 38, achieved notable successes against British warships; but because of the reactions of neutral powers (especially the United States) Germany hesitated before adopting unrestricted U-boat warfare against merchant ships. The decision to do so in February 1917 was largely responsible for the entry of the United States into the war. The U-boat campaign then became a race between German sinkings of merchant ships and the building of ships, mainly in the United States, to replace them. In April 1917, 430 Allied and neutral ships totaling 852,000 tons were sunk, and it seemed likely that the German gamble would succeed. However, the introduction of convoys, the arrival of numerous U.S. destroyers, and the vast output of American shipyards turned the tables. By the end of the war Germany had built 334 U-boats and had 226 under construction. The peak U-boat strength of 140 was reached in October 1917, but there were never more than about 60 at sea at one time. In 1914–18 the destruction—more than 10 million tons—caused by the U-boats was especially remarkable in view of the small size (less than 1,000 tons), frailty, and vulnerability of the craft.

WORLD WAR II

The Armistice terms of 1918 required Germany to surrender all its U-boats, and the Treaty of Versailles forbade it to possess them in the future. In 1935, however, Adolf Hitler's Germany repudiated the treaty and forcefully negotiated the right to build U-boats. Britain was ill-prepared in 1939 for a resumption of unrestricted submarine warfare, and during the early months of World War II the U-boats, which at that time numbered only 57, again achieved great successes. The first phase, during which the U-boats generally operated singly, ended in March 1941, by which time many merchant ships were sailing in convoy, trained escort groups were becoming available, and aircraft were proving their effectiveness as anti-U-boat weapons. In the next phase the Germans, having acquired air and U-boat bases in Norway and western France, were able to reach much farther out into the Atlantic, and their U-boats began to operate in groups (called wolf packs by the British). One U-boat would shadow a convoy and summon others by radio, and then the group would attack, generally on the surface at night. These tactics succeeded until radar came to the aid of the escorts and until convoys could be given continuous sea and air escort all the way across the Atlantic in both directions. In March 1943, as in April 1917, the Germans nearly succeeded in cutting Britain's Atlantic lifeline, but by May escort carriers and very-long-range reconnaissance bombers became available. After the U-boats lost 41 of their number during that month, they withdrew temporarily from the Atlantic.

In the next phase, U-boats were sent to remote waters where unescorted targets could still be found. Although at first they achieved considerable successes, especially in the Indian Ocean, the Allied strategy of striking at the U-boats' supply vessels and putting all possible shipping into convoys again proved successful. In the final phase the U-boats—then fitted with the snorkel (*schnorkel*) ventilating tube, which permitted extended underwater travel and greatly reduced the effectiveness of radar—returned to the coastal waters around the British Isles, but they sank few ships and themselves suffered heavy losses.

In World War II Germany built 1,162 U-boats, of which 785 were destroyed and the remainder surrendered (or were scuttled to avoid surrender) at the capitulation. Of the 632 U-boats sunk at sea, Allied surface ships and shore-based aircraft accounted for the great majority (246 and 245 respectively).

only a modest-sized German military force. After France's capitulation following the occupation of its capital, whole armies would move to the Eastern Front to drive the Russians out. Schlieffen died in 1913, and the plan was put in motion by General Helmuth von Moltke. As often happens in history, the plans of men may go awry in ironic ways. The western armies of Germany did, indeed, move through neutral Belgium but were stopped at the Battle of the Marne (September 1914) in northern France. Meanwhile, General Paul von Hindenburg was reactivated at age 67 and sent with Major General Erich Ludendorff to halt the Russian advance into East Prussia. There the Germans unexpectedly defeated two large Russian armies at the Battle of Tannenberg (August 1914).

The fighting on the Western Front turned into a war of attrition as the two sides built opposing trenches from the Swiss border to the English Channel. For three and a half years neither side moved more than 30 miles despite titanic battles at Verdun, the Somme, and Ypres. In the east the outmanned German forces, with the help of the Austrians, inflicted a series of costly military defeats on Russia, but, given the vastness of its territory and population, the Central Powers were unable to knock Russia out of the war until after the seizure of power by Vladimir Ilich Lenin in the October Revolution of 1917. In 1916 Ludendorff and Hindenburg became joint heads of all German land forces and recognized, as had their predecessor Erich von Falkenhayn, that the war would be won or lost on the Western Front. With Italy (1915) and Romania (1916) entering the war on the side of the Triple Entente, the Central Powers faced an almost impossible situation in a war of attrition. The two generals became de facto rulers of Germany and sought the mobilization of the whole society for total war. More than 11 million men, some 18 percent of the population, were in uniform, of whom almost two million were ultimately killed. Germany was unable to feed itself, and after the severe winter of 1916–17 malnutrition and even starvation were not uncommon.

On the diplomatic front the elites ruling Germany planned for vast annexations of Russian, Belgian, and French territory as well as for an African empire. The war costs were to be paid by the defeated powers of the Triple Entente. At no time during the war did the German government engage in serious negotiations to restore the sovereignty of Belgium or to return to the status quo before the start of the conflict. Nor were the Triple Entente and its allies very interested in a negotiated peace, but their situation was not as desperate as Germany's. In fact, every belligerent government found it safer to demand ever-greater efforts from its people than to admit that their earlier sacrifices had been in vain. As the stakes grew higher and the game more dangerous, no player felt able to leave the table.

Ludendorff and Hindenburg adopted an all-or-nothing policy in regard to victory. They created an independent state of Poland in 1916, which prevented serious negotiations with Russia for a separate peace. They adopted submarine warfare in 1917, despite the knowledge that it would bring the United States into the war because it offered a slim hope of quick victory if Triple Entente ships carrying men and supplies could be prevented from reaching France. Ludendorff also mounted a major offensive in April 1918, ignoring Woodrow Wilson's proposal of Fourteen Points for a future peace and failing to offer any peace terms of his own. When asked what would happen if the offensive failed, he replied, "Then, Germany will be destroyed."

In 1917 the Reichstag, following the lead of the Centre Party, passed a peace resolution that called for Germany to refrain from any annexations. Social Democrats and Progressives rallied to support the resolution. The military and civilian leadership ignored the resolution and enforced a draconian peace on Russia and Romania in 1917–18. When the major battle in the west was brewing in April 1918, there were more than a million soldiers in the east to enforce the Treaty of Brest-Litovsk with Russia.

Clearly, the military, agrarian, and industrial elites who ruled Germany considered themselves involved in two wars simultaneously, one against the Triple Entente and the other against the aspirations of the German people for full political emancipation. The latter conflict dictated victory at all costs on the military front. Defeat or a compromise peace on the battlefield would inevitably lead to democratization because it would lead to a loss of legitimacy for the elite that had demanded so many sacrifices from the many millions of workers, farmers, and artisans while denying them effective political power. In November 1914 Alfred Hugenberg, a major industrialist and subsequent ally of Adolf Hitler, told German entrepreneurs:

The consequences of the war will be unfavourable to employers and industry in many ways. One will probably have to count on a very increased sense of power on the part of the workers and labour unions, which will find expression in increased demands on the employer for legislation. It would, therefore, be well advised in order to avoid internal difficulties to distract the attention of the people and to give fantasies concerning the extension of German territory room to play.

William II felt compelled to promise an eventual end to the restrictive Prussian franchise in his Easter message of 1917. Shortly thereafter the Fatherland Party was established with enormous support from the elites. Its program included a commitment to fight for an unequivocal German victory, including annexations, and maintenance of the Prusso-German political system.

The Ludendorff offensive of April 1918 made great breakthroughs in the west. But the effects of four years of attrition were apparent. The military did not have the reserves to take advantage of the initial gains. With almost a million fresh American troops in France, the Allies launched a counterattack that quickly gave them the initiative. Slowly the German forces began retreating. On August 8 the German army suffered a severe defeat in northern France, and not long thereafter

William II installed a new, more liberal government in Berlin, headed by Maximilian, Prinz von Baden. The new ministers were informed that the war was virtually lost, and they were advised to seek an immediate armistice. Before the negotiations were successful, revolution broke out in the German navy on November 3, 1918, and spread to the military and urban workers. The government of Max von Baden resigned, and William II was forced to flee to the Netherlands on November 9, 1918. The Social Democrats declared a republic and took power at this appalling moment of defeat, while the former military and civilian leaders sought to escape responsibility for the calamity. A civilian, Matthias Erzberger of the Centre Party, signed the armistice, which took effect November 11, 1918.

THE WIEMAR REPUBLIC AND THE THIRD REICH

To say that German history was even more volatile in the next three decades would be a tremendous understatement. The postwar German government would weather a revolution from the left and putsches from the right, but, mired in economic depression in the 1930s, Germany ultimately lurched toward fascism. Led by Adolf Hitler and the Nazi Party, the country pursued bellicose territorial expansion that sparked another world war that would leave Germany vanquished, devastated, and burdened by the horrible legacy of the Holocaust.

THE RISE AND FALL OF THE WEIMAR REPUBLIC, 1918–33

The republic proclaimed early in the afternoon of Saturday, November 9, 1918, is often called the "accidental republic." When Friedrich Ebert, the leader of the so-called Majority Socialists, accepted the imperial chancellorship from Max von Baden, it was with the understanding that he would do his utmost to save the imperial system from revolution. Ebert believed that the only way to accomplish this would be by transforming Germany into a constitutional monarchy. Elections would have to be held for a constituent assembly, whose task it would be to draw up a new constitution.

DEFEAT OF REVOLUTIONARIES, 1918–19

Ebert, however, was faced with a precarious situation. The dangers confronting him were mounting all over the country. Four and a half years of seemingly futile combat and sacrifice had resulted in a disaffection with the war and discredited the imperial system, as well as its emperor. Shortages of food and fuel had rendered the population vulnerable to the influenza epidemic sweeping Europe. On October 18 alone Berlin authorities had reported 1,700 influenza deaths. Independent Socialists in Munich had forced the abdication on November 8 of Bavaria's King Louis III and proclaimed a Bavarian socialist republic. The port cities along the North Sea and the Baltic Sea were falling into the hands of sailors'

and workers' and soldiers' councils (Räte) in the wake of the naval mutiny at Kiel in early November. Karl Liebknecht and Rosa Luxemburg, leaders of the radical Spartacus League, were eager to transform Germany into a republic of workers' and soldiers' councils (a Räterepublik) in imitation of the soviet republic being established by the Bolshevik leaders in Russia. As Ebert was accepting the reins of government in the Reichstag building on November 9, Liebknecht was proclaiming a socialist republic at a rally of his own followers in front of the deserted Royal Palace about a mile away. Many Marxist revolutionaries believed that the Bolshevik Revolution was merely the spark that would set off the worldwide proletarian revolution that Karl Marx had predicted. Inevitably, that revolution would have to spread to Germany. Given this ideologically charged scenario, Liebknecht confidently anticipated his destiny to become the German Lenin.

While the Liebknecht rally was proceeding in front of the Royal Palace, an angry crowd was gathering before the Reichstag building, the seat of the government. Because Ebert had just left the building, his friend and fellow Majority Socialist Philipp Scheidemann felt called upon to address the crowd. To meet its inevitable demands for change and to forestall whatever Liebknecht might be telling his followers, Scheidemann in his speech used the phrase "Long live the German republic!" Once made, the proclamation of a republic could not be withdrawn. Ebert was furious when he learned of Scheidemann's "accidental" proclamation, but he realized that there was no turning back. He spent the afternoon seeking partners to form a provisional government to run the newly proclaimed republic. By nightfall he managed to persuade the Independent Socialists, a party that in 1917 had split from the Majority Socialists over the continuation of the war, to provide three members of a provisional government. To gain their cooperation, Ebert had to agree to name the provisional government the Council of Peoples' Commissars and to transform Germany into a vaguely defined social republic. Despite this promise, Ebert still hoped that elections to a constituent assembly would lead to the creation of a moderate democratic republic. The Independent Socialists, however, though not as radical as Liebknecht, held to their vision of a socialist Räterepublik. They hoped that workers and soldiers would elect a multitude of councils across the entire country during the following weeks, assuming these would establish the foundation for a genuinely socialist republic.

For the time being, however, Majority and Independent Socialists jointly formed a provisional government for the defeated German nation, which everywhere seemed on the verge of collapse. Although the armistice of November 11 ended the fighting, it did not end the Allied blockade. The winter of 1918–19 brought no relief in the shortages of food and fuel, and the flu epidemic showed no signs of abatement. Soldiers returning

from the military fronts by the hundreds of thousands were left stranded, jobless, hungry, and bitter—grist for the mill of revolution.

The push for revolution, led by an enthusiastic Liebknecht and a more reluctant Luxemburg, came on January 6, 1919, encouraged by Soviet Russia and further prompted by fear that Ebert's plans for the election of a constituent assembly, scheduled for January 19, might stabilize the German situation. The Spartacists, now officially the Communist Party of Germany, initiated massive demonstrations in Berlin and quickly seized key government and communications centres.

The events of "Spartacist Week," as the radical attempt at revolution came to be known, demonstrated that Germany was not nearly as ripe for revolution as leading radicals had believed. As Luxemburg had feared, mass support for communism did not exist among German workers; instead, most remained loyal to the Independent Socialists or to Ebert's more moderate and democratic vision of socialism. The German army, moreover, had recovered its nerve and was determined to prevent a further move to the left. In December the army had begun secretly to train volunteer units drawn from the sea of soldiers returning from the front. These so-called Freikorps ("Free Corps") units formed dozens of small right-wing armies that during the next years roamed the country, looking for revolutionary activity to suppress. The Spartacist revolt, which was confined largely to Berlin, was put down within a week by some 3,000 Freikorps members. When Liebknecht and Luxemburg were captured on January 15, they were both shot at the initiative of Freikorps officers. Although sporadic revolutionary activity continued elsewhere in Germany during the following months, its failure in Berlin clearly marked its doom. The proclamation on April 4, 1919, of a Räterepublik in Bavaria revived radical fortunes only briefly; Freikorps units put down the radical Bavarian republic by the end of the month.

The collapse of the Spartacist revolt greatly enhanced the chances for Ebert's vision of Germany's future to prevail. Moreover, the meeting of a national congress of workers' and soldiers' councils in mid-December 1918, upon which the Independent Socialists had pinned their own hopes for creating a socialist republic, proved to be far less radical than expected; it did nothing to interfere with Ebert's plans to elect an assembly to draw up a democratic constitution. The elections on January 19, 1919—the first German election in which women had voting rights—produced a resounding victory for Ebert's conception of democracy. Three of every four voters gave their support to political parties that favoured turning Germany into a democracy. After months of turmoil Germany was to become a democratic republic. The assembly began its deliberations on February 6, 1919, choosing to meet in Weimar, a small city that was considered less vulnerable to radical political interference than Berlin.

On January 18, 1919, representatives of the powers victorious over Germany began the deliberations in Paris that would establish a European peace settlement. Germany's new democratic leaders placed high hopes in the prospects for this settlement. U.S. President Woodrow Wilson's Fourteen Points seemed to promise Germans national self-determination as well as to encourage the efforts to transform Germany into a democracy. When the German constituent assembly met in Weimar for the first time, it immediately declared itself sovereign over all of Germany. It selected a provisional government—with Ebert as president and Scheidemann as chancellor—whose first major task was to prepare for the expected invitation to Paris to negotiate a peace treaty with the empire's former enemies.

But the invitation for a German delegation to come to Paris did not arrive until early April. Rather than being treated as a fellow—if fledgling—democracy, Germans soon learned that they were still viewed as the pariah of Europe. Wilson's idealism had been forced to yield to still-fresh wartime resentments being articulated by the leaders of the French, British, and Italian delegations. Instead of offering negotiations, the Allies forced Germany to sign the treaty with no alterations.

THE TREATY OF VERSAILLES

In its final form, the Treaty of Versailles contained many provisions that the

Germans had fully expected. That Alsace-Lorraine was to be handed back to France was no surprise; nor were the small territorial adjustments along the border with Belgium. The plebiscite allowing the Danish population of northern Schleswig to choose between joining Denmark or remaining with Germany was unarguably consistent with the principle of national self-determination. But this principle, the Germans expected, would also justify a union between Germany and the Germans of what now remained of Austria after the collapse of the previous November. More serious to Germany was the stipulation that its coal-rich Saar region was to be taken over by the League of Nations and the coal given to France to aid its postwar reconstruction. Eventually a plebiscite was to allow Saarlanders to choose whether or not they wished to rejoin Germany.

On its eastern frontier Germany was forced to cede to the newly independent Poland the province of West Prussia, thereby granting Poland access to the Baltic Sea, while Germany lost land access to the province of East Prussia. Danzig was declared a free city under the permanent governance of the League of Nations. Much of the province of Posen, which, like West Prussia, had been acquired by Prussia in the late 18th-century partitions of Poland, was likewise granted to the restored Polish state. Also transferred from Germany to Poland, as the result of a later plebiscite, was a significant portion of coal-rich and industrially developed Upper Silesia.

Overseas Germany was compelled to yield control of its colonies. Although these colonies had proven to be economic liabilities, they had also been symbols of the world-power status that Germany had gained in the 1880s and '90s. More damaging were the treaty's commercial clauses that took from Germany most of its foreign financial holdings and reduced its merchant carrier fleet to roughly one-tenth of its prewar size.

The treaty's provisions for disarming Germany were to be, the Allied leaders promised, merely the first step in a worldwide process of disarmament. To ensure that Germany would not revive as a military power, its army was to be reduced to 100,000 men and would not be allowed to produce tanks, poison gas, or military planes. Moreover, Germany's frontier with France was to be permanently demilitarized; German military forces were to remain behind a line 31 miles (50 km) east of the Rhine. The treaty also called for the dissolution of the German general staff, the German army's military command structure that the Allies believed to be the engine of German aggression. The navy, too, was to be dismantled and limited to 15,000 men, a half dozen battleships, and 30 smaller ships, with an absolute prohibition on the building of submarines. Germany's compliance with the treaty's terms was to be assured by an Allied occupation of the Rhineland and the presence of the Inter-Allied Commissions of Control.

The terms of the Treaty of Versailles that the Germans most resented, however, were the so-called honour clauses: Articles 227 through 230 gave the Allies the right to try individual Germans, including the former emperor, as war criminals; Article 231, often called the war guilt clause, provided the justification for Article 232, which established a commission to collect reparation payments, the total of which was eventually set at 132 billion gold marks. German bitterness over these honour clauses was nearly universal. Almost no German believed that Germany was responsible for the outbreak of war in 1914. Technically, Article 231 did not declare Germany alone as guilty for causing the war; rather, Germany was branded as responsible "for causing all the loss and damage" suffered by the Allies in the war "imposed upon them by the aggression of Germany and her allies." Germans read it as an accusation of guilt, however, and interpreted it as the cynical product of victors' justice.

Upon learning of the full terms of the treaty, the German provisional government in Weimar was thrown into upheaval. "What hand would not wither that binds itself and us in these fetters?" Scheidemann asked, and he resigned rather than accept the treaty. Army chief Paul von Hindenburg did the same, after declaring the army unable to resume the war under any circumstances. Only an ultimatum from the Allies finally brought a German delegation to Paris to sign the treaty on June 28, 1919, exactly five years after the assassination of Archduke Francis Ferdinand.

THE WEIMAR CONSTITUTION

In the month following the signing of the treaty, the Weimar constituent assembly completed a draft constitution for the new republic, resulting in what was hailed as the most modern democratic constitution of its day. The Weimar constitution provided for a popularly elected president who was given considerable power over foreign policy and the armed forces. Article 48 also gave the president emergency decree powers to protect the republic from crises initiated by its opponents on either the left or the right. The president was empowered to nominate the chancellor, whose government required the confidence of the lower house of the parliament, the Reichstag, which was elected by universal suffrage through a system of proportional representation. An upper house, the Reichsrat, comprised delegates appointed by the governments of the federal states, the Länder.

The Weimar constitution's most modern features, the provisions for popular referendum and initiative, were designed to enable the electorate, by way of petition, to introduce bills into the Reichstag and to force the body to vote on them. If the bill was voted down, the constitution prescribed a national referendum to allow the electorate to pass the bill into law against the wishes of the Reichstag. Through these provisions, it was thought, the government would never be allowed to ignore the wishes of the voters.

The Weimar constitution was promulgated formally on August 11, 1919, ending the provisional status of government in Germany that had begun with Scheidemann's proclamation of a republic the previous November. In September the government, judging the situation sufficiently safe in Berlin, returned to the capital. But it did not yet consider it sufficiently safe to risk nationwide elections for president or for a Reichstag to replace the constituent assembly. Instead the assembly prolonged Ebert's provisional term as president for three years; elections for the Reichstag were delayed until June 1920.

YEARS OF CRISIS, 1920–23

In its early years the new German democracy faced continuing turmoil. The Treaty of Versailles, quickly labeled "the Diktat" by the German public, galvanized the resentment that had accumulated during the war, much of which was turned back on the republic itself. Its enemies began to blame the hated treaty on the republic's socialist and democratic progenitors, whom they accused of having undermined Germany's efforts in the final stages of the war. A revived and radicalized right wing asked whether the German army might not have been stabbed in the back by traitors on the home front. Racist circles took seriously the notorious *Protocols of the Learned Elders of Zion,* a fraudulent document fabricated in Russia in 1895 and published in Germany in 1920, which suggested that all of recent history, including World War I, resulted from a conspiracy of Jews seeking to control the world. Roving Freikorps units contributed to the brutalization of German political life. In March 1920 one

of these units, under the command of the former naval captain Hermann Ehrhardt, succeeded in briefly seizing control of the government in Berlin. This so-called Kapp Putsch, named after the conservative politician Wolfgang Kapp, who had planned it, was thwarted not by the army but by a general strike of Berlin's socialist and communist workers. Threats by military figures succeeded in forcing the resignation of Bavaria's socialist government and its replacement by a conservative regime, however, and thereafter radical groups of the right found protection and a degree of nurture in this southern German state. By the end of 1922 there had been nearly 400 political assassinations, the vast majority of them traceable to rightists. The victims included prominent politicians such as Matthias Erzberger, who signed the armistice of 1918, and Walther Rathenau, the foreign minister.

The June 1920 elections to the first Reichstag reflected the difficulties in which the new democracy found itself. The Weimar coalition parties, the Social Democratic Party, the Centre Party, and the Democrats, which in January 1919 had together received more than 75 percent of the vote, this time managed to win only 43.5 percent. Contributing to the problems that the republic faced in the early 1920s was the escalating rate of inflation that was eventually to destroy the German mark. Although the inflation was rooted in the huge debt that Germany had amassed in financing its war effort, the hyperinflation of 1923 was triggered by the French-Belgian military occupation in January 1923 of the German industrial district in the Ruhr valley. The occupation occurred in retaliation for Germany's having fallen behind in its reparation payments and was intended to force German industry to provide compensation for the French and Belgian losses. Rather than accede quietly to the humiliation of occupation, the German government urged workers and employers to close down the factories. Idle workers were paid during the following months with a currency inflating so rapidly that printers gave up trying to print numbers on bills. By mid-1923 the German mark was losing value by the minute: a loaf of bread that cost 20,000 marks in the morning would cost 5,000,000 marks by nightfall; restaurant prices went up while customers were eating; and workers were paid twice a day. When economic collapse finally came on November 15, it took 4.2 trillion German marks to buy a single American dollar.

The social and political cost of the hyperinflation was high. Scholars note that the inflation did more to undermine the middle classes than the ostensibly socialist revolution of 1918. A lifetime of savings would no longer buy a subway ticket. Pensions planned for a lifetime were wiped out completely. Politically, the hyperinflation fueled radicalism on both the left and the right. The Communists, badly damaged by their failure in January 1919, saw greatly improved prospects for a successful revolution. In Munich the leader of the small National Socialist German Workers' (Nazi) Party, Adolf Hitler, used the turmoil to fashion an alliance with other right-wing groups and attempt a coup in November

Adolf Hitler at a Nazi party meeting in Munich, Germany, circa 1925. *Hulton Archive/Getty Images*

1923—the Beer Hall Putsch—that sought to use Bavaria as a base for a nationalist march on Berlin. He hoped to overthrow the democratic system of Weimar that he believed was responsible for Germany's political and economic humiliation. Neither the radicals of the right nor those of the left succeeded in imposing their will. In the short run they did not succeed because of ineptitude and miscalculation; in the long run they failed because the government sponsored a currency reform that restabilized the mark and also decided to end its policy of passive resistance in the Ruhr in exchange for an end to the occupation and a rescheduling of the reparation payments that it owed to the Allies.

THE WEIMAR RENAISSANCE

Amid the political and economic turmoil of the early 1920s, Germany's cultural and intellectual life was flowering. The so-called Weimar Renaissance brought the fulfillment of the Modernist revolution, which in the late 19th century had begun to transform the European aesthetic sensibility. The Modernist rejection of tradition perfectly suited the need of many Germans for new meanings and values to replace those destroyed by the war. "A world has been destroyed; we must seek a radical solution," said the young architect Walter Gropius upon his return from the front in late 1918. In 1919 Gropius became the founder and first director of the Bauhaus school of design in Weimar, the most important institution in Germany for the expression of Modernism's aesthetic and cultural vision. Bauhaus artists believed that they were creating a new world through their painting, poetry, music, theatre, and architecture. The legacy of German Modernism in general,

Still from Robert Wiene's classic Expressionist film The Cabinet of Dr. Caligari *(1919).* From a private collection

and of the Bauhaus in particular, is most immediately evident in the stark steel-and-glass high-rise buildings whose clear and clean lines have come to dominate the skylines of the world's cities. Moreover, the paintings and sculptures decorating them, as well as the designs of the furniture and the lighting fixtures, are heavily influenced by the aesthetic principles articulated in Weimar Germany during the 1920s.

Beyond the Bauhaus, painters such as George Grosz, Max Beckmann, and Otto Dix pursued an artistic approach known as Expressionism; they were interested in depicting their emotional responses to reality rather than reality itself. In music the rejection of tonality by composers such as Arnold Schoenberg, Anton von Webern, and Alban Berg broke a centuries-old tradition. At the juncture between popular and serious music, the composer Kurt Weill collaborated with the poet and dramatist Bertolt Brecht to create in 1928 *Die Dreigroschenoper* (*The Threepenny Opera*), a bitterly satiric musical play in which the world of modern capitalism was equated with that of underworld gangsterism. In films such as Robert Wiene's *Das Cabinet des Dr. Caligari* (1920; *The Cabinet of Dr. Caligari*) and Fritz Lang's *Metropolis* (1927), distorted sets and unusual camera angles probed for disturbing truths behind the surface appearances of reality.

Not everyone welcomed the Modernist attack on tradition. Angry audiences often interrupted opera performances and theatrical productions. Siegfried Wagner, the son of the composer Richard Wagner, deplored a Modernist version of his father's *Der fliegende Holländer* (1843; *The Flying Dutchman*), calling the production an example of "cultural bolshevism." Other artists—the novelist Thomas Mann, for example, winner of the 1929 Nobel Prize for Literature—chose to remain above the fray in the Olympian heights of German Kultur.

YEARS OF ECONOMIC AND POLITICAL STABILIZATION

The financial recovery that began with the restabilization of the German currency in late 1923 received a boost in 1924 when the Allies agreed to end their occupation of the Ruhr and to grant the German government a more realistic payment schedule on reparations. A committee of the Allied Reparations Commission headed by the American financier and soon-to-be vice president Charles Dawes had recommended these changes and urged the Allies to grant sizable loans to Germany to assist its economic recovery. The Dawes Plan marked a significant step in the upswing of the German economy that lasted until the onset of the Great Depression. The 800 million gold marks in foreign loans had by 1927 enabled German industrial production to regain its 1913 prewar high. That same year the Reichstag addressed the vital need for social and class reconciliation by voting for a compulsory unemployment insurance plan. Reconciliation on the political level seemed achieved in 1925 when the

77-year-old Hindenburg was elected to succeed the deceased Ebert as president. Although no democrat, the aged field marshal took seriously his duty to support the constitution and the republic.

The guiding spirit in German foreign policy from 1924 through 1929 was the foreign minister, Gustav Stresemann, who firmly believed that Germany was more likely to gain relief from the harshness of Versailles by trying to fulfill its terms than by stubbornly continuing to resist them. Stresemann's efforts ushered in what came to be known as "the era of fulfillment." It began in December 1925 when Germany signed the Pact of Locarno, in which it guaranteed to maintain the new postwar boundaries with France and Belgium and to submit to international arbitration any boundary disputes that might arise in the east with Poland or Czechoslovakia. Germany formally rejoined the family of nations by being granted membership in the League of Nations in September 1926. In 1928 Germany became party to the most dramatic symbolic gesture of postwar reconciliation, the Kellogg-Briand Pact, which promised to outlaw aggressive war; this agreement was signed by nearly all the world's major countries during the next year.

The May 1928 Reichstag elections seemed to reflect the economic and political stabilization of the Weimar Republic. The antirepublican parties of the left and right together received only 13 percent of the total vote, with the Communists receiving 10.6 percent and the Nazis taking only 2.6 percent. Germany's

reintegration into the international political structure advanced with the decision in early 1929 by the Allied Reparations Commission to settle the reparations question. Owen D. Young, an American business executive, headed the committee appointed to make recommendations in this matter. The Young Committee proposed that German reparations be reduced to about 37 billion gold marks, less than one-third of the 1921 total, and that payments be stretched until 1988. It also called for the dissolution of the Reparations Commission and for an immediate end to what remained of the Allied occupation of the Rhineland.

The German government, seeing the obvious advantages in the Young Plan, officially accepted its terms in August 1929. However, right-wing opposition parties saw the plan as nothing less than a renewal of Germany's humiliation. Led by the German National Peoples' Party (DNVP) and its leader Alfred Hugenberg, the press and movie-industry lord, the nationalist opposition seized upon the constitutional processes for popular initiative and referendum in order to force the government to reverse its acceptance of the plan. To run the opposition's anti-Young Plan campaign, Hugenberg engaged Hitler, the leader of the apparently moribund Nazi Party. The objective was to force the German government to repudiate the reparations debt as well as the war guilt clause of Versailles upon which the debt rested. German signatories to the Young Plan, moreover, were to become liable to the charge of treason.

The right wing's initiative did force the Reichstag into reconsidering its approval of the Young Plan but to no avail. The national plebiscite that necessarily followed found only 13.8 percent of the voters favouring the objectives of the right wing. The bitterness of the campaign, however, may have contributed to the illness and death of Stresemann during the campaign.

THE END OF THE REPUBLIC

An unintended effect of the anti-Young Plan campaign was to give widespread public exposure to Hitler, who used his access to the Hugenberg-owned press empire and to its weekly movie newsreels to give himself and his Nazi movement national publicity. An additional assist to Hitler's career came on October 29, 1929, with the stock market crash on Wall Street, an event that signaled the onset of what quickly became a worldwide depression. The crash had an immediate effect in Germany as American investors, anxious about their financial position, began withdrawing their loans to Germany. German indebtedness to these investors had by 1929 reached nearly 15 billion marks. Prices on the German stock exchanges fell drastically during the last month of the year. Business failures multiplied. Early in 1930 Germany's second largest insurance firm collapsed. Unemployment rose to three million during the course of the year. By the winter of 1932 it reached six million. Germany's industry was working at no more than 50 percent of its capacity, and the volume of German foreign trade fell by two-thirds between 1929 and 1932.

The first critically important political effect of the economic crisis came in March 1930 when the government coalition fell apart over the rising cost of maintaining the unemployment program adopted in 1927. The Social Democratic Party, representing labour, and the Peoples' Party, representing business, were unable to agree on the size of the government's contribution to the fund, and their coalition dissolved. When a new coalition could not be formed, parliamentary democracy in Germany came to an end.

Political instability forced President Hindenburg to invoke his emergency powers (Article 48), which he used to appoint Heinrich Brüning of the Catholic Centre Party as chancellor. For the next two years, until May 30, 1932, Brüning governed without a parliamentary majority, deriving his authority from the powers residing in the office of President Hindenburg. However well-intentioned, Brüning's deflationary economic policies were unable to stem the tide either of the depression or of its social and political ravages. His fateful decision to call for Reichstag elections in September 1930, moreover, inadvertently opened the door for the enemies of Weimar democracy. Together the Nazis and Communists gained nearly one of every three votes cast. In comparison to 1928, the Nazis increased their share of the vote sevenfold to 18 percent, while the Communists won 13 percent, a slight gain from their 10 percent share.

Although bitterly opposed to each other, during the next two years the Nazis and Communists succeeded in mobilizing the political and economic resentments generated by the depression. Hitler's charismatic appeal and the youthful energies of his movement were attractive to large segments of a populace fearful of being ruined by economic and social disaster. Hitler's record as a war veteran lent authority to the hypernationalism he expressed in racist terms. His identification of the Jew as the enemy responsible for all of Germany's ills, be it the defeat of 1918, the Treaty of Versailles, the reparations, the inflation, or now the depression, seemed plausible to many eager to find a scapegoat. The power of Hitler's appeal was reflected in the party's growing membership lists—from 170,000 members in 1929 to 1,378,000 in 1932—and in the swelling ranks of the Nazi Party's paramilitary SA (Sturmabteilung), the infamous storm troopers.

Unlike Hitler, the Communists found it difficult to extend their support beyond the German working classes. Moreover, Stalin's increasing control over the Communists limited their political flexibility. Nonetheless, their self-confidence rose substantially because the depression seemingly confirmed their prediction of the inevitable collapse of capitalism. To the Communists, Hitler and National Socialism were perceived merely as products of the last phase of capitalism.

The depression reached its depths in the winter of 1931–32. Unemployment was still rising; the succession of business failures resembled rows of falling dominoes. Brüning, helpless in the face of these problems, was dubbed "the hunger chancellor" by his critics. Some hope of breaking the

political impasse came with the series of critical state legislative elections scheduled for the spring of 1932 and with the presidential election required at the expiration of Hindenburg's first term. Hitler's opponents recognized that the 84-year-old Hindenburg, now fading into senility, was their only hope to prevent Hitler from winning the presidency, and, with great difficulty, they convinced Hindenburg, who wanted to retire, to seek a second term. The year 1932 was to be one of continuous election campaigning.

Although Hindenburg was eventually reelected, a runoff was necessary, and Hitler won 37 percent of the popular vote. His larger aim, however, had been to make himself the leading, or only, candidate for Brüning's position as chancellor. Hindenburg did choose to replace Brüning in May 1932 but named the political dilettante Franz von Papen rather than Hitler. Desperate to find a base in parliament, Papen called for Reichstag elections in July. The result was a disaster for Papen and another triumph for the Nazis, who took 37 percent of the vote, the largest total they were ever to acquire in a free election. The Communists won 15 percent of the vote. Thus the two parties dedicated to destroying German democracy held a majority in the Reichstag. Still, Hitler was not appointed chancellor. In November Papen called for another Reichstag election in the hope of gaining parliamentary backing. Again he failed, although the Nazi vote fell by 4 percent. By contrast, the Communist vote rose to nearly 17 percent. In early December, when Hindenburg decided to replace Papen, he again ignored Hitler, choosing instead a friend from the army, General Kurt von Schleicher.

In the Nazi camp there was bitter frustration at the end of 1932. The party was deeply in debt and demoralized by the year's endless campaigning. Putschist elements in the party, never persuaded that elections could bring the party to power, were growing increasingly restive. So deep was the frustration that on December 7 Gregor Strasser, second only to Hitler in the party, broke with the Nazis and retired from politics.

THE THIRD REICH, 1933–45

It was not long before the fortunes of the Nazis changed for the better. Within a year they not only took power but established the Third Reich, which Hitler predicted would last 1,000 years.

THE NAZI REVOLUTION

When Hitler finally became chancellor, on January 30, 1933, it was not on the crest of a wave of popular support but as the result of backroom political intrigue by Schleicher, Papen, and the president's son, Oskar von Hindenburg. Only Hitler, they believed, could bring together a coalition with Hugenberg's DNVP and possibly the Centre Party that could command a majority in the Reichstag. They assured the reluctant president that Hitler's radical tendencies would be checked by the fact that Papen would hold the vice-chancellorship and that other conservatives would control

Adolf Hitler, circa 1936. *Hulton Archive/Getty Images*

the crucial ministries, such as those of war, foreign affairs, and economics. The Nazis themselves were restricted to holding the chancellorship and the insignificant federal ministry of the interior. As a sop to the Nazis, Hermann Göring was granted ministerial status but given no portfolio; yet, significantly, he became interior minister in the state of Prussia, which gave him control over the largest police force in Germany.

The Nazis professed an ideology, national socialism, that purported to champion the common man, whom they portrayed as a victim in a world controlled by Jews. Anti-Semitism and notions of German racial superiority were at the core of this ideology, which, in its particulars, was also a catalog of resentments that had accumulated in German society since November 1918. Heading the list were the humiliations associated with Versailles, but not far behind were resentments of big business, big banks, big department stores, and big labour, as well as resentments of the divisiveness and inefficiencies that political parties seemed to foster.

Neither the 25-point party program of 1920 nor Hitler's autobiographical political manifesto, *Mein Kampf* ("My

Struggle," 1925), contained clear conceptions of the shape that German politics and society would take under the Nazis, but Hitler and his propagandists had communicated clearly that the changes would be fundamental and come at the expense of Germany's racial enemies. Racially superior Germans were to be gathered into a tightly knit Volksgemeinschaft, or racial community, in which divisions of party and class would be transcended in a spirit of racial harmony, a harmony that would necessarily exclude people of inferior blood. This goal logically required a solution to what the Nazis called "the Jewish problem." At the very least it called for a reversal of the trend, more than a century old, of Jewish assimilation into the allegedly superior German nation and into German cultural and economic life. As for Germany's position in international affairs, Hitler had long spoken of Germany's need for additional living space (Lebensraum) in the east. First, however, there was the continued need to break the chains of the hated Treaty of Versailles.

Whether the Nazis would ever get a chance to implement their ideological objectives depended, when Hitler became chancellor, upon whether they would be able to tighten their initially tenuous hold on the reins of power. Liberals, socialists, and communists remained bitterly opposed to Hitler; important segments of business, the army, and the churches were to varying degrees suspicious of the measures he might take. It was a combination, finally, of Hitler's

daring and brutality, of the weaknesses of his opponents, and of numerous instances of extraordinary good luck that allowed him to establish his totalitarian dictatorship. When the Centre Party refused to join the Nazi-DNVP coalition in January 1933, Hitler demanded elections for a new Reichstag. The elections of March 5, 1933, were preceded by a brutal and violent campaign in which Nazi storm troopers under the command of Ernst Röhm figured prominently. Hitler was also able to take advantage of the Reichstag fire (probably the work of a lone and deranged Dutch communist) of February 27 to suspend civil liberties and arrest communist as well as other opposition leaders. Despite this campaign of terror, the Nazis did not win a majority, gaining only 43.9 percent of the total. The 8 percent acquired by the DNVP, however, was sufficient for the two parties to wield a majority in the Reichstag. At its first meeting on March 23 the new Reichstag—under great pressure from the SA and the SS (Schutzstaffel; "Protective Echelon"), the elite corps of Nazis headed by Heinrich Himmler—voted in favour of the Enabling Act that allowed Hitler to ignore the constitution and to give his decrees the power of law. In this fashion, the Nazis established the regime they called the Third Reich, the presumed successor of the Holy Roman Empire (the First Reich) and of the German Empire ruled by the Hohenzollerns from 1871 to 1918 (the Second Reich).

The decree powers were the pseudolegal base from which Hitler carried

BERLIN 1936 OLYMPIC GAMES

The Berlin Games, held August 1–16, 1936, were the 10th occurrence of the modern summer Olympics. The Games were held in a tense, politically charged atmosphere. Two years after Berlin was awarded the Games, the Nazi Party had risen to power, and its racist policies led to international debate about a boycott of the Games. Fearing a mass boycott, the International Olympic Committee pressured the German government and received assurances that qualified Jewish athletes would be part of the German team and that the Games would not be used to promote Nazi ideology. Hitler's government, however, routinely failed to deliver on such promises. Only one athlete of Jewish descent was a member of the German team; pamphlets and speeches about the natural superiority of the Aryan race were commonplace; and the Reich Sports Field, a newly constructed sports complex that covered 325 acres (131.5 hectares) and included four stadiums, was draped in Nazi banners and symbols. Nonetheless, the attraction of a spirited sports competition was too great, and in the end 49 countries chose to attend the Olympic Games in Berlin.

The Berlin Olympics also featured advancements in media coverage. It was the first Olympic competition to use telex transmissions of results, and zeppelins were used to quickly transport newsreel footage to other European cities. The Games were televised for the first time, transmitted by closed circuit to specially equipped theatres in Berlin. The 1936 Games also introduced the torch relay by which the Olympic flame is transported from Greece.

Nearly 4,000 athletes competed in 129 events. The track-and-field competition starred American Jesse Owens, who won three gold medals individually and a fourth as a member of the triumphant U.S. 4 × 100-metre relay team. Altogether Owens and his teammates won 12 men's track-and-field gold medals; the success of Owens and the other African American athletes, referred to as "black auxiliaries" by the Nazi press, was considered a particular blow to Hitler's Aryan ideals.

However, the Germans did win the most medals overall, dominating the gymnastics, rowing, and equestrian events. Hendrika ("Rie") Mastenbroek of the Netherlands won three gold medals and a silver in the swimming competition. Basketball, an Olympic event for the first time in 1936, was won by the U.S. team. Canoeing also debuted as an Olympic sport.

The 1940 and 1944 Games, scheduled for Helsinki, Finland (originally slated for Tokyo), and London, respectively, were canceled because of World War II.

out the first steps of the Nazi revolution. Within two weeks of the passing of the Enabling Act, Nazi governors were sent out to bring the federal states into line, and a few months later the states themselves were abolished. On April 7, 1933, Nazis began to purge the civil service, along with the universities, of communists, socialists, democrats, and Jews. On May 2 the trade unions were disbanded and replaced by what the Nazis called a Labour Front. In the meantime Göring had begun refashioning the political arm of the Prussian police into a secret political police, the Gestapo (Geheime Staatspolizei), to serve the Nazi cause, a process that was being duplicated by Himmler with the Bavarian police.

The brutality with which Hitler met any presumed challenge to his authority became dramatically evident when on June 30, 1934, he ordered the murders of the SA leadership. Röhm's storm-trooper street thugs had provided useful muscle during the party's long years of struggle, but their continuing penchant for unruliness, Hitler feared, could invite the army's intervention and therewith his own overthrow. To head off this possibility, Hitler engaged the loyal Himmler, who used his SS during the so-called "Night of the Long Knives" to purge the SA of dozens of its top leaders, including Hitler's longtime friend Röhm. The penultimate step in Hitler's seizure of power came on August 2, 1934, when, upon the death of President Hindenburg, he appropriated the powers of the presidency and combined them with his own as chancellor. The final step came in February 1938 when Hitler took personal command of the three branches of the German armed forces.

THE TOTALITARIAN STATE

The main purpose and goal of the Nazi revolution was to establish a Volksgemeinschaft. Its creation required the purification and increase of the German "race" as well as its biological separation from the Jews, whose infusion of evil into the German bloodstream, the Nazis said, served to pollute and undermine Germany's well-being. Nazi efforts to purify the German race gained an air of scientific respectability from the pseudoscience of eugenics, the racial hygiene movement that flourished widely in the early decades of the 20th century. Nazi leaders spoke of their efforts to "reconstruct the German race." The Law for the Protection of Hereditary Health (July 14, 1933) allowed for the eventual sterilization of as many as two million people deemed unworthy of propagating. The Marriage Subsidy Law of July 1933 aimed to stimulate the birth rate by granting loans to newly married couples; these loans would be forgiven incrementally with the birth of each additional child. The Nazi idealization of mothers and the celebration of motherhood as a special service to the Reich had the same objective. Hitler spoke of an eventual doubling of the German population through these measures. The most notorious of the steps taken to purify the German race was also a milestone in the anti-Jewish legislation promulgated by the Nazis: the infamous Nürnberg Laws of September 1935, which forbade marriage or sexual relations between Jews and Germans and assigned to Jews a lower class of citizenship.

Nazi efforts to solve the "Jewish problem" were in fact products of a vicious anti-Semitism that propelled the Nazi regime toward increasingly extreme measures of persecution. SA terrorism,

NÜRNBERG LAWS

The Nürnberg Laws were two race-based measures depriving Jews of rights, designed by Hitler and approved by the Nazi Party at a convention in Nürnberg on September 15, 1935. One, the Reichsbürgergesetz ("Law of the Reich Citizen"), deprived Jews of German citizenship, designating them "subjects of the state." The other, the Gesetz zum Schutze des Deutschen Blutes und der Deutschen Ehre ("Law for the Protection of German Blood and German Honour"), usually called simply the Blutschutzgesetz ("Blood Protection Law"), forbade marriage or sexual relations between Jews and "citizens of German or kindred blood." These measures were among the first of the racist Nazi laws that culminated in the Holocaust.

Under these laws, Jews could not fly the German flag and were forbidden "to employ in domestic service female subjects of German or kindred blood who are under the age of 45 years." The first supplementary decree of November 14, 1935—one of 13 ordinances elaborating these laws—defined Jews as persons with at least one Jewish grandparent and declared explicitly that "a Jew cannot be a citizen of the Reich. He cannot exercise the right to vote; he cannot occupy public office." The other enactments completed the process of Jewish segregation. Before long Jewish passports were stamped with a red "J" (for Jude; "Jew"), and Jews were compelled to adopt "Jewish" names. Jewish communities were deprived of their legal status by the decree of March 28, 1938, and steps were taken to exclude Jews completely from the practice of medicine.

This racial definition meant that Jews were persecuted not for their religious beliefs and practices but for a so-called racial identity transmitted irrevocably through the blood of their ancestors. These laws resolved the question of definition and set a legal precedent. The Nazis later imposed the Nürnberg Laws on territories they occupied. The laws also provided a model for the treatment and eventual genocide of the Roma (Gypsies).

Although the Nürnberg Laws divided the German nation into Germans and Jews, neither the term *Jew* nor the phrase *German or kindred blood* was defined. Because the laws contained criminal provisions for noncompliance, the bureaucrats had the urgent task of spelling out what the words meant. Two basic Jewish categories were established. A full Jew was anyone with three Jewish grandparents. That definition was fairly simple. Defining part-Jews—Mischlinge ("mongrels")—was more difficult, but they were eventually divided into two classes. First-degree *Mischlinge* were people who had two Jewish grandparents but did not practice Judaism and did not have a Jewish spouse. Second-degree *Mischlinge* were those who had only one Jewish grandparent.

The efforts to prove one's non-Jewish ancestry generated a new cottage industry employing hordes of "licensed family researchers," offering their services to anxious Germans afraid of a skeleton in the family closet. These efforts also involved the Health Ministry and church offices, which had to provide birth and baptismal certificates.

legislation expelling Jews from the civil service and universities, boycotts of Jewish businesses and professionals, and the eventual expropriation of Jewish-owned properties had by 1938 led to the emigration of roughly half of the 1933 Jewish population of 500,000 people. Until the massive campaign of violence against Jews and Jewish property known as Kristallnacht ("Night of Broken Glass"), during the night of November 9–10, 1938, it still seemed possible for some Jews to remain in Germany, albeit in severely circumscribed circumstances. With Kristallnacht the Nazis ushered in a new level of persecution. In its aftermath Hitler put Göring in charge of Jewish policy. Göring coordinated the numerous party and governmental agencies competing for control of—and profit from—the persecutions of the Jews.

For the Nazis, to exclude Jews from the Volksgemeinschaft was as important as attracting the German working classes to it, in order to undo the long-standing alienation of the largely socialist-minded German worker from the nationalist consensus. Any success in this effort depended heavily upon the Nazis' ability to provide employment for the millions of jobless whom they inherited in 1933. Public spending on rearmament and on public works projects such as the super-highway, or autobahn, network helped create many of the jobs so desperately needed. By 1937 Germany was beginning to suffer from a labour shortage. It was equally important to inculcate workers with a sense of being an integral part of a racially based national community. For this the Nazis devised an elaborate program of subsidies for leisure-time activities for workers. Called "Strength through Joy," the program subsidized workers' vacations; it made possible excursions to mountain or seaside resorts and offered the possibility of cruises in the Mediterranean or the Baltic Sea. By providing leisure activities for workers until then reserved for their economic and social superiors, the government attempted to integrate them into the Volksgemeinschaft. A new, inexpensive automobile, the Volkswagen, was designed to give workers the opportunity to own a car, which had until then in Germany been a symbol of wealth and status largely reserved for the upper classes. Hitler once said that Henry Ford had done more than anyone else to obliterate class differences in America.

FOREIGN POLICY

Hitler kept tight control over foreign affairs, formulating himself both the strategy and the tactics calculated to achieve his goals. The immediate objective was to reestablish Germany's position in world affairs; by this Hitler meant ending the humiliations attending the Treaty of Versailles, such as the demilitarized Rhineland and the limitations on German armaments. The chains of that treaty needed to fall with a loud clang, he said. The larger objective, the one he had spoken about since his entry into politics in the early 1920s, was the conquest for

Germany of Lebensraum. Hitler believed that this space needed to be acquired in the east, at the expense of the Soviets, so as to secure for Germany the Ukrainian "breadbasket" and open up vast territories for German colonization. Hitler found justification for such conquests in his notions of German racial superiority over the Slavic peoples who inhabited the lands he coveted. Furthermore, he saw the Bolsheviks who now controlled the Soviet Union as the vanguard of the world Jewish conspiracy. Control of this territory was to become the foundation for Germany's economic and military domination of Europe and eventually, perhaps, of the world.

No such domination or expansion was possible without war, of course, and Hitler did not shrink from its implications. His rearming of Germany, begun in secret in 1933, was made public in March 1935 when he announced the creation of an air force and the reintroduction of general military conscription to provide the manpower for 36 new divisions in the army. In June of that same year he signed an agreement with the British that allowed a German naval buildup of up to 35 percent of Britain's surface naval strength and up to 45 percent of its tonnage in submarines. On March 7, 1936, he moved German forces into the demilitarized Rhineland. Versailles was dead. Neither the British nor the French had lifted a finger in its defense, choosing instead to sign agreements expressly negating the terms of Versailles. By 1936 Hitler was spending 10.2 billion marks

on rearmament, and Göring was placed in charge of a so-called Four-Year Plan to prepare the German economy for war. On November 5, 1937, Hitler gathered his general staff and admonished them to be prepared for war in the east no later than 1942 or 1943.

As a cover for his true intentions during the first years of power, Hitler spoke long and often of his desire for peace. All he wanted, he said, was a Germany allowed its rightful place in world affairs. As evidence of his pacific intentions, he signed in January 1934 a 10-year non-aggression pact with Poland. A truer picture of his intentions became evident in July 1934, however, when Hitler encouraged the Nazi Party in Austria to attempt an overthrow of the government of Chancellor Engelbert Dollfuss. A Nazi squad shot and killed Dollfuss, but the coup attempt was badly managed. Benito Mussolini's movement of Italian troops to the Austrian border forced Hitler to back away from supporting his Austrian partners.

Propaganda Minister Joseph Goebbels's anti-Bolshevik rhetoric helped Hitler to delude France and Britain, as well as the United States—which was leery of being drawn into another European quarrel—into accepting his claim to be the West's last bulwark against Bolshevik expansion. His agreement with the Japanese in 1936, the Anti-Comintern Pact, was directed against the Third Communist International. A year later Mussolini, after a year of German-Italian cooperation in aiding General Francisco

Franco's rebel forces in the Spanish Civil War, added his signature to the pact.

Hitler made two dramatic foreign policy moves in 1938 that helped clarify for the world the extent of his less-than-pacific intentions. In March he annexed Austria to the Reich, justifying the Anschluss ("Annexation") as a fulfillment of the principle of German national self-determination. Britain and France stood by quietly at this additional repudiation of the Versailles treaty. Next Hitler engineered a diplomatic crisis with Czechoslovakia, claiming Czech mistreatment of its German minority in the Sudetenland. Against considerable opposition from his own military, Hitler was determined to go to war with the Czechs. Only through the intervention of Britain's Prime Minister Neville Chamberlain, who offered to come to Germany to appease Hitler and who managed to persuade the Czechs to yield to all of Hitler's demands, was war avoided. Chamberlain's intervention resulted in the Munich agreement in late September 1938, in which the Italians, the French, and the British ceremoniously handed the Sudetenland over to Hitler. Since that time the very word Munich has come to symbolize caving in to the demands of a dictator.

Certain that Britain and France would do nothing to stop him, Hitler decided to move up his timetable for conquests in the east. On March 15, 1939, Hitler seized what remained of Czechoslovakia, reshaping its pieces into a Bohemian and Moravian protectorate and a nominally independent state of Slovakia. Within a week he annexed from Lithuania the city of Memel and the surrounding countryside, territory lost to Germany in the Memel dispute as a consequence of Versailles. When Britain and France countered these moves by guaranteeing armed assistance to Poland—clearly next on Hitler's agenda—in the event of German aggression, a furious Hitler ordered his military to prepare an invasion of that country. Poland was critical to Hitler's long-range strategy for the conquest of Lebensraum in the east; any invasion of the Soviet Union required that Polish territory be available as a staging area. Until the British-French guarantee, he had hoped to enlist Poland, mostly through bombast and threat, as an ally in an attack on the Soviet Union, and he believed Poland could be dealt with summarily after the defeat of the Soviet Union. When Poland refused to play the role he had assigned it, Hitler began looking for allies in his resolution of the Polish problem. In late May 1939 he signed his "Pact of Steel" with Mussolini. Then came the most sensational diplomatic rapprochement of the 20th century. Shortly after signing the pact with Italy, Hitler put out feelers to Soviet leader Joseph Stalin about the possibility of dividing eastern Europe, Poland included, into German and Soviet spheres of influence. These negotiations led to the notorious German-Soviet Nonaggression Pact of August 24, 1939, a pact that secretly sealed Poland's doom and delayed Hitler's unbending determination to conquer Lebensraum from the Soviets for almost two years. On

September 1, 1939, Hitler launched his invasion of Poland. Two days later Britain and France declared war on Germany.

WORLD WAR II

World War II is appropriately called "Hitler's war." Germany was so extraordinarily successful in the first two years that Hitler came close to realizing his aim of establishing hegemony in Europe. But his triumphs were not part of a strategic conception that secured victory in the long run. Nonetheless, the early successes were spectacular. After the defeat of Poland within a month, Hitler turned his attention westward. He believed that it was necessary to defeat Britain and France before he could again turn eastward to the territories that were to become the "living space" for his new empire. The attack on the Western Front began in the spring of 1940. Hitler took Denmark and Norway during the course of a few days in April, and on May 10 he attacked France, along with Luxembourg, Belgium, and the Netherlands. Once again his armies achieved lightning victories; Luxembourg, Belgium, and the Netherlands were overrun in a few days, and France capitulated on June 21. Only the British, now alone, obstructed Hitler's path to total victory in the west.

Hitler determined that he could take Britain out of the war with air power. German bombers began their attack in August 1940, but the British proved intractable. The vaunted German air force (Luftwaffe) failed to bring Britain to its knees partly because of the strength of the British air force, partly because the German air force was ill-equipped for the task, and partly because the British were able to read German code. Yet Hitler had been so confident of a quick victory that, even before the attack began, he had ordered his military planners to draw up plans for an invasion of the Soviet Union. The date he had set for that invasion was May 15, 1941.

Although the defeat of the Soviet Union was central to Hitler's strategic objective, during the early months of 1941 he allowed himself to be sidetracked twice into conflicts that delayed his invasion. In both instances he felt obliged to rescue his ally Mussolini from military difficulties. Mussolini had invaded Greece in October 1940, despite the fact that he was already in difficulty in North Africa, where he was unable to cut off Britain's Mediterranean lifeline in Egypt. In February 1941 Hitler decided to reinforce Mussolini in North Africa by sending an armoured division under the command of General Erwin Rommel. When Mussolini's invasion of Greece also bogged down, Hitler again decided to send reinforcements. To reach Greece, German troops had to be sent through the Balkan countries, all of them officially neutral. Hitler managed to bully these countries into accepting the passage of German troops, but on March 27 a coup in Yugoslavia overthrew the government, and the new rulers reneged on the agreement. In retaliation Hitler launched what he called Operation Punishment against

BLITZKRIEG

Tested by the Germans in 1938 during the Spanish Civil War and against Poland in 1939, the military tactic known as blitzkrieg ("lightning war") proved to be a formidable combination of land and air action. The essence of blitzkrieg is the use of mobility, shock, and locally concentrated firepower in a skillfully coordinated attack to paralyze an adversary's capacity to coordinate his own defenses, rather than attempting to physically overcome them, and then to exploit this paralysis by penetrating to his rear areas and disrupting his whole system of communications and administration. The tactics, as employed by the Germans, consisted of a splitting thrust on a narrow front by combat groups using tanks, dive-bombers, and motorized artillery to disrupt the main enemy battle position at the point of attack. Wide sweeps by armoured vehicles followed, creating large pockets of trapped and immobilized enemy forces. These tactics were remarkably economical of both lives and matériel, primarily for the attackers but also, because of the speed and short duration of the campaign, among the victims.

Blitzkrieg tactics were used in the successful German invasions of Belgium, the Netherlands, and France in 1940. They were used by the German commander Erwin Rommel during the desert campaigns in North Africa and by U.S. General George Patton in the European operations of 1944. More recent manifestations of blitzkrieg were the combined air and ground attacks by Israeli forces on Syria and Egypt in June 1967 and the Israeli counterattacks and final counteroffensive against the same adversaries in October 1973.

the Yugoslavs. Yugoslav resistance collapsed quickly, but the effect was to delay for another month the planned invasion of the Soviet Union.

When the invasion of the Soviet Union finally came, on June 22, 1941, it did so with both campaigns against the British, across the English Channel and in the Mediterranean, still incomplete. Hitler was prepared to take the risk that fighting on multiple fronts entailed because he was convinced that the war against the Soviet Union would be over by the onset of the Russian winter. The spectacular German advances during the first weeks of the invasion seemed proof of Hitler's calculation. On July 3 his army chief of staff wrote in his war diary that the war had been won. The German Army Group North was approaching Leningrad; Army Group Centre had broken through the Soviet defenses and was rushing toward Moscow; and Army Group South had already captured vast reaches of Ukraine. The prospect of capturing the summer harvest of Ukraine along with the oil fields of the Caucasus led Hitler to transfer troops driving toward Moscow to reinforce those operating in the south.

Hitler's generals later considered this decision a turning point in the war. The effect was to delay until October the drive toward Moscow. By then an early winter had set in, greatly impeding the German advance and finally bringing it to a halt at the outskirts of Moscow in early December. Then, on December 6, the Soviets, having had time to regroup, launched a massive counteroffensive to relieve their capital city. On the following day the Japanese, nominally Germany's ally, launched their attack on the U.S. naval base at Pearl Harbor in Hawaii. Although they had not bothered to inform Hitler of their intentions, he was jubilant when he heard the news. "Now it is impossible for us to lose the war," he told his aides. On December 11 he declared war on the United States.

Though his plans for a quick defeat of the Soviet Union had not been realized, Hitler's troops at the end of 1941 controlled much of the European territory of the Soviet Union. They stood at the outskirts of Leningrad and Moscow and were in control of all of Ukraine. To prepare for what would now have to be the campaign of 1942, Hitler dismissed a number of generals and assumed himself the strategic and operational command of the armies on the Eastern Front.

At the high point of Hitler's military successes in the Soviet Union, members of the Nazi leadership were, with Hitler's understanding, feverishly planning for the new order they intended to impose on the conquered territories. Its realization called both for the removal of obstacles to German settlements and for a solution to the "Jewish problem." Nazi planners were drafting an elaborate scheme, General Plan East, for the future reorganization of eastern Europe and the western Soviet Union, which called for the elimination of 30 million or more Slavs and the settlement of their territories by German overlords who would control and eventually repopulate the area with Germans. During the fall of 1941 Himmler's

Children in the Auschwitz concentration camp. *Keystone/Hulton Archive/Getty Images*

SS expanded and refurbished with gas chambers and crematoriums an old Austrian army barracks near the Polish rail junction at Auschwitz. Here was to continue, with greater efficiency, the Holocaust—the mass murder of Jews that had begun with the June invasion, when SS Einsatzgruppen ("deployment groups") began rounding up Jews and shooting them by the thousands. The assurance of victory in the east, the heartland of European Jewry, convinced the Nazis that they could implement a "final solution" to the "Jewish problem." Experts estimate that ultimately some six million Jews were murdered in the death factories of eastern Europe. At least an equal number of non-Jews died of murder and starvation in places like Auschwitz, including two and a half million Soviet prisoners of war and countless others from eastern European nationalities.

The success of Nazi armies until the end of 1941 had made it possible to spare German civilians on the home front from the misery and sacrifices demanded of them during World War I. Hitler's imagination, however, was haunted by the memory of the collapse of the home front in 1918, and, to avoid a repetition, the Nazis looted the occupied territories of food and raw materials as well as labour. Food shortages in Germany were not serious until late in the war. Women were allowed to stay at home, and the energies of the German workforce were not stretched to their limits because eventually some seven million foreign slave labourers were used to keep the war effort going.

Through much of 1942 an ultimate German victory still seemed possible. The renewed offensive in the Soviet Union in the spring at first continued the successes of the previous year. Once again Hitler chose to concentrate on the capture of the Caucasus and its oil at the expense of the Moscow front. The decision entailed a major battle over the industrial centre at Stalingrad (now Volgograd). Elsewhere, by midsummer of 1942, Rommel's Afrika Korps advanced to within 65 miles (105 km) of Alexandria in Egypt. In the naval battle for control of the Atlantic sea lanes, German submarines maintained their ability to intercept Allied shipping into mid-1943.

By early 1943, however, the tide had clearly begun to turn. The great winter battle at Stalingrad brought Hitler his first major defeat. His entire Sixth Army was killed or captured. In North Africa Rommel's long success ended in late 1942 when the British broke through at El Alamein. At the same time, a joint British-American force landed in northwestern Africa, on the coast of Morocco and Algeria. By May 1943 the German and Italian forces in North Africa were ready to surrender. That same summer the Allies broke the back of the German submarine campaign in the Atlantic. On July 10 the Allies landed in Sicily. Two weeks later Mussolini was overthrown, and in early September the Italians withdrew from the war.

The addition of an Italian front made the rollback of German forces on all fronts that much more likely. In the Soviet Union, German forces were stretched across 2,500 miles (4,000 km). They had lost their air superiority when Allied bombing raids on German cities forced the withdrawal of large numbers of fighter planes. British and American bombings reached a high point in midsummer when a raid on Hamburg killed 40,000 of its inhabitants. Similar air raids killed hundreds of thousands of German civilians and leveled large areas of most German cities. Shortages of food, clothing, and housing began to afflict German cities as inevitably as did the Allied bombers.

The rollback of German forces continued inexorably during 1944. On June 6 the Allies in the west launched their invasion of France across the English Channel. In the east the Soviet army was advancing along the entire 2,500-mile front. By the end of the year, it stood poised on the eastern frontiers of prewar Germany. In the west, British and American troops stood ready to attack across the western borders.

On the German home front, 1944 became a year of acute suffering. On July 20, officers carried out a plot, part of a long-simmering opposition to Hitler from within German military and civilian circles, but Hitler managed to escape the dramatic attempt on his life practically unharmed. He attributed his survival of the July Plot to his selection by fate to succeed in his mission of restoring Germany to greatness.

Fate did not again intervene on Hitler's behalf. In mid-January of 1945 he withdrew underground into his bunker in Berlin where he remained until his suicide on April 30. By that time Soviet soldiers were streaming into Berlin. All that remained of the Reich was a narrow wedge of territory running southward from Berlin into Austria.

With the Soviet army in control of Berlin and the Western Allies within striking distance to the west and the south, there was no prospect of dividing them. Nonetheless, when Hitler's successor, Grand Admiral Karl Dönitz, sought to open negotiations for a surrender a few days after Hitler's death, he still hoped that a separate surrender to the British and Americans in the west might allow the Reich to rescue something from the Soviets in the east. The Western Allies, fearful of any move that might feed the suspicions of Stalin, refused to consider the German proposal, insisting that a German surrender be signed with all the Allies at the same time. Early in the morning of May 7, 1945, a German delegation came to U.S. General Dwight D. Eisenhower's headquarters in Rheims, France, and at 2:41 AM signed the surrender documents. Despite the fact that a Soviet major general signed for the Soviet Union, Stalin insisted that a second surrender ceremony take place in Soviet-occupied Berlin. This second surrender was signed in a Berlin suburb the following afternoon.

PARTITION, REUNIFICATION, AND BEYOND

For purposes of occupation, the Americans, British, French, and Soviets divided Germany into four zones. The American, British, and French zones together made up the western two-thirds of Germany, while the Soviet zone comprised the eastern third. Berlin, the former capital, which was surrounded by the Soviet zone, was placed under joint four-power authority but was partitioned into four sectors for administrative purposes. An Allied Control Council was to exercise overall joint authority over the country.

ALLIED OCCUPATION AND THE FORMATION OF THE TWO GERMANYS, 1945–49

These arrangements did not incorporate all of prewar Germany. The Soviets unilaterally severed the German territories east of the Oder and Neisse rivers and placed these under the direct administrative authority of the Soviet Union and Poland, with the larger share going to the Poles as compensation for territory they lost to the Soviet Union. The former provinces of East Prussia, most of Pomerania, and Silesia were thus stripped from Germany. Since virtually the entire German population of some 9.5 million in these and adjacent regions was expelled westward, this amounted to a de facto annexation of one-fourth of Germany's territory as of 1937, the year before the beginning of German expansion under Hitler. The Western Allies acquiesced in these actions by the Soviets, taking consolation in the expectation that these annexations were merely temporary expedients that the final peace terms would soon supersede.

As a result of irreconcilable differences among the Allied powers, however, no peace conference was ever held. The issue of German reparations proved particularly divisive. The Soviet Union, whose population and territory had suffered terribly at the hands of the Germans, demanded large-scale material compensation. The Western Allies initially agreed to extract reparations but soon came to resent the Soviets' seizures of entire German factories as well as current production. Under the terms of inter-Allied agreements, the Soviet zone of occupation, which encompassed much of German agriculture and was less densely populated than those of the other Allies, was to supply foodstuffs to the rest of Germany in return for a share of reparations from the Western occupation zones. But when the Soviets failed to deliver the requisite food, the Western

Allies found themselves forced to feed the German population in their zones at the expense of their own taxpayers. The Americans and British therefore came to favour a revival of German industry so as to enable the Germans to feed themselves, a step the Soviets opposed. When the Western powers refused in 1946 to permit the Soviets to claim further reparations from their zones, cooperation among the wartime allies deteriorated sharply. As day-by-day cooperation became more difficult, the management of the occupation zones gradually moved in different directions. Even before a formal break between East and West, opposing social, political, and economic systems had begun to emerge.

Despite their differences, the Allies agreed that all traces of Nazism had to be removed from Germany. To this end, the Allies tried at Nürnberg 22 Nazi leaders; all but three were convicted, and 12 were sentenced to death. The Soviets summarily removed former Nazis from office in their zone of occupation; eventually, antifascism became a central element of East Germany's ideological arsenal. But, since the East German regime denied any connection to what happened in Germany during the Nazi era, there was little incentive to examine Nazism's role in German history. The relationship of Germans to the Nazi past was more complex in West Germany. On the one hand, many former Nazis survived and gradually returned to positions of influence in business, education, and the professions, but West German intellectuals were also critically engaged with the burdens of the past, which became a central theme in the novels of Heinrich Böll, Günter Grass, and many others.

On into the 21st century, the Holocaust casts a dark shadow across German politics and culture. Historians have debated the place of anti-Semitism in German history: How much did the German people know about the murder of the Jews? How many approved of the "final solution" carried out by the Nazi government? Was the Holocaust the result of a uniquely powerful and deeply rooted German hatred of Jews, as some historians have argued (e.g., Daniel Goldhagen in *Hitler's Willing Executioners: Ordinary Germans and the Holocaust* [1996])? Or, did the Holocaust arise within the violent context of war, leading ordinary men to commit crimes that would otherwise have been unthinkable?

Beginning in the summer of 1945, the occupation authorities permitted the formation of German political parties in preparation for elections for new local and regional representative assemblies. Two of the major leftist parties of the Weimar era quickly revived: the moderate Social Democratic Party (Sozialdemokratische Partei Deutschlands; SPD) and the German Communist Party (Kommunistiche Partei Deutschlands; KPD), which was loyal to the Soviet Union. These were soon joined by a new creation, the Christian Democratic Union (Christlich-Demokratische Union; CDU), with its Bavarian sister party, the Christian Social Union (Christlich-Soziale Union; CSU). The leaders of this Christian Democratic coalition had for the most part been active in the moderate parties of the Weimar Republic, especially the Catholic Centre Party. They sought to win popular support on the basis of a nondenominational commitment to Christian ethics and democratic institutions. Germans who favoured a secular state and laissez-faire economic policies formed a new Free Democratic Party (Freie Demokratische Partei; FDP) in the Western zones and a Liberal Democratic Party in the Soviet zone. Numerous smaller parties were also launched in the Western zones.

Under pressure from the occupation authorities, in April 1946 the Social Democratic Party leaders in the Soviet zone agreed to merge with the Communists, a step denounced by the Social Democrats in the Western zones. The resulting Socialist Unity Party (SED) swept to victory with the ill-concealed aid of the Soviets in the first elections for local and regional assemblies in the Soviet zone. However, when in October 1946 elections were held under fairer conditions in Berlin, which was under four-power occupation, the SED tallied fewer than half as many votes as the Social Democratic Party, which had managed to preserve its independence in the old capital. Thereafter the SED, which increasingly fell under communist domination as Social Democrats were systematically purged from its leadership ranks, avoided free, competitive elections by forcing all other parties to join a permanent coalition under its leadership.

The occupying powers soon approved the formation of regional governmental units called Länder (singular Land), or states. By 1947 the Länder in the Western zones had freely elected parliamentary assemblies. Institutional developments followed a superficially similar pattern in the Soviet zone, but there the political process remained less than free because of the dominance of the Soviet-backed SED.

When it had become apparent by 1947 that the Soviet Union would not permit free, multiparty elections throughout the whole of Germany, the Americans and British amalgamated the German administrative organs in their occupation zones in order to foster economic recovery. The resulting unit, called Bizonia, operated through a set of German institutions located in the city of Frankfurt am Main. Its federative structure would later serve as the model for the West German state.

In the politics of Bizonia, the Social Democrats and the Christian Democrats quickly established themselves as the major political parties. The Social Democrats held to their long-standing commitment to nationalization of basic industries and extensive government control over other aspects of the economy. The Christian Democrats, after initially inclining to a vaguely conceived "Christian socialism," swung to espousal of a basically free-enterprise orientation. In March 1948 they joined with the laissez-faire Free Democrats to install as architect of Bizonia's economy

Ludwig Erhard, a previously obscure economist who advocated a "social market economy," essentially a free-market economy with government regulation to prevent the formation of monopolies or cartels and a welfare state to safeguard social needs.

When repeated meetings with the Soviets failed to produce four-power cooperation, the Western occupying powers decided in the spring of 1948 to move on their own. They were particularly concerned about the deteriorating economic conditions throughout occupied Germany, which burdened their own countries and awakened fears of renewed political extremism among the Germans. The Western powers therefore decided to extend to their occupation zones American economic aid, which had been instituted elsewhere in western Europe a year earlier under the Marshall Plan. To enhance the effectiveness of that aid, the Americans, British, and French effected a currency reform in their zones that replaced Germany's badly inflated currency (the Reichsmark) with a new, hard deutsche mark, or DM. Western Germany's economy responded quickly, as goods previously unavailable for nearly worthless money came onto the market.

The Soviets responded angrily to the currency reform, which was undertaken without their approval. When the new deutsche mark was introduced into Berlin, the Soviets protested vigorously and boycotted the Allied Control Council. Then in June 1948 they blockaded land routes from the Western zones to the Western sectors of the old capital, which were surrounded by territory occupied by the Soviet Red Army and lay about 100 miles (160 km) from the nearest Western-occupied area. By sealing off the railways, highways, and canals used to deliver food and fuel, as well as the raw materials needed for the factories of Berlin's Western sectors, with a population of more than two million people, the Soviets sought to drive out their erstwhile allies and to force the Western sectors to merge economically and politically with the Soviet zone that surrounded them. They were thwarted, however, when the Western powers mounted an around-the-clock airlift that supplied the West Berliners with food and fuel throughout the winter of 1948–49. In May 1949 the Soviets relented and lifted the blockade.

FORMATION OF THE FEDERAL REPUBLIC OF GERMANY

Instead of halting progress toward the political integration of the Western zones, as the Soviets apparently intended, the Berlin blockade accelerated it. In April 1949 the French began to merge their zone into Bizonia, which became Trizonia. That September a Parliamentary Council of 65 members chosen by the parliaments of the Länder began drafting a constitution for a West German government. Twenty-seven seats each in this council were held by the Social Democrats and the Christian Democrats, five by the Free Democrats, and the rest by smaller parties, including two by the

Communists. The Council completed its work in the spring of 1949, and the Federal Republic of Germany (Bundesrepublik Deutschland), commonly known as West Germany, came into being in May 1949 after all the Länder except Bavaria had ratified the Grundgesetz (Basic Law), as the constitution was called to underline the provisional nature of the new state. Indeed, this document specified that it was designed only for temporary use until a constitution had been freely adopted by the German people as a whole.

The Basic Law was approved by the Western Allied military governors with certain reservations, notably the exclusion of West Berlin, which had been proposed as the federation's 12th Land. The 11 constituent Länder of West Germany, then, were Bavaria, Bremen, Hamburg, Hessen, Lower Saxony, North Rhine–Westphalia, Rhineland-Palatinate, Schleswig-Holstein, Baden, Württemberg-Baden, and Württemberg-Hohenzollern (the last three were merged in 1952 to form Baden-Württemberg, and in 1957 Saarland became the 10th Land).

By the terms of the Basic Law, the Federal Republic of Germany was established with its provisional capital in the small city of Bonn. The West German state took shape as a federal form of parliamentary democracy. An extensive bill of rights guaranteed the civil and political freedoms of the citizenry. In keeping with German traditions, many spheres of governmental authority were reserved for the individual Länder. The key locus of power at the federal level lay in the

Germany, 1952–90.

lower legislative chamber, the Bundestag, elections for which had to take place at least every four years. The deputies were chosen by a voting procedure known as "personalized proportionality," which combined proportional representation with single-seat constituencies. In order to minimize the proliferation of smaller political parties that had helped to discredit democracy in the Weimar Republic, a party had to win a minimum of 5 percent of the overall vote to gain representation in the Bundestag. The Länder were represented in the upper legislative chamber, the Bundesrat, whose members were designated by the governments of the Länder, their number varying according to the states' populations. The chancellor, elected by the Bundestag, headed the government; however, in response to the misuse of presidential power in the Weimar Republic, the constitution greatly reduced the powers of the president, who was chosen indirectly by a federal convention. The final key institution of the Federal Republic was the Federal Constitutional Court. Independent of both the legislative and executive branches, it successfully introduced into German practice for the first time the American principle of judicial review of legislation. Its seat was established in the city of Karlsruhe.

Initially, West Germany was not a sovereign state. Its powers were circumscribed by an Occupation Statute drawn up by the American, British, and French governments in 1949. That document reserved to those powers ultimate authority over such matters as foreign relations, foreign trade, the level of industrial production, and all questions relating to military security. Only with the permission of the Western occupation powers could the Federal Republic legislate or otherwise take action in those spheres. Alterations in the Basic Law required the unanimous consent of the three Western powers, and they reserved veto power over any legislation they deemed unconstitutional or at variance with occupation policies. In the event of an emergency that endangered the new West German government, the Western Allies retained the right to resume their full authority as occupying powers.

FORMATION OF THE GERMAN DEMOCRATIC REPUBLIC

When it became clear that a West German government would be established, a so-called election for a People's Congress was held in the Soviet occupation zone in May 1949. But instead of choosing among candidates, voters were allowed only the choice of approving or rejecting—usually in less-than-secret circumstances—"unity lists" of candidates drawn from all parties, as well as representatives of mass organizations controlled by the communist-dominated SED. Two additional parties, a Democratic Farmers' Party and a National Democratic Party, designed to attract support from farmers and from former Nazis, respectively, were added with the blessing of the SED. By ensuring that communists predominated in

STASI

The Stasi (official name Ministerium für Staatsicherheit; "Ministry for State Security"), or secret police, was one of the most hated and feared institutions of the East German communist government. It developed out of the internal security and police apparatus established in the Soviet zone of occupation in Germany after World War II. The law establishing the ministry, whose forerunner was the Kommissariat 5 (modeled along the lines of the Soviet KGB), was passed by the East German legislature on February 8, 1950, four months after the establishment of the German Democratic Republic. The Stasi, whose formal role was not defined in the legislation, was responsible for both domestic political surveillance and foreign espionage, and it was overseen by the ruling Socialist Unity Party. Its staff was at first quite small, and its chief responsibilities were counterintelligence against Western agents and the suppression of the last vestiges of Nazism. Soon, however, the Stasi became known for kidnapping former East German officials who had fled the country; many of those who were forcibly returned were executed.

Under Erich Mielke, its director from 1957 to 1989, the Stasi became a highly effective secret police organization. Within East Germany it sought to infiltrate every institution of society and every aspect of daily life, including even intimate personal and familial relationships. It accomplished this goal both through its official apparatus and through a vast network of informants and unofficial collaborators (inoffizielle Mitarbeiter), who spied on and denounced colleagues, friends, neighbours, and even family members. By 1989 the Stasi relied on 500,000 to 2,000,000 collaborators as well as 100,000 regular employees, and it maintained files on approximately 6,000,000 East German citizens—more than one-third of the population.

In addition to domestic surveillance, the Stasi was also responsible for foreign surveillance and intelligence gathering through its Main Administration for Foreign Intelligence (Hauptverwaltung Aufklärung). Its foreign espionage activities were largely directed against the West German government and the North Atlantic Treaty Organization. Under Markus Wolf, its chief of foreign operations from 1958 to 1987, the Stasi extensively penetrated West Germany's government and military and intelligence services, including the inner circle of West German Chancellor Willy Brandt (1969–74); indeed, the discovery in April 1974 that a top aid to Brandt, Günter Guillaume, was an East German spy led to Brandt's resignation two weeks later.

The Stasi also had links to various terrorist groups, most notably the Red Army Faction (RAF) in West Germany. During the 1970s and '80s, the Stasi worked closely with the RAF and cooperated with Abū Niḍāl, Ilich Ramírez Sánchez (commonly known as Carlos, or "the Jackal"), and the Palestine Liberation Organization. The Stasi also allowed Libyan agents to use East Berlin as a base of operations for carrying out terrorist attacks in West Berlin. Following the bombing of a discotheque in West Berlin (April 1986) that killed two U.S. servicemen, the Stasi continued to allow Libyan agents to use East Berlin as both a base of operations and a safe haven.

Soon after the opening of the Berlin Wall in 1989, the East German legislature passed a law to reconstitute the Ministry of State Security as the Office for National Security (Amt für Nationale Sicherheit); however, because of public outcry, the office was never established, and the Stasi was formally disbanded in February 1990. Concerned that Stasi officials were destroying the organization's files, East German citizens occupied its main headquarters in Berlin on January 15, 1990. In 1991, after considerable debate, the unified German parliament (Bundestag) passed the Stasi Records Law, which granted to Germans and foreigners the right to view their Stasi files. By the early 21st century, nearly two million people had done so.

these unity lists, the SED determined in advance the composition of the new People's Congress. According to the official results, about two-thirds of the voters approved the unity lists. In subsequent elections, favourable margins in excess of 99 percent were routinely announced.

In October 1949, following the formation of the Federal Republic, a constitution ratified by the People's Congress went into effect in the Soviet zone, which became the German Democratic Republic (Deutsche Demokratische Republik), commonly known as East Germany, with its capital in the Soviet sector of Berlin. The People's Congress was renamed the People's Chamber, and this body, together with a second chamber composed of officials of the five Länder of the Soviet zone (which were abolished in 1952 in favour of centralized authority), designated the communist Wilhelm Pieck of the SED as president of the German Democratic Republic on October 11, 1949. The next day, the People's Chamber installed the former Social Democrat Otto Grotewohl as premier at the head of a cabinet that was nominally responsible to the chamber. Although the German Democratic Republic was constitutionally a parliamentary democracy,

decisive power actually lay with the SED and its boss, the veteran communist functionary Walter Ulbricht, who held only the obscure position of deputy premier in the government. In East Germany, as in the Soviet Union, the government served merely as the agent of an all-powerful communist-controlled party, which was in turn ruled from above by a self-selecting Politburo.

POLITICAL CONSOLIDATION AND ECONOMIC GROWTH, 1949–69

The government that emerged from the Federal Republic's first general election in August 1949 represented a coalition of the Christian Democrats with the Free Democrats. Konrad Adenauer of the Christian Democratic Union, a veteran Roman Catholic politician from the Rhineland, was elected the country's first chancellor by a narrow margin in the Bundestag. Because of his advanced age of 73, Adenauer was expected by many to serve only as an interim officeholder, but in fact he retained the chancellorship for 14 years. Theodor Heuss of the Free Democratic Party was elected as West Germany's first president. As economics minister in the Adenauer cabinet, Ludwig Erhard launched the Federal Republic on a phenomenally successful course of revival as a social market economy. His policies left the means of production mainly in private hands and allowed market mechanisms to set price and wage levels. The government promoted social justice with measures designed to ensure an equitable distribution of the wealth generated by the pursuit of profit. Under these policies, industrial output rapidly recovered, living standards steadily rose, the government soon abolished all rationing, and West Germany became renowned for its Wirtschaftswunder, or "economic miracle."

One of the most urgent internal problems for Adenauer's first administration was the resettlement of refugees. By 1950 West Germany had become the new home of 4.5 million Germans from the territory east of the Oder-Neisse line; 3.4 million ethnic Germans from Czechoslovakia, prewar Poland, and other eastern European countries; and 1.5 million from East Germany. The presence of these refugees put a heavy social burden on West Germany, but their assimilation proved surprisingly easy. Many of the refugees were skilled, enterprising, and adaptable, and their labour proved an important contributor to West Germany's economic recovery.

In East Germany the SED regime concentrated on building a viable economy in a territory that lacked rich natural resources, was less than one-half the size of the Federal Republic, and had

a population (17 million) only one-third as large. The regime used its centralized control over a planned economy to invest heavily in the construction of basic industries at the expense of the production of consumer goods. Moreover, war reparations required that much productive capacity be diverted to Soviet needs. Despite an impressive rate of industrial growth, the standard of living remained low, lagging far behind that of West Germany. Even food was a problem, as thousands of farmers fled to West Germany each year rather than give in to mounting pressure to merge their land (which many had only recently obtained through the postwar agrarian reform) into the collective farms favoured by the communist regime. Food rationing had to be continued long after it had ended in West Germany. The resulting material hardships, along with relentless ideological indoctrination, repression of dissent, and harassment of churches by a militantly atheistic regime, prompted many thousands of East Germans to flee to West Germany every year. In 1952 East Germany sealed its borders with West Germany, but East Germans continued to leave through Berlin, where free movement still prevailed between the Soviet and Western sectors of the city.

In West Germany Adenauer followed a resolute policy of linking the new state closely with the Western democracies, even at the cost of perpetuating Germany's division for the time being. In 1951 the chancellor succeeded in gaining membership for West Germany in the

European Coal and Steel Community, which later served as the core of the European Economic Community, the precursor of the European Union. In that same year the Americans, British, and French agreed to a revision of the Occupation Statute that substantially increased the internal authority of the Federal Republic. Skillfully exploiting the Western fears of a communist assault on Europe, which had been awakened by the Korean War, Adenauer gained further concessions from the Western occupying powers in return for his agreement to rearm West Germany within the context of a western European defense system. In 1955 West Germany became a full member of the North Atlantic Treaty Organization (NATO) and gained sovereignty over its foreign relations as the Occupation Statute expired.

With West Germany's impressive economic recovery continuing, the voters confirmed the policies of the Adenauer government. In 1953 the coalition of the Christian and Free Democrats increased its previously thin majority. In 1957 the chancellor's party achieved the first and only absolute majority ever recorded by a German party in a free general election. The FDP, who had left the government in 1956 over policy disputes, remained in opposition, along with the SPD.

Mounting dissatisfaction with the SED regime in East Germany led to the first popular uprising in the postwar Soviet bloc when workers in East Berlin, the seat of government, went on strike on June 17, 1953, to protest against increased production quotas. When the regime failed to respond, the workers took to the streets and demanded a change in government. The rebellion quickly spread throughout East Germany and was quelled only when Soviet troops intervened, killing at least 21 people and wounding hundreds of others. In the wave of retribution that followed, some 1,300 were sentenced to prison for taking part in the uprising, which the East German government portrayed as a plot by West Germany and the United States.

In the wake of the uprising, Stalin's successors in the leadership of the Soviet Union upgraded the status of the German Democratic Republic. In 1954 Moscow ceased to demand reparations and proclaimed East Germany a sovereign state. In 1955 it became a charter member of the Warsaw Pact, the Soviet bloc's military alliance. The SED leadership loosened ideological controls on artistic and intellectual activities somewhat, increased the production of consumer goods, and relaxed pressure on farmers to enter collective farms. Agricultural yields improved, and the last food rationing ended in 1958. Within a few years, however, the government resumed its repressive measures and again shifted its economic priorities to favour the collectivization of agriculture and investment in heavy industry at the expense of consumer goods. The flight of refugees through Berlin continued, with a high proportion of technicians, managers, and professionals among them.

BERLIN WALL

The Berlin Wall surrounded West Berlin and prevented access to it from East Berlin and adjacent areas of East Germany during the period from 1961 to 1989. In the years between 1949 and 1961, about 2.5 million East Germans had fled from East to West Germany, including steadily rising numbers of skilled workers, professionals, and intellectuals. Their loss threatened to destroy the economic viability of the East German state. In response, East Germany built a barrier to close off East Germans' access to West Berlin (and hence West Germany). This barrier, the Berlin Wall, was first erected on the night of August 12–13, 1961, as the result of a decree passed on August 12 by the East German Volkskammer ("Peoples' Chamber"). The original wall, built of barbed wire and cinder blocks, was subsequently replaced by a series of concrete walls (up to 15 feet [5 metres] high) that were topped with barbed wire and guarded with watchtowers, gun emplacements, and mines. By the 1980s this system of walls, electrified fences, and fortifications extended 28 miles (45 km) through Berlin, dividing the two parts of the city, and extended a further 75 miles (120 km) around West Berlin, separating it from the rest of East Germany.

The Berlin Wall came to symbolize the Cold War's division of East from West Germany and of eastern from western Europe. About 5,000 East Germans managed to cross the Berlin Wall (by various means) and reach West Berlin safely, while another 5,000 were captured by East German authorities in the attempt and 191 more were killed during the actual crossing of the wall.

East Germany's hard-line communist leadership was forced from power in October 1989 during the wave of democratization that swept through eastern Europe. On November 9 the East German government opened the country's borders with West Germany (including West Berlin), and openings were made in the Berlin Wall through which East Germans could travel freely to the West. The wall henceforth ceased to function as a political barrier between East and West Germany.

In 1961 the flow of refugees to West Germany through Berlin increased dramatically, bringing the total number of East Germans who had fled since the war to some three million. On August 13, 1961, the East German government surprised the world by sealing off West Berlin from East Berlin and surrounding areas of East Germany, first with barbed wire and later by construction of a concrete wall through the middle of the city and around the periphery of West Berlin. East Germans could no longer go to the West through the tightly guarded crossing points without official permission, which was rarely granted. East Germans who sought to escape by climbing over the wall risked being shot by East German guards under orders to kill, if need be, to prevent the crime of "flight from the republic." By thus imprisoning the population, the SED regime stabilized the economy of East Germany, which eventually became the most prosperous of the Soviet bloc but which nevertheless continued to lag behind that of West Germany in both the quantity and quality of its consumer goods. Under party boss Ulbricht, the East German government also tightened the repressive policies of what had become a totalitarian communist dictatorship. Upon the death of President Pieck in 1960, Ulbricht had assumed the powers of the presidency as head of a newly created Council of State. In 1968 he imposed a new constitution on East Germany that sharply curtailed civil and political rights.

In West Germany's national election in 1961 the Christian Democrats suffered losses for the first time. The SPD, which had broadened its appeal by jettisoning the last remnants of its Marxist past and accepting the existing economic system in its Bad Godesberg program of 1959, scored impressive gains. Adenauer managed to retain the chancellorship by forming another coalition with the Free Democrats, but his position was weakened. He had tarnished his image in 1959 when he announced his candidacy for the presidency only to withdraw in favour of a lacklustre party colleague, Heinrich Lübke, when he realized that under the Basic Law the president had little power. The elderly chancellor was further weakened when in 1962 his defense minister, Franz Josef Strauss of the Bavarian Christian Social Union, adopted high-handed methods in bringing about the arrest of the editors

of the popular weekly news magazine *Der Spiegel*—which had been critical of Strauss—in connection with an alleged security leak. At the insistence of the Free Democrats, Adenauer relinquished the chancellorship in October 1963 to Erhard. Although the Erhard cabinet held its own in the election of 1965, the architect of the "economic miracle" himself fell from power in November 1966 when the Free Democrats withdrew their support because of disagreements over how to respond to a recession. For the next three years the Federal Republic was governed by a grand coalition of the two largest parties, the Christian Democrats and the Social Democrats, with Christian Democrat Kurt Georg Kiesinger as chancellor and Social Democrat Willy Brandt as foreign minister.

OSTPOLITIK AND RECONCILIATION, 1969–89

When the SPD scored impressive gains in the election of 1969 and its candidate, Gustav Heinemann, also captured the presidency, West Germany underwent its first full-scale change of government. After 20 years of CDU-CSU domination, the SPD captured the chancellorship for Brandt in coalition with the FDP, whose leader Walter Scheel became foreign minister. This so-called social-liberal coalition carried through a number of domestic reforms, but its principal impact was on the Federal Republic's relations with East Germany and the communist-ruled countries of eastern Europe. While confirming West Germany's commitment to the Western alliance, the new government embarked upon a bold new "eastern policy," or Ostpolitik.

Previously, West Germany had refused to recognize even the existence of the East German government. And by the terms of the Hallstein Doctrine (named for one of Adenauer's key foreign-policy aides, Walter Hallstein), the Bonn authorities had refused to maintain diplomatic relations with all those countries (other than the Soviet Union) that recognized the German Democratic Republic. Now the Brandt-Scheel cabinet reversed these policies by opening direct negotiations with East Germany in 1970 to normalize relations between the two German states. In 1970 the government entered into treaties with the Soviet Union and Poland that required Bonn to recognize the Oder-Neisse line as Germany's eastern boundary. After the Soviet Union joined in 1971 with the Americans, British, and French in a Four Power Agreement that regularized Berlin's status and opened the way for an easing of the West Berliners' lot, in 1972 the Brandt-Scheel cabinet and East Germany concluded the Basic Treaty, which regularized the relations of the two German states. By its terms each side recognized, and agreed to respect, the other's authority and independence. Each foreswore any title to represent the other internationally, which meant West Germany's abandonment of its long-standing claim to be the sole legitimate spokesman of the German people. The two agreed to exchange "permanent missions," which meant that their relations stopped short of full diplomatic recognition.

The new Ostpolitik met with bitter resistance within West Germany from the Christian Democrats, who denounced it as a surrender on many points that should await settlement by a peace treaty, including the status of the eastern territories that were severed from Germany in 1945. The Christian Democrats especially objected to the appearance that West Germany had given legitimacy to a dictatorial East Germany that refused to allow free elections, maintained the Berlin Wall, and ordered its border guards to shoot fleeing citizens. The Christian Democrats therefore pledged not to ratify the Basic Treaty if they regained power in the election of November 1972. The voters endorsed the Brandt government's Ostpolitik, however, by making the SPD the largest party in the Bundestag (for the first time) and by strengthening their coalition partner, the FDP. The Basic Treaty was signed at the end of 1972, and in the following year both German states gained admission to the United Nations.

West Germany's original overtures toward East Germany had met with resistance from Ulbricht, but the path for negotiations was cleared by a withdrawal of Soviet support that led to Ulbricht's replacement by another communist functionary, Erich Honecker, as East German leader in 1971. In his last years, Ulbricht had experimented with a decentralization of economic decision making, but under Honecker East Germany reverted to Soviet-style centralized planning.

East Germany benefited greatly from the Basic Treaty. Once Bonn had accorded East Germany recognition, the Western democracies followed suit, so that the East German state at last enjoyed the international acceptance that it had long sought. Economically, the Basic Treaty also proved a boon to East Germany. Spurred by West German credits, trade between the two German states increased, yielding valuable West German currency for East Germany. The latter derived further income from annual fees paid to it by West Germany for Western travelers' use of the highways through East Germany to Berlin and from ransoms paid by West Germany for the release of political prisoners held in East Germany. The larger number of West Germans allowed to visit East Germany also brought in hard currency. Each year the East German government reported impressive leaps in productivity, which, after the regime's collapse, proved to be largely fictional. In actuality, the material gap between the two parts of Germany widened. In order to concentrate its resources on industrial production for export purposes, the East German government neglected to maintain the country's infrastructure, which became increasingly apparent as East Germany's roads, railways, and buildings deteriorated. An acute housing shortage also persisted. Waiting periods of years were still required for the purchase of major consumer items such as automobiles, which continued to be crudely manufactured according to standards of the early postwar period, while those of West Germany ranked high in the world for quality and advanced design.

The benefits of international recognition were offset by the dangers posed to the dictatorial East German government by increased contact with democratic West Germany as a result of the Basic Treaty's easing of restrictions on visits by West Germans to East Germany. In an effort to deal with the subversive effects of such contacts, the East German government repeatedly sought to reduce the influx of West German visitors by raising the fees it charged for visas. It classified some two million of its citizens as "bearers of secrets" and forbade them personal contact with Westerners. To stifle dissent at home, the government tightened its already repressive ideological controls on artists and intellectuals, imprisoning some and stripping others of their citizenship and banishing them to West Germany. To emphasize the distinctness of the German Democratic Republic, an amended constitution was adopted in 1974 that minimized the use of the word "German" and stressed the socialist nature of the East German state and its irrevocable links with the Soviet Union.

In West Germany, Brandt resigned in May 1974 after one of his trusted aides was unmasked as a spy for East Germany. Brandt's successor as chancellor was fellow Social Democrat Helmut Schmidt, who continued the SPD-FDP coalition. When Walter Scheel of the FDP was elected federal president in 1974, his party colleague Hans-Dietrich Genscher succeeded him as foreign minister. Because the FDP's laissez-faire elements resisted increases in the government's role in the economy, the SPD was able to achieve little of its program for expanding the welfare state. In 1976 both the SPD and the FDP suffered electoral losses, but the coalition retained its majority; four years later, however, the coalition regained some ground.

The social-liberal coalition came to an end in October 1982 when the FDP, which had been suffering losses in local and regional elections, defected and formed a coalition with the Christian Democrats. The new chancellor was the veteran CDU politician Helmut Kohl, who had been the unsuccessful candidate of his party for that office in the 1976 election. To confirm the change of government, Kohl arranged for early elections in March 1983. The election yielded sizable gains for the Christian Democrats but heavy losses for the FDP, many of whose former supporters favoured collaboration with the SPD. The SPD also suffered heavy losses, most of which went to the new ecological party, the Greens, who gained entry to the Bundestag only a few years after their movement had formed in protest against the government's indifference to environmental degradation.

Faced with mounting dissent at home, Honecker's East German government sought to enhance its claims to legitimacy by seeking further recognition from West Germany. It was therefore buoyed when Chancellor Schmidt paid an often-postponed official visit to East Germany in December 1981. At that time Schmidt ignored Honecker's demand that Bonn treat East Germans as foreigners and cease to bestow West German citizenship automatically on those who fled to the West. Nevertheless, after Schmidt's visit East Germany began making it easier for its citizens to visit West Germany. By 1986 nearly 250,000 East Germans were visiting West Germany each year. As only one family member at a time was permitted to go, virtually all returned home. The East German government also began granting some of its dissatisfied citizens permission to emigrate to the West, an opportunity utilized each year in the 1980s by a few tens of thousands who managed to surmount formidable bureaucratic obstacles. These concessions were reciprocated by West Germany's guarantee of several large Western bank loans to East Germany. In 1987 the East German government realized a long-held ambition when, after many postponements, Honecker was at last received in Bonn by Chancellor Kohl with full state honours, seemingly confirming West Germany's acceptance of the permanence of the East German state.

But behind the Honecker government's facade of stability, East Germany was losing its legitimacy in the eyes of the overwhelming majority of its citizenry. Particularly among younger East

Germans, the new opportunities for travel to West Germany produced discontent rather than satisfaction. There they experienced a much more advanced, consumer-oriented society that provided its citizens with an abundance of far higher-quality goods than were available at home. While in West Germany, they chafed at having to depend materially on Western relatives because their own currency was virtually worthless outside East Germany. They also experienced full freedom of expression and an open marketplace of ideas and opinions that contrasted sharply with the rigid censorship and repression of deviant views at home. Once these East Germans had traveled or even heard of others' travel, the Berlin Wall and the other border fortifications designed to restrict their movements seemed more onerous than ever. In protest against the East German government's indifference to the damage its outdated industries were inflicting on the environment, a clandestine ecological movement came into being, and an underground independent peace movement took shape in protest against the regime's manipulation of the cause of peace for propaganda purposes. Both of these movements found sanctuary in the churches of predominantly Protestant East Germany.

THE REUNIFICATION OF GERMANY

The swift and unexpected downfall of the German Democratic Republic was triggered by the decay of the other communist regimes in eastern Europe and the Soviet Union. The liberalizing reforms of President Mikhail Gorbachev in the Soviet Union appalled the Honecker regime, which in desperation was by 1988 forbidding the circulation within East Germany of Soviet publications that it viewed as dangerously subversive. The Berlin Wall was in effect breached in the summer of 1989 when a reformist Hungarian government began allowing East Germans to escape to the West through Hungary's newly opened border with Austria. By the fall, thousands of East Germans had followed this route, while thousands of others sought asylum in the West German embassies in Prague and Warsaw, demanding that they be allowed to emigrate to West Germany. At the end of September, Genscher, still West Germany's foreign minister, arranged for their passage to West Germany, but another wave of refugees from East Germany soon took their place. Mass demonstrations in the streets of Leipzig and other East German cities defied the authorities and demanded reforms.

In an effort to halt the deterioration of its position, the SED Politburo deposed Honecker in mid-October and replaced him with another hard-line communist, Egon Krenz. Under Krenz the Politburo sought to eliminate the embarrassment occasioned by the flow of refugees to the West through Hungary, Czechoslovakia, and Poland. On the evening of November 9, Günter Schabowski, a communist functionary, mistakenly announced at a televised news conference that the government would allow East Germans unlimited passage to West Germany, effective "immediately." While the government had in fact meant to require East Germans to apply for exit visas during normal working hours, this was widely interpreted as a decision to open the Berlin Wall that evening, so crowds gathered and demanded to pass into West Berlin. Unprepared, the border guards let them go. In a night of revelry tens of thousands of East Germans poured through the crossing points in the wall and celebrated their new freedom with rejoicing West Berliners.

The opening of the Berlin Wall proved fatal for the German Democratic Republic. Ever-larger demonstrations demanded a voice in government for the people, and in mid-November Krenz was replaced by a reform-minded communist, Hans Modrow, who promised free, multiparty elections. When the balloting took place in March 1990 the SED, now renamed the Party of Democratic Socialism (PDS), suffered a crushing defeat. The eastern counterpart of Kohl's CDU, which had pledged a speedy reunification of Germany, emerged as the largest political party in East Germany's first democratically elected People's Chamber. A new East German government headed by Lothar de Maizière, a long-time member of the eastern Christian Democratic Union, and backed initially by a broad coalition, including the eastern counterparts of the Social Democrats and Free Democrats, began negotiations for a treaty of unification. A surging tide of refugees from East to West Germany that threatened to cripple East Germany added urgency to those negotiations. In July that tide was somewhat stemmed by a monetary union of the two Germanys that gave East Germans the hard currency of the Federal Republic.

The final barrier to reunification fell in July 1990 when Kohl prevailed upon Gorbachev to drop his objections to a unified Germany within the NATO alliance in return for sizable (West) German financial aid to the Soviet Union. A unification treaty was ratified by the Bundestag and the People's Chamber in September and went into effect on October 3, 1990. The German Democratic Republic joined the Federal Republic as five additional Länder, and the two parts of divided Berlin became one Land. (The five new Länder were Brandenburg, Mecklenburg–West Pomerania, Saxony, Saxony-Anhalt, and Thuringia.)

In December 1990 the first all-German free election since the Nazi period conferred an expanded majority on Kohl's coalition. After 45 years of division, Germany was once again united, and the following year Kohl helped negotiate the Treaty on European Union, which established the European Union (EU) and paved the way for the introduction of the euro, the EU's single currency, by the end of the decade.

The achievement of national unification was soon shadowed by a series of difficulties, some due to structural problems in the European economy, others to the costs and consequences of unification itself. Like most of the rest of Europe, Germany in the 1990s confronted increased global competition, the increasing costs of its elaborate social welfare system, and stubborn unemployment, especially in its traditional industrial sector. However, it also faced the staggering added expenses of unifying the east and west. These expenses were all the more unsettling because they were apparently unexpected. Kohl and his advisers had done little to prepare German taxpayers for the costs of unification, in part because they feared the potential political consequences but also because they were themselves surprised by the magnitude of the task. The core of the problem was the state of the eastern German economy, which was far worse than anyone had realized or admitted. Only a handful of eastern firms could compete on the world market; most were woefully inefficient and also environmentally destructive. As a consequence, the former East German economy collapsed, hundreds of thousands of easterners faced unemployment, and the east became heavily dependent on federal subsidies. At the same time, the infrastructure—roads, rail lines, telephones, and the like—required massive capital investment in order to provide the basis for future economic growth. In short, the promise of immediate prosperity and economic equality, on which the swift and relatively painless process of unification had rested, turned out to be impossible to fulfill. Unemployment, social dislocation, and disappointment continued to haunt the new Länder more than a decade after the fall of the Berlin Wall.

The lingering economic gap between the east and west was just one of several difficulties attending unification. Not surprisingly, many easterners resented what they took to be western arrogance and insensitivity. The terms Wessi ("westerner") and Ossi ("easterner") came to imply different approaches to the world: the former competitive and aggressive, the product of what Germans call the West's "elbow society"; the latter passive and indolent, the product of the stifling security of the communist regime. The PDS became the political voice of eastern discontents, with strong if localized support in some of the new Länder. Moreover, the neofascist German People's Union (Deutsche Volksunion), led by millionaire publisher Gerhard Frey, garnered significant support among eastern Germany's mass of unemployed workers. In addition to the resentment and disillusionment over unification that many easterners and some westerners felt, there was also the problem of coming to terms with the legacies left by 40 years of dictatorship. East Germany had developed a large and effective security apparatus (the Stasi), which employed a wide network of professional and amateur informants. As the files of this organization began to be made public, eastern Germans discovered that many of their most prominent citizens, as well as some of their friends, neighbours, and even family members, had been on the Stasi payroll. Coming

Gerhard Schröder, 1999. NATO photos

to terms with these revelations—legally, politically, and personally—added to the tension of the postunification decade.

Despite the problems attending unification, as well as a series of scandals in his own party, Kohl won a narrow victory in 1994. In 1996 he surpassed Adenauer's record as the longest-serving German chancellor since Bismarck. Nevertheless, his popularity was clearly ebbing. Increasingly intolerant of criticism within his own party, Kohl suffered a humiliating defeat when his first choice for the presidency was rejected. Instead, Roman Herzog, the president of the Federal Constitutional Court, was elected in May 1994 and fulfilled his duties effectively and gracefully. As Germany prepared for the 1998 elections, its economy was faltering—unemployment surpassed 10 percent and was double that in much of eastern Germany—and some members of Kohl's party openly hoped that he would step aside in favour of a new candidate; instead the chancellor ran again and his coalition was defeated, ending his 16-year chancellorship. Kohl was replaced as chancellor by Gerhard Schröder, the pragmatic and photogenic leader of the SPD, which formed a coalition with the Green Party.

Schröder's government got off to a rocky start, the victim of the chancellor's own indecisiveness and internal dissent from his party's left wing. The coalition also suffered from internal dissension within Foreign Minister Joschka Fischer's Green Party, which was divided between pragmatists such as Fischer and those who regarded any compromise as a betrayal of the party's principles. In 1999 the government's problems were swiftly overshadowed by a series of revelations about illegal campaign contributions to the CDU, which forced Kohl and his successor, Wolfgang Schäuble, to resign their leadership posts. In April 2000 the CDU selected as party leader Angela Merkel, who became the first former East German and first woman to lead a major political party in Germany.

Schröder's government focused much of its efforts on reforming the German social welfare system and economy. In particular, the government wanted to reduce the costs of the generous but bloated welfare system; as the population was aging, the number of beneficiaries was increasing at a rate exceeding the number of contributors, threatening the solvency of the system. Moreover, the government attempted to relieve the burden on businesses of the country's high taxes and labour costs, which had driven away foreign investment and encouraged German firms to close German plants and move them overseas. The government also aimed to eliminate the country's reliance on nuclear power, agreeing to phase out its use by about 2022. In 2010 the government extended that deadline into the 2030s.

When the 2002 election campaign began, the government's efforts to improve the economy had not succeeded. Economic growth remained sluggish, and

ANGELA MERKEL

As a young child, Angela Merkel (born July 17, 1954, Hamburg, West Germany) moved with her family to East Germany so that her father, a Protestant pastor, could work in his native Brandenburg. After earning a doctorate in physics at the University of Leipzig in 1978, she settled in East Berlin, where she worked at the Academy of Sciences as a quantum chemist. In 1989 she became involved in the democracy movement, and in 1990, shortly before Germany's reunification, she became a member of the conservative Christian Democratic Union (CDU). Elected as a Bundestag (lower house of parliament) deputy later that year, she became noted for her political skill. Chancellor Helmut Kohl made her minister of family affairs, senior citizens, women, and youth (1991–94) and minister of environment, conservation, and reactor safety (1994–98).

In 1998 Kohl and the CDU lost the elections to Gerhard Schröder and the Social Democratic Party of Germany (SPD). The following year a finance scandal hit the CDU, and Merkel became a vocal detractor of Kohl, her onetime mentor. Merkel's stance greatly increased her visibility and popularity with the German public, although it upset Kohl loyalists.

In 2000 Merkel was elected head of the CDU, becoming the first woman and the first non-Catholic to lead the party. She was also the first CDU leader to come from the party's liberal wing, which was particularly problematic for the CDU's sister party in Bavaria, the ultraconservative Christian Social Union (CSU). As CDU leader, Merkel faced the lingering effects of the finance scandal and a divided party. In 2002 she ceded the nomination for the general election to Edmund Stoiber of the CSU, who later lost to Schröder.

Merkel received the party's nomination for the 2005 election, and among her campaign promises were reforms to the country's ailing economy and improved relations with the United States, which had become strained by Schröder's opposition to the Iraq War. The CDU-CSU alliance won the general election, but it was unable to form a majority government with its preferred coalition partner, the centrist Free Democratic Party (FDP). After several weeks of talks, a deal was reached with the SPD that gave Merkel the chancellorship, at the head of a grand coalition. She took office on November 22, 2005, becoming not only the first woman to hold the office but also the first East German. In Germany's parliamentary elections on September 27, 2009, Merkel's mandate as chancellor was renewed, this time with the CDU-CSU and the FDP winning enough seats to form a coalition without the SPD. In 2011 she was awarded the U.S. Presidential Medal of Freedom.

unemployment (particularly in eastern Germany) remained high. Faced with a vigorous challenge from Edmund Stoiber, the head of Bavaria's government, Schröder based much of his campaign on opposition to U.S. policy regarding the Iraqi regime of Ṣaddām Ḥussein—a view that was widely shared throughout Germany. As a result, Schröder and the Greens were able to win a narrow victory in September 2002. The new government attempted to build a consensus for economic reforms, which would require sacrifices from trade unions and other important parts of the Social Democrats' constituency. At the same time, Schröder sought to repair the damaged relationship with the United States, though he opposed U.S.-led military action against

Iraq in 2003. As the country's economy continued to worsen, early elections were held in 2005. The CDU and CSU won a narrow victory, and a coalition government was formed with Merkel as chancellor; she became the first woman to hold that office.

At the start of the new millennium, Germany remained a leader in Europe and was the key to the continent's security, stability, and prosperity. For more than 50 years, from Adenauer to Kohl, Schröder, and Merkel, Germans had played an important role in the creation of European institutions. Germany remains essential to the success of both the EU's ambitious program of economic and political integration and its efforts to expand to include members from the former Soviet bloc. Germany will also be an important part of European efforts to craft a new security strategy, based on an enlarged NATO and a revised relationship with the United States.

In Germany's parliamentary elections on September 27, 2009, Merkel's mandate as chancellor was renewed, this time with the CDU-CSU and the FDP winning enough seats to form a coalition. The SPD, which since 2005 had served as the junior partner in a grand coalition with the CDU-CSU, thus was forced into opposition. Germany comfortably weathered the debt crisis that shook the rest of the euro zone, and Merkel and French Pres. Nicolas Sarkozy brokered a series of deals that were intended to contain the damage to the single currency.

While Merkel's international presence was on the rise, she suffered domestically. The resignations of Pres. Horst Köhler in 2010, Defense Minister Karl-Theodor zu Guttenberg in 2011, and Pres. Christian

East German border guards demolish a section of the Berlin Wall on November 11, 1989. *AFP/Getty Images*

Wulff in 2012 were all blows to Merkel's prestige. After Japan's Fukushima nuclear accident in March 2011, Merkel pledged to phase out nuclear power in Germany by 2022, but this move came too late to boost the CDU's performance in state elections later that month. In contrast, the Green Party, which had long opposed nuclear power, captured enough support to form a government in Baden-Württemberg, a CDU stronghold since 1953. Joachim Gauck was elected president of Germany in March 2012, becoming the third person to hold that office in as many years. Unaffiliated with any political party, Gauck was a popular choice for the largely ceremonial role because of his history as a pro-democracy dissident in East Germany and his supervision of the Stasi archives after the fall of the Berlin Wall. For the first time since Germany's reunification, the posts of both chancellor and president were held by individuals from the former East Germany.

CONCLUSION

Much of Germany's post-World War II success has been the result of the renowned industriousness and self-sacrifice of its people, about which novelist Günter Grass, winner of the Nobel Prize for Literature in 1999, remarked, "To be a German is to make the impossible possible." He added, more critically,

> For in our country everything is geared to growth. We're never satisfied. For us enough is never enough. We always want more. If it's on paper, we convert it into reality. Even in our dreams we're productive.

This devotion to hard work has combined with a public demeanour—which is at once reserved and assertive—to produce a stereotype of the German people as aloof and distant. Yet Germans prize both their private friendships and their friendly relations with neighbours and visitors, place a high value on leisure and culture, and enjoy the benefits of life in a liberal democracy that has become ever more integrated with and central to a united Europe.

GLOSSARY

BASIN A large or small depression in the surface of the land.

CABINET A body of advisers of a head of state.

CALVINISM The theological system of Calvin and his followers marked by strong emphasis on the sovereignty of God, the depravity of humankind, and the doctrine of predestination.

CAPITAL Relating to or being assets that add to the long-term net worth of a corporation.

CHAMBER A hall for the meetings of a deliberative, legislative, or judicial body.

COMMUNISM A political system in which goods are owned in common and are available to all as needed.

COOPERATIVE An enterprise or organization owned by and operated for the benefit of those using its services.

CURRENCY Something (as coins, treasury notes, and banknotes) that is in circulation as a medium of exchange.

DEMOCRACY A government in which the supreme power is vested in the people and exercised by them directly or indirectly through a system of representation usually involving periodically held free elections.

DEMOGRAPHIC The statistical characteristics of human populations.

DIALECT A regional variety of language distinguished by features of vocabulary, grammar, and pronunciation from other regional varieties and constituting together with them a single language.

DUKE A sovereign male ruler of a continental European duchy.

INFLATION A continuing rise in the general price level usually attributed to an increase in the volume of money and credit relative to available goods and services.

INTEREST The profit in goods or money that is made on invested capital.

JURISDICTION The power, right, or authority to interpret and apply the law.

LEGISLATION The exercise of the power and function of making laws.

MARKET The area of economic activity in which buyers and sellers come together and the forces of supply and demand affect prices.

MIGRATION The act of moving from one country, place, or locality to another.

OCCUPATION The act or process of taking possession of a place or area.

PARLIAMENT The supreme legislative body of a usually major political unit that is a continuing institution comprising a series of individual assemblages.

PEASANT A usually uneducated person of low social status.

PENINSULA A portion of land nearly surrounded by water and connected with a larger body by an isthmus.

PLATEAU A usually extensive land area having a relatively level surface raised sharply above adjacent land on at least one side.

PROTESTANT A member of any of several church denominations denying the universal authority of the Pope and affirming the Reformation principles of justification by faith alone, the priesthood of all believers, and the primacy of the Bible as the only source of revealed truth.

ROMAN CATHOLICISM The largest denomination of Christianity, with more than one billion members.

SOCIALISM Any of various economic and political theories advocating collective or governmental ownership and administration of the means of production and distribution of goods.

TRIBUTARY A stream feeding a larger stream or a lake.

BIBLIOGRAPHY

GENERAL WORKS

Akademie der Wissenschaften der DDR, *Information GDR: The Comprehensive and Authoritative Reference Source of the German Democratic Republic*, 2 vol. (1989), is a comprehensive work on former East Germany. Eric Solsten (ed.), *Germany: A Country Study*, 3rd ed. (1996), provides an excellent overview of all aspects of life in Germany.

LAND

A simple but useful portrayal of Germany in maps is Bernhard Schäfers et al., *The State of Germany Atlas* (1998; originally published in German, 1997).

PEOPLE

Publications that provide an overview of population issues in Germany and Europe include Rainer Münz and Myron Weiner (eds.), *Migrants, Refugees, and Foreign Policy: U.S. and German Policies Toward Countries of Origin* (1997); and Heinz Fassmann and Rainer Münz (eds.), *European Migration in the Late Twentieth Century: Historical Patterns, Actual Trends, and Social Implications* (1994).

ECONOMY

Sources of recent information on Germany include the German government's Federal Ministry of Economics and Technology and *OECD Economic Surveys: Germany* (annual).

GOVERNMENT AND SOCIETY

German politics in the post-World War II period is the subject of David P. Conradt, *The German Polity*, 7th ed. (2001); and Manfred G. Schmidt, *Political Institutions in the Federal Republic of Germany* (2003). Mike Dennis, *The Rise and Fall of the German Democratic Republic 1945–1990* (2000), provides a political history of the former East Germany.

CULTURAL LIFE

Intellectual life, arts, and culture in former West Germany are treated in Gordon A. Craig, *The Germans* (1982, reprinted 1991). Postwar literature is the subject of Lowell A. Bangerter, *German Writing Since 1945: A Critical Survey* (1988). A historical overview of film is provided in Sabine Hake, *German National Cinema* (2002).

HISTORY

ANCIENT GERMANY

Herbert Schutz, *The Prehistory of Germanic Europe* (1983), offers a good, well-illustrated general account of the early period. Tim Cornell and John Matthews, *Atlas of the Roman World* (1982, reissued 1987), clarifies with maps and illustrations the social and economic background of Roman-German interaction.

MEROVINGIANS AND CAROLINGIANS

Patrick J. Geary, *Before France and Germany: The Creation and Transformation of the Merovingian World* (1988), examines the period from the perspective of the unity of late antiquity. Rosamond McKitterick, *The Frankish Kingdoms Under the Carolingians, 751–987* (1983), presents a general survey of Carolingian Europe, with an emphasis on cultural history.

MEDIEVAL GERMANY TO 1250

G. Barraclough, *The Origins of Modern Germany*, 3rd ed. (1988), is a good analysis of medieval German history. General surveys include Alfred Haverkamp, *Medieval Germany, 1056–1273*, 2nd ed. (1992; originally published in German, 1984); and Timothy Reuter, *Germany in the Early Middle Ages, c. 800–1056* (1991).

FROM 1250 TO 1493

Joachim Leuschner, *Germany in the Late Middle Ages* (1980; originally published in German, 1975), provides a basic introduction to political history. A valuable supplement is the more complex F.R.H. Du Boulay, *Germany in the Later Middle Ages* (1983). Gerhart Hoffmeister (ed.), *The Renaissance and Reformation in Germany: An Introduction* (1977), offers a fine overview of intellectual life.

FROM 1493 TO *C.* 1760

An excellent guide to this period is Thomas A. Brady, Jr., Heiko A. Oberman, and James D. Tracy (eds.), *Handbook of European History, 1400–1600: Late Middle Ages, Renaissance, and Reformation*, 2 vol. (1994–95). Bob Scribner and Sheilagh Ogilvie (eds.), *Germany: A New Social and Economic History*, 2 vol. (1996), is a good collection on the society and economy of the Renaissance and Reformation.

FROM *C.* 1760 TO 187

A good survey of the period is James J. Sheehan, *German History, 1770–1866* (1989, reissued 1993). David Blackbourn, *The Long Nineteenth Century: A History of Germany, 1780–1918* (also published as *Fontana History of Germany, 1780–1918: The Long Nineteenth Century*, 1997), covers Germany's emergence as a nation-state. The best account of Germany's place in the international system is Paul W. Schroeder, *The Transformation of European Politics, 1763–1848* (1994, reissued 1996).

A balanced and up-to-date overview of the German Confederation is Thomas Nipperdey, *Germany from Napoleon to Bismarck, 1800–1866* (1996; originally published in German, 1983).

Otto Pflanze, *Bismarck and the Development of Germany*, 2nd ed., 3 vol. (1990), portrays the architect of the new Germany and his impact on the European balance of power. An excellent work on the Franco-Prussian war is Michael Howard, *The Franco-Prussian War: The German Invasion of France, 1870–71*, 2nd ed. (2001).

FROM 1871 TO 1918

A general historical survey of the period is Hans-Ulrich Wehler, *The German Empire, 1871–1918* (1985, reissued 1997; originally published in German, 1973), which stresses the continuity between the empire and the Nazi era. James J. Sheehan, *German Liberalism in the Nineteenth Century* (1978, reissued 1995), analyzes the activities of the two liberal parties on the local and national levels and describes their growing acceptance of the empire. Margaret Lavinia Anderson, *Practicing Democracy: Elections and Political Culture in Imperial Germany* (2000), examines the relationship between political participation and authority from 1867 to 1914. Roger Chickering (ed.), *Imperial Germany: A Historiographical Companion* (1996), is a useful guide to further reading.

Economic developments of the period are surveyed in Fritz Stern, *Gold and Iron: Bismarck, Bleichröder, and the Building of the German Empire* (1977, reissued 1987). Cultural and social issues are addressed in Fritz Stern, *The Politics of Cultural Despair: A Study in the Rise of the Germanic Ideology* (1961, reprinted 1974), a study of intellectuals' disenchantment with modern industrial society and their hopes for a spiritual revolution. A good introduction to Germany at war is Roger Chickering, *Imperial Germany and the Great War, 1914–1918* (1998).

FROM 1918 TO 1945

Dietrich Orlow, *A History of Modern Germany: 1871 to Present*, 4th ed. (1999), offers a good survey of Germany's difficult 20th century. Hans Mommsen, *The Rise and Fall of Weimar Democracy*, trans. by Elborg Forster and Larry Eugene Jones (1996; originally published in German, 1989), is a fine synthesis of the republic's tragic history. Peter Gay, *Weimar Culture: The Outsider as Insider* (1968, reprinted 1988), provides a stimulating introduction to the cultural and intellectual brilliance of Germany during the 1920s. An excellent guide to further reading on Weimar culture is Anton Kaes, Martin Jay, and Edward Dimendberg (eds.), *The Weimar Republic Sourcebook* (1994). Ian Kershaw, *Hitler, 1889–1936: Hubris* (1998, reissued 2000), and *Hitler, 1936–45: Nemesis* (2000), together constitute the definitive biography of the dictator. One of the best single-volume treatments of World War II is Gerhard L. Weinberg, *A World at Arms: A Global History of World War II* (1994). Raul Hilberg, *The Destruction of the European Jews*, rev. ed., 3 vol. (1985), remains the standard and most comprehensive study of the efforts by the Nazis to exterminate the Jewish people. Michael Berenbaum (ed.), *Witness to the Holocaust* (1997), contains 94 basic documents on 21 major themes, from the Nazi rise to power to the Nürnberg trials, including consideration of the non-Jewish victims of the Holocaust. Daniel Jonah Goldhagen, *Hitler's Willing Executioners: Ordinary Germans and the Holocaust* (1996), is a controversial interpretation of culpability for the Holocaust.

AFTER 1945

A survey of the history of both German states is V.R. Berghahn, *Modern Germany: Society, Economy, and Politics in the Twentieth Century*, 2nd ed. (1987, reissued 1993). An excellent treatment of the collapse of East Germany is Charles S. Maier, *Dissolution: The Crisis of Communism and the End of East Germany* (1997, reissued 1999). Also of value is Philip Zelikow and Condoleezza Rice, *Germany Unified and Europe Transformed: A Study in Statecraft* (1995, reissued 1997), which traces the diplomatic events leading to German reunification. Examinations of the post-unification era are presented by Winand Gellner and John D. Robertson, *The Berlin Republic: German Unification and a Decade of Changes* (2003); and Klaus Larres, *Germany Since Unification*, 2nd ed. (2001).

Index